D0914686

⊕ *BARTHOLOMEW*
WORLD ATLAS

⊕ *BARTHOLOMEW*
WORLD ATLAS

THIS EDITION PRODUCED EXCLUSIVELY FOR
GALLEY PRESS

Published in this edition by Galley Press, an imprint of
W.H. Smith & Son Limited,
Registered No. 237811 England.
Trading as WHS Distributors, St. John's House,
East Street, Leicester, LE1 6NE.

Printed in Scotland by John Bartholomew & Son Ltd

ISBN 0 86136 669 7
G1131

CONTENTS

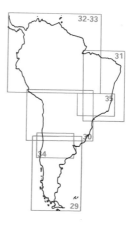

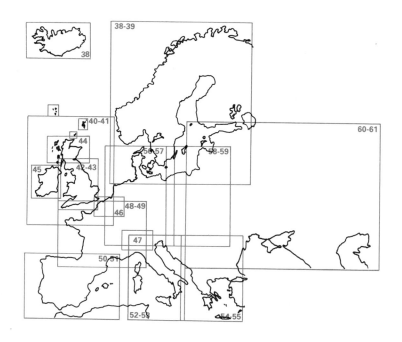

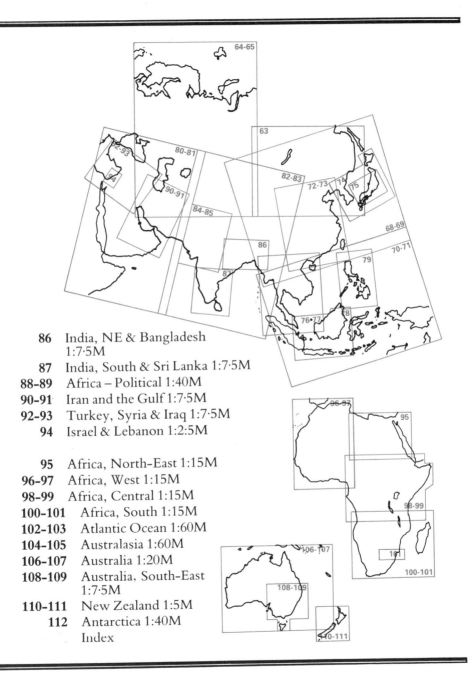

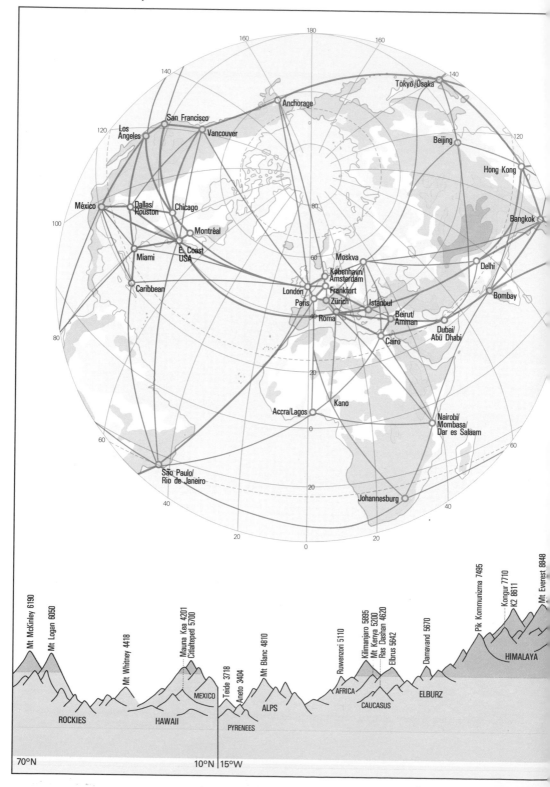

160 180 160
140 140
Tōkyō/Ōsaka
Anchorage
San Francisco
Los Angeles Vancouver
Beijing
120 120
Hong Kong
México Dallas/Houston Chicago
Montréal Bangkok
100 Moskva
E. Coast USA Delhi
Miami København/Amsterdam
Caribbean London Frankfurt Bombay
Paris Zürich İstanbul
Roma Beirut/Amman
80 Cairo Dubai/Abū Dhabi

Accra/Lagos Kano
Nairobi/Mombasa/Dar es Salaam
60 60
São Paulo/Rio de Janeiro
Johannesburg
40 40
20 20
0

Mt McKinley 6190
Mt Logan 6050
Mt Whitney 4418
Mauna Kea 4201
Citlaltepetl 5700
MEXICO
Teide 3718
Aneto 3404
Mt Blanc 4810
Ruwenzori 5110
Kilimanjaro 5895
Mt Kenya 5200
Ras Dashan 4620
Elbrus 5642
AFRICA
Damavand 5670
CAUCASUS
ELBURZ
Pik Kommunizma 7495
Kongur 7710
K2 8611
Mt Everest 8848
HIMALAYA

ROCKIES
HAWAII
PYRENEES
ALPS

70°N 10°N 15°W

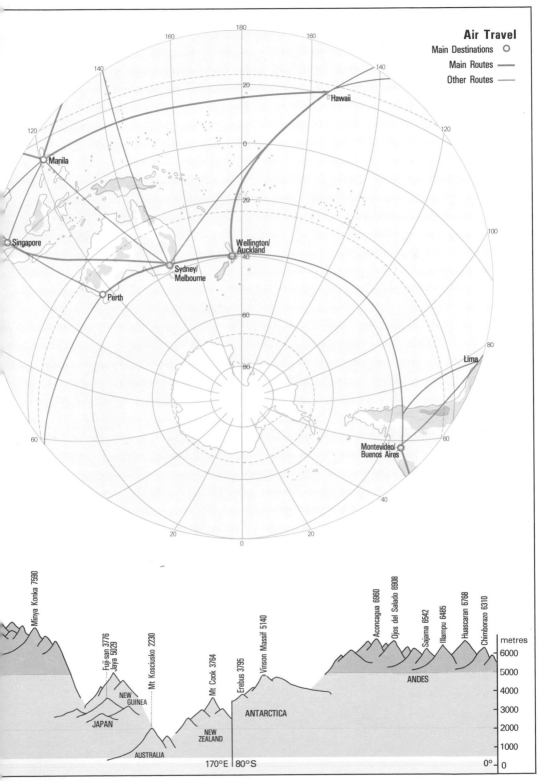

Air Travel

Main Destinations ○
Main Routes ——
Other Routes ——

180
160   160
140   140
120   120
100
0
20
20
80
60   60
40
20   20
0

Hawaii

Manila

Singapore

Wellington/
Auckland

Sydney/
Melbourne

Perth

Lima

Montevideo/
Buenos Aires

Minya Konka 7590

Fuji-san 3776
Jaya 5029

Mt Kosciusko 2230

Mt Cook 3764

Erebus 3795

Vinson Massif 5140

Aconcagua 6960
Ojos del Salado 6908

Sajama 6542

Illampu 6485

Huascaran 6768

Chimborazo 6310

metres
6000
5000
4000
3000
2000
1000
0

ANDES

NEW
GUINEA

JAPAN

AUSTRALIA

NEW
ZEALAND

ANTARCTICA

170°E 80°S   0°

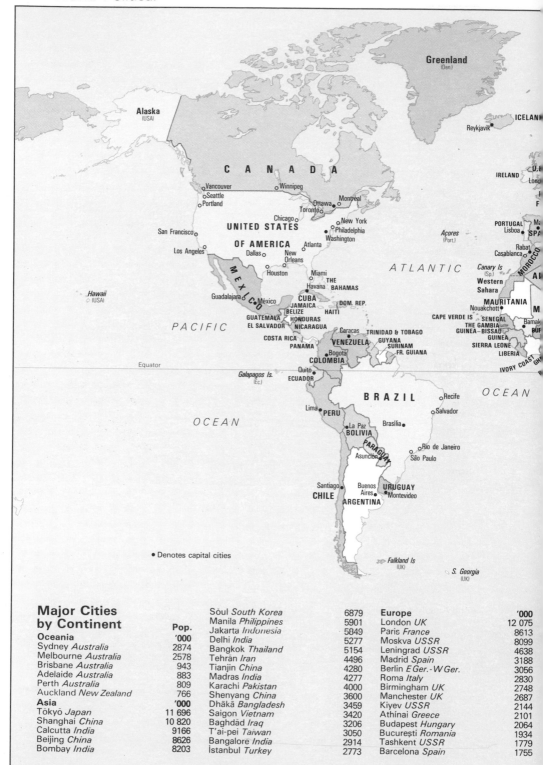

Greenland
(Den.)

ICELAND

Reykjavik

Alaska
(USA)

C A N A D A

IRELAND   U.K
Lond

Vancouver   Winnipeg
Seattle
Portland   Ottawa   Montréal
                  Toronto

Chicago   New York
San Francisco   Philadelphia
UNITED STATES   Washington
OF AMERICA   Atlanta

Los Angeles   Dallas   New
                    Orleans
        Houston   Miami

PORTUGAL   Ma
Lisboa   SPA

Rabat
Casablanca   MOROCCO

Açores
(Port.)

ATLANTIC

Canary Is
(Sp.)
Western
Sahara

Hawaii
(USA)

Guadalajara   México
CUBA
JAMAICA   DOM. REP.
BELIZE   HAITI
GUATEMALA   HONDURAS
EL SALVADOR   NICARAGUA

THE
Havana   BAHAMAS

MAURITANIA
Nouakchott   M

CAPE VERDE IS   SENEGAL
THE GAMBIA   Bamak
GUINEA-BISSAU   BUF
GUINEA
SIERRA LEONE
LIBERIA

PACIFIC

COSTA RICA
PANAMA

Caracas   TRINIDAD & TOBAGO
VENEZUELA   GUYANA
Bogotá   SURINAM
COLOMBIA   FR. GUIANA

IVORY COAST   GH

Equator

Galapagos Is.
(Ec.)

Quito
ECUADOR

OCEAN

Lima   PERU

B R A Z I L

Recife

OCEAN

La Paz   Brasília
BOLIVIA

Salvador

OCEAN

PARAGUAY
Asunción

Rio de Janeiro
São Paulo

Santiago   Buenos
CHILE   Aires   URUGUAY
ARGENTINA   Montevideo

● Denotes capital cities

Falkland Is
(UK)

S. Georgia
(UK)

Major Cities by Continent

	Pop. '000
Oceania	**'000**
Sydney *Australia*	2874
Melbourne *Australia*	2578
Brisbane *Australia*	943
Adelaide *Australia*	883
Perth *Australia*	809
Auckland *New Zealand*	766
Asia	**'000**
Tōkyō *Japan*	11 696
Shanghai *China*	10 820
Calcutta *India*	9166
Beijing *China*	8626
Bombay *India*	8203

	'000
Sòul *South Korea*	6879
Manila *Philippines*	5901
Jakarta *Indonesia*	5849
Delhi *India*	5277
Bangkok *Thailand*	5154
Tehrān *Iran*	4496
Tianjin *China*	4280
Madras *India*	4277
Karachi *Pakistan*	4000
Shenyang *China*	3600
Dhākā *Bangladesh*	3459
Saigon *Vietnam*	3420
Baghdād *Iraq*	3206
T'ai-pei *Taiwan*	3050
Bangalore *India*	2914
İstanbul *Turkey*	2773

Europe	**'000**
London *UK*	12 075
Paris *France*	8613
Moskva *USSR*	8099
Leningrad *USSR*	4638
Madrid *Spain*	3188
Berlin *E Ger.–W Ger.*	3056
Roma *Italy*	2830
Birmingham *UK*	2748
Manchester *UK*	2687
Kiyev *USSR*	2144
Athínai *Greece*	2101
Budapest *Hungary*	2064
Bucureşti *Romania*	1934
Tashkent *USSR*	1779
Barcelona *Spain*	1755

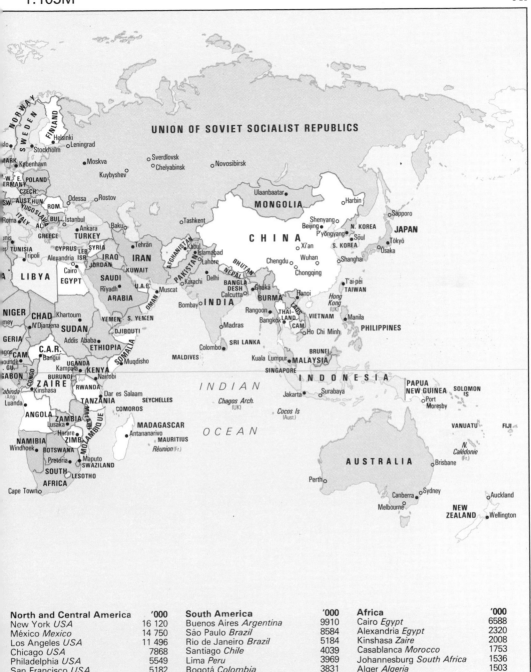

North and Central America	'000	South America	'000	Africa	'000
New York *USA*	16 120	Buenos Aires *Argentina*	9910	Cairo *Egypt*	6588
México *Mexico*	14 750	São Paulo *Brazil*	8584	Alexandria *Egypt*	2320
Los Angeles *USA*	11 496	Rio de Janeiro *Brazil*	5184	Kinshasa *Zaire*	2008
Chicago *USA*	7868	Santiago *Chile*	4039	Casablanca *Morocco*	1753
Philadelphia *USA*	5549	Lima *Peru*	3969	Johannesburg *South Africa*	1536
San Francisco *USA*	5182	Bogotá *Colombia*	3831	Alger *Algeria*	1503
Detroit *USA*	4618	Caracas *Venezuela*	2576	Lagos *Nigeria*	1477
Boston *USA*	3448	Belo Horizonte *Brazil*	1815	El Gîza *Egypt*	1247
Houston *USA*	3102	Salvador *Brazil*	1526	Addis Ababa *Ethiopia*	1133
Washington *USA*	3060	Medellin *Colombia*	1442	Cape Town *South Africa*	1108
Toronto *Canada*	2999	Fortaleza *Brazil*	1339	Dar es Salaam *Tanzania*	870
Dallas *USA*	2975	Montevideo *Uruguay*	1314	Durban *South Africa*	851
Cleveland *USA*	2834	Recife *Brazil*	1241	Abidjan *Ivory Coast*	850
Montréal *Canada*	2828	Brasília *Brazil*	1203	Ibadan *Nigeria*	847
Miami *USA*	2640	Pôrto Alegre *Brazil*	1159	Nairobi *Kenya*	835

22 -10	23 -11	24	1 +11	2 +10	3 +9	4 +8	5 +7	6 +6	7 +5	8 +4	9 +3	10 +2	11 +1

DATE LINE

Anchorage

Monday
Sunday

Vancouver
Winnipeg
8.30
Ottawa

Denver
Washington
Londo
Pa

Los Angeles

New Orleans
Raba

Miami

México

Dakar

Pánamá Caracas
8.30
Abidja

Equator

2.30

Lima

La Paz

3.30

São Paulo

Zone Times are the Standard Times
kept on land and sea compared with
12 hours (noon) Greenwich Mean Time.
Daylight Saving Time (normally one
hour in advance of local Standard
Time), which is observed by certain
countries for part of the year,
is not shown on the map.

Buenos
Aires

Greenwich Meridian

180°	165°	150°	135°	120°	105°	90°	75°	60°	45°	30°	15°

Journey Times

Sail (via Cape)
164 days

Steam (via Cape)
43 days

Steam (via Suez)
30 days

Supertanker
(via Cape)
28 days

Singapore ⟵

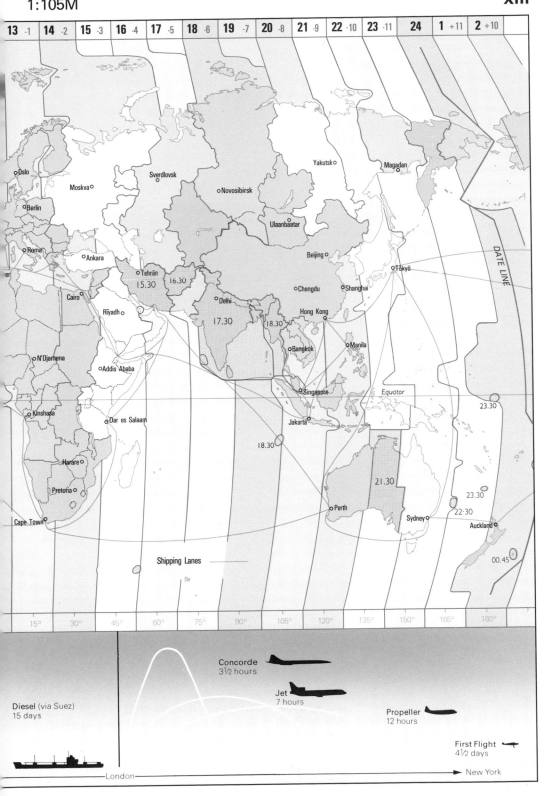

DATE LINE

Oslo

Moskva

Berlin

Sverdlovsk

Yakutsk

Magadan

Novosibirsk

Roma

Ankara

Tehrān
15.30

16.30

Ulaanbaatar

Beijing

Tōkyō

Cairo

Rīyadh

Delhi

Chengdu

Shanghai

Hong Kong

17.30

18.30

Addis Ababa

N'Djamena

Bangkok

Manila

Equator

Singapore

23.30

Kinshasa

Dar es Salaam

Jakarta

Harare

18.30

21.30

Pretoria

23.30

Cape Town

Perth

Sydney

22·30

Auckland

00.45

Shipping Lanes

15°   30°   45°   60°   75°   90°   105°   120°   135°   150°   165°   180°

Concorde
3½ hours

Jet
7 hours

Propeller
12 hours

Diesel (via Suez)
15 days

First Flight
4½ days

London ————————————————————→ New York

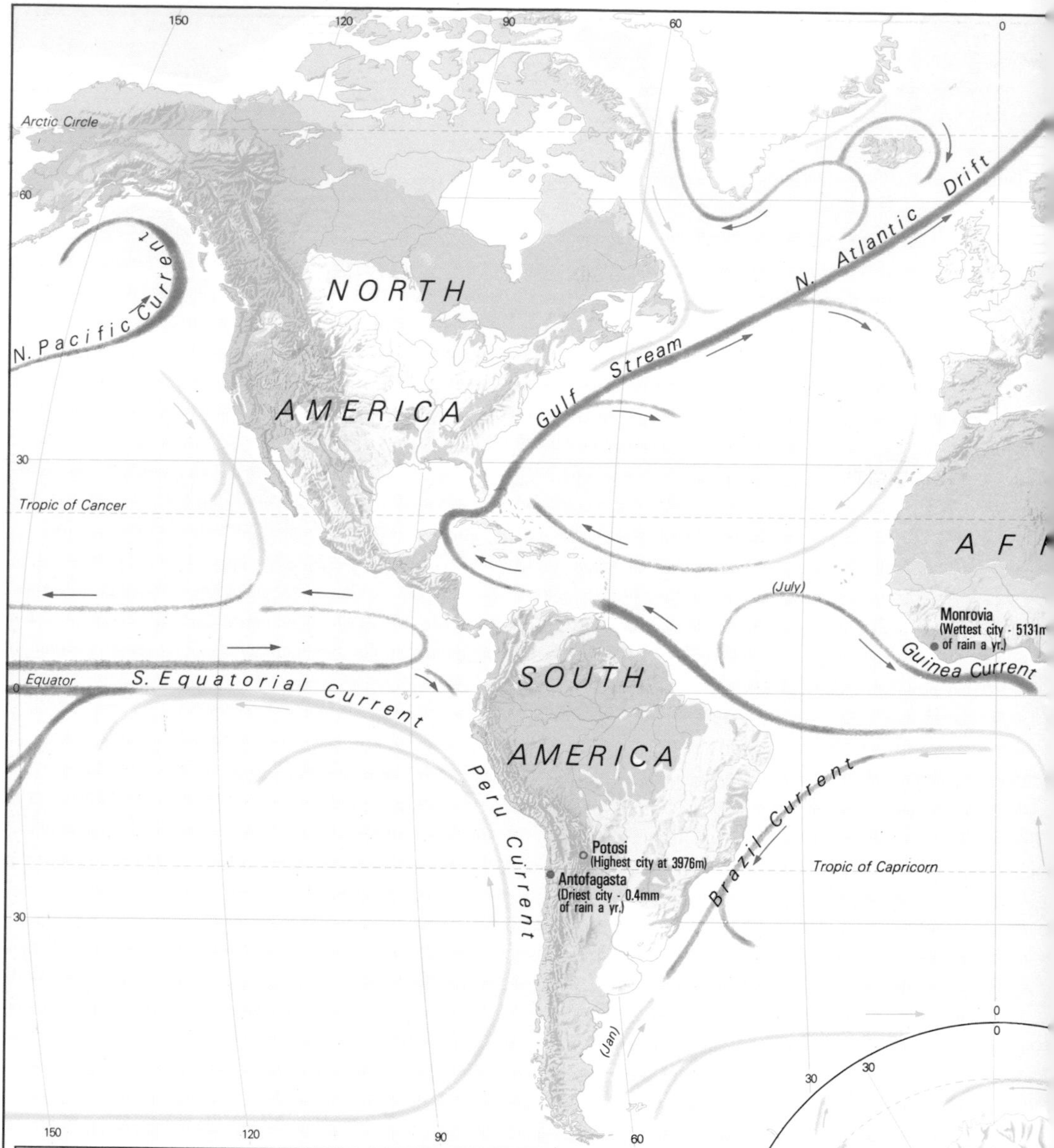

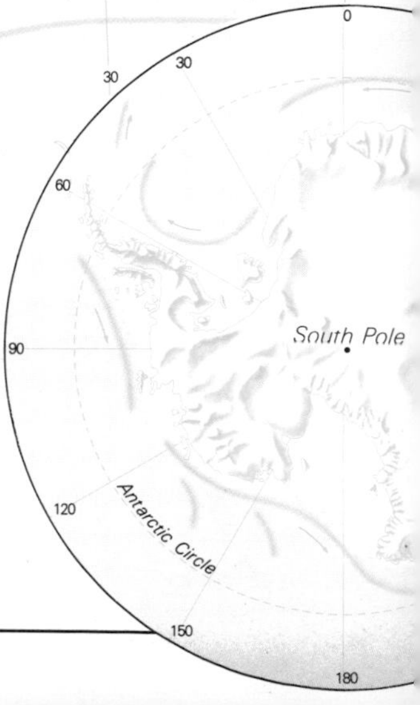

Arctic Circle

150   120   90   60   0

60

N. Pacific Current

N. Atlantic Drift

N. Pacific Current

N O R T H

A M E R I C A

Gulf Stream

30

Tropic of Cancer

A F R

(July)

Monrovia
(Wettest city - 5131m
of rain a yr.)

Equator   *S. Equatorial Current*

0

S O U T H

A M E R I C A

Guinea Current

Peru Current

Brazil Current

Potosi
(Highest city at 3976m)

Antofagasta
(Driest city - 0.4mm
of rain a yr.)

Tropic of Capricorn

30

(Jan)

150   120   90   60

0   0

30   30

60

Tundra

Flat areas frozen over except during brief summers when flooding occurs. Habitat of compact, wind resistant plants; lichens and mosses: animals ; lemmings and reindeer.

Woodland and Grass

Temperate areas of richer soils, its forest characterised by deciduous trees - oak, beech, maple. Region most exploited by man for intensive farming, settlements and industry.

90

South Pole

Northern Forest

Extensive coniferous forest area where winters are severe, summers brief. Conifers include spruce, fir, giant redwoods. Habitat of beavers, squirrels and red deer.

Grassland

Hot summers, cold winters, moderate rainfall. Vast area of grassland and 'black' soils. Ideal for growing grain crops, grazing beef cattle. Also called steppe, veld, pampas, prairie.

120

Antarctic Circle

150

180

30 60 90 120 150 180

Noril'sk
(Coolest city with -10.9°C
mean annual temp.)

60

ROPE

A S I A

30

Jericho
(Lowest city
at -270m)

Al Aziziyah
Highest recorded
temp. of 57.8°C)

I C A

Kuro-Shio

(July)

Monsoon Drift

N Equatorial Current

Djibouti
(Warmest city with 30°C
mean annual temp.)

(Jan)

(July)

(July)

(July)

Indian Counter Current

(Jan)

0

(July)

Equatorial Current (Jan)

(July)

(Jan)

AUSTRALIA

30

West Wind Drift

30 30

● ○ Places with extreme
climatic conditions

Ocean Circulation

Continental shelf

Surface currents-warm

Ice shelf

Surface currents-cold

120 150 180

60

Scrub
Areas of long, hot, dry summers and
short warm winters where crop
growing and grazing have destroyed
original tree cover. Now habitat of
evergreen scrub–vines and olives.

Savanna
Habitat supports tall coarse grasses
with thorny, flat-topped trees. Grazed
by giraffes and zebras. Drought is
common and plants are adapted to
recover quickly from ravages of fire.

90

Vostok Station
(Lowest recorded
temp. of -88.3°C)

Desert
Environment includes bare mountains,
rocky waste, sand dunes. Plants (wiry
grass, thorn bushes, cacti) and animals
(lizards, camels) must be well adapted
to extremes of heat and drought.

Rainforest
Hot and wet–without marked seasons.
Habitat of luxuriant trees, lianas,
monkeys and tigers. Five vegetation
layers– high trees, tree canopy, open
canopy, shrubs, ground herbs.

120

150

BOUNDARIES

▬▬▬▬	International
▬ ▬ ▬	International under Dispute
▪ ▪ ▪ ▪	Cease Fire Line
────	Autonomous or State/ Administrative
▬ ▬ ▬	Maritime (National)
─ ─ ─ ─	International Date Line

COMMUNICATIONS

══════	Motorway/Under Construction
────────	Major/Other Road
─ ─ ─ ─	Under Construction
··········	Track
⇉═════⇇	Road Tunnel
─·─·─	Car Ferry
────────	Main/Other Railway
─ ─ ─ ─ ─	Under Construction
··········	Rail Ferry
→─────←	Rail Tunnel
─┴─┴─┴─	Canal
⊕ ✈	International/Other Airport

LANDSCAPE FEATURES

	Glacier, Ice Cap
	Marsh, Swamp
	Sand Desert, Dunes
	Freshwater
	Saltwater
	Seasonal
	Salt Pan

OTHER FEATURES

	River/Seasonal
≍	Pass, Gorge
	Dam, Barrage
	Waterfall, Rapid
	Aqueduct
	Reef
. 217 ▲ 4231	Spot Height, Depth/ Summit, Peak
⌣	Well
△ ▲	Oil/Gas Field
───Gas/Oil───	Oil/Natural Gas Pipeline
⌐ Gemsbok Nat. Pk ⌐	National Park
∴ UR	Historic Site

LETTERING STYLES

CANADA	Independent Nation
FLORIDA	State, Province or Autonomous Region
Gibraltar (U.K.)	Sovereignty of Dependent Territory
Lothian	Administrative Area
LANGUEDOC	Historic Region
Loire **Vosges**	Physical Feature or Physical Region

TOWNS AND CITIES

Square symbols denote capital cities			*Population*
■	●	**New York**	over 5 000 000
■	●	**Montréal**	over 1 000 000
□	○	Ottawa	over 500 000
■	●	**Québec**	over 100 000
□	○	St John's	over 50 000
□	○	Yorkton	over 10 000
□	○	Jasper	under 10 000

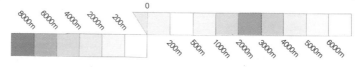

Built-up-area

Depth	Sea Level 0	Height

8000m 6000m 4000m 2000m 200m   200m 500m 1000m 2000m 3000m 4000m 5000m 6000m

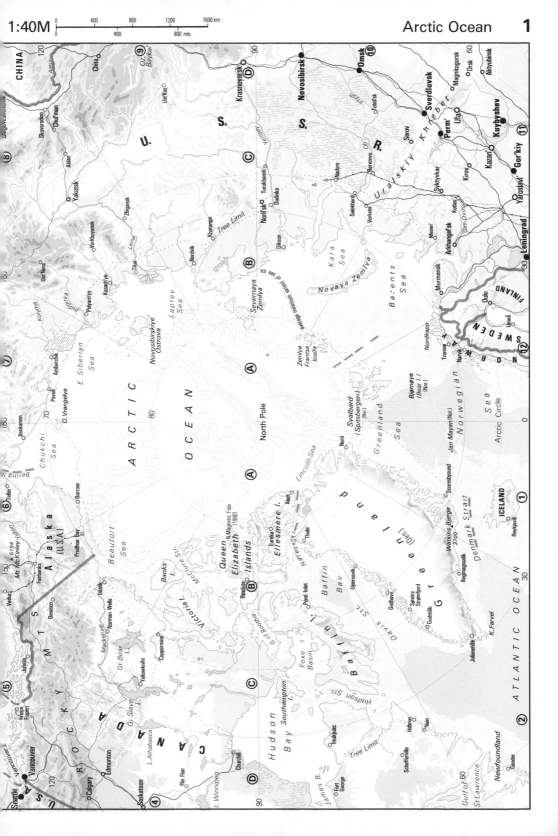

400   800   1200   1600 km
400   800 mls

CHINA

Argun

Shilka
Chita

Oz. Baykal ⑨

Ust'Kut

Krasnoyarsk Ⓓ

90

Novosibirsk

Omsk ⑩

Sverdlovsk

Magnitogorsk

60

Omsk   Aktyubinsk

U.   S.   S.   R.

Tobol'sk

Irtysh

Serov

Perm'   Ufa

Uralskiy Khrebet

Kuybyshev ⑪

Nadym

Berezovo

Syktyvkar

Kazan'   Kirov

Gor'kiy

120

Storvadino

Aldan

Yakutsk

Verkhoyansk

Vilyuy

Lena

Turukhansk Ⓒ

Yenisey

Dudinka

Nor'ilsk

Salekhard

Vorkuta

Kotlas

Sev. Dvina

Mezen'

Yaroslavl'

30

Leningrad

Khatanga

Tree Limit Ⓑ

Dikson

Kara
Sea

Sev. Dvina

Arkhangel'sk

FINLAND

SWEDEN ⑫

⑧

Chul'man

Zhigansk

Taksi

Norinsk

Moyero

Novaya Zemlya

Murmansk

Oulu

Barents

Sea

Ⓒ

Ust'Nera

Indigirka

Polyarn'yy

Novosibirskiye
Ostrova

Laptev
Sea

Severnaya
Zemlya

minimum extent of sea ice

Zemlya
Frantsa-
Iosifa

Nordkapp

Tromsø

NORWAY

Upali

Kazach'ye

average

Bjørnøya
(Bear I.)
[Nor.]

Narvik

⑦

Ambarchik

Kolyma

E. Siberian
Sea

Ⓐ

Svalbard
(Spitsbergen)
[Nor.]

Greenland

Sea

Norwegian

Sea

Arctic Circle

0

①

ICELAND

Reykjavík

Pevek

O. Vrangelya

ARCTIC

80

North Pole

Ⓐ

Lincoln Sea

Nord

Jan Mayen [Nor.]

Scoresbysund

30

ⒸⒸ

Vankarem

70

OCEAN

Denmark Strait

Watkins Bjerge
3700

Teller ⑥

Chukchi
Sea

Bering Str.

Barrow

Beaufort
Sea

Alert

Eureka

Thule

Nares Str.

Queen
Elizabeth Islands

Ellesmere I.

G r e e n l a n d   (Den.)

Angmagssalik

Denmark Strait

Prudhoe Bay

N.Magnetic Pole
(1980)

Upernavik

⑤

Mt McKinley
▲6194

Fairbanks

Alaska
(U.S.A.)

Valdez

Dawson

Inuvik

Mackenzie

Norman Wells

Banks I.

McClure Str.

Resolute

Victoria I.

Ⓑ

Godhavn

Sandre
Stromfjord

K. Farvel

Prince Rupert

Juneau

ROCKY   MTS

Gt. Bear L.

Coppermine

G. of Boothia

Foxe
Basin

Baffin

Bay

Godthåb

Julianehåb

ATLANTIC OCEAN

Yellowknife

Ⓒ

Davis Str.

Pond Inlet

②

Seattle
Vancouver

Edmonton

Calgary

120

Gt. Slave L.

CANADA

L. Athabasca

Ⓒ

Saskatoon

Fin Flon

L. Winnipeg

Churchill

④

90

Hudson
Bay

Southampton I.

Hudson Str.

Ⓓ

Tree Limit

Ivujivac

Schefferville

Hebron

Fort
George

James B.

Gulf of
St. Lawrence

60

Newfoundland

Gander

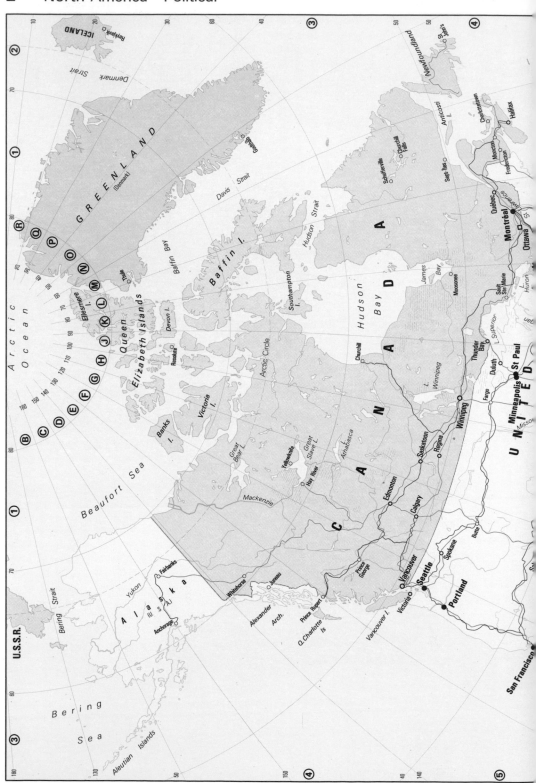

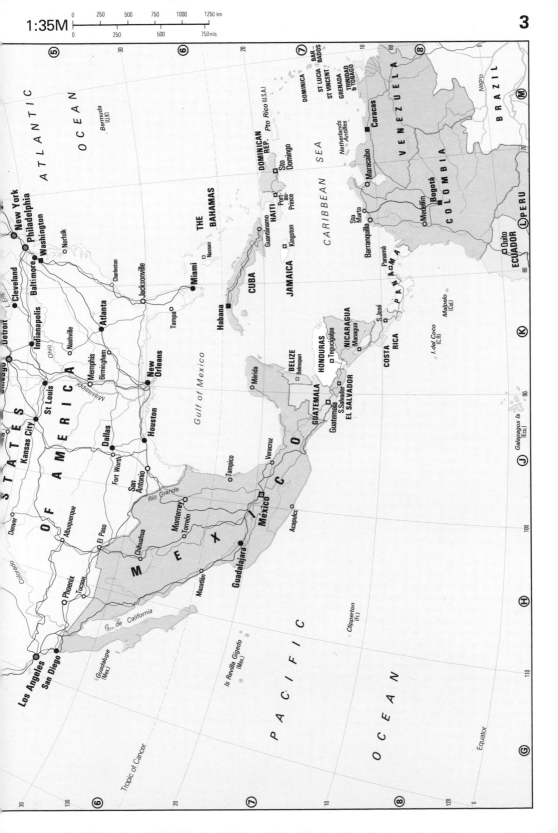

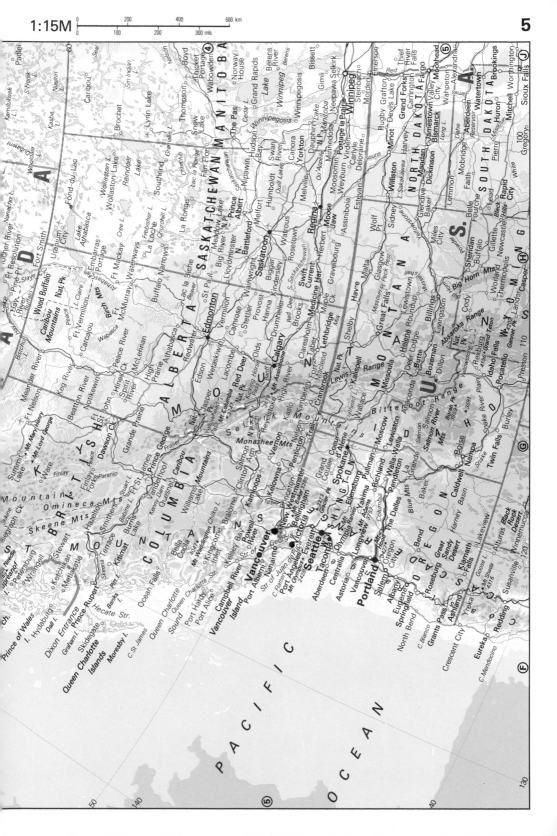

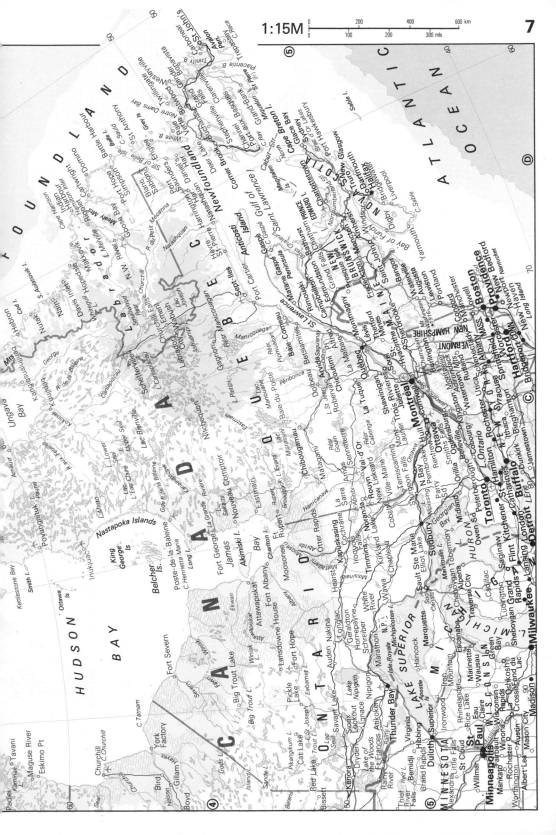

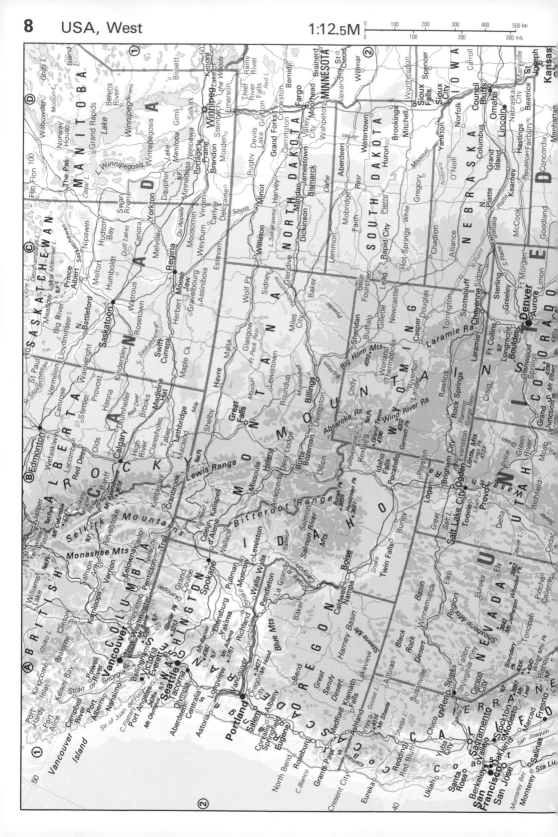

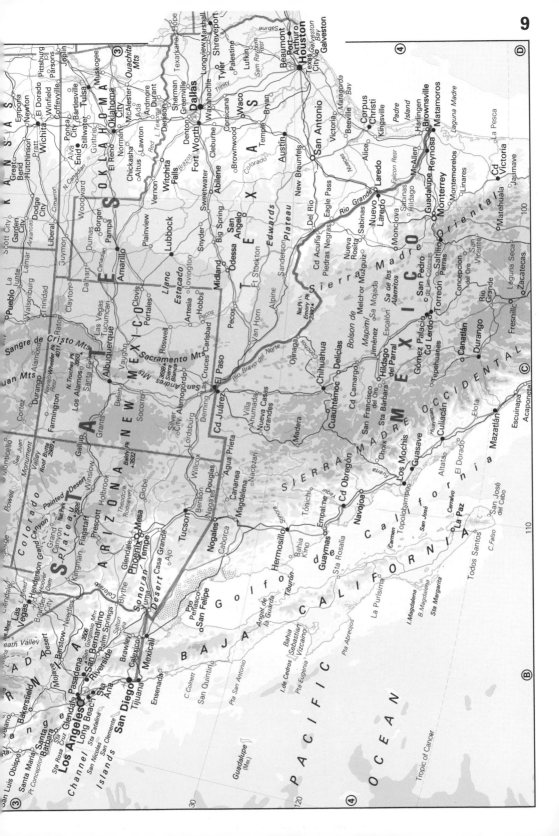

0 100 200 300 400 500 km
0 100 200 300 mls

ATLANTIC OCEAN

THE BAHAMAS

Eleuthera · Cat · San Salvador · Rum Cay · Crooked · Acklins
Little Abaco · Great Abaco · Berry Is · New Providence · Nassau · Great Bahama Bank · Andros · Great Exuma · Long · Gt Ragged · Banes
Grand Bahama · West Palm Beach · Ft Lauderdale · Hollywood · Miami Beach · Arch. de Camagüey · Cayo Romano · Ciego de Avila · Camagüey · Holguín
Exuma Sound · Bahama · Cayo Romano · Sta Clara · Santi Spiritus · Cienfuegos · Colón · Cárdenas · Matanzas · CUBA
Florida · Miami · The Everglades · Nat Pk · C. Sable · Florida Keys · Key West · Marquesas Keys
Straits of Florida · Habana (Havana) · Guane · Pinar del Rio · G. de Batabanó

GULF OF MEXICO

Tropic of Cancer

80 · 90 · 30 · 70

ATLANTIC OCEAN

C. Hatteras · C. Lookout · C. Fear · Myrtle Beach · New Bern · Wilmington · Lumberton · Fayetteville · Elizabeth City · Portsmouth · Albemarle Sound · Roanoke · Rocky Mt · Kitty Hawk

NORTH CAROLINA · SOUTH CAROLINA · Charleston · Georgetown · Port Royal Sound · Florence · Sumter · Columbia · Rock Hill · Charlotte · Raleigh · Durham · Greensboro · Winston-Salem · High Point · Danville

Savannah · Brunswick · Jacksonville · St Augustine · Daytona Beach · Melbourne · Fort Pierce · C. Canaveral · Cape Canaveral · Sanford · Orlando · Tampa · St Petersburg · Clearwater · Ocala · Gainesville · Lake Okeechobee · Ft Myers · Tampa B

FLORIDA · Apalachee Bay · Tallahassee · Valdosta · Waycross · Jesup · Cordele · Albany · Dothan · Panama City · Pensacola · Mobile · Mobile Bay · Biloxi

GEORGIA · Atlanta · Macon · Columbus · Phenix City · Griffin · Athens · Gainesville · Rome · Anniston · La Grange · Marietta

ALABAMA · Montgomery · Birmingham · Bessemer · Tuscaloosa · Gadsden · Decatur · Florence · Huntsville · Chattanooga · Atmore · Tombigbee · Alabama

TENNESSEE · Nashville · Knoxville · Asheville · Cleveland · Oak Ridge · Johnson City · Bristol · Kingsport · Mt Mitchell · Chickamauga

KENTUCKY · Owensboro · Bowling Green · Middlesboro · Frankfort · Lexington · Hopkinsville · Paducah

MISSISSIPPI · Jackson · Meridian · Hattiesburg · Laurel · Columbus · Greenwood · Greenville · Clarksdale · Natchez · Brookhaven · Vicksburg · Yazoo City · Bogalusa

LOUISIANA · New Orleans · Baton Rouge · Lafayette · Lake Charles · Alexandria · Natchitoches · Monroe · Morgan City · Atchafalaya B.

ARKANSAS · Little Rock · Pine Bluff · Hot Springs · Conway · Searcy · Jonesboro · Forrest City · Helena · Camden · El Dorado · Crossett · Hope · Texarkana · Fayetteville · Ouachita Mts · Boston Mts · Fort Smith

MISSOURI · St Louis · Springfield · Joplin · Rolla · Poplar Bluff · Sikeston · Cairo · Cape Girardeau · Jefferson City · Lake of the Ozarks · Ozark Plateau

KANSAS · Wichita · Emporia · Newton · Coffeyville · Winfield · El Dorado · Pittsburg

OKLAHOMA · Oklahoma City · Tulsa · Muskogee · McAlester · Ardmore · Durant · Ada · Norman · Stillwater · Ponca City · Bartlesville

TEXAS · Dallas · Fort Worth · Houston · Austin · Waco · Galveston · Beaumont · Port Arthur · Orange · Lufkin · Tyler · Longview · Marshall · Palestine · Corsicana · Temple · Bryan · Victoria · Beeville · Corpus Christi · Kingsville · Harlingen · Brownsville · Matamoros · Padre Island · Laguna Madre · Matagorda Bay · Galveston Bay · Sabine · Cleburne · Denton · Sherman · Denison · Greenville · Waxahachie · Colorado · Brazos · Trinity · San Bernard · Toledo Bend Resr · Red

Memphis · Dyersburg · Blytheville · W. Plains · Parsons

① ② ③ ④ Ⓐ Ⓑ Ⓒ Ⓓ

1:10M

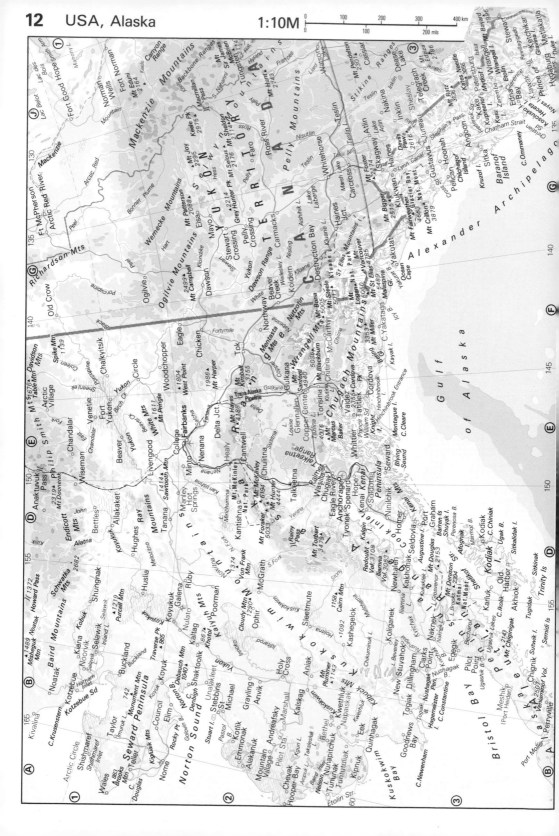

1:7.5M

0 100 200 300 km
0 50 100 150 mls

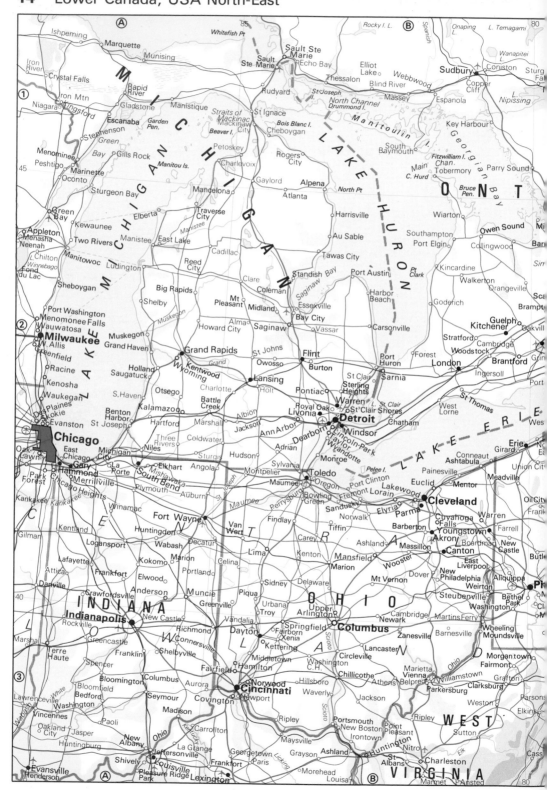

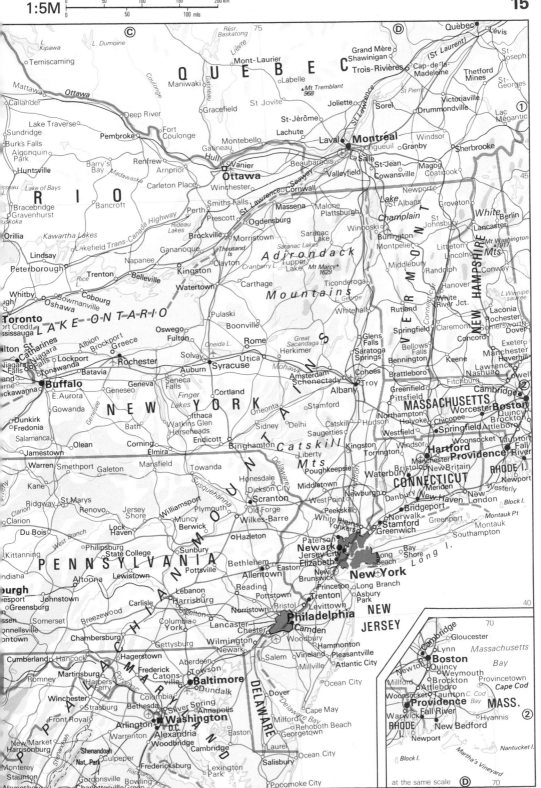

25 50 75 100 km
0 25 50 mils

Cobleskill · Cohoes · Watervliet · Troy · Hinsdale · Readsboro · Winchester · 72 · Greenville · Haverhill · Newburyport
Richmondville · Schoharie · Rensselaer · Adams · N. Adams · Northfield · Winchendon · Nashua · Methuen · Ipswich
Stamford · Albany · Williamstown · Greenfield · Turners Falls · Fitchburg · Dracut · Lawrence · Gloucester
Middleburgh · Ravena · Mt Greylock 1064 · Shelburne · Millers · Gardner · Leominster · Lowell · Salem · Beverly
① Grand Gorge · Prattsville · Coxsackie · Cheshire · S. Deerfield · Falls · Clinton · Marlboro · Newton · Lynn · Marblehea
Chatham · Lenox · Dalton · Northampton · Amherst · Barre · Quabbin · Worcester · Framingham · Brookline · Boston
NEW · Catskill · Hudson · Stockbridge · Easthampton · Chester · Resr · Oxford · Southbridge · Franklin · Quincy · Bay
Saugerties · Gt Barrington · Otis · Westfield · Chicopee · Monson · Webster · Mansfield · Weymouth
Shandaken · Mt Everett 793 · Springfield · Stafford Springs · Woonsocket · Brockton · Plymouth
42 · Slide Mtn 1281 · Canaan · Thompsonville · Putnam · Central Falls · Taunton · Bridgewater · Attleboro · Middleboro
YORK · Kingston · Millerton · Winsted · Windsor · Rockville · Storrs · Providence · Pawtucket
Liberty · Rhinebeck · Torrington · Locks · New Britain · Willimantic · Cranston · Warren · Somerset · Warehar
Ellenville · New Paltz · Hyde Park · Amenia · Hartford · Manchester · Moosup · Jewett · Warwick · Fall River
Monticello · Poughkeepsie · Bristol · CONNECTICUT · City · RHODE · Bristol · New
Otisville · Wappingers · New Milford · Waterbury · Meriden · Middletown · Norwich · ISLAND · Bedford
Walden · Falls · Naugatuck · Wallingford · Uncasville · Jamestown · Newport · Falmouth
② Newburgh · Beacon · Candlewood · Southington · Wakefield · Buzzards
Middletown · Carmel · Brewster · Seymour · Deep River · Mystic · Westerly · Bay · Vineyard
Port Jervis · Highland · Danbury · Hamden · New Haven · New London · Block Island Sd · Haven
Milford · Falls · West Point · Bethel · Derby · Old Lyme · Fishers I. · Block Island · Martha's Vineyard
Sussex · Warwick · Peekskill · Bridgeport · Milford · Clinton · Rhode Island Sound · Nomans Lanc
Hamburg · Haverstraw · New Canaan · Stratford · Long Island Sound · Gardiners I. · ②
Franklin · Pompton · Suffern · Ossining · Fairfield · Greenport · Montauk Pt
Newton · Lakes · Ramsey · Tarrytown · Norwalk · Mattituck · Sag Harbor · Montauk
Butler · White Plains · Stamford · Pt Jefferson · Riverhead · East Hampton
Dover · Paterson · Greenwich · Port Chester · Huntington · Southampton · ATLANTIC
Morristown · Clifton · Yonkers · Kings Park · OCEAN
NEW · E.Orange · Passaic · Bronx · Center Moriches
Newark · Queens · Bay Shore · Sayville · Long Island
JERSEY · Jersey City · New York · Brooklyn · Great South Bay
Bernardsville · Elizabeth · Staten I. · Long Beach
Somerville · ⒷⒸ · 72 · Ⓓ

Milton · Bloomsburg · Catawissa · Hazleton · 76 · Stroudsburg · Ⓑ · Newton · Butler · White Plains · Ⓒ · Port
Lewisburg · Danville · Lehigh · Bangor · Hackettstown · Netcong · Paterson · Chester
Sunbury · Mt Carmel · Mahanoy · Lehighton · Palmerton · Belvidere · Morristown · Dover · Clifton · Yonkers
Milroy · Middleburg · Shamokin · Frackville · City · Tamaqua · Washington · Bernardsville · Passaic · Bronx
Burnham · McClure · Herndon · Minersville · Phillipsburg · Newark · E.Orange · New York
Lewistown · Mifflintown · Lykens · Tremont · Pottsville · Whitehall · Easton · Clinton · Jersey City · Queens
Newport · Pine Grove · Schuylkill · Allentown · Bethlehem · Somerville · New Brunswick · Elizabeth · Brooklyn
Duncannon · Millersburg · Haven · Hamburg · Emmaus · Flemington · Perth Amboy · Staten I.
PENN. · Dauphin · Lebanon · Womelsdorf · Quakertown · Lambertville · South River · Amboy · Atlantic Highlands
Harrisburg · Palmyra · Boyertown · Doylestown · Princeton · Raritan Bay · Long
Newville · Steelton · Hershey · Shillington · Reading · Souderton · Hightstown · Red Bank · Long Branch
Carlisle · Middletown · Lansdale · Warminster · Morrisville · Freehold · Asbury Park
Mt Holly · Dillsburg · Lititz · Elizabethtown · Ephrata · Pottstown · Norristown · Trenton · Lakewood · Manasquan
Springs · Manchester · Columbia · Phoenixville · Levittown · Bordentown · Lakehurst · Point Pleasant
Shippensburg · York · Lancaster · Coatesville · Philadelphia · Burlington · Breton Woods
Gettysburg · Hanover · Red Lion · Parkesburg · Downingtown · Willingboro · Mt Holly · Toms River · ② · 40
Waynesboro · Littlestown · Glen Rock · W. Chester · Chester · Camden · Woodbury · Chatsworth · Seaside Park
Emmitsburg · Stewartstown · Kennett Square · Wilmington · NEW · Barnegat
Westminster · Rising Sun · Penns Grove · Glassboro · Atco · Bay · Barnegat
③ Reisterstown · Elkton · Newark · Woodstown · JERSEY · Surf City
Frederick · Bel Air · Havre de Grace · Salem · Hammonton · Tuckerton · Beach Haven
Mt Airy · Towson · Aberdeen · Elmer · Egg Harbor City · Little Egg Harbor
MARYLAND · Cockeysville · Edgewood · Middletown · Vineland · Mays Landing · Great Bay
Ellicott City · Baltimore · Cecilton · Bridgeton · Pleasantville · Atlantic City · ③
Damascus · Catonsville · Dundalk · Smyrna · Millville · Somers Point
Columbia · Glen Burnie · Chestertown · Woodbine · Port Norris · Ocean City
Rockville · Laurel · Centreville · Dover · Delaware
Leesburg · Wheaton · Silver Spring · College · Queenstown · Annapolis · Frederica · Bay · Stone Harbor
Bethesda · Park · Bowie · Mayo · Harrington · ATLANTIC
Arlington · Queen Anne · Milford · Cape May · OCEAN
Fairfax · Washington · Greensboro · Wildwood
Alexandria · D.C. · Ⓐ · St Michaels · 76 · Greenwood · Ⓑ · C.Henlopen · 74 · Ⓒ · C. May Pt

New York · Catskill Mountains · Ashokan Resr · Mink · Hudson · Berkshire Hills · Housatonic · Massachusetts · Massachusetts Bay
Delaware · Blue Mtn · Susquehanna · Juniata · Shenandoah · Catoctin Mtn · South Mtn · Potomac

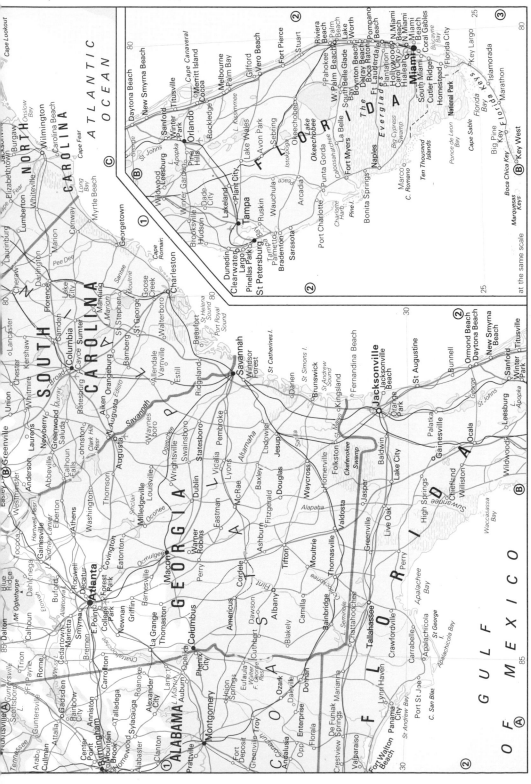

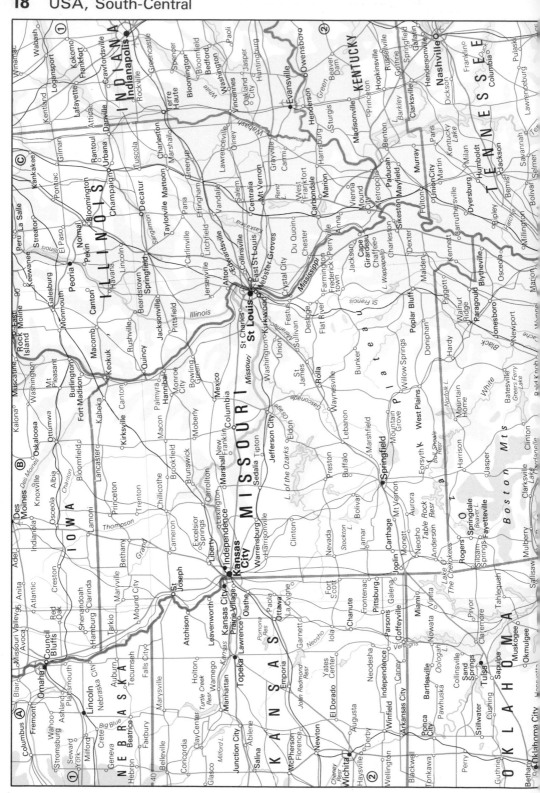

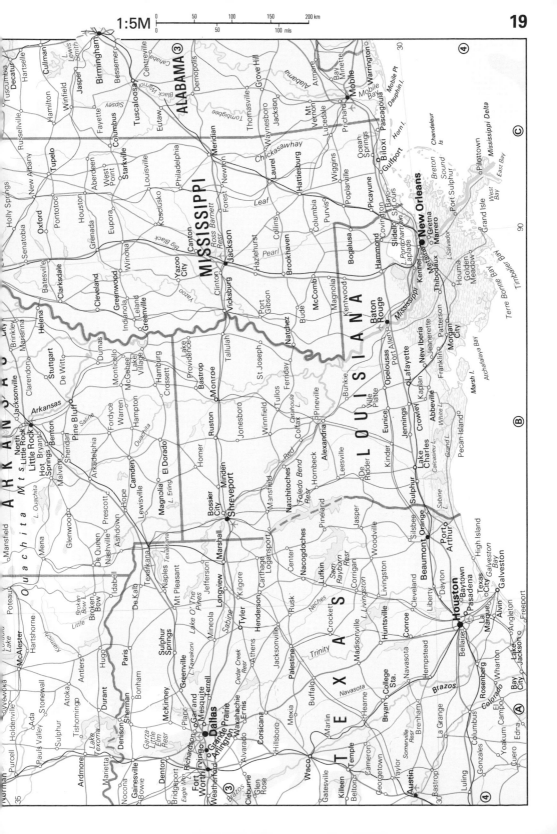

1:5M

0 50 100 150 200 km
0 50 100 mls

A 125 Parksville Gibsons Vancouver 120 C
Port Horseshoe Bay Hammond Hope Princeton Okanagan Kettle Castlegar Salmo
Alberni Nanaimo **Vancouver** Mission Agassiz Falls Oliver Grand Trail Creston
New City Chilliwack C A N A D A Osoyoos Forks
Barkley Sd Ladysmith Westminster Blaine Abbotsford 2627 Metaline
Bamfield Duncan Cowichan Ferndale North Skagit Mtn Keremeos Lakeview Mt Falls Bonners
Port Sidney Bellingham Mt Baker Cascades 2356 Okanogan Ione Ferry
Renfrew Esquimalt Anacortes 3285 Ross L. Oroville Tonasket Priest
C. Flattery San Juan Burlington Nat. Mt Logan Republic Colville River
Str of Juan de Fuca Is Concrete Park 2733 Omak Franklin Sandpoint
Victoria Mt Vernon Skagit Columbia Okanogan D. Roosevelt Coeur
Forks Marysville Glacier Peak Brewster Grand Lake Newport Priest d'Alene
Olympic Everett 3221 Chelan Coulee River Spirit Lake
Nat. Park Snohomish Banks Wilbur Spokane Kellogg
Mt Olympus Edmonds Monroe L. Coeur 1
2428 Bellevue W A S H I N G T O N Medical d'Alene L.
Bremerton **Seattle** Chelan Lake Cheney St Joe
Port Orchard Renton Wenatchee Odessa Plummer St
1 Kent Snoqualmie Ephrata Ritzville Maries
Shelton **Tacoma** Auburn Pass Yakima Moses Lake Colfax Potlatch
Puyallup Ellensburg Othello Pullman Moscow I
Olympia Mt Rainier Mount Rainier Wenatchee Eltopia Kendrick D
Hoquiam 4392 Nat. Park Naches Selah Dayton Clarkston Lewiston A
Aberdeen Centralia Yakima Richland H
Grays Harb. Raymond Chehalis Cowlitz Toppenish Sunnyside Pasco O
South Bend Winlock Mt St Helens Mt Adams Kennewick Walla Walla
C. Disappointment Longview 2950 3751 Goldendale Columbia Walla
Astoria Kelso White Umatilla Echo Pendleton Blue Grande Ronde Wallowa
Seaside Rainier Salmon Arlington Mountains Enterprise Riggins
St Helens Woodland Hood Condon La Grande Hells He
Tillamook Portland Camas River The Dalles Ukiah Wallowa Canyon Devil
Hillsboro Vancouver John Baker Mts Mtn
McMinnville Lake Oswego Gresham Mt Hood Day Sacajawea 2997 2863
Newberg Oregon City 3427 Spray Pk
45 Lincoln City Woodburn Mt Wilson Long Creek Baker 45
Salem 1707 Deschutes Condon Midvale
Newport Stayton Mt Jefferson Dayville P Weiser
Corvallis Albany 3199 Madras John Day L Payette Ontario
Yachats Lebanon Prineville Canyon City Unity A Vale Nyssa
Sweet Redmond Emmett
Florence Eugene Home Three Sisters Bend Brothers T Caldwell
Springfield 3156 Burns Drewsey E Nampa
Lowell La Pine Crane A Murphy
Reedsport Cottage O R E G O N High Harney Basin Jordan U Owyhee Mts
Grove Desert Valley
Coos Bay Oakland Crescent Silver Lake Harney L. Malheur L.
N.Bend Coos Oakridge
C. Blanco Myrtle Bay Mt Thielsen High Desert Steens Mtn
Point Roseburg 2799 Santa Rosa Ra.
Port Orford Myrtle Creek Crater L. McDermitt
2 Canyonville Nat. Mt Scott Chiloquin Bly Valley Falls Denio Osgood Mts
Gold Prospect Pk 2721 Golconda
Beach Wolf Creek Mt Upper Lakeview Warner Mts
Grants McLoughlin Klamath Winnemucca Humboldt
Brookings Pass 2894 L. Black Rock Desert
Central Point Ashland Klamath N E V A D A Battle
O'Brien Medford Falls Rye Patch Mountain
Hornbrook Dorris Willow Ranch Resr Imlay
Pt St George Crescent City Yreka Clear L. Goose L.
C. Klamath Weed Resr Middle Mt Tobin
Mendocino Klamath Mts Mt Shasta Canby Alturas Upper L. 2979
4317 Adin Alkali L.
Dunsmuir Mount Pit
C A L I F O R N I A Shasta
Humboldt Bay Arcata Weaverville Burney
Eureka L.
Fortuna Project City Lassen Pk Eagle L.
B 120 Redding Nat. Pk 3167 C
Susanville

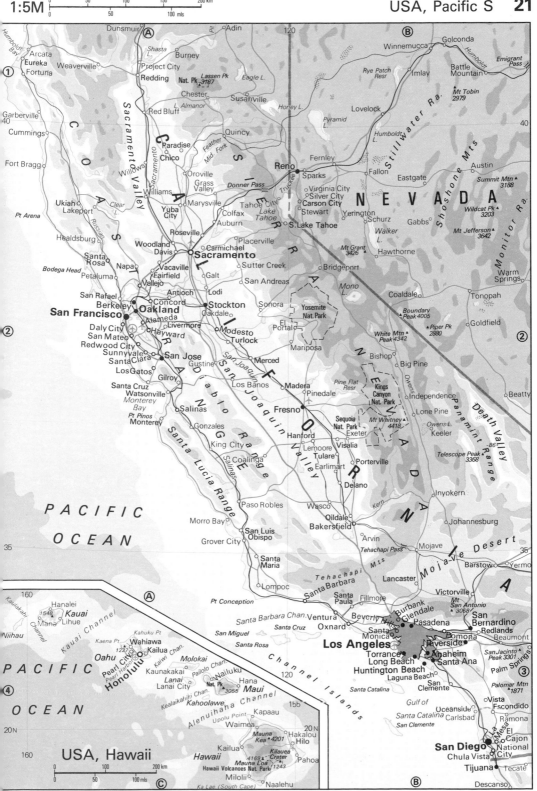

50   100   150   200 km
50   100 mls

USA, Pacific S

Dunsmuir
Shasta
Burney
Adin
120
A
Golconda
Winnemucca
B
Emigrant Pass
Humboldt
Arcata
Eureka
Weaverville
Project City
Redding
Nat. Pk.
Lassen Pk. 3187
Eagle L.
Rye Patch Resr
Imlay
Battle Mountain
Humboldt
Fortuna
Chester
Susanville
Mt Tobin 2979
Austin
Garberville
Cummings
Red Bluff
L. Almanor
Honey L.
Pyramid L.
Humboldt-water Ra.
40
Summit Mtn 3188
40
Fort Bragg
Paradise
Chico
Oroville
Quincy
Reno
Fernley
Fallon
Eastgate
Lovelock
Wildcat Pk. 3203

PACIFIC OCEAN
USA, Hawaii

0 25 50 75 100 km
0 25 50 mls

Lytton, Calistoga, Healdsburg, L.Berryessa, Woodland, Folsom L., Folsom, Placerville, Camino, Diamond Springs, Markleeville, Topaz
Forestville, St Helena, Winters, Davis, Sacramento, Plymouth, Highland Pk 3333, Coleville
Sebastopol, Santa Rosa, Sonoma, Yountville, Vacaville, Dixon, Carmichael, Elk Grove, Sutter Ck, Mokelumne, Bear Valley, Dardanelle, Devils Gate 2301, Bridgeport Resr
Petaluma, Napa, Elmira, Galt, Jackson, West Pt, Mokelumne Hill, Arnold, Sonora Pass 2933, Bridgeport
Novato, Vallejo, Fairfield, Lodi, Clements, San Andreas, Murphys, Pinecrest, Excelsior Mtn 3790
San Rafael, Mill Valley, S. Pablo B., Pittsburg, Isleton, Angels Camp, Bellota, Mokelumne Aqueduct, Melones Resr, L. Eleanor, Yosemite, Hetch Hetchy Resr, Tioga Pass, Lee Vining
Berkeley, Richmond, Concord, Oakley, Antioch, Brentwood, Stockton, Farmington Resr, Stanislaus, Sonora, Groveland, Mather, Tuolumne Mdws, Mt Dana 3978, June Lake
San Francisco, Golden Gate, Alameda, Oakland, Mt Diablo 1173, Byron, Manteca, Oakdale, Don Pedro Resr, Coulterville, El Portal, National, Mt Lyell 3997, Mt Ritter 4010
Daly City, S.San Francisco, San Leandro, San Francisco Bay, Hayward, Tracy, Ripon, Modesto, Riverbank, Modesto Resr, L.McClure, Park, Devil Postpile N.M.
San Mateo, Redwood City, Pleasanton, Livermore, Vernalis, Ceres, Turlock L., Snelling, Wawona, Mariposa, Fish Camp, Mammoth Pool Resr, Bass Lake
Palo Alto, Mountain View, Fremont, Patterson, Turlock, Merced, Yosemite, Mariposa Resr, Lakeshore 3146, Huntington L.
San Gregorio, Santa Clara, Sunnyvale, Mt Hamilton 1284 (Lick Observatory), Newman, Atwater, Merced, Planada, Kaiser Pk, Shaver L.
Pescadero, San Jose, Coyote, Gustine, Los Banos, Chowchilla, Raymond, Fresno, Millerton L., Friant Dam, Friant, Humphreys, Patterson Mtn 2489
Boulder Creek, Los Gatos, Morgan Hill, Volta, S. Luis Resr, Dos Palos, Berenda, Madera, Herndon, Pinedale, Pine Flat Resr, Piedra, Kings
Davenport, Soquel, Gilroy, Firebaugh, Mendota, Clovis, Minkler
Santa Cruz, Watsonville, Laveaga Pk 1154, Hollister, Tres Pinos, San Juan Bautista, Kerman, Helm, Sanger, Badger
Monterey Bay, Castroville, Salinas, Alisal, Pinnacles N.M., Selma, Reedley, Dinuba
Pacific Grove, Seaside, Monterey, Carmel, Gonzales, Kingsburg

Santa Cruz Mts, Diablo Range, Gabilan Ra., San Joaquin Valley, SIERRA NEVADA, Yosemite

Los Alamos, Sta Ynez, Lompoc, Buellton, Solvang, Los Olivos, San Rafael Mts, Big Pine Mtn 2081, L Cachuma, Santa Barbara Resr, Piru Ck, Gorman, Lake Hughes, California Aqueduct, Lancaster, Rosamond L., Helendale
Pt Arguello, Pt Conception, Gaviota, Goleta, Santa Ynez Mts, Carpinteria, Ojai, Fillmore, Castaic, Acton, Palmdale, Littlerock, Adelanto, Victorville, Hesperia
Santa Barbara, Santa Paula, Santa Clara, Newhall, Moorpark, San Fernando, Wrightwood, San Gabriel Mts 3068, Mojave
San Miguel, Santa Barbara Channel, Ventura, Oxnard, Camarillo, Burbank, Glendale, Pasadena, Monrovia, Upland, San Bernardino, Highland
Port Hueneme, Los Angeles, Hollywood, Mt Wilson 1740, Mt San Antonio 3068, Pomona, Ontario, Colton, Redlands
Santa Rosa, Santa Cruz, Anacapa Is, Santa Monica, Beverly Hills, Inglewood, Whittier, Riverside, Corona, Perris
San Nicolas, Channel Islands, Torrance, Redondo Beach, Lakewood, Fullerton, Orange, Santa Ana, Santiago Pk 1736, Sta Ana Mts, Elsinore
Long Beach, Garden Grove, Anaheim, Costa Mesa, Elsinore L.
Santa Barbara, Huntington Beach, Newport Beach, Laguna Beach, San Clemente, S.Onofre, Fallbrook
San Catalina, Santa Catalina, Avalon, Gulf of Santa Catalina, Santa Margarita, Oceanside, Vista
San Clemente, Outer Santa Barbara Channel, San Pedro Channel, Carlsbad, Encinitas
Del Mar, La Jolla, San Diego

PACIFIC OCEAN

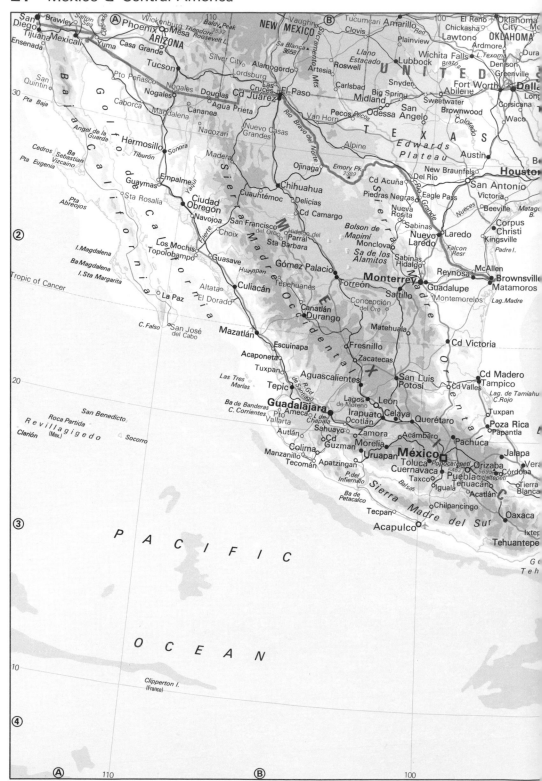

200   400   600 km
100   200   300 mls

Ft Smith
Memphis
Huntsville Chattanooga
Springs Little Rock
ARKANSAS Gainesville
Pine
Bluff
Greenwood
Greenville MISSISSIPPI
Monroe Jackson Meridian
Shreveport Vicksburg
Natchez Jackson
LOUISIANA
Alexandria Hattiesburg
Lake Baton
Charles Rouge
Orange Biloxi
Pt Arthur Lafayette New Orleans
Galveston

Tupelo
Gadsden Atlanta Athens
Birmingham Tuscaloosa ALABAMA
Columbus
Columbus Montgomery Phenix
City
Dothan Albany
Tallahassee Valdosta
Mobile Apalachee Bay Gainesville
Pensacola Panama City
Ocala

SOUTH Florence Columbia
CAROLINA
Augusta Orangeburg
Macon Charleston
GEORGIA
Savannah
Waycross
Brunswick
Jacksonville
St Augustine
Daytona Beach
Orlando
C. Canaveral
Melbourne
Ft Pierce
W.Palm
Beach
Lake Worth
Hollywood
Miami Beach
Nassau
Cat
San
Salvador

C. Fear

Little Abaco
THE
BAHAMAS
Great Abaco
Berry Is
New
Providence
Andros
Eleuthera
Exuma Sound
Great
Exuma
Rum
Cay
Long

Clearwater Tampa
St Petersburg
Tampa Bay
Ft Myers
Lake
Okeechobee
Ft Lauderdale
Miami
The Everglades
C. Sable
Key West
Marquesas Keys

GULF OF
MEXICO

Straits of Florida
Great Bahama Bank

Progreso Tizimin
Mérida
Ticul Valladolid
Peto I. de
Cozumel
B. de la Ascensión
Campeche Yucatan
Escárcega Chetumal
Bco Chinchorro
Cd del Ambergris Cay
Carmen Turneffe I.
Frontera L. de Términos
Coatzacoalcos Villahermosa
Minatitlán Belize
Istmo Tenosique Belmopan BELIZE
de Stann Creek
Tuxtla Flores Pta Gorda G. of
Gutiérrez Honduras
San Cristóbal Pto
Comitán Cortés
Tonalá Sumacinta
Huixtla GUATEMALA Pto
Tapachula Cobán Barrios
Quezaltenango Guatemala
Escuintla STA ANA
San José San Salvador
Sonsonate S Miguel La Unión
EL SALVADOR Matagalpa
Chinandega León
Managua
Masaya Granada
San Juan
del Sur
G. de Papagayo
Pen. de
Nicoya Puntarenas
San José
Cartago
COSTA
G.de Nicoya RICA
Pto Cortés
Pen. de Osa
G.Dulce Pto
Armuelles
Santiago
G. de
Chiriquí

Habana Matanzas
(Havana) Cardenas
Colón Sta Clara
Pinar del Rio Cienfuegos
Guane Sancti Spíritus
G. de Batabanó
I. de la
Juventud
I. de
Pinos

Arch. de
Camagüey Cayo Romano
Morón Ciego de Ávila
Camagüey
CUBA Holguín Banes
Victoria de Bayamo
las Tunas Guantánamo
Jardines Manzanillo
de la Reina Santiago
C. Cruz de Cuba
G. de Guacanayabo

C. San Antonio
C.Catoche
Pto
Juárez
C. San Antonio

Yucatan Channel

Little Cayman
(U.K.)
Grand Cayman
(U.K.)
Cayman Brac

CARIBBEAN

Montego Bay
Spanish Town
JAMAICA
Kingston
Port
Antonio
Pedro Cays
(Jam.)

Serrana Bank
(U.S.A. & Col.)
Cayos Miskitos
I. de Caratasca
Pto Cabezas
HONDURAS
Comayagua Juticalpa
Tegucigalpa Paraca
San Salvador
La Ceiba Trujillo
Sta Rosa Yoro
S. Pedro Sula I. de la Bahía
Tela
Pto
Cortés
Coco
(Segovia)
Bonanza
NICARAGUA
L. de Managua Bluefields
Juigalpa
Rio Grande
L. de
Nicaragua San Juan del Norte
San Juan
Prinzapolca
I. de Providencia
(Col.)
I. de San Andrés
(Col.)
Is del Maíz
(Nic. & U.S.A.)

SEA

Alajuela Limón
Colón Pta S. Blas
La Chorrera PANAMA
Panamá
David Arch.
de
las Perlas
Chitré
Golfo
de
Panamá
Pen.
de Azuero
Pta
Solano

90   80

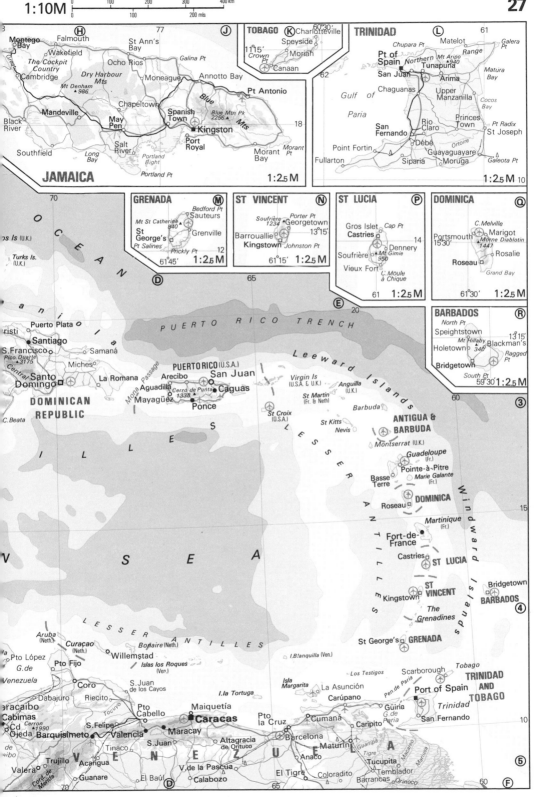

100   200   300   400 km
100   200 mls

JAMAICA

Montego Bay   Falmouth   St Ann's Bay
Wakefield   Galina Pt
The Cockpit Country   Ocho Rios
Cambridge   Dry Harbour Mts   Moneague   Annotto Bay
Mt Denham 986   Blue   Pt Antonio
Chapelton   Mts
Mandeville   Spanish   Blue Mtn Pk 2256
May Pen   Town   18
Black River   Kingston
Southfield   Salt River   Port Royal
Long Bay   Portland Bight   Morant Pt
Portland Pt   Morant Bay

1:2.5 M

TOBAGO   Charlotteville
Speyside
Crown   Moriah   60°30'
Canaan   11°15'

TRINIDAD   61
Chupara Pt   Matelot   Galera Pt
Pt of Spain   Northern   Mt Aripo 940   Range
San Juan   Tunapuna
Chaguanas   Arima   Matura Bay
Gulf of Paria   Upper Manzanilla   Cocos Bay
San Fernando   Rio Claro   Princes Town   Pt Radix
Point Fortin   Débé   St Joseph
Fullarton   Siparia   Guayaguayare
Moruga   Galeota Pt

1:2.5 M   10
62

GRENADA
Bedford Pt
Mt St Catherine 840   Sauteurs
St George's   Grenville
Pt Salines   Prickly Pt   12
61°45'   1:2.5 M

ST VINCENT
Soufrière   Porter Pt
1234   Georgetown
Barrouallie   13°15'
Kingstown   Johnston Pt
61°15'   1:2.5 M

ST LUCIA
Gros Islet   Cap Pt
Castries   14
Soufrière   Mt Gimie 950
Dennery
Vieux Fort   C. Moule à Chique
61   1:2.5 M

DOMINICA
C. Melville
Portsmouth   Marigot
15°30'   Morne Diablotin 1447
Roseau   Rosalie
Grand Bay
61°30'   1:2.5 M

BARBADOS
North Pt
Speightstown   13°15'
Holetown   Mt Hillaby 340   Blackman's
Bridgetown   Ragged Pt
South Pt
59°30'   1:2.5 M

Turks Is. (U.K.)
ris Is (U.K.)

O C E A N

Puerto Plata   70
risti
S.Francisco   Santiago   Samaná
Pico Duarte 3175   Miches
Central   Santo Domingo   La Romana
DOMINICAN REPUBLIC
C. Beata

PUERTO RICO TRENCH
20
Leeward Islands

Mona Passage
PUERTO RICO (U.S.A.)
Arecibo   San Juan
Aguadilla   Cerro de Punta 1338   Caguas
Mayagüez   Ponce

Virgin Is (U.S.A. & U.K.)   Anguilla (U.K.)
St Martin (Fr. & Neth.)

St Croix (U.S.A.)   Barbuda

St Kitts   **ANTIGUA & BARBUDA**
Nevis
Montserrat (U.K.)

Guadeloupe (Fr.)
Pointe-à-Pitre
Basse   Marie Galante (Fr.)
Terre
Roseau   **DOMINICA**

Martinique (Fr.)
Fort-de-France

Castries   **ST LUCIA**

Kingstown   **ST VINCENT**

The Grenadines

St George's   **GRENADA**

15

A N T I L L E S   **L E S S E R**

C A R I B B E A N   **S E A**

L E S S E R   **A N T I L L E S**

Aruba (Neth.)   Curaçao (Neth.)   Bonaire (Neth.)
Willemstad   Islas los Roques (Ven.)   I.B!anquilla (Ven.)
Pto López   Pto Fijo   Los Testigos
G.de   Coro   Scarborough   Tobago
Venezuela   S.Juan de los Cayos   Isla Margarita   La Asunción   Pen de Paria   **TRINIDAD AND**
Dabajuro   Riecito   Pto Cabello   I.la Tortuga   Carúpano   **TOBAGO**
aracaibo   Maiquetía   Güiria   Port of Spain
Cabimas   Cerron 1990   S.Felipe   **Caracas**   Pto la Cruz   Cumaná   G.de Paria   Trinidad
Cd Ojeda   Barquisimeto   Valencia   Maracay   Caripito   San Fernando   10
aibo   S.Juan   Altagracia de Ortuco   Barcelona   Maturín
Valera   Tinaco   Anaco   Guanipa   Tigre
Trujillo   Acarigua   **V E N E Z U E L A**   Tucupita   Macareo
Cord. de Mérida   Guanare   V. de la Pascua   El Tigre   Tremblador
Valera   El Baúl   Calabozo   Coloradito   Barrancas   Orinoco
70   65   60

1:40M

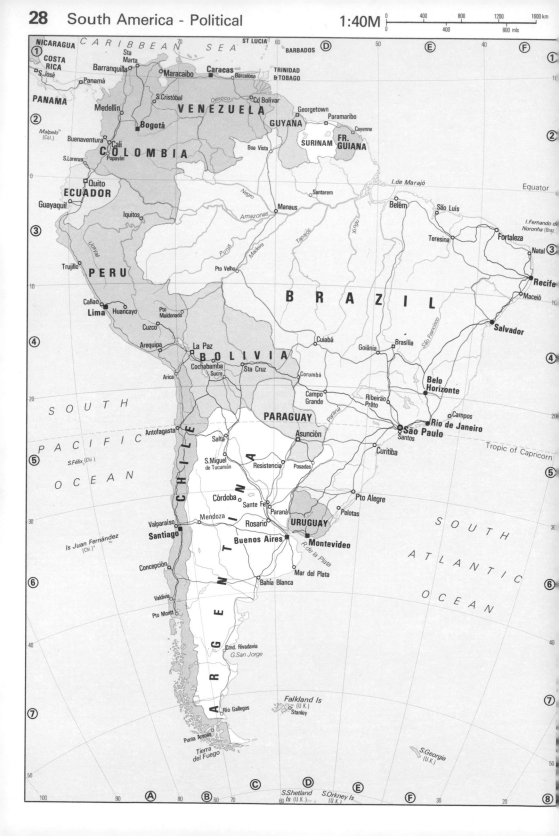

1:15M

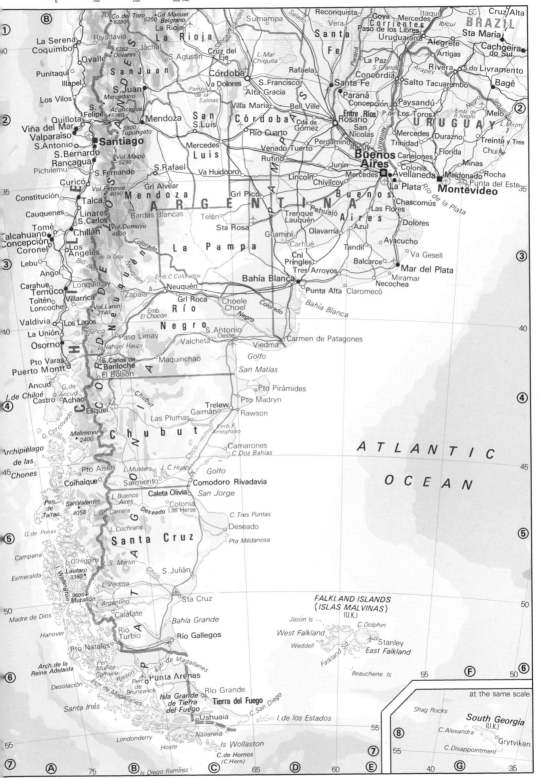

ATLANTIC

OCEAN

FALKLAND ISLANDS
(ISLAS MALVINAS)
(U.K.)

West Falkland

East Falkland

Stanley

at the same scale

South Georgia
(U.K.)

Grytviken

1:15M

200   400 km
100   200

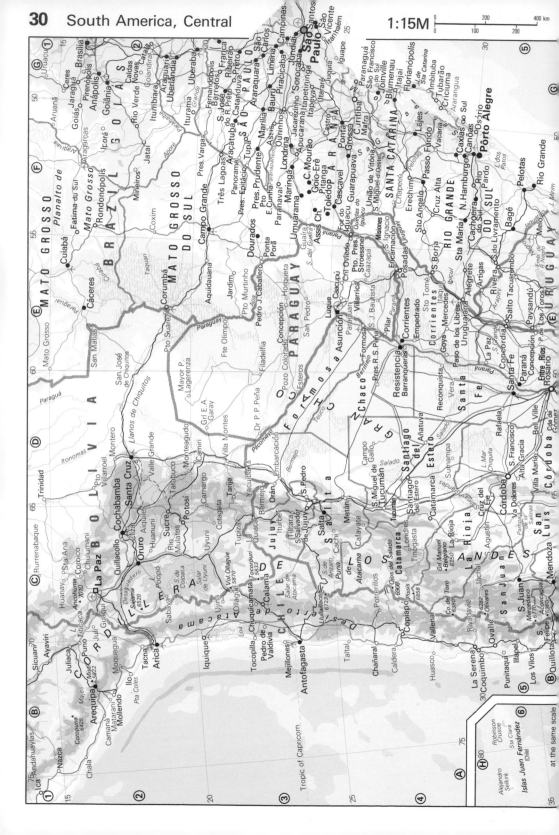

1:15M

| 200 | 400 | 600 km |
| 100 | 200 | 300 mls |

Equator

PARÁ
MARANHÃO
CEARÁ
RIO GRANDE DO NORTE
PARAÍBA
PERNAMBUCO
PIAUÍ
BRAZIL
BAHIA
ALAGOAS
SERGIPE
GOIÁS
MINAS GERAIS
ESPÍRITO SANTO
SÃO PAULO

A T L A N T I C   O C E A N

Tropic of Capricorn

C. Maguarinho
I. de Marajó
B. de Marajó
Salinópolis
Bragança
Pará
Belém
Capanema
Abaetetuba
Cametá
Alcântara
Pinheiro
São Luís
Rosário
Parnaíba
Camocim
Acaraú
Tucuruí
Monção
Chapadinha
Coroatá
Bacabal
Codó
Caxias
Campo Maior
Teresina
Castelo
Crateús
Sta Quitéria
Sobral
Itapipoca
Caucaia
Fortaleza (Ceará)
Canindé
Aracati
Morada N
Nova Russas
Quixadá
Piripiri
Oeiras
Floriano
Picos
J. do Norte
Crato
Mombaça
Tauá
Iguatu
Acopiara
Patu
Caicó
Sousa
Patos
Sa Talhada
Salgueiro
Ouricuri
Paulistana
S.Raimundo Nonato
Petrolina
Juàzeiro
Garanhuns
Palmeira dos Ind
Propriá
Penedo
Lagarto
Arapiraca
Maceió
Aracaju
Estância
Serrinha
Jacobina
R.de Jacuipe
Feira de S.
Iaçu
Castro Alves
Cachoeira
Alagoinhas
Salvador (Bahia)
Valença
Jequié
Ipiaú
Itabuna
Ilhéus
Canavieiras
Belmonte
Pôrto Seguro
Itamaraju
Nanuque
São Mateus
Linhares
Colatina
SANTO
Vitória
Vila Velha
Cachoeiro de Itapemirim
S.João da Barra
Campos
Nova Friburgo
Petrópolis
Magé
Niterói
Rio de Janeiro
São Paulo
Santos
São Vicente
Itanhaém
Juquiá
Iguape
São Francisco do Sul
Paranaguá
Curitiba
Mafra
União de Vitória
Guarapuava
Ponta Grossa
Castro
Itararé
Itapeva
Itapetininga
Sorocaba
Jundiaí
Campinas
Jacarezinho
Apucarana
Londrina
Ourinhos
Assis
Pres. Prudente
Araçatuba
Marília
Bauru
Piracicaba
Limeira
Araraquara
São Carlos
Catanduva
Barretos
Franca
Ribeirão Prêto
Poços de Caldas
Lavras
Barbacena
Juiz de Fora
Volta Redonda
Barra Mansa
S.João del Rei
Divinópolis
Belo Horizonte
Sete Lagoas
Carátinga
Manhuaçu
Ponte Nova
Cariacica
Fabriciano
Cnl
Gov. Valadares
Teófilo Otôni
Diamantina
Itabira
Lafaiete
Carangola
Itaperuna
Caetité
Vitória da Conquista
Araçuai
Itapetinga
Itambacuri
Montes Claros
Salinas
Porteirinha
São Francisco
Januária
Brasília
Anápolis
Pirenópolis
Goiânia
Ceres
Formosa
Jaraguá
Goiás
Uruaçu
Aruanã
Rio Verde
Caldas Novas
Goiandira
Catalão
Araguari
Uberlândia
Ituiutaba
Paracatu
Pirapora
Corinto
Curvelo
Patos de Minas
João Pinheiro
Araxá
Uberaba
Iturama
Fernandópolis
S.José do R.Prêto
Barra
Ibotirama
Bom Jesus da Lapa
Barreiras
Marabá
Imperatriz
Grajaú
Pto Franco
Carolina
Balsas
Araguaína
Jatobá
.do Araguaia
C.do Araguaia
Ilha do Bananal
S.Félix
Jataí
póra
Itumbiara
Pres. Vargas
Araçuai
Sa do Chifre
Morro do Espinhaço
Serra do Espinhaço
Serra de Mantiqueira
Sa da Mantiqueira
Chapada Diamantina
Tocantins
Araguaia
Paranã
Grande
Paraná
São Francisco
Contas
Jequitinhonha
Doce
Velhas
Paraíba
Paranaíba
Gurupi
Pindaré
Capim
Mearim
Parnaíba
B. de São Marcos
Camocim
Rocas
I. Fernando de Noronha
Areia Branca
Macau
Pta do Calcanhar
Natal
Cabedelo
João Pessoa
Campina Grande
Limoeiro
Caruaru
Olinda
Recife (Pernambuco)
Caboatão
Palmares
Barreiros
Pt do Borborema
Sa do Borborema
Garanhuns
Cach de P.Alfonso
Sen.do Bonfim
B. de T. os Santos
Mossoró
Aracaú
Mombaça
Caldas Novas

Pres. Vargas
0
5
10
15
20
25

A   B   C   D   E
50   45   40   35

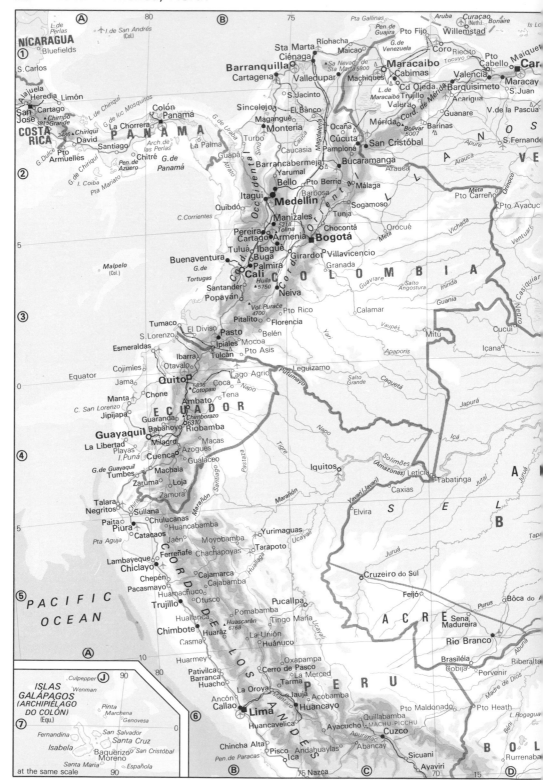

ISLAS GALÁPAGOS (ARCHIPIÉLAGO DO COLÓN) (Equ.)

at the same scale

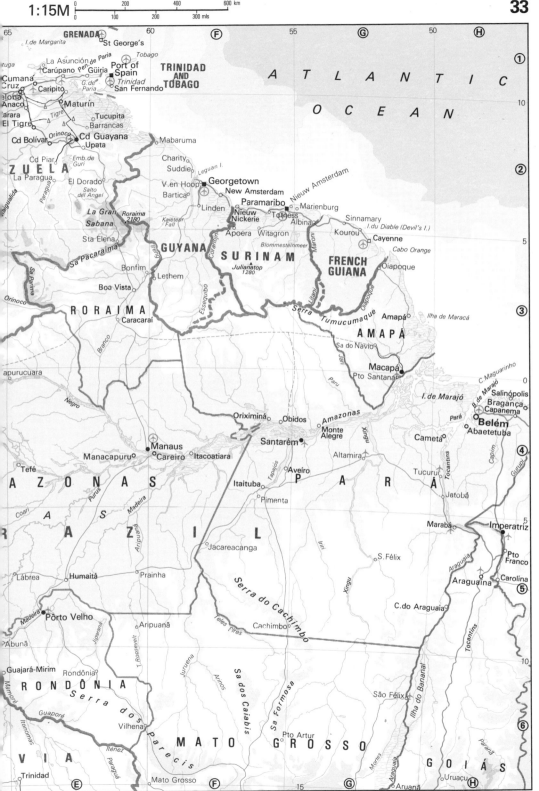

200   400   600 km
100   200   300 mls

65   60   F   55   G   50   H

GRENADA
St George's
I. de Margarita
La Asunción Pen de Paria Güiria Tobago
Carúpano Port of Spain   **TRINIDAD**
Cumaná   Trinidad   **AND**
Cruz G. de Paria San Fernando   **TOBAGO**
Caripito
Anaco
ararа Maturín
El Tigre Tucupita
Tigre Barrancas
Cd Bolívar Orinoco Cd Guayana
Upata Mabaruma
Cd Piar Emb. de Guri
ZUELA La Paragua   Charity
El Dorado   Suddie
Salto del Angel V. en Hoop Leguan I. Georgetown
Roraima 2180   Bartica New Amsterdam
La Gran   Linden Nieuw Amsterdam
Sabana Kaieteur Fall   Nieuw Paramaribo Marienburg
Sta Elena Nickerie Totness
Sa Pacaraima Julianatop Albina Sinnamary
GUYANA 1280   I. du Diable (Devil's I.)
Sa Parima Bonfim   **SURINAM** Kourou
Lethem Apoera Witagron   Cayenne
Boa Vista Blommesteinmeer   Cabo Orange
FRENCH
Orinoco   **GUIANA**
RORAIMA   Serra Tumucumaque Oiapoque
Caracaraí   Amapá Ilha de Maracá
Branco   Sa do Navio **AMAPÁ**
apurucuara   Jari
Macapá
Negro   Paru Pto Santana C. Maguarinho
0
I. de Marajó Salinópolis
Oriximiná Obidos Pará B. de Marajó Bragança
Amazonas Capanema
Manaus Santarém Monte **Belém**
Manacapuru Careiro Itacoatiara Alegre Cametá Abaetetuba
AZONAS Altamira
Tefé Aveíro **PARÁ** Tucuruí
Purus Itaituba Tapajós Jatobá
Madeira Pimenta 5
Coari **BRAZIL** Marabá Imperatriz
Aripuanã Jacareacanga Iriri Pto
Lábrea Humaitá Prainha S. Félix Franco
Xingu Araguaína Carolina
Madeira Pôrto Velho Teles Pires **Serra do Cachimbo** C. do Araguaia 5
Guajará-Mirim Aripuanã Cachimbo 10
Abunã Rondônia **RONDÔNIA** Serra dos Caiabis São Félix
Guaporé Sa dos parecis Sa Formosa 6
Itenez Vilhena Pto Artur
Juruena Arinos
VIA **MATO** **GROSSO** **GOIÁS**
Trinidad Mato Grosso Aruanã Uruaçu
E   F   15   G   H

ATLANTIC
OCEAN
10

1

2

5

3

4

10

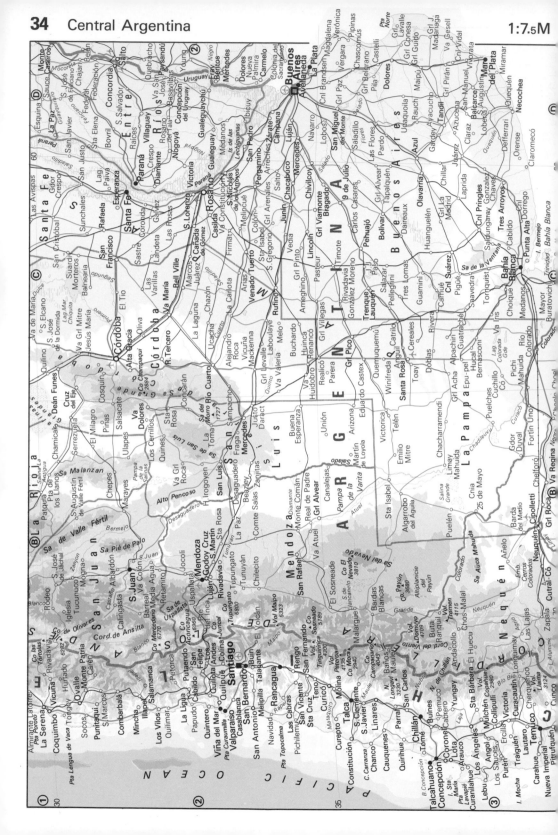

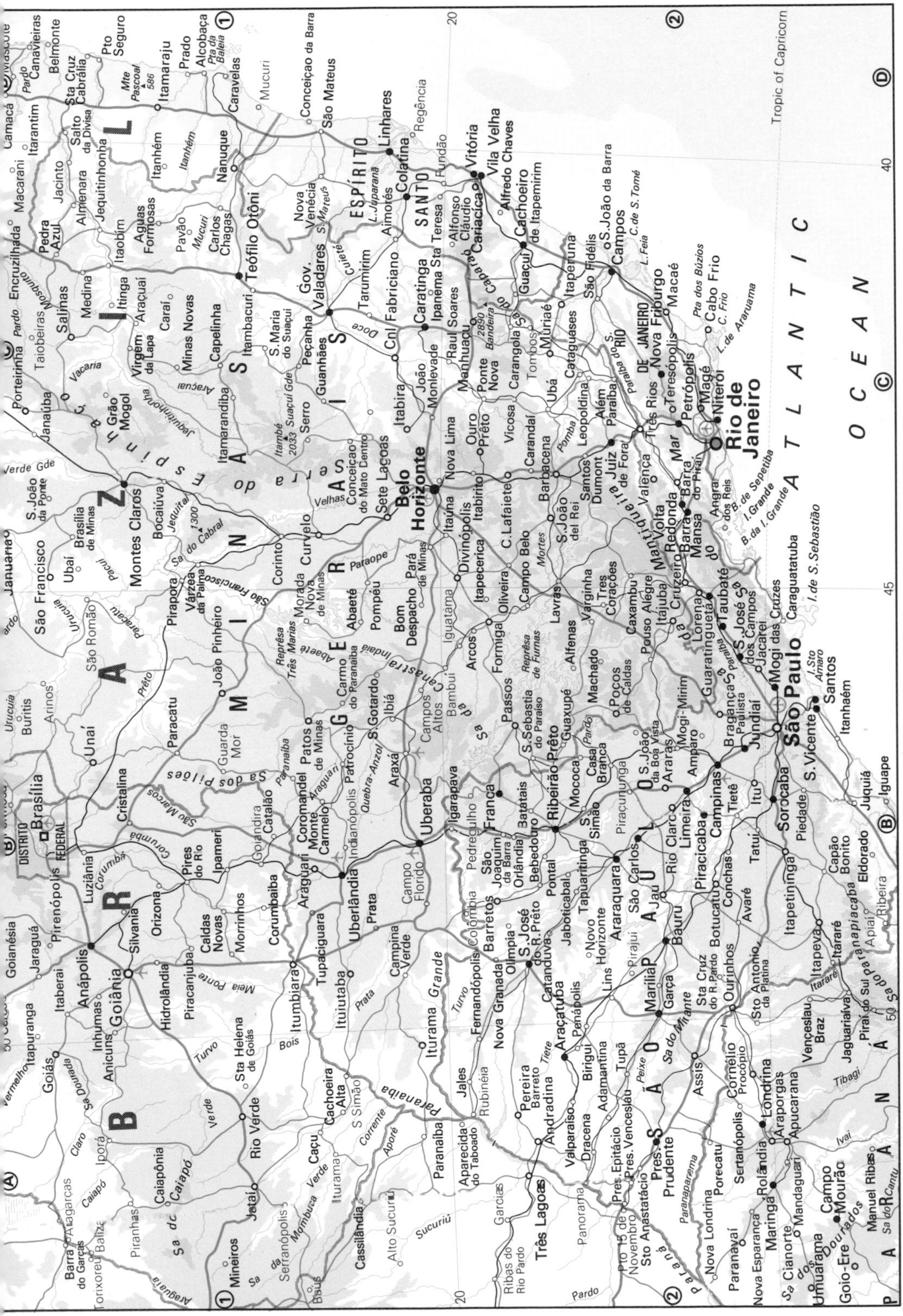

Scale: 0 — 100 — 200 — 300 km
0 — 50 — 100 — 150 mls

Tropic of Capricorn

A T L A N T I C   O C E A N

Rio de Janeiro — Niterói — Magé — Petrópolis — Teresópolis — Nova Friburgo — Macaé — Cabo Frio — C. Frio — Pta dos Búzios — L. de Araruama

Belo Horizonte — São Paulo — São Vicente — Santos — Santo Amaro — Itanhaém

ESPÍRITO SANTO — Vitória — Vila Velha — Colatina — Linhares — São Mateus — Conceição da Barra — Cachoeiro de Itapemirim — Alfredo Chaves — Afonso Cláudio — Sta Teresa — Nova Venécia

MINAS GERAIS — Montes Claros — Teófilo Otoni — Gov. Valadares — Itabira — Curvelo — Sete Lagoas — Diamantina — Januária — Pirapora — Uberaba — Uberlândia — Araguari — Patos de Minas — Araxá — Patrocínio — Juiz de Fora — Ubá — Viçosa — São João del Rei — Lavras — Poços de Caldas — Varginha — Passos — Divinópolis — C. Lafaiete — Barbacena

SERRA DO ESPINHAÇO

RIO DE JANEIRO — Campos — São Fidélis — São João da Barra — C. de S. Tomé — Volta Redonda — Barra Mansa — Resende — Barra do Piraí — Valença — Três Rios — Angra dos Reis — I. Grande — B. da I. Grande

SÃO PAULO — Campinas — Sorocaba — Jundiaí — Piracicaba — Ribeirão Prêto — Franca — Bauru — Marília — Presidente Prudente — Araçatuba — Araraquara — São José do Rio Prêto — São Carlos — Botucatu — Jaú — Avaré — Itapetininga — Taubaté — São José dos Campos — Guaratinguetá — Lorena — Cruzeiro — Caraguatatuba — I. de S. Sebastião

PARANÁ — Londrina — Maringá — Apucarana — Cornélio Procópio — Jacarèzinho

DISTRITO FEDERAL — Brasília — Anápolis — Goiânia — Goiás — Pirenópolis — Luziânia — Cristalina — Catalão

Rios: São Francisco — Paranaíba — Grande — Paranapanema — Tietê — Paraná — Doce — Paraíba — Paranã — Ivaí — Tibagi

(1:7.5M — South-East Brazil — 35)

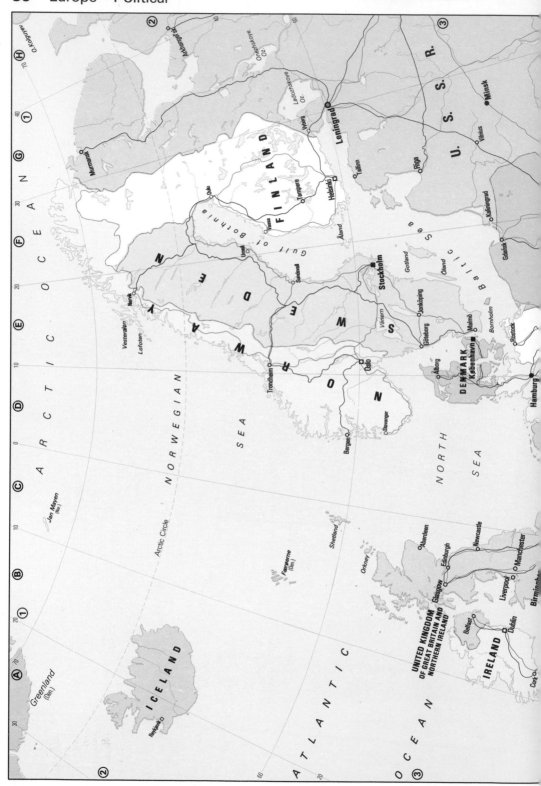

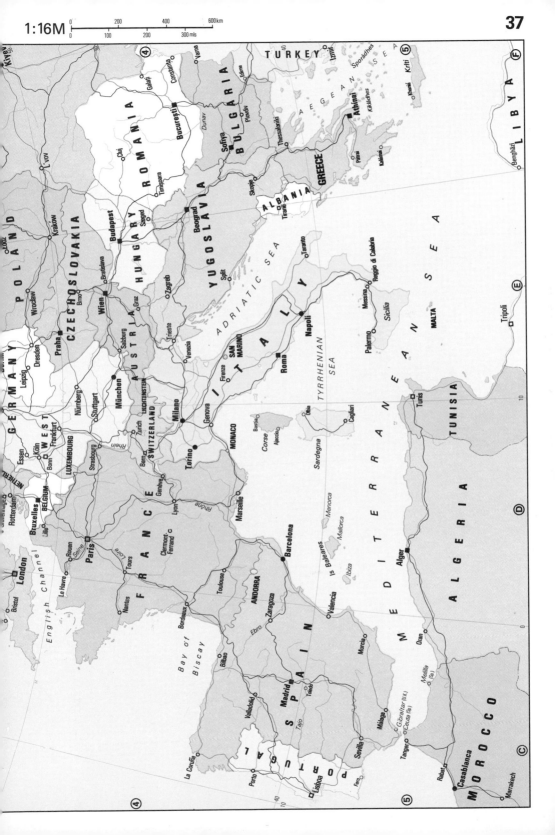

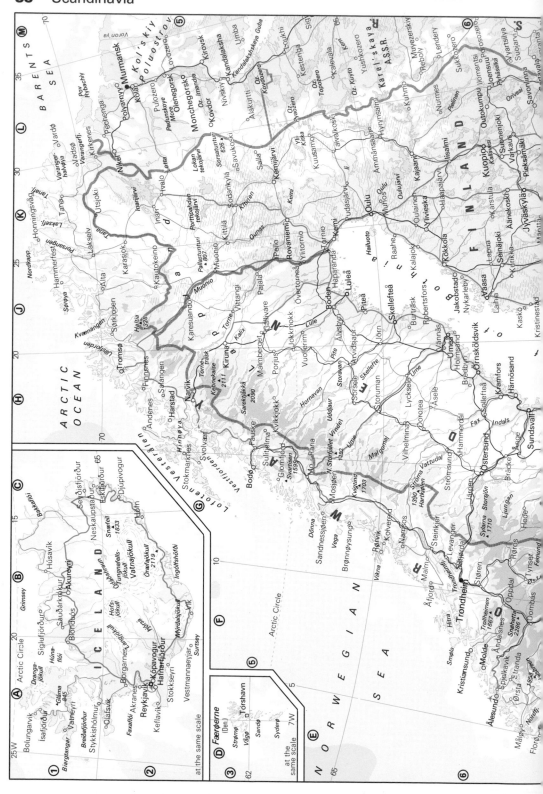

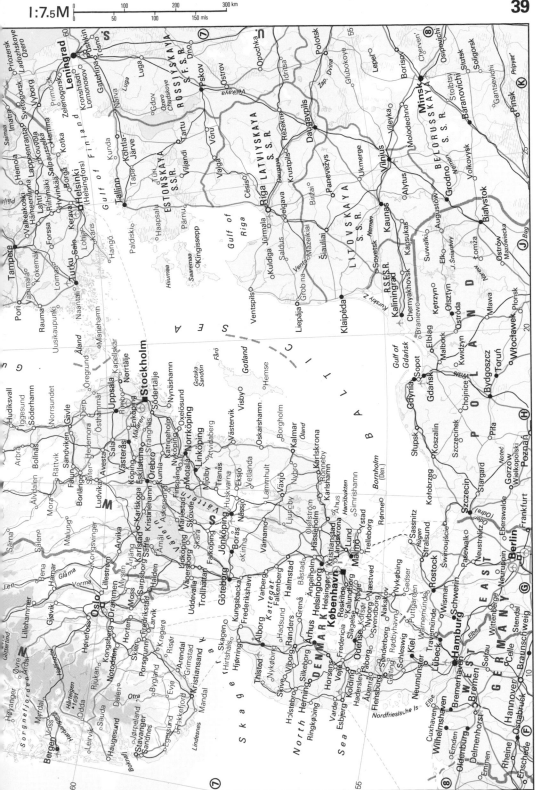

100 200 300 km

50 100 150 mls

⑦

⑧

S
U.

Priozersk
Ladozhskoye
Ozero
Priozersk
Svetogorsk
Kronshtadt
Leningrad Pushkin
Lomonosov Gatchina

Imatra
Heinola
Valkeakoski
Hämeenlinna
Lappeenranta
Kouvola
Lahti
Salpausselkä
Hyvinkää
Borgå
Vyborg
Primorsk
Zelenogorsk
Vuoksa
Luga
Luga
Gatchina
Oredezh
Chyeven
Osipovichi
Slutsk
Soligorsk

Pskov
Ostrov
Dno
Opochka
Polotsk
Borisov
Minsk
Stolbtsy
Baranovichi
Gantsevichi
Pinsk
Pripyat'

Tampere

Pori
Rauma
Naantali
Turku
Helsinki
(Helsingfors)

Hangö
Paldiski
Haapsalu
Pärnu
Viljandi
Tartu
Vōru
Valga
Valmiera
Rēzekne
Daugavpils
Vitebsk

ROSSIYSKAYA S.F.S.R.

ESTONSKAYA S.S.R.
Tallinn

Hiiumaa
Saaremaa
Okingissepp
Gulf of Riga

Ventspils

LATVIYSKAYA S.S.R.
Riga
Jūrmala
Jelgava
Kuldīga
Venta
Saldus
Grob na Mazeikiai
Šiauliai
Panevēžys
Biržai
Krustpils

Liepāja
Klaipēda
Sovetsk
Taurage
Kapsukas
Kaunas
Jonava
Vilnius
Ukmergė
Molodechno
Vileyka
Molodechno

LITOVSKAYA S.S.R.

R.S.F.S.R.
Kaliningrad
Chernyakhovsk
Braniewo
Elbląg
Malbork

BELORUSSKAYA S.S.R.
Grodno
Alytus
Lida
Baranovichi
Volkovysk
Slonim
Nyeman
Mosty
J.Bug

Suwałki
Augustów
Ełk
Łomża
Ostrów Maz.
Grajewo
Białystok
Bielsk

Olsztyn
Ostróda
Mława
Ciechanów
Płońsk
Włocławek

K
J
H

Gulf of Finland
BALTIC SEA

Öland
Åland
Mariehamn

Stockholm
Uppsala
Södertälje
Nynäshamn
Norrtälje
Norrköping
Linköping

Gotland
Visby
Fårö
Gotska Sandön

Gdynia
Gdańsk
Sopot
Wisła
Słupsk
Koszalin
Kołobrzeg
Szczecinek
Chojnice
Piła
Bydgoszcz
Toruń
Gorzów Wielkopolski
Poznań
Stargard
Szczecin

POLAND

Bornholm (Den.)

Berlin
EAST GERMANY
WEST GERMANY

København
DENMARK

North Sea
Skagerrak
Kattegat

Oslo
Bergen
Stavanger

N
M
S
U

Sorgnefjorden
Glitterlind
Galdhøpiggen

60
55
55
25
20
15
10

1:5M

③ Esbjerg

's-Gravenhage (Den Haag) Rotterdam
NETHERLANDS
Antwerpen Mechelen
Brugge Bruxelles (Brussel)
Oostende Gent Roubaix Mons Valenciennes
Vlissingen Zeebrugge Kortrijk Tournai Denain
BELGIUM Lille Douai
Dunkerque Tourcoing Cambrai
Calais St-Omer Arras Laon
Dover St-A Béthune PICARDIE Soissons Château-Thierry
Canterbury Boulogne Montreuil Abbeville Amiens Compiègne
Folkestone Hastings Le Tréport Beauvais Senlis St-Quentin Provins
Eastbourne Dieppe Neufchâtel Mondidier Oise Melun Sézanne Romilly-s-S
Brighton Fécamp Bolbec Rouen Mantes Cergy Pontoise Meaux Paris Sens
English Channel Le Havre Elbeuf Louviers Versailles FRANCE Fontainebleau
Deauville Lisieux Evreux Dreux Chartres Etampes Rambouillet
Cherbourg Bayeux Caen Argentan Alençon Mayenne
pte de Barfleur Valognes St-Lô Coutances NORMANDIE Orne Domfront Mont-St-Michel
C. de la Hague Alderney Guernsey Sark St Helier Granville St-Malo Fougères
Channel Is (U.K.) Jersey Golfe de St-Malo Dinan Dinard Dol St-Michel
Prawle Pt Roscoff Morlaix St-Brieuc Carhaix Plouguer
Lizard Pt Brest I. d'Ouessant

's-Gravenhage Rotterdam Harwich Felixstowe
Great Yarmouth Lowestoft
Norwich
King's Lynn The Wash Newmarket Cambridge Ipswich Colchester Chelmsford Southend-on-Sea
Peterborough Bedford Luton Maidstone Crawley Guildford
Leicester Northampton Oxford Windsor Reading Winchester Southampton
Coventry ENGLAND Swindon Bath Salisbury Bournemouth Portsmouth Isle of Wight
Birmingham Gloucester Bristol Weston-super-Mare Taunton Weymouth Torbay
WALES Worcester Wye Newport Cardiff Bristol Chan.
Aberystwyth Builth Wells Brecon Swansea Barnstaple Bude Exeter Dartmoor Plymouth Torbay
Cardigan Bay Carmarthen Pembroke Fishguard St David's Hd Newquay Truro Falmouth
St George's Chan. Land's End Penzance
Isles of Scilly

Middlesbrough Scarborough
Yorkshire Moors Flamborough Hd
York Hull Humber Grimsby
Leeds Bradford Huddersfield Doncaster Lincoln
Harrogate Manchester Sheffield Nottingham Derby
Blackpool Preston Bolton Stoke-on-Trent Trent
Morecambe Barrow-in-Furness Kendal Scafell Pike 977
Lancaster Liverpool Birkenhead Chester Crewe Shrewsbury Wolverhampton
Isle of Man Douglas Holyhead Bangor Anglesey Snowdon Dee
IRISH SEA Pwllheli

Portadown Armagh Newry Dundalk Drogheda
Monaghan Cavan Dublin (Baile Átha Cliath) Dun Laoghaire Bray Wicklow Arklow
Enniskillen Longford Mullingar Wicklow Mts Wexford Rosslare
Sligo B. Sligo Boyle Roscommon Athlone Monasterevan Port Laoise Carlow Kilkenny Barrow
REP. OF IRELAND Limerick Tipperary Clonmel Waterford Dungarvan
Galway Ennis L. Derg Dingle Tralee Killarney Cork Youghal
Achill I. Clew B. L. Mask L. Corrib Galway B. Aran Is Carrauntoohill 1041 Bantry Old Hd of Kinsale
Slyne Hd Dingle B. Bantry B. C. Clear

1:2.5M

0 25 50 75 100 km
0 25 50 mils

Shetland (inset 1)
Herma Ness, Unst, Fetlar, Yell, Whalsay, Bressay, Out Skerries, Lerwick, Brae, Scalloway, St Magnus Bay, Hillswick, Isbister, The Faither, Papa Stour, Sumburgh Hd, Fitful Hd, Fair Isle, Foula, Shetland

Orkney (inset 2)
Papa Westray, N. Ronaldsay, Sanday, Stronsay, Eday, Shapinsay, Westray, Rousay, Birsay, Mainland, Kirkwall, Burray, S. Ronaldsay, Stromness, Scapa Flow, Hoy, Pentland Firth, Dunnet Hd, John o' Groats, Thurso

at the same scale

Mainland
N O R T H   S E A
Long Forties
Buchan Deep

Aberdeen, Girdle Ness, Stonehaven, Montrose, Arbroath, Fife Ness, Dundee, St Andrews, North Berwick, Haddington, Berwick-upon-Tweed, St Abb's Hd, Eyemouth, Lammermuir Hills, Duns

Fraserburgh, Peterhead, Buchan Ness, Kinnairds Hd, Banff, Inverurie, Huntly, Keith, Dufftown, Elgin, Lossiemouth, Forres, Nairn, Cromarty, Spey, Ythan, Don, Dee, Banchory, Ballater, Braemar, Brechin, Forfar, A. Esk

Grampian, Grantown-on-Spey, Cairngorms, Ben Macdui ▲1310, Lochnagar ▲1155, Aviemore, Kingussie, Pitlochry, Blair Atholl, Aberfeldy, Crieff, Blairgowrie, Perth, Cupar, Glenrothes, Methil, Kirkcaldy, Dunfermline, Edinburgh, Loch Leven, Kinross, Tayside, Central, Lothian

Grampian Mountains, Monadhliath Mts, Highland, Findhorn, Black Isle, Inverness, Loch Ness, Glen More, Fort Augustus, Ben Nevis ▲1344, Fort William, Ballachulish, Loch Rannoch, L. Ericht, L. Tummel, L. Tay, Loch Tay, Ben Lawers ▲1214, Killin, Crianlarich, Callander, Stirling, Falkirk, Livingston, Coatbridge, Glasgow, Hamilton, Motherwell, Paisley, Dumbarton

Wick, Lybster, Helmsdale, Brora, Beatrice, Thurso, Dunnet Hd, Pentland Firth, Hoy, Burray, S. Ronaldsay, John o' Groats Firth, Dornoch Firth, Tarbat Ness, Tain, Dornoch, Lairg, L. Shin, Ben More Assynt ▲998, Ben Kilbreck ▲961, Ben Hope ▲927, Tongue, Durness, C. Wrath, Eriboll, L. Eriboll, Oykel, Ben Dearg ▲1081, Ben Wyvis ▲1045, Alness, Dingwall, Beauly, Ben Attow ▲1031, Kyle of Lochalsh, Strath, Farrar, Glen

Scotland

Ullapool, Lochinver, Enard Bay, Eddrachillis Bay, Greenstone Pt, Gairloch, L. Maree, L. Broom, Rubha Hunish, L. Torridon, L. Ewe, Applecross, Raasay, Sd of Raasay, Portree, Cuillin Hills, Isle of Skye, L. Snizort, L. Bracadale, Broadford, Kyle of Lochalsh, Sd of Sleat, Mallaig, L. Hourn, L. Nevis, Knoydart, Arisaig, L. Morar, L. Shiel, Loch Linnhe, Morvern, Ardnamurchan Pt, Mull, Tobermory, Ulva, Staffa, Iona, Oban, Firth of Lorn, Loch Etive, Loch Awe, Loch Fyne, Inveraray, Arrochar, Helensburgh, Greenock, Rothesay, Bute, Largs, Firth of Clyde

Western Isles, Flannan Is, Butt of Lewis, Broad B., Stornoway, Loch Roag, Lewis, Harris, Tarbert, Scarp, Taransay, Pabbay, Sd of Harris, North Uist, Monach Is, Benbecula, South Uist, Lochmaddy, Lochboisdale, Eriskay, Barra, Castlebay, Barra Hd, Little Minch, The Minch, North Minch, Sea of the Hebrides, Eigg, Muck, Rum, Canna, Coll, Tiree, Colonsay, Jura, Islay, Sd of Jura, Port Askaig, Tarbert, Ardrishaig, Sd of Barra

56   58   60

1:2.5M

0   25   50   75   100 km
0   25   50 mils

NETHERLANDS

WESTFALEN

GERMANY

RHEINLAND

PFALZ

SAARLAND

BELGIQUE — BELGIË

LUXEMBOURG

Moselle

Meuse

Ardennes

Aisne

Somme

Oise

Marne

Seine

Pas-de-Calais

Nord

NORTH SEA

Rotterdam • Dordrecht • Gorinchem

Dortmund • Bochum • Essen • Duisburg • Düsseldorf • Wuppertal • Köln (Cologne) • Bonn

Mannheim • Ludwigshafen • Wiesbaden am Main • Frankfurt am Main • Mainz • Worms • Speyer

Karlsruhe • Baden-Baden

Saarbrücken • Metz • Nancy • Thionville

Antwerpen (Anvers) • Bruxelles (Brüssel) • Gent (Gand) • Liège • Namur • Charleroi • Mons

Maastricht • Aachen • Eindhoven • Breda • Tilburg

Lille • Roubaix • Tourcoing • Arras • Valenciennes • Douai

Reims • Épernay • Châlons • Soissons • Laon • St-Quentin • Amiens • Beauvais

Paris • St-Denis • Versailles

Calais • Boulogne • Dunkerque • Dover • Deal • Margate • Ramsgate

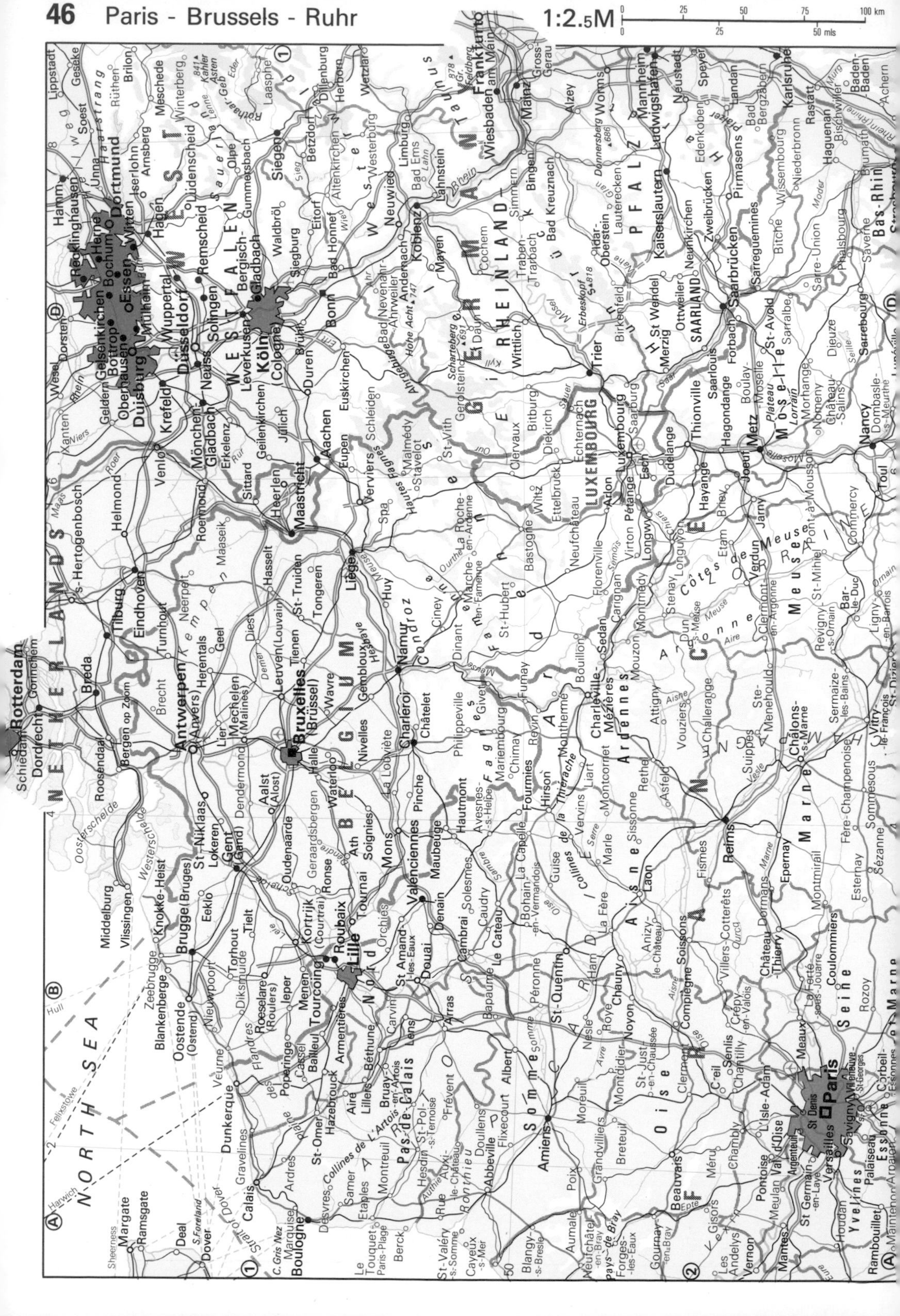

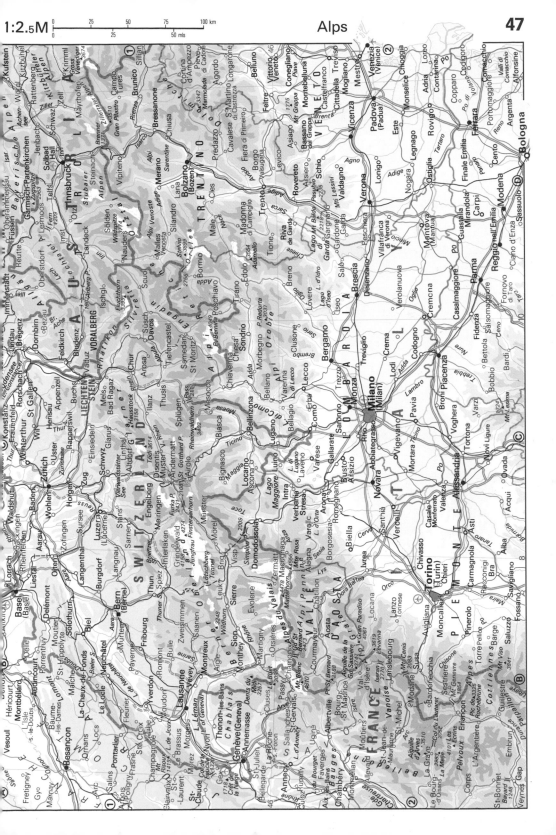

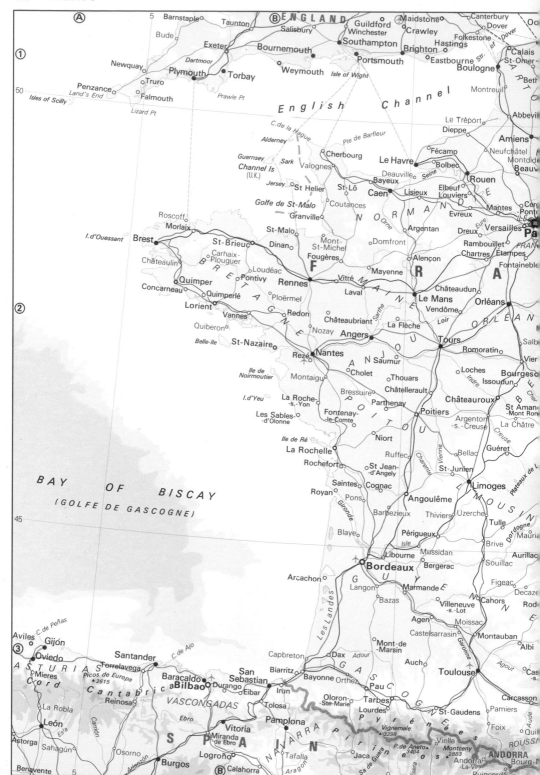

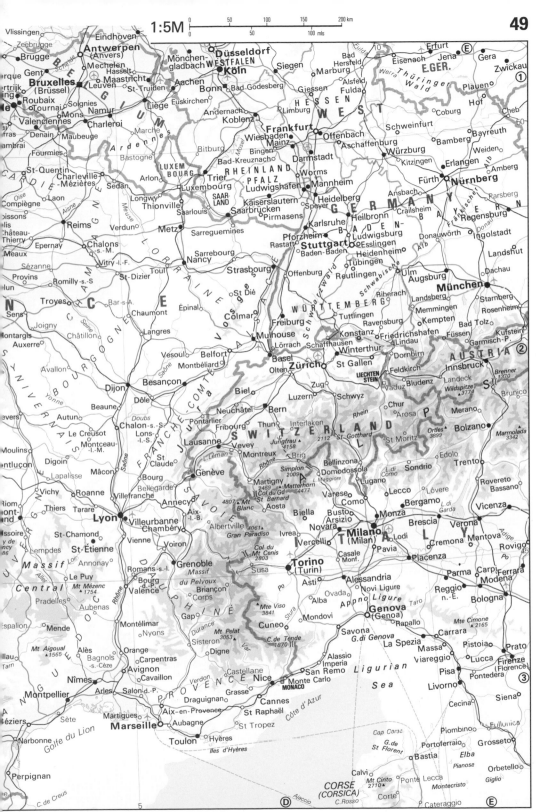

1:5M

50 100 150 200 km
50 100 mls

Vlissingen
Zeebrugge
Brugge
Antwerpen
(Anvers)
Eindhoven
Mönchen-
gladbach
Düsseldorf
WESTFALEN
Köln
Bad
Hersfeld
Eisenach
Erfurt
Jena
Gera
Zwickau
Gent
Mechelen
Maastricht
Aachen
Bonn
Bad-Godesberg
Siegen
Marburg
Alsfeld
Fulda
Coburg
Schweinfurt
Bamberg
Bayreuth
Weiden
E.GER.
Plauen
Hof
Cheb
50
Bruxelles
(Brüssel)
Leuven
Hasselt
St-Truiden
Liège
Euskirchen
Andernach
Koblenz
Limburg
Giessen
Wiesbaden
Mainz
Offenbach
Frankfurt
Aschaffenburg
Würzburg
Kitzingen
Erlangen
Fürth
Nürnberg
Amberg
Roubaix
Tournai
Soignies
Namur
Mons
Charleroi
Marche
Bitburg
Bad-Kreuznach
Darmstadt
Worms
Mannheim
Heidelberg
Speyer
Ansbach
Crailsheim
Regensburg
Rarsberg
Valenciennes
Denain
Maubeuge
Fourmies
Bastogne
LUXEM
BOURG
Trier
Luxembourg
Arlon
RHEINLAND
PFALZ
Ludwigshafen
Kaiserslautern
Pirmasens
Karlsruhe
Heilbronn
Ludwigsburg
Pforzheim
Donauwörth
Ingolstadt
Landshut
St-Quentin
Charleville-
Mézières
Sedan
Longwy
Thionville
SAAR
LAND
Saarbrücken
Saarlouis
Sarreguemines
Stuttgart
Esslingen
Baden-Baden
Heidenheim
Dachau
München
Compiègne
Laon
Reims
Verdun
Metz
Sarrebourg
Rastatt
Offenburg
Reutlingen
Tübingen
Ulm
Augsburg
Starnberg
Aisne
Épernay
Châlons
-s.-M.
Vitry-l.-F.
Nancy
Strasbourg
Freiburg
Schwäbische
Alb
Landsberg
Memmingen
Rosenheim
Sézanne
Troyes
Bar-s.-A.
Chaumont
Épinal
St Dié
Colmar
Mulhouse
Lörrach
Schaffhausen
Konstanz
Friedrichshafen
Lindau
Kempten
Füssen
Bad Tölz
Garmisch-P.
Kufstein
Provins
Sens
Joigny
Langres
Vesoul
Belfort
Montbéliard
Basel
Olten
Zürich
Winterthur
St Gallen
Dornbirn
Feldkirch
Innsbruck
Brenner
1370
Auxerre
Avallon
Besançon
Biel
Neuchâtel
Bern
Luzern
Zug
Schwyz
Vaduz
Bludenz
LIECHTEN
STEIN
Landeck
Wildspitze
3774
Brunico
AUSTRIA
Dijon
Dôle
Pontarlier
Fribourg
Thun
Interlaken
Rhein
Chur
Arosa
Merano
Beaune
Autun
Le Creusot
Chalon-s.-S.
Lons-
-l.-S.
Lausanne
Vevey
Montreux
Jungfrau
4158
Brig
2112
St-Gotthard
St Moritz
Ortles
3899
Bolzano
Marmolada
3342
Moulins
Digoin
Lapalisse
Mâcon
Bourg
Bellegarde
Genève
L'Léman
Martigny
Simplon
2009
Bellinzona
Domodossola
Edolo
Trento
Rovereto
Bassano
Vichy
Roanne
Villefranche
Annecy
Aix-
-l.-B.
Mt
Blanc
4807
St Bernard
Col du Gd
2469
Matterhorn
4477
L. Maggiore
Lugano
Lecco
Lovère
Vicenza
Thiers
Tarare
Lyon
Villeurbanne
Chambéry
Albertville
Gran Paradiso
4061
Aosta
Biella
Ivrea
Busto
Arsizio
Varese
Como
Bergamo
L. di
Garda
Brescia
Verona
St-Chamond
St-Étienne
Vienne
Voiron
Novara
Vercelli
Milano
(Milan)
Monza
Lodi
Cremona
Mantova
Rovigo
Le Puy
Mt Mézenc
1754
Annonay
Romans-s.-l.
Bourg
-d.-P.
Valence
Grenoble
Col du
Mt Cenis
2803
Susa
Torino
(Turin)
Asti
Casale
Monf.
Pavia
Piacenza
Parma
Carpi
Ferrara
Modena
Massif
Central
Pradelles
Aubenas
Privas
Montélimar
Nyons
Massif
du Pelvoux
Briançon
Corps
Gap
Po
Alessandria
Novi Ligure
Ovada
Alba
Appno
Ligure
Taro
Reggio
n.-E.
Bologna
Mende
Mt Aigoual
1565
Alès
Bagnols
-s.-Cèze
Orange
Carpentras
Cavaillon
DAUPHINÉ
Mt Pelat
3053
Digne
Mte Viso
3841
Mondovì
Cuneo
Savona
Genova
(Genoa)
G. di Genova
Rapallo
Mte Cimone
2165
Carrara
Pistoia
Prato
Nîmes
Arles
Salon-d.-P.
PROVENCE
Castellane
Draguignan
Grasse
Nice
Monte Carlo
MONACO
C. de Tende
1870
Alassio
San Remo
La Spezia
Massa
Viareggio
Lucca
Pisa
Pontedera
Firenze
(Florence)
Livorno
Siena
Montpellier
Béziers
Sète
Martigues
Aix-en-Provence
Aubagne
Marseille
Toulon
Hyères
Îles d'Hyères
St Raphaël
St Tropez
Cannes
Côte d'Azur
Cecina
Cap Corse
G. de
St Florent
Piombino
Portoferraio
Bastia
Elba
Pianosa
Grosseto
Narbonne
Golfe du Lion
Perpignan
C. de Creus
CORSE
(CORSICA)
Ajaccio
C. Rosso
Mt Cinto
2710
Ponte Lecca
Corte
Calvi
Montecristo
Orbetello
Giglio
Fullonica
Cateraggio

BELGIUM
ARDENNE
CHAMPAGNE
BOURGOGNE
NIVERNAIS
LORRAINE
ALSACE
FRANCHE-COMTÉ
JURA
VALAIS
SAVOIE
SWITZERLAND
HESSEN
WEST
GERMANY
BADEN-
WÜRTTEMBERG
BAYERN
Fränkische
Alb
Schwarzwald
Thüringer Wald
Rhein
Mosel
Main
Donau
Neckar
Rhône
Saône
Doubs
Seine
Yonne
Loire
Durance
Po
Ligurian
Sea
ITALY
Ligure
Fuldа

①
②
③
D
E

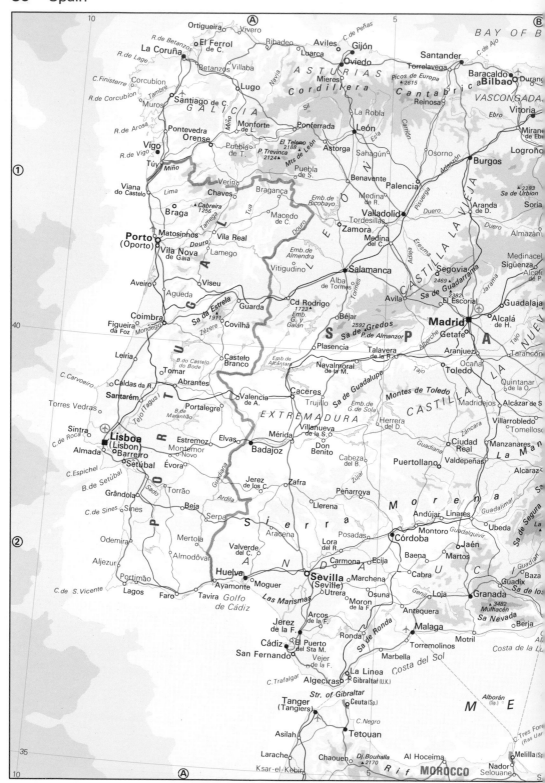

50   100   150   200 km
50   100 mls

CAY
Capbreton
Mont-de-Marsin
Dax
Auch
Albi   C
Toulouse
Nîmes
Arles   Salon-d.-P.   D
Montpellier
Aix-en-Provence
Aubagne
San Sebastian
Biarritz
Bayonne   Orthez
Pau
Castres-s.l'A
Béziers
Sète
Martigues
Marseille
Toulon   Hyères
Irun
Oloron-Ste-Marie
Tarbes
St-Gaudens
Carcassonne
Narbonne
Golfe du Lion
Tolosa
Lourdes
Pamiers
Aude
Foix
Quillan
Perpignan
FRANCE
GASCOGNE
Pamplona
Pyrénées
Vignemale ▲3298
P. de Aneto ▲3404
Viella
Monteny 2883
Andorra-La-Vª
ANDORRA
Bourg-Madame
ROUSSILLON
C. de Creus
NAVARRA
Jaca
Puigcerdá
Figueras
Costa Brava
Tafalla
Aragon
Huesca
Sa del Codi
Gerona
San Feliu de G.
Calahorra
Tudela
Barbastro
Ter
Vich
Alfaro
Ebro
Segre
Tarazona
Alagón
Lérida
Sabadell
Matanó
Granollérs
Zaragoza
Tarrasa
Badalona
Calatayud
CATALUÑA
Reus
Barcelona
Daroca
Caspe
Valls
Villanueva-y-G.
Emb. de Mequinenza
Tarragona
Alcaniz
Golfo de San Jorge
Monreal del C.
Tortosa
Amposta
C. de Tortosa
Sa de Gudar
Vinaroz
Benicarló
Torreblanca
Teruel
▲2019 Penarroya
Sarrión
Castellon de la P.
Villarreal
Is Columbretes
C. Formentor
C. de Caballeria
Menorca   40
Ciudadela   Mahón
Segorbe
Sagunto
C. Binibeca
Mallorca
Alcudia
Mayor ▲1445
Capdepera
Cuenca
Emb. de Alarcón
Turia
VALENCIA
Motilla del P.
Utiel
Cabriel
VALENCIA
Golfo de
Palma de Mallorca
Manacor
La Roda
Jucar
Alcira
Játiva
Santañy
C. de Salinas
Cabrera
Albacete
Gandia
Ontenient
Ibiza
S. Antonio Abad
Ibiza
ISLAS BALEARES
(BALEARIC ISLANDS)
(Sp.)
Almansa
Denia
Villena
Alcoy
C. de la Nao
Formentera
MURCIA
Hellín
Elda
Benidorm
Cieza
Alicante
Caravaca
Elche
Orihuela
Costa Blanca
Murcia
Totana
C. de Palos
Lorca
G. de Mazarrón
Cartagena
Húercal Overa
Aguilas
Vera

Alger (Algiers)
Harrach
Dellys
Bejaïa (Bougie)
Almeria
C. de Gata
Cherchell
Boufarik
Tizi Ouzou
Kherrata
Ténès
Blida
Bouïra
Djurdjura
Beni Mansour
Sétif
Miliana
Médéa
Bir Rabalou
Isser
Bosquet
Dahra
Cheliff
Khemis
El Asnam
Massif de l'Ouarsenis
Ksar El Boukhari
Sbisseh
Bj bou Arréridj
Mts du Hodna
M'Sila
C. Ferrat
Mers el Kebir
Arzew
Mostaganém
Relizane
Ouassel
Aïn Oussera
Aïn el Hadjel
Chott el Hodna
Barikao
Oran
Sig
O. Tlélat
Mohammadia
Mina
Tiaret
Plat. du Sersou
Z. Chergui
Bou Saâda
Beni-Saf
Aïn Témouchent
Mascara
Frenda
C
Monts des Ouled Nail
Ghazaouet
Sidi-bel-Abbès
35
5
MEDITERRANEAN SEA
ALGERIA

MURCIA
I   N   S   I   L   A

① ② ③

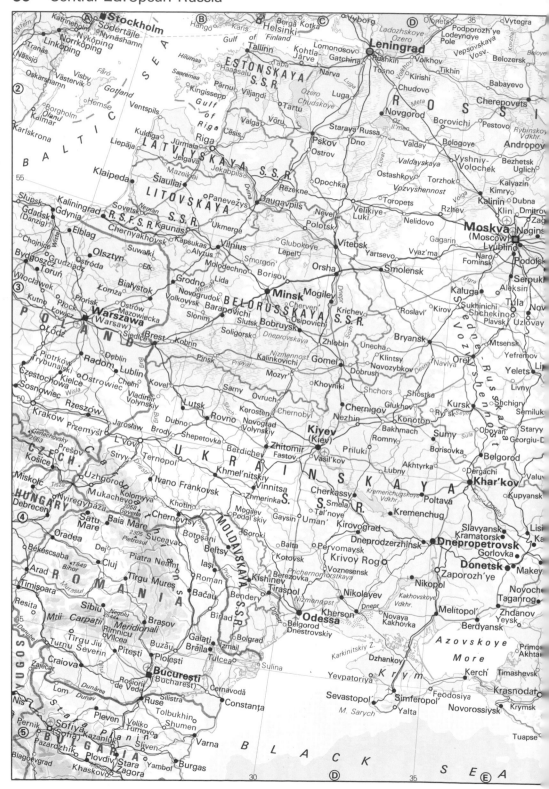

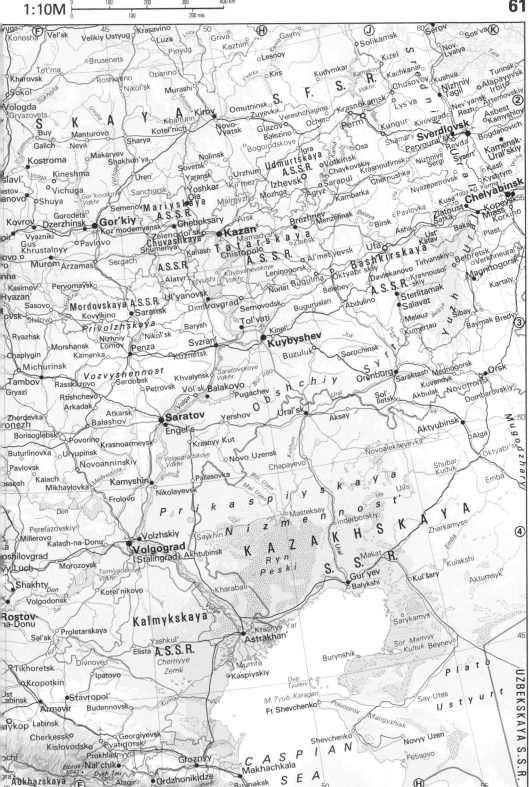

1:10M

100   200   300   400 km
100   200 mls

F   Vel'sk   Konosha   45   Krasavino   50   Griva   H   Gayny   J   Solikamsk   60   Serov   Sos'va   K
Velikiy Ustyug   Luza   Kazhim   Kudymkar   Kizel   Nov. Lyalya   ②
Vologda   Tot'ma   Brusenets   Pinyug   Lesnoy   Kachkanar   Chusovoy   Kushva   Turinsk
Gryazovets   Roslyatino   Oparino   Vyatka   Kirs   Krasnokamsk   Kungur   Nizhniy Tagil   Alapayevsk   Irbit
Buy   Manturovo   Nikol'sk   Murashi   Omutninsk   Zuyevka   Vereshchagino   Ochero   Perm   Kirovgrad   Nev'yansk   Artemovskiy
Kostroma   Makaryev   Shakhun'ya   Novo-Vyatsk   Glazov   Balezino   Osa   Shamary   Revda   Sverdlovsk   Pervoural'sk   Bogdanovich   Asbest   Kamyshlov
Galich   Neya   Sharya   Kirov   Bogorodskoye   Igra   Votkinsk   Krasnoufimsk   Nizhniye Sergi   Sysert'   Kamensk-Ural'skiy
Kineshma   Sovetsk   Nolinsk   Udmurtskaya   Chaykovskiy   Chernushka   Nyazepetrovsk   Kasli   Kyshtym
Vichuga   Yaransk   Urzhum   A.S.S.R.   Izhevsk   Sarapul   Agryz   Kambarka   Kusa   Zlatoust   Kopeysk
Shuya   Uren'   Yoshkar-Ola   Kil'mez'   Mozhga   Chelyabinsk   Korkino
Gor'kiy   Semenov   Mariyskaya   Malmyzh   Brezhnev   Menzelinsk   Ufa   Bashkirskaya   Asha   Ust'-Katav   Satka   Plast
Dzerzhinsk   Koz'modemyansk   A.S.S.R.   Arsk   Belaya   Pavlovka   Miass
Kovrov   Gorodets   Cheboksary   Kazan'   Al'met'yevsk   Birsk   Oktyabr'skiy   Davlekanovo   Krasnousol'skiy   Magnitogorsk   Verkhneural'sk

1:45M

ARCTIC OCEAN

Bering Sea

INTERNATIONAL DATELINE

Petropavlovsk Kamchatskiy

Sea of Okhotsk

Sakhalin

Kuril'skiye Ostrova

Sea of Japan

JAPAN

Sapporo

Hokkaido

Nagoya

Tokyo

Osaka

Shikoku

Kyūshū

Kita-Kyūshū

Vladivostok

Khabarovsk

N. KOREA

Pyŏngyang

S. KOREA

Sŏul

Pusan

Harbin

Changchun

Shenyang

Lüda

Qingdao

Yellow Sea

Shanghai

Nanjing

Huang He

Beijing

Tianjin

Zhengzhou

Xi'an

Taiyuan

Lanzhou

Ulaanbaatar

MONGOLIA

INNER MONGOLIA

C H I N A

SINKIANG

Ürümqi

Alma Ata

Kashmir

Islamabad

Kabul

AFGHANISTAN

Herat

Mashhad

Ashkhabad

Tashkent

Karaganda

Aral Sea

Kerman

IRAN

Tehrān

Eşfahān

Tabrīz

Kermān

Arctic Circle

Severnaya Zemlya

Zemlya Frantsa Iosifa

Novosibirskiye Ostrova

Noril'sk

Yakutsk

Magadan

Yenisey

Ob'

Lena

U N I O N   O F   S O V I E T   S O C I A L I S T   R E P U B L I C S

Krasnoyarsk

Novosibirsk

Barnaul

Omsk

Sverdlovsk

Chelyabinsk

Olonma

Sergino

Ufa

Kazan

Gor'kiy

Kuybyshev

Saratov

Svalbard (Nor.)

Zemlya Novaya

Barents Sea

Murmansk

Arkhangel'sk

NORWAY

SWEDEN

FINLAND

Helsinki

Leningrad

Moskva

Stockholm

Oslo

Riga

Minsk

København

DENMARK

Kiyev

Dnepropetrovsk

Khar'kov

Donetsk

Rostov

Volgograd

Astrakhan'

Caspian Sea

Baku

Tbilisi

Yerevan

Faerøerne (Den.)

Edinburgh

UNITED KINGDOM

IRELAND

Dublin

London

Paris

NETH.

BEL.

W. GERMANY

LUX.

POLAND

Warszawa

CZECHOSLOVAKIA

AUSTRIA

HUNGARY

YUGOSLAVIA

ROMANIA

București

BULGARIA

Odessa

Black Sea

Istanbul

Ankara

T U R K E Y

CYPRUS

SYRIA

Halab

Damascus

LEB.

Beirut

JOR.

Amman

IRAQ

Mosul

Baghdād

Başra

Abādān

KUWAIT

The Gu

SAUDI ARABIA

Adana

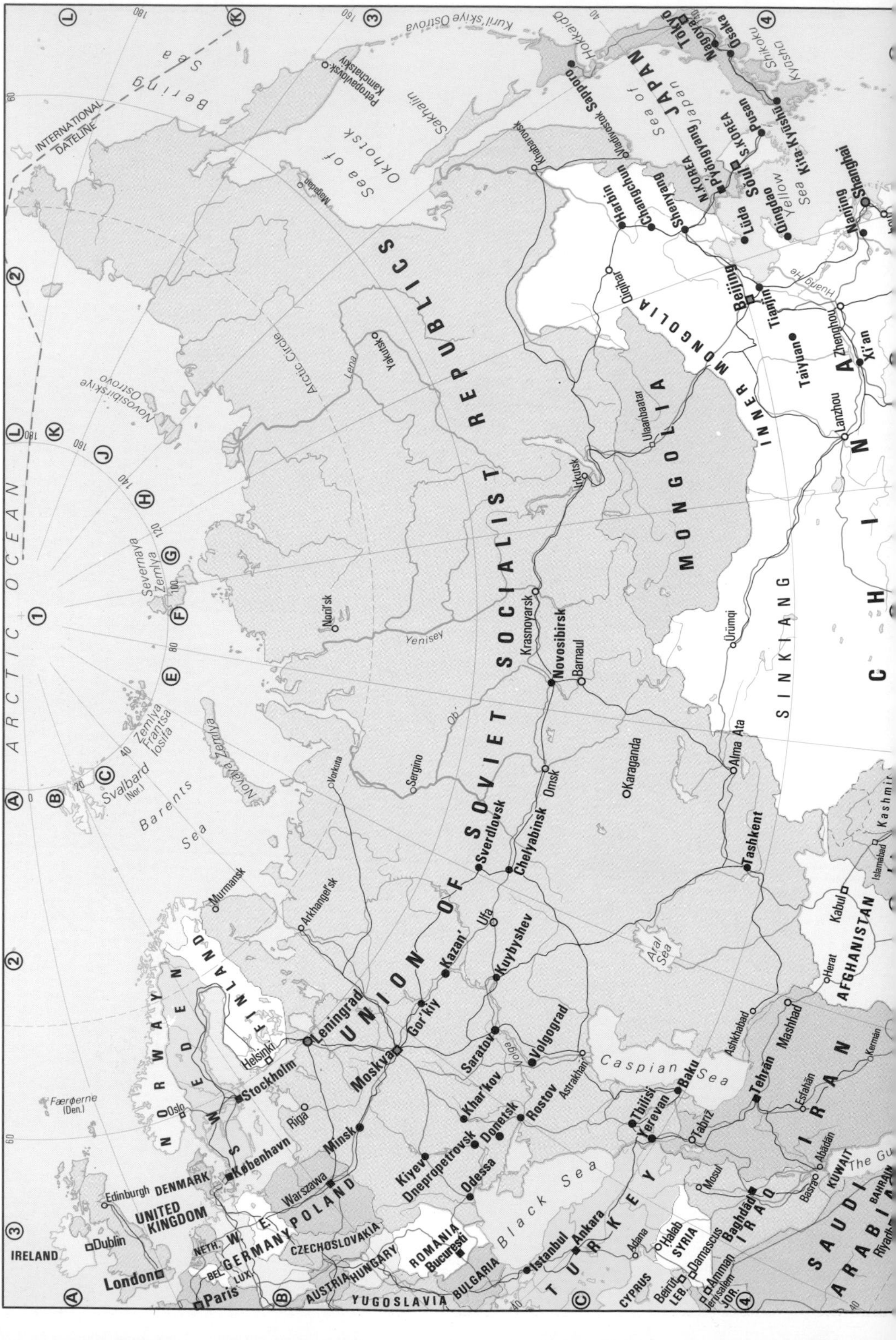

200 400 600 800 km
200 400 mls

ROSSIYSKAYA S.F.S.R.

SAKHALIN
Yuzhno-Sakhalinsk
Aleksandrovsk-Sakhalinskiy
Komsomol'sk-na-Amure
Nikolayevsk
Sikhote Alin'
Sovetskaya Gavan'
Khabarovsk
Proliv Tatarskiy

Sredne Sibirskaya Ploskogor'ye

Stanovoy Khrebet
Aldan
Yakutsk
Ust'-Maya

Vilyuy
Lensk
Kirensk
Bratsk
Tayshet
Achinsk
Kansk
Krasnoyarsk
Uyar
Abakan
Minusinsk

Bratskoye
Baykal'skiy Khrebet
Chita
Ulan-Ude
Irkutsk
Angarsk
Cheremkhovo

Tomsk
Anzhero-Sudzhensk
Leninsk-Kuznetskiy
Prokop'yevsk
Novokuznetsk
Biysk
Gorno-Altaysk
Kemerovo

ALTAY
TUVINSKAYA A.S.S.R.
Kyzyl

BURYATSKAYA A.S.S.R.

MONGOLIA
Ulaanbaatar

CHINA
Harbin
Qiqihar
Changchun
Shenyang
Beijing
Tianjin

KOREA
NORTH KOREA
SOUTH KOREA
Pyongyang
Seoul
Pusan
Taegu

JAPAN
SEA OF JAPAN
YELLOW SEA

Arctic Circle

200   400   600   800 km
200   400 mls

Tym   Napas   Ket   Iskitim   ④   Barnaul   Biysk   Gorno-Altaysk   ⑤   Manas   Manas   Usu   Manas   Yanqi   ⑥
Laryak   Vakh   Kolpashevo   Chulym   Junga   Zmeinogorsk   Zyryanovsk   Oz Zaysan   Tacheng   Qitai   Korla   K
Surgut   Kargasok   Tomsk   Kamen'-   Aleysk   Leninogorsk   Aktogay   Pik Pobedy   Yanqi   SINKIANG
Khanty-Mansiysk   Kuybyshev   na-Obi   Kulunda   Ayaguz   Panfilov   Aksu   7439   Kuga   Tarim Pendi
Vasyugan   Mogochin   Novosibirsk   Step   Semipalatinsk   Karagaly   Dzhungarskiy   Yining   Kashio   80
konda   Dem'yanskoye   Barabinsk   Slavgorod   Ust'-Kamenogorsk   50   Alatau   Alma Ata   T   i   e   n   S   h   a   n   J
Lozva   Tavda   Tatarsk   Oz Chany   Tara   Mikhaylovka   Pavlodar   Ekibastuz   Balkhash   Ozero Balkhash   Kashi   ⑥   K
Serov   Sos'va   Ishim   Barabinskaya   Tselinograd   Temirtau   KIRGIZSKAYA S.S.R.   Frunze   Andizhan   Murgab   7546
Bereznik   Ivdel   Tyumen   Tobol'sk   Shchuchinsk   Alekseyevka   Temirtau   Molnty   Chu   Tokmak   Naryn   TADZHIKSKAYA   Pik Kommunizma   Feyzabad
Kizel   Nizhniy   Tobol   Ishim   Atbasar   Kokchetav   Karaganda   Kzyl Orda   Chimkent   Leninabad   Samarkand   Dushanbe   7495
Nizhniy Tagil   Sverdlovsk   Kurgan   Petropavlovsk   Kustanay   Atasu   Betpak-Dala   Muyun Kum   Dzhambul   Tashkent   Denau   Feyzabad   70
Glazov   Kushva   Troitsk   Kartaly   Ishim   Turgay   Karsakpay   Kara tau   Turkestan   Kattakurgan   Kitab   Termez   Mazar-i-Sharif
Perm'   Chelyabinsk   Magnitogorsk   Tobol   Karsakpay   KAZAKHSKAYA S.S.R.   Syrdar'ya   Chimkent   Leninabad   Kagan   Karshi   AFGHANISTAN   H
Ol'khovsk   Zlatoust   Sibay   Orsk   Dombarovskiy   Aralskoye   Aral'sk   Novokazalinsk   UZBEKSKAYA   Kerki   Andkhoy   Meymaneh
Sarapul   Ufa   BASHKIR A.S.S.R.   Gor'ltask   Temir   Aktyubinsk   Mugodzhary   Aral'skoye More   Nukus   Chardzhou   Amu-Dar'ya   Mazar-i-Sharif   Herat
Chebotsary   Kuybyshev   Orenburg   Chelkar   Emba   Kara-Kalpakskaya   KARA-KALPAKSKAYA   Urgench   TURKMENSKAYA S.S.R.   Tedzhen
Gor'kiy   Ulyanovsk   Buzuluk   Uralsk   Emba   Dossor   Ustyurt   A.S.S.R.   Tashauz   Karakumy   Ashkhabad   Kushka   Herat
Kazan   Kuznetsk   Vol'sk   Kul'sary   Sagiz   Ustyurt   Plato   Urgench   Kyzyl Arvat   Mary   Tedzhen   60
Arzamas   Penza Syzran   Engel's   Gur'yev   Buzachi   Pov Mangyshlak   Krasnovodsk   Nebit-Dag   Kopet Dag   Mashhad
Tambov   Saratov   Kamyshin   Astrakhan'   Zaliv Kara Bogaz Gol   TURKMENSKAYA   Ashkhabad   Mashhad   Emamrud
Voronezh   Balashov   Mikhaylovka   Volga   Fort Shevchenko   Shevchenko   Krasnovodsk   Kizyl Arvat   Dasht-e-Kavir
Borisoglebsk   Volgograd   Kalmykskaya A.S.S.R.   Pov Mangyshlak   C   A   S   P   I   A   N   Nebit-Dag   Babol   Yazd   G
Kursk   Belgorod   Millerovo   Tsimlyanskoye   Divnoye   Kuma   Makhachkala   S   E   A   Krasnovodsk   Tehrān   Dasht-e-Kavir
Kharkov   Rostov-na-Donu   Stavropol   Groznyy   Dagestanskaya   Baku   Alborz   Qazvin   Rasht   Esfahan   Yazd
Poltava   Shakhty   Kropotkin   Ordzhonikidze   A.S.S.R.   AZERBAYDZHANSKAYA   Lenkoran'   Tabriz   Ardabil   Qom   Kashan   G
Dnepropetrovsk   Donetsk   Taganrog   Krasnodar   Kislovodsk   Bol'shoy   Kavkaz   Kirovabad   Tbilisi   Tabriz   Rasht   Esfahan   I   R   A   N
Zaporozhye   Zhdanov   Azovskoye More   Maykop   Sochi   Elbrus   Malyy Kavkaz   ARMYANSKAYA S.S.R.   Erzurum   Namak   Yazd
Krivoy Rog   Kharkovskaya   Kerch   GRUZINSKAYA S.S.R.   Sukhumi   Tbilisi   Yerevan   Tabriz   Esfahan
Kherson   Melitopol   Zhdanov   Batumi   Leninakan   Yerevan   Vagharshapat   Nakhichevan   IRAQ   40
Odessa   Simferopol   Sevastopol   Krym   Trabzon   Erzurum   Van   Diyarbakir   Mosul   Arbil   Sulaymaniyah
Galaţi   B   L   A   C   K   S   E   A   30   Samsun   Kelkit   T   U   R   K   E   Y   Urfa   Al Hasakah   Kirkuk   ⑤   G

R.S.F.S.R.
1   Chuvashskaya A.S.S.R.
2   Checheno-Ingushskaya A.S.S.R.
3   Severo-Osetinskaya A.S.S.R.
4   Kabardino-Balkarskaya A.S.S.R.
GRUZINSKAYA S.S.R.
5   Abkhazskaya A.S.S.R.
6   Adzharskaya A.S.S.R.
AZERBAYDZHANSKAYA S.S.R.
7   Nakhichevanskaya A.S.S.R.

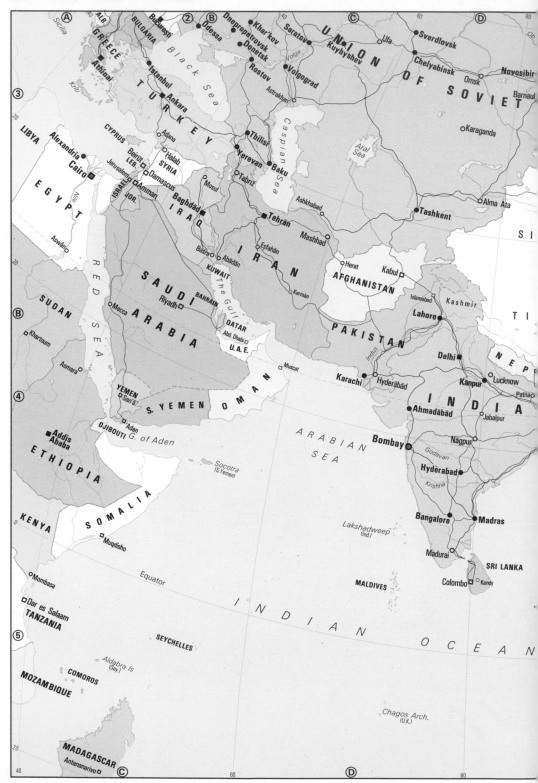

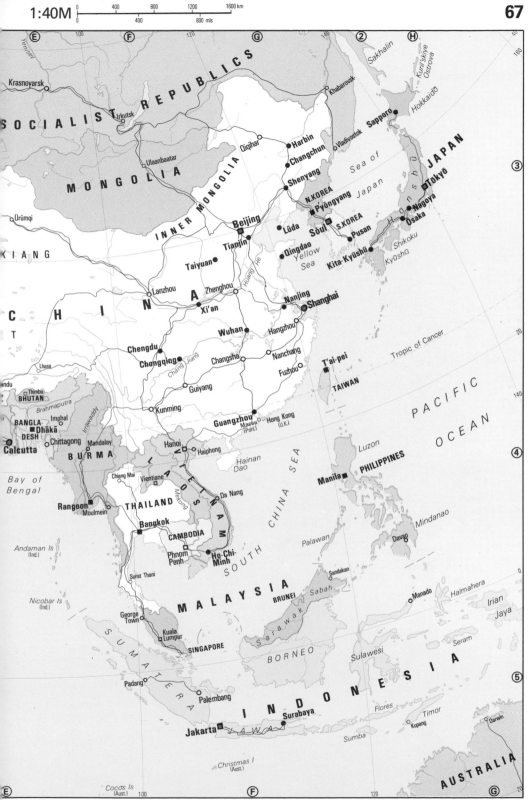

400 800 1200 1600 km
0
400 800 mls
0

Krasnoyarsk

Yenisey

SOCIALIST REPUBLICS

Irkutsk

Khabarovsk

Sakhalin

Kurl'skiye
Ostrova

Ulaanbaatar

MONGOLIA

INNER MONGOLIA

Qiqihar

Harbin

Changchun

Shenyang

Vladivostok

Sapporo

Hokkaidō

Sea of

JAPAN

Ürümqi

KIANG

CHINA

Beijing

Tianjin

Taiyuan

Lanzhou

Zhenghou

Xi'an

Huang He

Lhasa

Thimbu
BHUTAN

Brahmaputra

BANGLA
DESH

Dhākā

Calcutta

Chittagong

Mandalay

BURMA

Imphal

Irrawaddy

Chengdu

Chongqing

Chang Jiang

Changsha

Guiyang

Kunming

Nanjing

Wuhan

Hangzhou

Nanchang

Fuzhou

Guangzhou

Macao
(Port.)

Hong Kong
(U.K.)

N.KOREA

Pyŏngyang

Sŏul

S.KOREA

Pusan

Lüda

Qingdao

Yellow
Sea

Japan

Honshū

JAPAN

Tōkyō

Nagoya

Osaka

Kita-Kyūshū

Kyūshū

Shikoku

T'ai-pei

TAIWAN

Tropic of Cancer

PACIFIC

OCEAN

140

Luzon

PHILIPPINES

Manila

Mindanao

Davao

Bay of
Bengal

Rangoon

Moulmein

Chiang Mai

Vientiane

THAILAND

Mekong

LAOS

VIETNAM

Hanoi

Haiphong

Hainan
Dao

Da Nang

Bangkok

CAMBODIA

Phnom
Penh

Ho-Chi-
Minh

SOUTH

CHINA

SEA

Palawan

Sandakan

Manado

Halmahera

Irian
Jaya

Seram

Andaman Is
(Ind.)

Surat Thani

MALAYSIA

BRUNEI

Sabah

Sarawak

Nicobar Is
(Ind.)

George
Town

Kuala
Lumpur

SINGAPORE

SUMATERA

BORNEO

Sulawesi

Padang

Palembang

INDONESIA

JAWA

Jakarta

Surabaya

Flores

Timor

Kupang

Sumba

Darwin

Christmas I
(Aust.)

Cocos Is
(Aust.)

AUSTRALIA

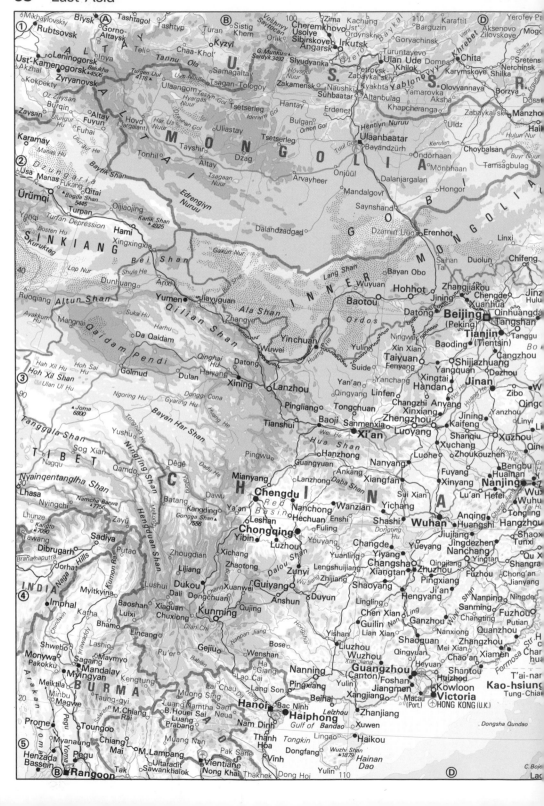

1:20M

200 400 600 800 km
200 400 mls

SEA OF OKHOTSK

Skovorodino 130 Tugur
Zeya Ekimchan Moskal'vo Okha
Ozhalinda Ovsyanka Peliny Nikolayevsk-na-Amure 150 Opala 50
Tygda Ushumun Osipenko Bogorodskoye Mys Lopatka
Guqigu Shimanovsk Norsk Ust'-Umal'ta Oz.Chukchagirskoye De Kastri Katangli Paramushir
Mangui Huma Svobodnyy Chiekunda Amgun Tymovskoye Onekotan
Ergun Zuoqi Kumara Belogorsk Komsomol'sk Aleksandrovsk-Sakhalinskiy Shiashkotan
Anhui Blagoveshchensk na-Amure SAKHALIN Rasshua
Nenjiang Zavitinsk Bolon Pobedino
Butha Qi Bei'an Ling Bureya Litovko Oz.Bolon' Poronaysk Simushir
Qiqihar Yichun Obluch'ye Khabarovsk Uglegorsk Zaliv
Anda Hailun Birobidzhan Khor Vanino Terpeniya Urup
Changchun Hegang Leninskoye Sovetskaya Il'inskiy
Shuangyashan Vyazemskiy Gavan' Yuzhno-
MANCHURIA Harbin Jiamusi Bikin Nel'ma Sakhalinsk Kuril'skiye Ostrova
Jixi Dal'nerechensk Gornozavodsk Korsakov (Kuril Islands) Vityaz Depth
Wuchang Hulin Lesozavodsk Svetlaya Mys Aniva 10542 40
Mudanjiang Oz.Khanka Plastun La'Perouse Strait Iturup
Jilin Spassk Rudnaya Wakkanai
Shuangliao Songhua Turiy Rog Pristan' Abashiri Kunashir
Siping Ussuriysk Dal'niy Olga Rumoi Asahi Dake Shikotan
Tieling Liaoyuan Vladivostok Nakhodka Asahikawa 2290 Nemuro
Fushun Yanji Zaliv Otaru Muroran
Anshan Benxi Linjiang Petra Velikogo Sapporo Erimo-misaki HOKKAIDO 2
Dandong Tonghua Ch'ongjin Hakodate Uchiura-wan
Sinuiju Manpo Najin Tsugaru-kaikyo
Hamhung Hyesan Songjin Aomori
NORTH Soho-ri Hirosaki Hachinohe
Luda Anju Hungnam SEA OF Noshiro Morioka
P'yongyang KOREA Wonsan JAPAN Akita
Yantai Haeju Sakata Ishinomaki
Chengshan Kaesong Ch'unch'on Kangnung Yamagata Sendai
Jiao Inch'on Soul Ullung do Niigata Fukushima
Chonan (Seoul) Tok-do Nagaoka
SOUTH Ch'ongju Takaoka Utsunomiya
Taejon KOREA Hoki Fukui Kanazawa Mito
Kunsan Chonju Matsue Tottori Kyoto Gifu Fuji-san Tokyo
Taegu Nagoya Yokohama
Kwangju Masan Hiroshima Osaka Sakai Shizuoka
Mokp'o Pusan Tsushima Kure Wakayama Toyohashi
YELLOW Korea Strait Kita- Matsuyama Kochi Miyake
SEA Cheju haehyop Shimonoseki Kyushu Kii-suido Hachijo
Cheju Fukuoka Shikoku
Cheju do Sasebo Kumamoto Bungo-suido Myojin
Nagasaki Kyushu Miyazaki Sumisu
Shanghai Kagoshima Osumi-kaikyo Tori Ramapo Deep
Ningbo Yaku Tanega Sofu Gan 10374

EAST CHINA SEA

Tokara Retto Muko-jima
Amami Chichi-jima Ogasawara Gunto
Tokuno Nishino-shima (Bonin Islands)
Okinawa Haha-jima (Jap.)
Naha Okinawa Kitalo
Senkaku Gunto gunto Daito Is Iwo Jima Kazan Retto Fleming Deep
Chi-lung Sakishima Miyako (Volcano Is) 8651
Ishigaki (Jap.)
Iriomote Tropic of Cancer
T'ai-pei gunto
Hua-lien RYUKYU Northern
TAIWAN (FORMOSA) Parece Vela Marianas
(China Nat. Rep.) PACIFIC

OCEAN

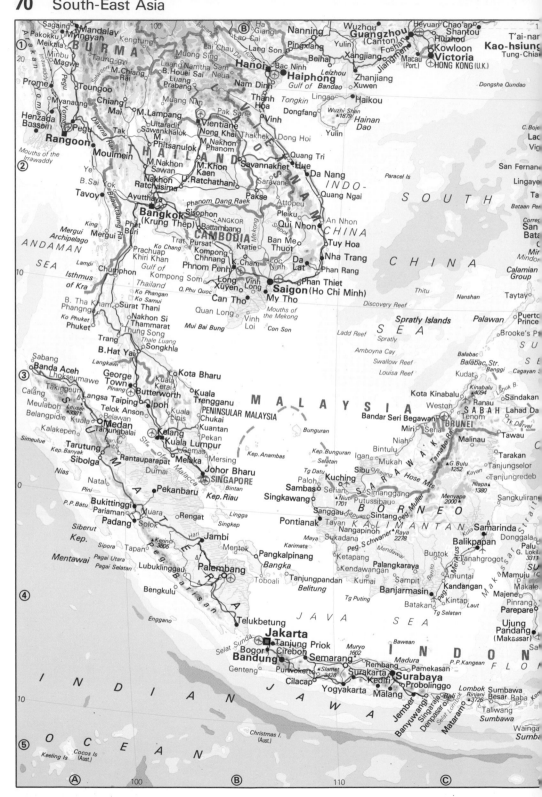

200   400   600   800 km
200   400 mls

P A C I F I C

130   (E)   140   (F)

TAIWAN (FORMOSA) (D)
-ai-tung (China Nat. Rep.)
g-tung

Farallon de Pajaros
Maug Is   20

Parece Vela

Asuncion

Agrihan

Batan Is

Pagan
Alamagan

Northern
Marianas

Guguan
Sarigan
Anatahan

Babuyan Is

C. Engaño
Aparri
Tuguegarao

Farallon
de Medinilla

Saipan (2)
Tinian

llagan
guio LUZON
upan
Baler
abanatuan
uezon City
Polillo Is

Rota

Manila
Daet Catanduanes
Naga
Legazpi

PHILIPPINES

O C E A N

Guam
(U.S.A.)
Nero Deep
9637

Boac
Bulan
mblon

Catarman

Masbate
Masbate
Catbalogan
Ilollo
Bacolod
Negros

Oras

Samar

Guiuan

Leyte

Dinaget
10265

Roxas
Tacloban
Cebu

J 10497

Bohol
Sea Siargao
Surigao
Butuan

Mansyu Deep
9818

Challenger Deep
11033

10

Ulithi

Fais

Gaferut

Yap

Faraulep

Siaton
Manukan

Cagayan de Oro
Ozamiz Marawi
L. Lanao Malanbang
Cotabato Davao
Digos

MINDANAO

Ngulu

Sorol

Woleai

Lamotrek

Ifalik

ela
amboanga
olo
Jolo Moro
Gulf

General
Santos Tinaca Pt

Davao G.

Palau
Islands Koror

Trust Terr. of the PACIFIC ISLANDS (USA)

Eauripik

ISLANDS

ulu Arch

Kepulauan
Talaud Karakelong

Rep. of Belau

CAROLINE

Fed. States of
Micronesia (3)

E B E S

Tahuna
Sangine

Sonsorol

Pulo Anna
Merir

Kepulauan
Sangihe

Morotai

Tobi

Helen Reef

S E A

Buol
Manado
Kuandang
Belang Bacan

Tobelo
Ternate Halmahera

Mapia

Equator 0

Gorontalo
Kep. Togian
Luwuk

Teluk
Weda

Waigeo

Ninigo Group

Wuvulu

MOLUCCAS

Sorong

Selat Dampier Kwoka
3000 Manokwari
Cendrawasih
Peg. Arfak
2839

Biak
Numfoor Yapen

Supiori

Tg d'Urville

Jayapura

Aitape Schouten Is

Wewak (4)

Karkar

Peleng Taliabu Mangole
Teluk
Tolo
Danau
Towuti
Kep. Banggai

Obi Misool

Teluk
Cendrawasih

Sarmi

PAPIK

PAPUA

Kendari
Kolaka
mpone
Muna

Wowoni

Butung

Kep
Sula

CERAM SEA

Piru 3019
Namlea
Seram
Ambon

Bula Fakfak

Teluk Berau

Kaimana

Dom
1340
Angemuk
3741

IRIAN

Pegunungan Maoke
Pk Jaya
5029

Pk Mandala
4702

NEW

Mendi

Mt
Hagen
Central Ra.
Kubor
4359

Long I.

NEW GUINEA

Madang

Goroka
inschafen

Baubau Kep.
Tukangbesi

BANDA SEA

Buru

Kep. Banda

Dobo
Kobroör

Kep.
Aru

Wokam

Trangan

Tk Flamingo

JAYA

Kokonau

Tanahmerah

GUINEA

Digul

L. Murray

Kikori

PAPUA

Bulolo
Wau
Salar

Kerema

Morobe

Mt Victoria 4073
Kokoda

S I A

Nila
Damar Teun

Wetar
Romang

Yamdena
Babar

Kepulauan
Tanimbar

P. Kolepom

Merauke

Fly

Daru

Gulf of
Papua

Albert
Edward
3993

Port (4)
Moresby

ores
Lomblen Alor
Dili
Ende Atambua
TIMOR

Selat Wetar Kep. Leti
Sermata

Saumlaki
Selaru

Tg Vals
Komoran

Saibai

Mulgrave I.

Banks I.
Thursday I. C. York
Pr. of Wales I. Somerset

Torres Strait

Great Barrier Rf.

C. Grenville

CORAL

(5)

Savu Sea
wu Kupang
Roti

A R A F U R A   S E A

Iron
Range

Weipa

Albatross B.

SEA

TIMOR (D) SEA

C. V. Diemen
Bathurst I.

Melville

Coburg Pen.

Dundas Str.
Croker I.

Clarence Str. Darwin

Wessel Is
Gove
Pen. C. Arnhem
Nhulunbuy

AUSTRALIA (E)

Arnhem Land 140

(F)

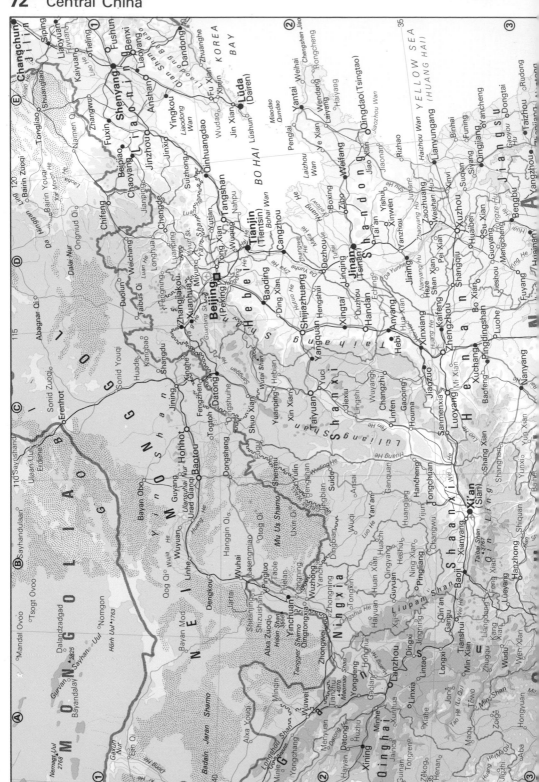

1:10M

0   100   200   300   400 km
0   100   200 mils

SOUTH CHINA SEA

GULF OF TONGKIN

Shanghai
Songjiang
Ma'anshan
Wuhu
Wuxi
Suzhou
Hangzhou
Shaoxing
Ningbo
Zhoushan Qundao
Linhai
Wenling
Wenzhou
Fuding
Fuzhou (Foochow)
Putian
Quanzhou
Xiamen (Amoy)
Zhangzhou
Shantou (Swatow)

TAIWAN
Chi-lung
T'ai-pei
T'ai-chung
Chia-i
Tai-nan
Kao-hsiung
P'ing-tung
T'ai-tung

Zhejiang
Jiangxi
Fujian
Wuyi Shan

Nanchang
Jingdezhen
Shangrao
Quzhou

Wuhan
Huangshi
Jiujiang
Changsha
Zhuzhou
Xiangtan

Hunan
Hubei

Hengyang
Shaoyang

Guangzhou (Canton)
Foshan
Victoria
HONG KONG (U.K.)
Kowloon
Macau (Port.)
Zhongshan

Guangdong
Shaoguan
Heyuan
Huizhou
Shenzhen

Guilin
Liuzhou
Nanning

Guangxi

Guiyang
Anshun

Guizhou

Chongqing (Chungking)
Fuling
Neijiang
Zigong
Yibin
Luzhou

Sichuan
Chengdu
Leshan
Emei

Daxue Shan

Yunnan
Kunming

VIETNAM
Hanoi
Haiphong
Hon Gai
Red River (Hong)

LAOS
Luang Prabang

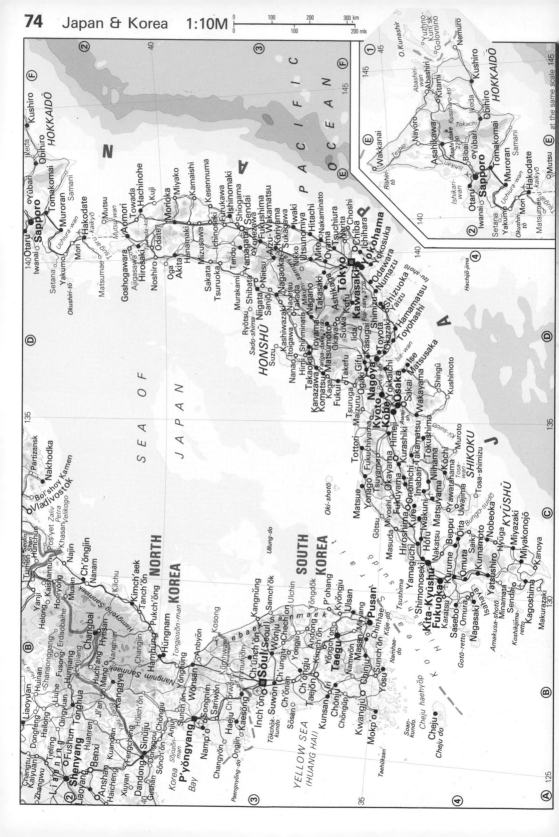

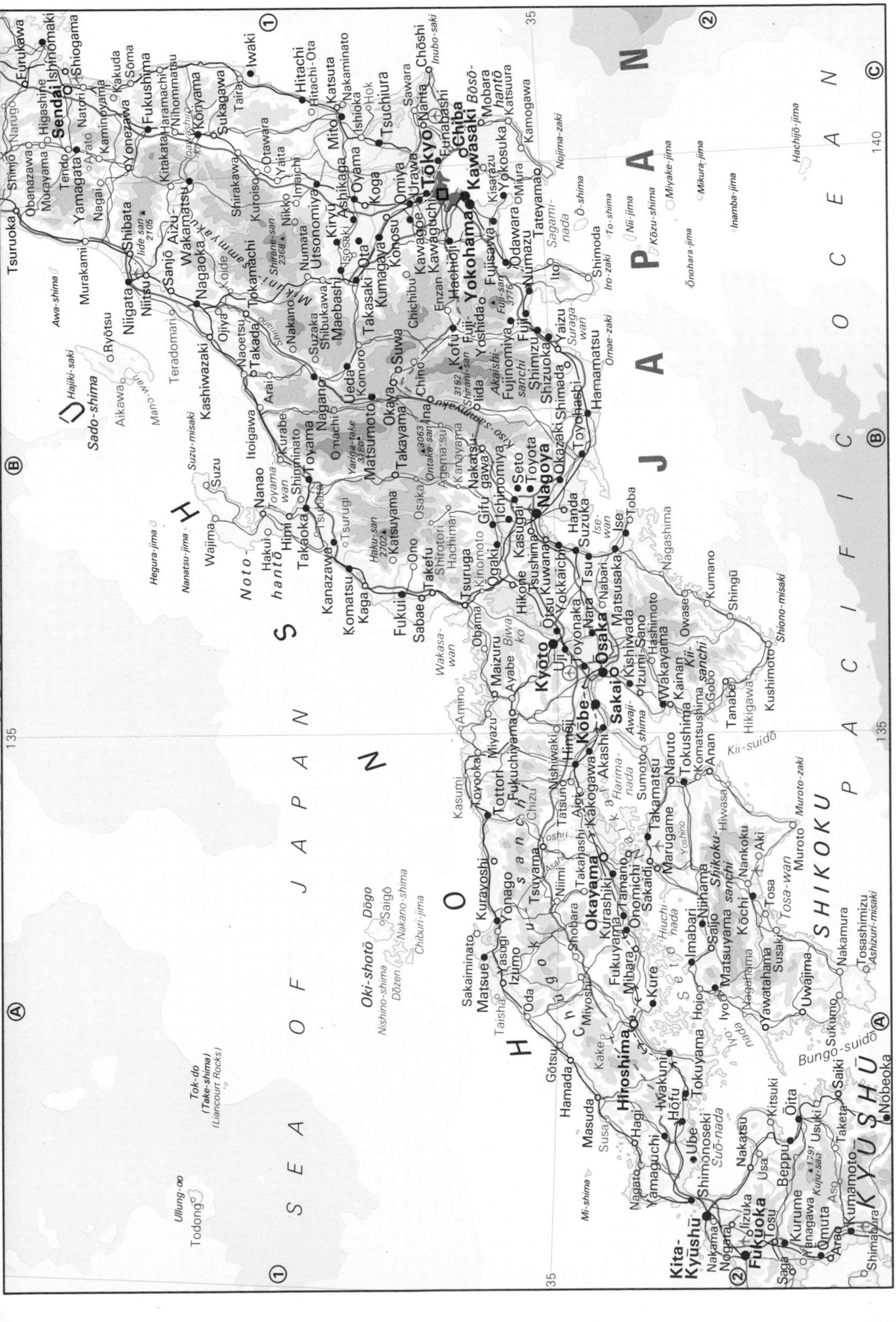

Scale: 0 50 100 150 200 km
0 50 100 mls

Major labels and place names:

SEA OF JAPAN

PACIFIC OCEAN

JAPAN

SHIKOKU

KYUSHU

Sado-shima

Oki-shotō

Tok-do (Take-shima) (Liancourt Rocks)

Ullung-do / Todong

Cities and towns (north/northeast):
Funakawa, Shinomaki, Shiogama, Sendai, Natori, Higashine, Murayama, Kakuda, Kaminoyama, Yamagata, Tendo, Yonezawa, Nagai, Shibata, Fukushima, Nihommatsu, Sōma, Haramachi, Kōriyama, Taira, Iwaki, Hitachi, Hitachi-Ōta, Katsuta, Nakaminato, Mito, Ishioka, Tsuchiura, Sawara, Narita, Chōshi, Inubo-saki, Mobara, Katsuura, Kamogawa

Central:
Tsuruoka, Sakata, Obanazawa, Narugo, Shimojō, Niigata, Niitsu, Shibata, Sanjō, Nagaoka, Takada, Naoetsu, Tōkamachi, Nakano, Nagano, Ueda, Komoro, Matsumoto, Suwa, Chino, Kōfu, Fuji, Numazu, Mishima, Odawara, Fujisawa, Kawasaki, Yokohama, Tōkyō, Chiba, Funabashi, Kawaguchi, Hachiōji, Urawa, Ōmiya, Kōnosu, Kumagaya, Takasaki, Maebashi, Utsunomiya, Nikkō, Kiryū, Ōta, Ashikaga, Koga, Tochigi

West central:
Kanazawa, Komatsu, Kaga, Fukui, Sabae, Takefu, Ono, Toyama, Takaoka, Himi, Nanao, Wajima, Noto-hantō, Suzu, Suzu-misaki

Gifu, Ichinomiya, Nagoya, Okazaki, Toyota, Seto, Toyohashi, Hamamatsu, Shizuoka, Shimizu, Shimada, Yaizu, Ōmaezaki, Irō-zaki, Shimoda

Kansai:
Kyōto, Ōsaka, Kōbe, Sakai, Ōtsu, Uji, Nara, Wakayama, Kainan, Himeji, Akashi, Kakogawa, Kishiwada, Naruto, Tokushima, Tanabe, Shingū, Shiono-misaki, Kushimoto, Muroto, Muroto-zaki

West (San'in/San'yō):
Tottori, Yonago, Matsue, Izumo, Ōda, Hamada, Masuda, Hagi, Yamaguchi, Ube, Shimonoseki, Kita-Kyūshū, Fukuoka, Kurume, Ōmuta, Kumamoto, Ōita, Beppu, Nobeoka

Okayama, Kurashiki, Fukuyama, Onomichi, Mihara, Kure, Hiroshima, Iwakuni, Tokuyama, Hōfu

Takamatsu, Marugame, Kōchi, Matsuyama, Imabari, Saijō, Niihama, Uwajima, Yawatahama, Sukumo, Nakamura

Seas/bays/physical features:
Ise-wan, Suruga-wan, Sagami-nada, Wakasa-wan, Toyama-wan, Harima-nada, Kii-suidō, Bungo-suidō, Tosa-wan, Ashizuri-misaki, Bōsō-hantō, Nojima-zaki

Islands:
Ō-shima, Nii-jima, Kōzu-shima, Miyake-jima, Mikura-jima, Hachijō-jima, Inamba-jima, Ōnohara-jima, Hegura-jima, Nanatsu-jima, Awa-shima, Hajiki-saki, Dōgo, Dōzen

1:10M

100 200 300 400 km

100 200 mls

④ ⑤ ⑥

S O U T H   C H I N A   S E A

M A L A Y S I A

SARAWAK
(Malaysia)

Kuching
Sambas
Singkawang
Pontianak

B O R N E O

Kalimantan

I N D O N E S I A

Vung Tau
Phu Vinh
Vinh Long
Can Tho
Khanh Hung
Rach Gia
Xuyen
Nam Can

Mouths of
the Mekong

Con Son

Vinh Loi

Quan Long

Mui Bai Bung
Hon Khoai
O.Phu Quoc

Kep. Bunguran
Seletan

Bunguran

Binjai

Midai

Kep. Anambas

Letong

Jemaja

Serasan

Tg Datu

Subi

Tg Sirik

Serian
Sanggau
Balaikarangan
Saratok
Nut
Tayan

Telukbatang
Sukadana
Nangataytap
Ketapang

Mempawah
Palobi
Kertamulia

Maya
T.k.Sukadono

Karimata

THAILAND

Kuala Trengganu

PENINSULAR
MALAYSIA

SINGAPORE
Str.of Singapore

Kota Bharu
Tumpat
Narathiwat
Pattani
Songkhla
Yala
Gerik
Ipoh
Taiping
Butterworth
George Town
Penang
Port Weld
Kangar
Alor Setar
Ban Hat Yai

Nakhon Si Thammarat
Ban Pak Phanang
Trang
Ban Kantang
Thung Song
B.Tha Kham
M.Luang
Phangnga
Kapoe
Ranong
Ban Khok Kloi
Ko Lanta
Ko Phuket
Phuket

Isthmus
of Kra

Ko Phangan
Ko Samui
Surat Thani
Ban Na San

Hale Luang

Kuala Dungun
Chukai
Kuantan
Pekan

Redang

Gua Musang
Kuala Krai
Kuala Lipis
Kuala Kubu Baharu
Kampar
Kuala Lumpur
Kelang
Pelapohon
Kuala Kelang
Port Dickson
Temerloh
Seremban
Gemas
Segamat
Melaka
Muar
Batu Pahat
Johor Baharu
Keluang
Mersing
Tioman

G.Tahan
2189

Pahang
G.Batu Puteh
2130

Kukup

Bintan
Tanjungpinang
Kep. Riau
Sawang
Burung
Tembelan

Kep. Tambelan

Kep. Badas

Kep. Lingga

Singkep

Lingga

Jambi

Bangka

Belinyu

Bukittinggi
Padangpanjang
Padang
Pariaman
Solok

Pekanbaru
Bangkinang
Payakumbuh
G.Kulabu
2912
G.Talakmau
2174

Tembilahan
Rengat
Sungaipenuh
Muaratebo
Muara

Tigapuluh
772 Peg.

Pematang
Perawang
Sebanga
Bengkalis
Dumai
Rupat
Minas
Daludalu
Rantauparapat
Padangsidempuan
Tarutung

Kerinci
3805

Selat Berhala

Hari

Tg Jabung

Siberut

Selat Mentawi

Pematangsiantar
Danau Toba
Samosir
Medan
Belawan
Binjai
Kuala
Kalakepen
Langsa
Seruwai
Kualasimpang

Tebingtinggi
Kisaran

Sibolga
Barus
Tapaktuan
Bakungan
Sinabang

Gunungsitoli
Lahewa
Telukdalam

Nias

P.P.Banyak
Tuangku

Simeulue

Sigep
Pulauteio
P.P.Batu
Tailełeo
Pini
Sigep

Equator

Banda Aceh
Sigli
Lhokseumawe
Geumpang
G.Geureudong
2885
Takingeun
G.Leuser
3381
Uwak
Alas

A C E H

Sabang

Calang
Meulaboh
Belangpidie

Tg Jambuair

Langkawi

Kedah

Perak

Gerai

Kelantan

M A L A Y

Kemaman

T I M O R

NICOBAR ISLANDS
(India)

Koihoa
Great Nicobar
Little Nicobar
Henhoaha

S t r a i t   o f   M a l a c c a

0 100 200 300 400 km
0 100 200 mls

Celebes Sea

Flores Sea

Makassar Strait (M a k a s s a r)

SULAWESI (CELEBES)

Tarakan
Tanjungselor
Tanjungredeb
G. Bulu 1252
Kayan
Konjikemul G. Niapa 1305
Longnawan
G. Menyapa 2000
Merah
Samarinda
Balikpapan
Sangkulirang
Seguntur
Tg Mangkalihat
Maratua

Pasangkayu
Karossa
Mamuju
Onang
Majene
Polewali
Mandar
Ujung Pandang (Makassar)
Pattallassang
Bk Gandadiwata
P.P. Postilyon
Kep. Sabalana
P.P. Kangean

KALIMANTAN

BORNEO

Equator
Bangsalsembera
Tanahgrogot
Tenggarong
Intu
Muaratewah
Tanjung
G. Sarempaka
Dayyu
G. Besar 1892
Amuntai
Barabai
Kandangan
Pagatan
Kotabaru
Martapura
Banjarmasin
Batakan
Tg Selatan
Kintap
Jorong
Tg Layar
Pleihari
Kadapongan
Matasiri
Kalembau

SARAWAK

Bintulu
Mukah
Igan
Sibu
Kapit
Balui
G. Mulu 2377
Peg. Muller
Bt Batubrok 2240
Putussibau
Lubok Antu
D. Luar
Simanggang
Semitau
Sintang
Sanggau
Nangapinoh
Peg. Schwaner 2278
Raya
Kotabaharu
Buntok
Palangkaraya
Mendawai
Muarateweh

Kuching
Serian
Sambas
Singkawang
Pontianak
Kertamulia
Paloh
Sambas

Hose Mts
Kapuas Hulu
Pegunungan Iran
Long Akah
Duit Ra.
Kelai
G. Kinabalu
Niut 1701

I N D O N E S I A

J A V A   S E A

Bawean
P.P. Karimunjawa
Tg Bugel
Rembang
Blora
Cepu
Gresik
Madiun
Mojokerto
Surabaya
Pasuruan
Probolinggo
Situbondo
Panarukan
Banyuwangi
Madura
Sumenep
Pamekasan
Sampang
Bangkalan
Malang
Kediri
Blitar
Tulungagung
Pacitan
Ponorogo
G. Lawu 3265
G. Slamet
Magelang
Yogyakarta
Purworejo
Wonosari
Surakarta
Semarang
Kudus
Pekalongan
Tegal
Brebes
Pemalang
Cirebon
Indramayu
Bandung
Tasikmalaya
Garut
Purwokerto
Cilacap
Ciamis
Sukabumi
Bogor
Cianjur
Jakarta
Tanjung Priok
Labuhan
Serang
Pameungpeuk
Genteng
Pelabuhanratu
Kalianda
Telukbetung
Kotaagung
Menggala
Kotabumi
Sukadana
Teginening
Serang

J A W A

Denpasar
Singaraja
Bali
Tabanan
Bayan
Mataram
Praya
Sumbawa Besar
Taliwang
Lombok
Sumbawa
Dompu
Raba
Sape
Bima
Sangeang
P.P. Kangean

S U M A T E R A

Pangkalpinang
Bangka
Kep. Lingga
Kep. Riau
Tanjungpinang
Bintan
Singtep
Mentok
Belinyu
Toboali
Kep. Bangka
Palembang
Belitung
Tanjungpandan
Manggar
Dendang
Karimata
Selat Karimata
Kep. Bunguran Selatan
Kep. Anambas
Kep. Tambelan
Kep. Badas

SINGAPORE

MALAYSIA
Kuala Lumpur
Klang
Seremban
Melaka
Muar
Johor Baharu
Batu Pahat
Keluang
Mersing
Tioman
Bengkalis
Dumai
Pekanbaru
Minas
Perawang
Rengat
Tembilahan
Jambi
Muarabungo
Lubuklinggau
Lahat
Muaraenim
Baturaja
Martapura
Kotabumi
Krui
Bintuhan
Bengkulu
Manna
Tais
Lais

Pgunungan Barisan
G. Resag 2232
G. Besar
G. Patah 2817
G. Gedang 2446
Enggano
Rakata (Krakatau)
Selat Sunda

BRUNEI
Bandar Seri Begawan
Miri
Seria
Labuan
Kota Kinabalu
Weston
Beaufort
Tenom
Keningau
Bingkor
Kudat
Tawau
Kalabakan
Tarakan
SABAH
Mt Magdalena
Tambunan
Ranau
Sandakan
Lahad Datu
Semporna

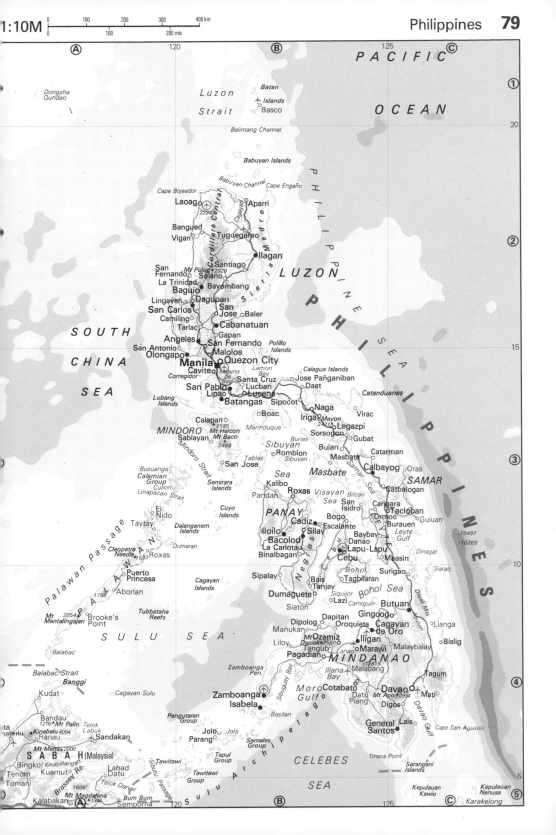

1:10M

100 200 300 400 km
0 100 200 mls

A · 120 · B · 125 · C

PACIFIC
OCEAN

① 20

Dongsha Qundao

Luzon
Strait

Batan
Islands
Basco

Balintang Channel

Babuyan Islands

Babuyan Channel Cape Engaño

Cape Bojeador
Laoag ⊕ Aparri
2234 Tuguegarao
Bangued
Vigan Ilagan

Cordillera Central

② San
Fernando
La Trinidad Solano Santiago
Baguio Bayombang
Lingayen Dagupan
San Carlos San Jose Baler
Camiling Cabanatuan
Tarlac Gapan
Angeles San Fernando
San Antonio Malolos Polillo
Olongapo Islands
Manila Quezon City
Corregidor Cavite Lamon
Laguna de Bay Calagua Islands
San Pablo Santa Cruz Jose Pañganiban
Lipao Lucban Daet
Lucena
Batangas Sipocot
Boac Naga Virac
Iriga Catanduanes
Marinduque Mayon

LUZON

Sierra Madre

Mt Pulog 2929
San

PHILIPPINE SEA

SOUTH
CHINA
SEA

Lubang
Islands

Calapan
2585
Mt Halcon
Sablayan Mt Baco
2488
MINDORO
San Jose
Tablas
Romblon
Sibuyan

Sorsogon
Bulan
Masbata Gubat
Catarman
Calbayog Oras

Legazpi

Sibuyan
Sea
Masbate

SAMAR

③

Busuanga
Calamian
Group
Culion
Linapacan Strait

Kalibo
Pandan
Roxas

Visayan
Sea

San
Isidro

Catbalogan

Cadiz

Biliran
Carigara
Cariga
Tacloban
Ormoc
Burauen

Guiuan

Cuyo
Islands

El
Nido

Taytay

Dalanganem
Islands

Dumaran

PANAY

Bogo
Iloilo Silay Escalante
Bacolod Danao
La Carlota Lapu-Lapu
Binalbagan Cebu

Baybay
Leyte
Gulf

10497
10265

Dinagat

Maasin

P
A
L
A
W
A
N

Cleopatra
Needle 1593

Roxas

Puerto
Princesa
Aborlan

Cagayan
Islands

Sipalay

Negros

Bohol
Bais
Tanjay
Tagbilaran

Surigao

Siquijor
Siarao

Palawan passage

Mt 2054
Mantalingajan
Brooke's
Point

Tubbataha
Reefs

Dumaguete
Lazi
Siaton

Camiguin

Bohol Sea

Butuan
Gingoog

Dinat Mts

Lianga

④

Balabac

Balabac Strait

Banggi

Kudat

Cagayan Sulu

SULU SEA

Dapitan
Dipolog Oroquieta Cagayan
de Oro
Mañukan
Liloy Dapiak 2560 Iligan
Tangub Malaybalay
Pagadian Marawi
MINDANAO
Zamboanga Malabang
Pen. 2815
Illana Malabang
Bay

Mt Ozamiz

Bislig

Agusan

Davao Mts

Zamboanga
Isabela

Basilan

Cotabato
Moro
Gulf

Datu
Piang

Mt Apo 2994
Digos

Davao
Tagum
Mati

Cape San Agustin

Pangutaran
Group

Jolo
Jolo
Parang

Samales
Group

Tapul
Group

Tawitawi
Group

Sulu
passage

Sulu Archipelago

General
Santos

Lais

Tinaca Point

Sarangani
Islands

Bandau
1216 Mt Palin
Kinabalu 4094 Ranau
Mt Meltas 2000
SABAH (Malaysia)
Bingkor Kinabatangan
Tenom
Tomani
Kuamut
Sandakan
Lahad
Datu
Brassey Ra.
1606
Mt Magdalena 1346
Kalabakan Bum Bum Sempoma

CELEBES
SEA

Kepulauan
Kawio

Kepulauan
Nenusa

Karakelong

⑤ 5

A · 120 · B · 125 · C

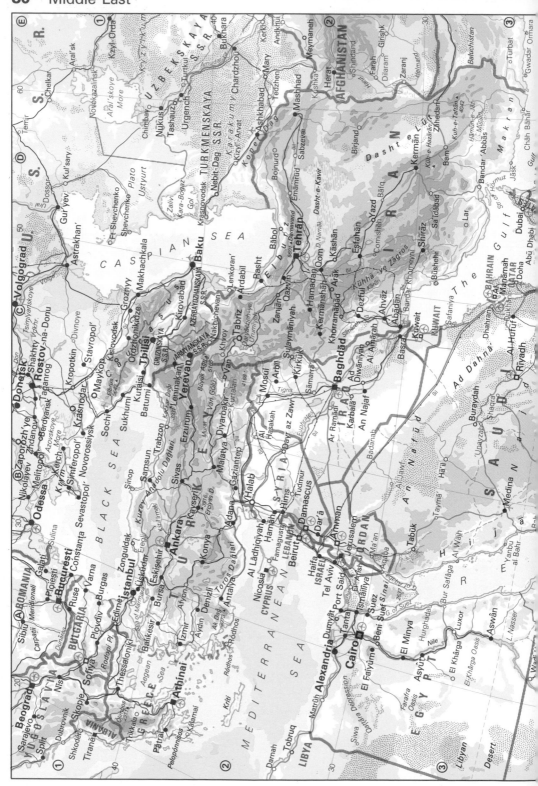

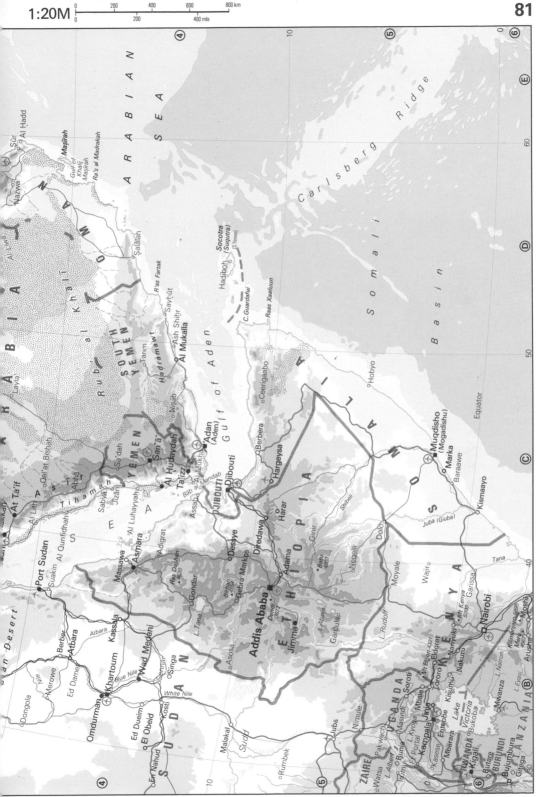

1:20M

200   400   600   800 km
200   400 mils

Sūr
Al Hadd
Nazwā
Maşīrah
Gulf of
Khalīf
Maşīrah
Ra's al Madrakah
A R A B I A N
S E A
Carlsberg Ridge
Layla
Qal'at Bishah
Ra's al Madrakah
Ṣalālah
Rub' al Khālī
O M A N
Y E M E N
S O U T H
Y E M E N
Socotra
(Suqutra)
(S.Yemen)
Hadiboh
C. Guardafui
Raas Xaafuun
Somali
Basin
Ra's Fartak
Sayhūt
Ash Shihr
Al Mukalla
Hadramawt
Tarīm
Nişāb
Gulf of Aden
Ceerigaabo
Hobyo
Equator
At Tā'if
Al Līth
Al Qunfidhah
Abhā
Sa'dah
Al Luhayyah
San'ā
Ta'izz
Al Hudaydah
Jīzan
Sablah
A S I R
Tihamah
S E A
Mukhā
Adan
(Aden)
Bāb al Mandab
Assab
Djibouti
Berbera
Hargeysa
Muqdisho
(Mogadishu)
Marka
Baraawe
S O M A L I A
Kismaayo
Juba (Giuba)
Port Sudan
Suakin
Massawa
Asmara
Adigrat
Dessye
Dire dawa
Harar
Giniir
Shibeli
Doloo
Dolo
Negelli
Wajīr
Garissa
Tana
Berbera
Ras Dashan
4620
Gondar
Debra Markos
E T H I O P I A
Adama
Bātu
4307
Moyale
Mt Kenya
5200
Nairobi
Moshi
Kilimanjaro
5895
Meru
4567
Arusha
Dongola
Merowe
Berber
Atbara
Kassala
Singa
Ed Damer
Atbara
Nile
Ed Damer
Khartoum
Omdurman
Wad Medani
Blue Nile
White Nile
Kosti
S U D A N
Ed Dueim
El Obeid
En Nahud
Malakal
Sobat
Rumbek
Jūbā
Nimule
Pakwach
L. Albert
Watsa
Bunia
Arua
Gulu
U G A N D A
Soroti
Mbale
Tororo
Kisumu
Eldoret
Nakuru
Namyuki
K E N Y A
Addis Ababa
Jimma
Asosa
L. Tana
Dendi
3072
L. Abaya
Gardulla
L. Rudolf
Debra Markos
Z A I R E
Kasese
Masindi
Jinja
Kampala
Entebbe
Lake Victoria
Bukoba
Mbarara
Mwanza
L. Eyasi
L. Natron
Butare
Bujumbura
Kigali
Gitega
Mbale
T A N Z A N I A
R W A N D A
B U R U N D I
L. Albert
L. Kyoga
Portal
Kabale
Sudan Desert

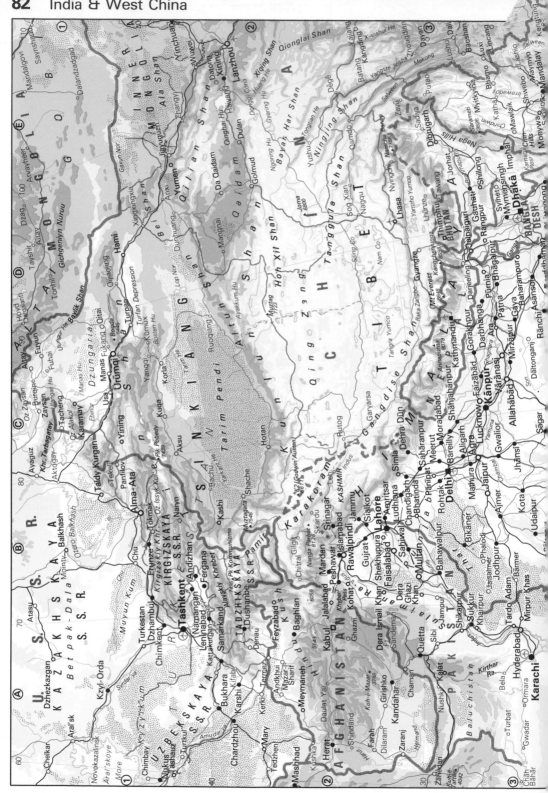

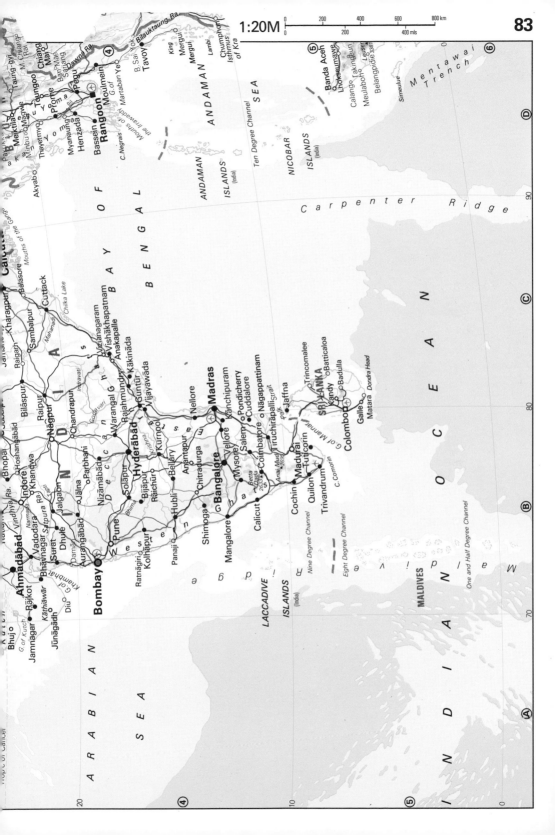

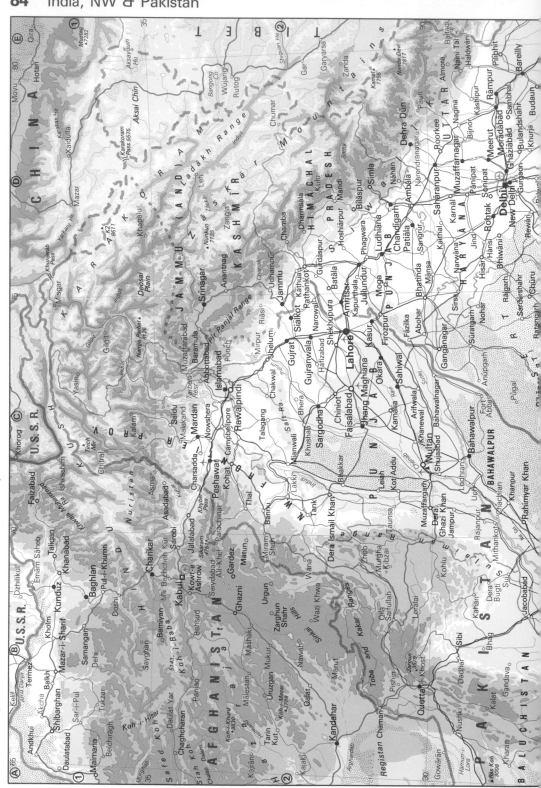

1:7.5M

100 200 300 km
50 100 150 mils

1:7.5M

100   200   300 km
50   100   150 mls

Thāne   Kalyān
Bombay Ⓐ
Alībāg   Lonāvale
Srīvardhan   Pune MAHARASHTRA
Mahād   (Poona)
Wai   Daund
Chiplūn   Phaltan   Bārāmati
Satāra   Pandharpur
Karād   Vite
Ratnāgiri ①
Sāngli   Miraj
Kolhāpur   Ichalkaranji
Mālvan   Bijāpur
Vengurla   Belgaum
Panaji   Goa,
Madgaon   Daman
   & Diu   KARNATAKA
Kārwār   Dandeli   Hubli
Sirsi   Gadag
Kumta   Hāveri
Bhatkal   Rānibennur   Hirlhar
Coondapoor   Davangere
Udupi   Chitrādurga
Kārkal   Shimoga
Mangalore   Bhadrāvati   Tarikere
Kāsaragod   Chikmagalūr   Kādūr   Arsikere
Hole Narsipur   Hassan
Cannanore   Madikeri   Mandya
Tellicherry   Mysore   Nanjangūd
Badagara   Chāmrājnagar
Calicut   Mahe
(Kozhikode)   Ootacamund
Beypore   Coonoor
Coimbatore
Ponnāni   Tiruppur
Trichūr   Pālghat
Shoranūr
Cochin   Pollāchi   Erode
Ernākulam   Palani
Kottayam   Bodināyakkanūr
Alleppey   Kambam   Dindigul
Kāyankulam   Madurai
Quilon   Virudunagar
Puliyangudi   Aruppukkottai
Tenkāsi   Rājapālaiyam
Tirunelveli   Tuticorin
Trivandrum   Palayankottai
Nāgercoil   Tiruchchendūr
Kanniyākumari   C.Comorin

Ahmadnajar   Parbhani   Purna   Nānded
Bīr   Nirmal
Parli   Bodhan   Nizāmābad
Udgir   Jagtial   Mancheral
Lātūr   Karimnagar
Barsi   Bidar   Siddipet   Warangal
Solāpur   Sangāreddi   Yellandu
Homnābad   Bhongir
Akalkot   Gulbarga   HYDERABAD
Shāhābād   Nalgonda   Suriapet
Yādgir   ANDHRA   Khammam
Shorāpur   Mahbūbnagar   Krishna   Vijayawāda
Jamkhandi   Nārāyanpet   Mācherla   Guntūr
Bāgalkot   Rāichur   Wanparti   Narasarāopet
Guledagudda   Narasarāopet   Tenāli
Gajendragarh   Kurnool   PRADESH   Chilakalūrupet
Koppal   Adoni   Nandyāl   Kani   Bāpatla
Hospet   Dhone   Giddalūr   Giri   Chīrāla
Bellary   Guntakal   Ongole
Swāmihalli   Gooty   Kondukūr
Rāyadurg   Tādpatri   Kavali
Kalyandurg   Proddatūr
Dhamavaram   Anantapur   Cuddapah   Nellore
Kadiri   Venkatagiri   Gūdūr
Hindupur   Tirupati   Sri Kālahasti
Sira   Chik   Kolar   Chittoor
Tumkūr   Ballapur   Arakkonam
Dod Ballāpur   Kolar   Vellore   MADRAS
Tiptūr   BANGALORE   Gold Fields   Kānchipuram
Krishnagiri   Amhūr
Tiruppattūr   Javadi Hills
Dharmapuri   Tiruvannāmalai   Tindivanam
Stanley Resr   Salem   Villupuram   Pondicherry
Mettūr   Cuddalore
Doda Betta   Vriddhāchalam   Chidambaram
Erode
TAMIL NĀDU   Kumbakonam
Cāuvery   Kāraikāl
Tiruchchirāppalli   Thanjāvūr   Nāgappattinam
Pudukkottai   Mannārgudi
Kodikkarai   Pt Calimere
Paramakkudi   Pt Pedro
Rāmanāthapuram   Jaffna
Talaimannar   Havankulam   Palk Strait
Mannar   Adam's Bridge   Mullaittvu
Gulf of   Vavuniya   Trincomalee
Mannār   Anurādhapura

Kotapad
Ⓒ Jagdalpur
Sironcha   Dantewāra
Bijāpur
Belampalli   Sukma
Jagtial
Bhadrāchalam
Kottagūdem
Rājahmundry
Elūru   Kākināda
Yanām
Bhīmavaram
Machilīpatnam

Nagercoil   Puttalam   Dambulla   Batticaloa
SRI LANKA   CEYLON
Chilaw   Matale
Kurunegala   Kandy
Negombo   Gampola   Badulla
Colombo   Adam's Pk   Nuwara-Eliya
Dehiwala-Mt Lavinia   2243   Ratnapura
Moratuwa   Opanake
Ambalangoda   Galle   Hambantota
Matara   Dondra Hd

Nine Degree Channel
Minicoy
Androth
Kalpeni
Eight Degree Channel
MALDIVES

Coromandel Coast
Malabar Coast
Pulicat L.
Penner
Krishna
Tungabhadra
Jog Falls
Bhadra Resr
Nilgiri Hills
Anaimalai Hills
Vembanad L.
Koyna Resr

15   15
①   ①
②   ②
③   ③
75   Ⓐ   Ⓑ

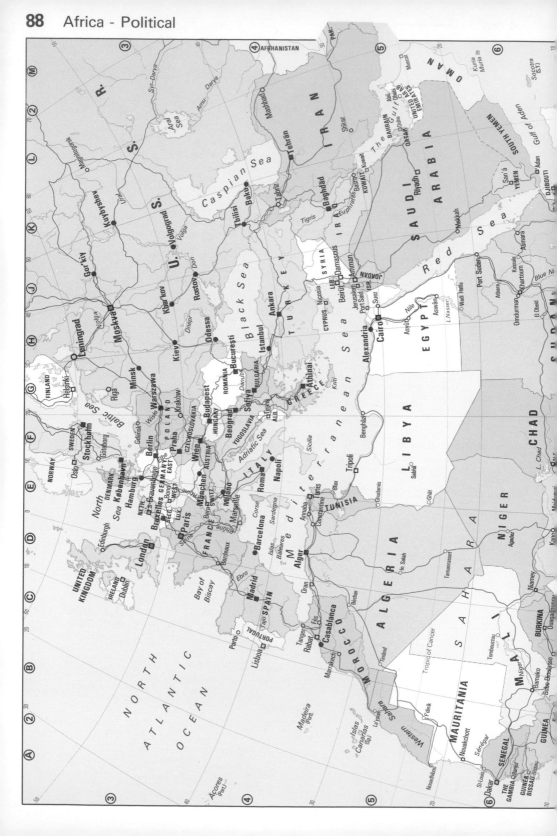

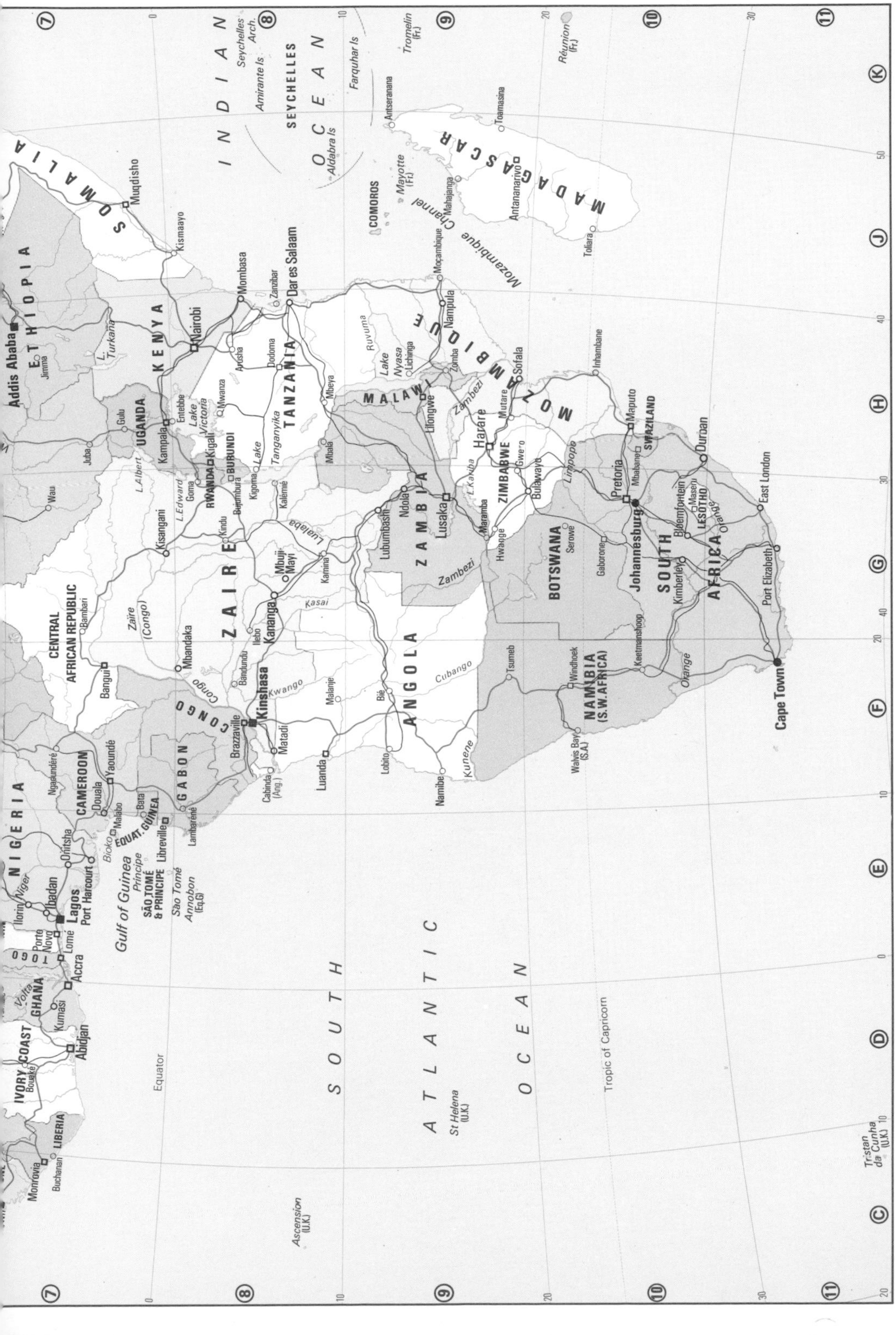

INDIAN

OCEAN

SEYCHELLES

Seychelles
Seychelles Arch.
Amirante Is.
Farquhar Is.

Tromelin (Fr.)

Réunion (Fr.)

Antseranana

Toamasina

MADAGASCAR

COMOROS
Mayotte
Mahajanga
Mozambique Channel

Antananarivo

Toliara

SOMALIA

Muqdisho

Kismayo

Mombasa
Zanzibar
Dar es Salaam

ETHIOPIA

Addis Ababa

Jimma

Gulu
L. Turkana

KENYA

Nairobi
Arusha

UGANDA
Kampala
Entebbe
Jinja
Lake Victoria
Mwanza

Juba

Wau

Ruvuma
Lake Nyasa
L. Uchinga

MOZAMBIQUE

Nampula

Sofala

Mutare
Beira

Lake Tanganyika
L. Edward
L. Albert
Goma
Kigoma
Kalemie
Kigali
RWANDA
BURUNDI
Bujumbura

Dodoma
TANZANIA
Tabora
Mbeya

MALAWI
Lilongwe
Blantyre

Zambezi

ZIMBABWE
Harare
Gweru
Bulawayo

Kisangani
Kindu

ZAIRE

Mbuji-Mayi
Kananga
Kamina

Kasai

Luanda
Likasi
Lubumbashi
ZAMBIA
Ndola
Lusaka

L. Kariba
Kafue
Hwange
Maramba

Kabwe

Limpopo

SWAZILAND
Maputo
Mbabane

Pretoria
Johannesburg

Durban

East London

Bangui

CENTRAL AFRICAN REPUBLIC

Bambari

Zaire (Congo)

Mbandaka

Ikeo
Bandundu

Kinshasa
Brazzaville
Matadi
Kwango

CONGO

GABON
Libreville
Lambaréné
Port-Gentil

Cabinda (Ang.)

ANGOLA
Malanje
Bié
Lobito

Benguela

Cubango

Kunene

NAMIBIA (S.W. AFRICA)
Windhoek
Tsumeb
Walvis Bay (S.A.)
Namibe

BOTSWANA
Serowe
Gaborone
Kanye

Orange

SOUTH AFRICA

Kimberley
Bloemfontein
LESOTHO
Maseru

Port Elizabeth

Cape Town

CAMEROON
Douala
Yaoundé
Malabo
Bioko
Bata
EQUAT. GUINEA

SÃO TOMÉ & PRÍNCIPE
Príncipe
São Tomé
Annobon (Eq.G.)

Gulf of Guinea

NIGERIA
Lagos
Ibadan
Ilorin
Onitsha
Port Harcourt
Ngaoundéré

Niger

Porto Novo
Lomé
Accra
GHANA
Kumasi
Volta

IVORY COAST
Abidjan
Bouaké

LIBERIA
Monrovia
Buchanan

St Helena (U.K.)

ATLANTIC OCEAN

SOUTH

Ascension (U.K.)

Tristan da Cunha (U.K.)

Tropic of Capricorn

Equator

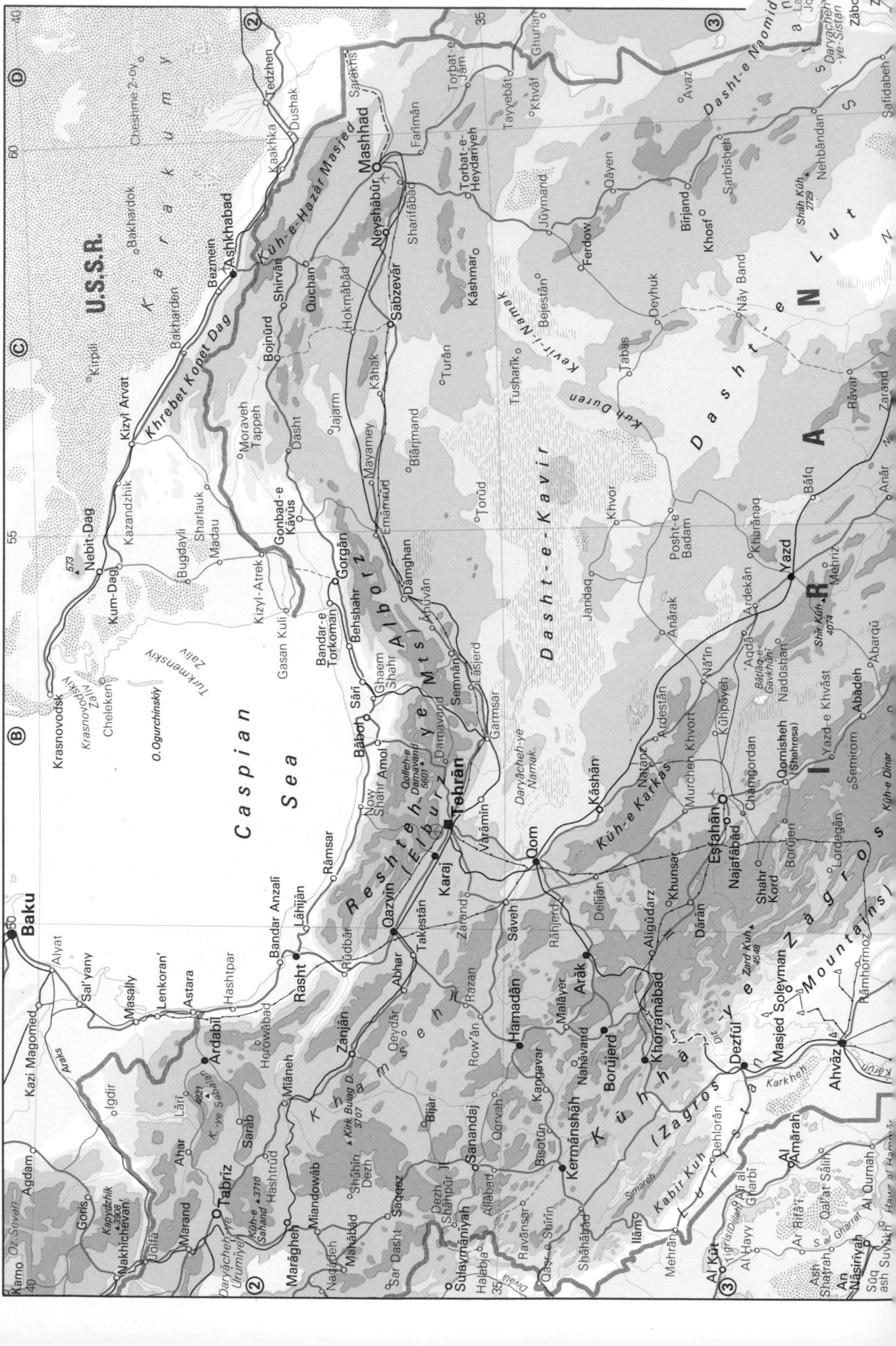

This is a map of Iran and the Gulf region.

U.S.S.R.

Baku, Kazi Magomed, Aliyat, Sal'yany, Masally, Lenkoran', Astara, Hashtpar, Ardabil, Helowābād, Rasht, Lāhījān, Bandar Anzali, Rāmsar

Karakum, Chesme-z-oy, Tedzhen, Dushak, Kaakhka, Bezmein, Ashkhabad, Bakhardok, Bakharden, Kirpili, Kizyl Arvat, Kazandzhik, Sharlauk, Madau, Kum-Dag, Nebit-Dag, Bugdayli, Krasnovodsk, Krasnovodskiy Zaliv, Cheleken, O.Ogurchinskiy, Turkmenskiy Zaliv, Gasan Kuli, Kizyl-Atrek

Caspian Sea

Kizyl Arvat, 573, Moraveh Tappeh, Dasht, Gonbad-e Kāvus, Bandar-e Torkeman, Behshahr, Gorgān, Sārī, Bābol, Shāhī, Amol, New Shahr, Ghaem Shahr

Shirvān, Bojnūrd, Quchan, Hokmābād, Mashhad, Neyshābūr, Sabzevār, Sharifābād, Farīmān, Sarakhs, Torbat-e Jām, Torbat-e Heydarīyeh, Tāyebād, Khvāf

Kūh-e-Hazar Masjed, Khrebet Kopet Dag, Reshteh-ye Alborz (Elburz Mts)

Jajarm, Miāndasht, Kāhak, Mayāmey, Biārjmand, Turān, Torud, Khvor, Jandaq

Dāmghan, Emāmrūd, Semnān, Tāsjerd, Garmsār, Varāmīn, Tehrān, Qom, Kāshān, Natanz

Dasht-e-Kavir, Kavir-i-Namak, Kuh Duren, Dasht-e Naomid, Dasht-e Lut, Kevir-i-Namak

Kāshmar, Bejestān, Ferdow, Deyhuk, Tabas, Posht-e Badam, Jūymand, Birjand, Khosf, Sarbisheh, Shāh Kūh 2729, Nāy Band, Ghurian, Avaz, Nehbandan, Lash-o-Joveyn, Zābol, Darvācheh-ye Sistan, Safidabeh, Zirani

I R A N

Na'īn, Ardekān, Anārak, Nadūshan, Yazd, Mehriz, Shir Kūh 4074, Abārqū, Bāfq, Kharānaq

Daryācheh-ye Namak, Kūh-e Karkas, Murchen Khvort, Ardestān, Aqda, Kūhpāyeh, Qamisheh (Shahreza), Semirom

Esfahān, Najafābād, Shahr Kord, Borūjen, Lordegān, Dārān

Qazvin, Takestān, Karaj, Zarand, Sāveh, Delijān, Khūnsar, Aligūdarz, Alīābād

Rūdbār, Abhar, Zanjān, Mīāneh, Qeydār, Bijār, Razan, Row'ān, Hamadān, Malāyer, Arāk, Nahāvand, Borūjerd, Khorramābād, Rāhjerd, Kāpgovar

Tabriz, Maragheh, Miandowāb, Mahābād, Saqqez, Sar Dasht, Sulaymānīyah, Halabja, Qasr-e Shīrīn

Ahar, Sarāb, Hashtrūd, Shāhīn Dezh, Dezh Shāhpūr, Bāneh, Alīābād, Ravānsar, Sanandaj, Oqreveh, Bisotūn, Kermānshāh, Mehrān

Kūh-e Sahand 3710, Kirk Bueg D. 3707, K.-ye Sabalan 4821

Kūhhā-ye Zagros (Zagros Mountains), Zard Kūh 4548, Kūh-e Dinar, Shir Kūh

Dezfūl, Masjed Soleyman, Kabir Kuh, Rāmhormoz, Ahvāz, Bandar-e, Khorramshahr

Al Kūt, Al Ḥayy, Al ʿAmārah, ʿAli al Gharbī, Qal'at Sālih, Al Qurnah, An Nāsirīyah, Ash Shatrah

Tigris/Dijla, Shatt al ʿArab, Dehlorān, Simareh, Karkheh, Diz, Karun

Agdam, Goris, Kapydzhik 3906, Nakhichevan, Iğdır, Oz. Sevan, Kamo, Marand, Nadūshan, Daryācheh-ye Urumīyeh (L. Urmia), Hashtrūd

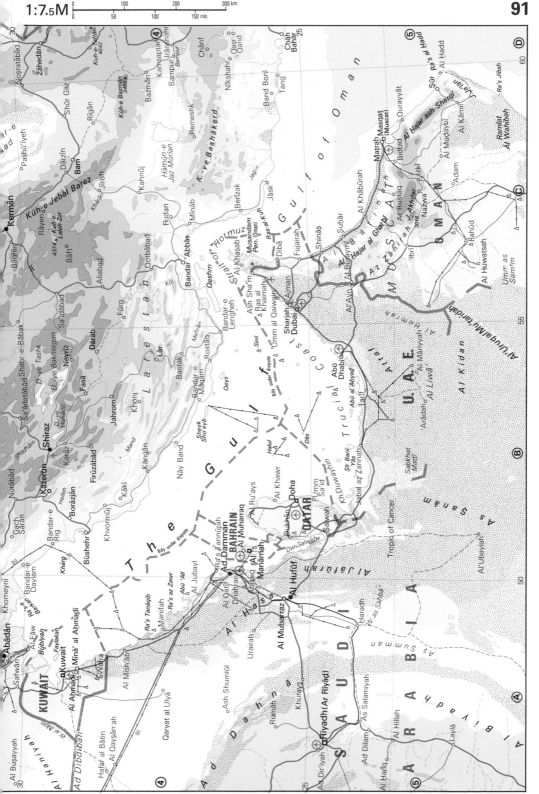

100
50
200
100
300 km
150 mls
0
0

Nosratābād
Zāhedān
Kūh-e Taftān
4042
Kamsaptān
Chānf
Qasr-e Qand
Chāh Bahār
25
⑤
Sūr Ra's al Hadd
Ra's Jibsh
Ⓓ
30
Pashū'iyeh
Shūr Gaz
Rīgān
Bazmān
Kūh-e Bazmān
3489
Bampur
Qasr-e Nīkshahr
Band Boni
Tang
Masqat (Muscat)
Al Hadd
60
Dārzīn
Bam
Remeshk
Kahnūj
Hāmūn-e
Jaz Mūrian
K.-ye Bashākerd
Jagin
Jask
Gulf of Oman
Matrah
Masqat
Bidbid
Qurayyāt
Al Hajar ash Sharqī
Ramlat Al Wahībah
Al Khābūrah
Ⓒ

Kermān
Kūh-e Jebāl Barez
Rāyen
4374
Kūh-e
Laleh Zār
Khārd Jiroft
Rudan
Mināb
Benzzak
Ras al-Kuh
Musandam Pen. (Oman)
Ras al Khasabb
Dibā
Fujairah
Suḥār
Ar Rustāq
J. Akhdar
3018
Naẓwā
Izki
Adam
 Al Kāmil
Al Mudaybi
Al Huwatsah

Bāghīn
Bāft
Ootbābād
Bandar 'Abbās
Qeshm
Strait of Hormuz
Ash Shām
Ras al Khaimah
Shinās
Al Buraymī
Al Khatwah
Az Zāhirah
Al Hajar al Gharbī
Ibrī
OMAN
Fahūd
Ⓒ

Sa'dātabād Shahr-e-Bābak
D.-ye Tashk
Fūrg
Bandar-e Lengheh
Sirri
Umm al Qaiwain
Al 'Ayn
Al 'Ayn
Umm as Samīm

Shiraz
Nēyrīz
Fasā
Lār
Rostāq
Sharjah
Dubai
Abū Dhabi
U.A.E.
Al Manīyah
Arādah
Al Kidan

Kāzerūn
Jahrom
Khonj
Kāngān
Nāy Band
Qeys
Bdy under dispute
Das
Abū al Abyad
Tarif
Al Liwā
Sābkhat Matti
As Sanam

Gāch Sarān
Borāzjān
Kākī
Sheyk Sho'eyb
Halul
Str. Banī Yās
Jabal aẓ Zannah
Khor

Būshehr
Khvormūj
Ra's Tannūrah
Ru'ays
Al Khawr
Doha
Umm Sa'id
Kh. Duwayhin
As Sanam

Kharg
Ra's az Zawr
Al Jubayl
Al Khawr
BAHRAIN
Al Muharraq
Manāmah
Bukhah
Salwah
Tropic of Cancer

Bandar-e Rig
Ra's Tanāqib
Manifah
Abū 'Alī
Al Qatif
Dhahran
Ḥawār
QATAR
Al Hufūf
Dw Salwah
Al Jafūrah
Al 'Ubaylah

Bandar-e Daylam
Ra's al Khafji
Faylakah
Mīnā' al Aḥmadī
Ra's Tanāqib
Al Qatif
Urairah
Salwah
Haradh
W. as Sahbā

Abādān
Safwān
Būbiyan
Kuwait
Al Miṣh'āb
Al Mubarraz
Harādh
As Summan
Yemen

KUWAIT
Al Aḥmadī
Al Wafrā
Ash Shumlūl
Qaryat al Ulyā
Rumāh
As Salāmiyah
Al Hillah
Laylā

30
Al Buṣayyah
Al Hafr al Bātin
Al Qaysūmah
Khuraysh
Rīyadh (Ar Rīyād)
SAUDI
ARABIA
Ad Diba
Ad Dir'iyah
Ad Dam
As Salamiyah
Ad Dilam
25
Ⓐ
④
⑤

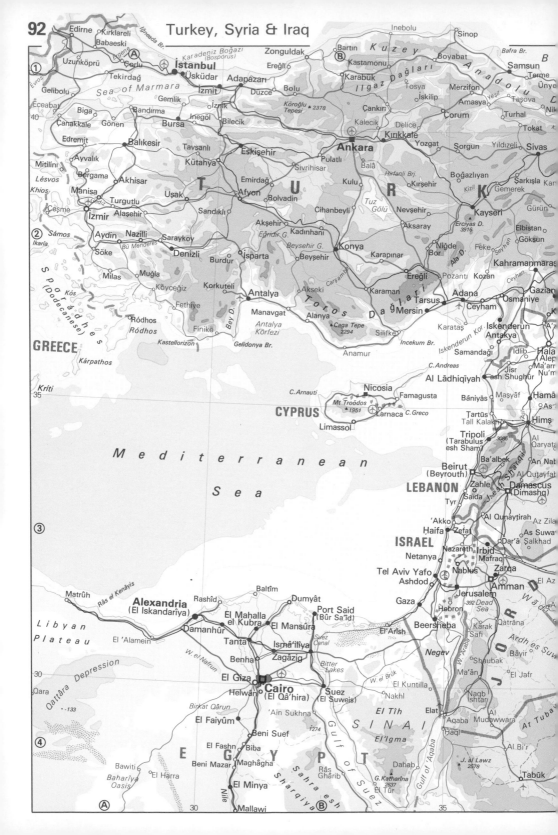

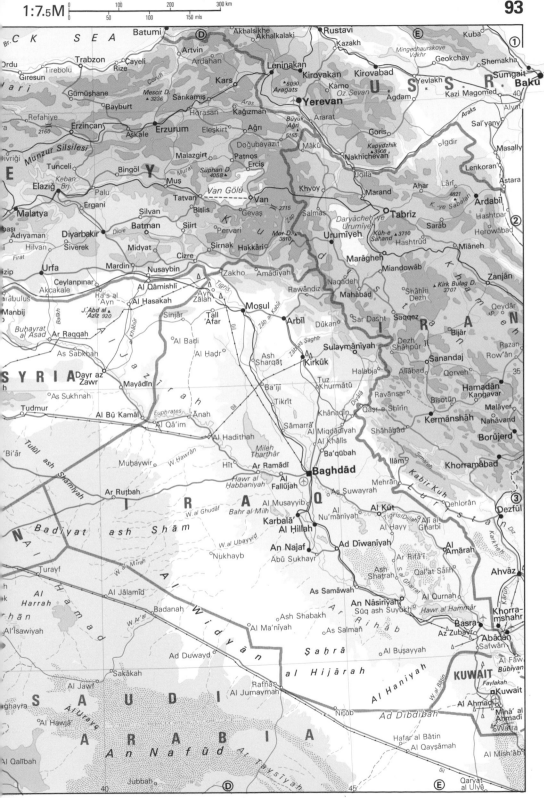

0 25 50 75 100 km
0 25 50 mls

CYPRUS

Paleokhorio Larnaca
Lefkara Larnaca Bay
Zyyi C.Kiti
Limassol
Akrotiri Bay
C.Gata

34 C.Greco

(B)

Tartūs Duraykish Kafrūn Bashūr
Arwad An Nāsirah Tall Bīsah
Hamīdīyah Tall Kalakh Qal'at al Hisn (KRAK DES CHEVALIERS)
Kleiat Kebir Qoûbayat Shinshr
Halba Al Qusayr Jūsīy
El Mīna El Hermel Hisy

Tripoli
(Tarābulus esh Shām) Zghorta
Batroun Amioune Qornet es Saouda 3086 Labouê
Jubail Kartaba Deir el Ahmar Dayr 'Atīy
BYBLOS Rhazir Ba'albek An Nabk
LEBANON Bikfaya 2628 Yabrūd
Jounié Al J.Ma'lūla
Baie de St Georges 2659 Qutayfan
Beirut Zahle Rayak Duma 'Adhra
(Beyrouth) Ba'abda Zahle
Aley Az Zabdāni 1910
Damour 'Ayn al Fijah
Beit ed Dine At Tall **Damascus**
Machgharab Barāda (Dimāshq)
Saïda Rachaya Qatana Al Kiswah
(Sidon)
Jezzine J.ash Shaykh (Mt Hermon)
Hāsbaiya A'waj Al Hijānah

MEDITERRANEAN

Marjayoun Baniyas
Tyr Q.Shemona Mas'adah CEASE FIRE LINES 1974
(Tyre, Sour) Jouai'ya Al Qunaytirah Ghabāghib Burāq
Bennt Yesud As Sanamayn
Enn Nâqoûra Jbail 1208 Hama'ala Khushnīyah Mismīyah
Har Meron Khabab
SEA Nahariya Ma'alot Tarshiha Zefat Al Lajāh Shaqc
'Akko Rama (Safad) Tiberias Nawa Izra' Shahbā
(Acre) (Yam Kinneret) Jabal 'Ar 17:
B.of Haifa Q.Yam Shefar'am (Sea of Galilee) Shaykh Miskīn
Haifa Q. Fīq As Suwaydā
(Hefa) 'Ata Tiberias
'Atlit Nazareth Ma'agan
528 Afula Deir Abu Dar'a
Zikhron Ya'aqov Mt Carmel MEGIDDO Sa'id Irbid Ramtha
CAESAREA ARMAGEDDON Beyt Shean Husn
Pardes Hanna Jenin Ajlūn Mafraq
Hadera Qabatiya Tubas J.Um ed Jarash
Netanya Tulkarm Daraj 1247 Es Samrā Sabhā
Herzliyya Sabastiya Zarqa Er Rummān
Kefar Sava Nablus Salt Suweilih Qa Khanna
ISRAEL Petah Tiqwa Ba'al Hazor Karama **Zarqa**
Ramat Gan Sarida 1016 Wadi es Sir Marka
Tel Aviv Ramallah **Amman** Sahāb
Yafo (Jaffa) Lod Jericho Qasr el Kharana
Rishon le Zion Ramla (Arīhā) Jiza Dab'a Jebel Mudeisisat
Rehovot Latrun **Jerusalem** (El Quds) Mādabā Wad adh
Ashdod Beit Jala (Yerushalayim)
Ashqelon Bethlehem Dhībān Khan ez Zabīb
Qiryat (Bayt Lahm)
Gat Bet Guvrin Hebron En Gedi
Gaza Sederot (El Khalil) Mazra Rabba
Gaza Strip LACHISH Dūra Yatta El Lisān Qatrāna
Khan Yunis Edh Dhahiriya
Rafah Ofaqim Beersheba MEZADA Karak
Zeelim (Be'er Sheva) Arad Safi 1253
Nevatim Sedom T.el Meise Qa'el Hafira
Ras Burūn Mazār Manzil
Sabkhet el Bardawīl Revivim **Dimona** MAMSHIT
El 'Arîsh Yeroham Safi Tafileh
Quezigt Sede Boqer Oron **JORDAN**
NIZANA Zin Hazeva Hāsā Qa'el Jinz
AVEDAT 1356 J.Qasred Deir Jurf ed Darāwīsh
G.Libni El Quseima **N e g e v** Rashādīya Danā Jebel Ithriy
463 Mizpe Negarot Ein 1641 Jebel
G.Maghâra Ramon Yahav J.el Atā'ita 1082
735 892 G.Halâl 1305 W.Fidan Shaubak
Har Ramon Nijil
Bir Gifgâfa Har Saggi Har Hakippa 1615 Jum Suwwāna Uneisa
EGYPT Bir Hasana 1006 467 (C)

(A) 34 36

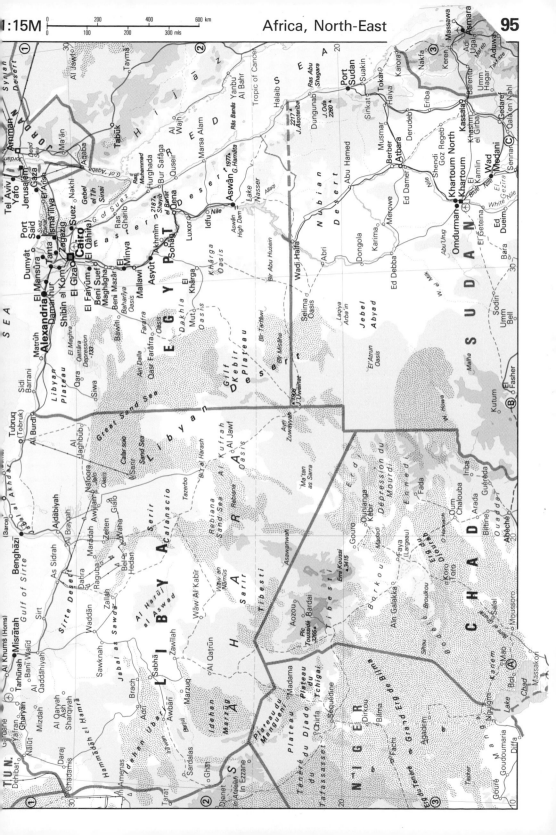

1:15M

200   400   600 km
100   200   300 mils

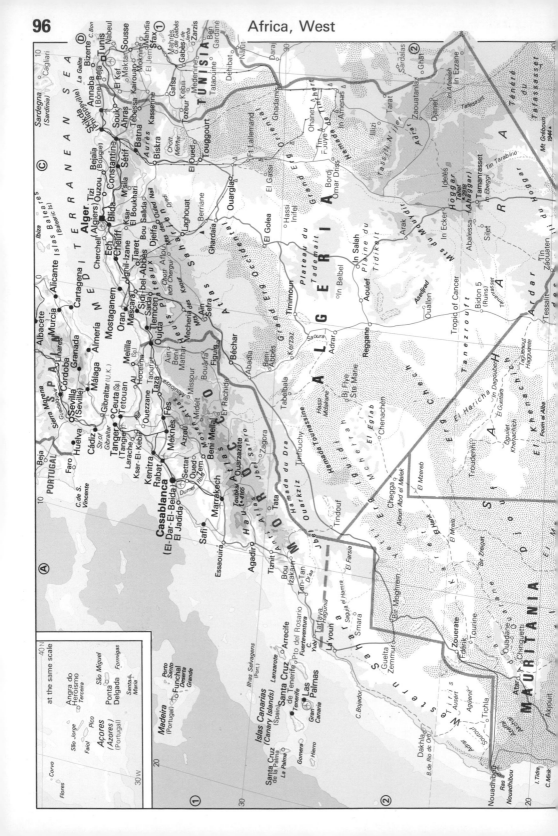

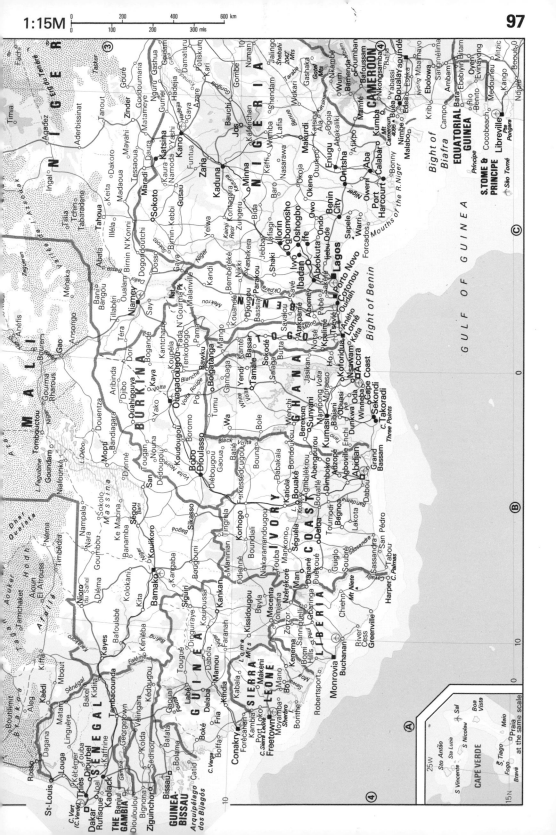

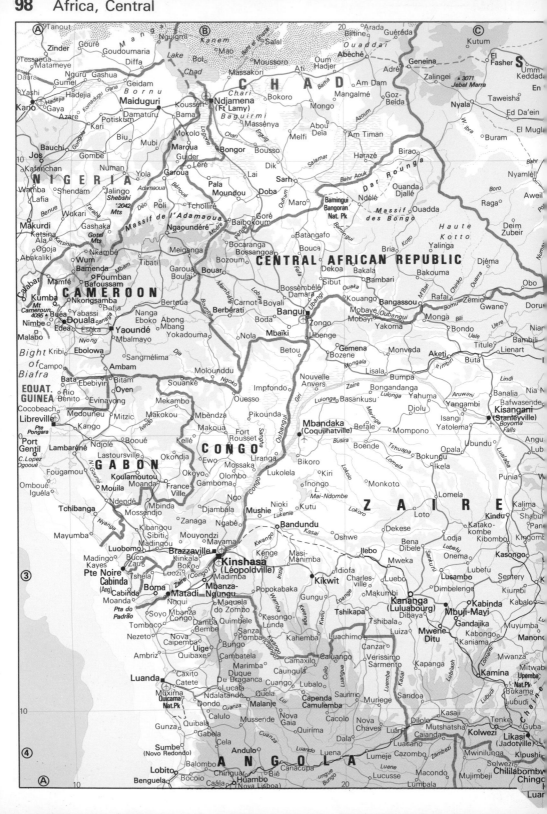

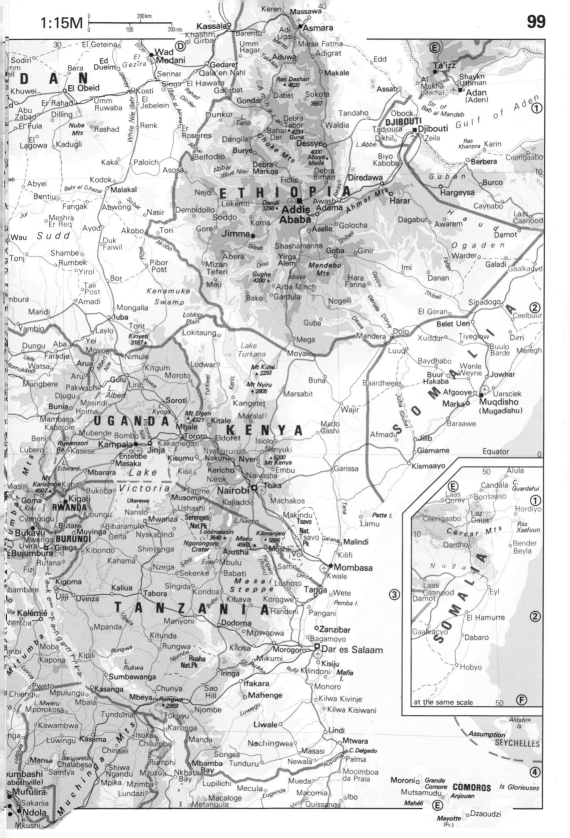

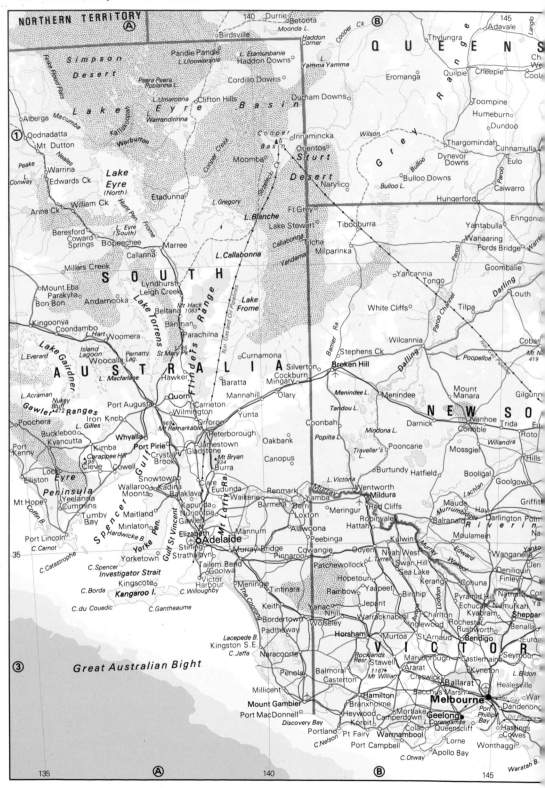

100 200 300 km
50 100 150 mls

LAND

Augathella © Mt Hutton 914 Injune Dawson Taroom Mundubbera Maryborough
Morven Mitchell Eurombah Wandoan Gayndah Biggenden
Mungallala Muckadilla Roma Wallumbilla Miles Gulguba Wondai Murgon Goomer Gympie
Angellala Ck Jackson Nat Gas Pipeline Chinchilla Kingaroy Nanango Brooloo Cooroy Tewantin
Surat Condamine Jandowae Yarraman Kilcoy Nambour Maroochydore
Glenmorgan Meandarra Tara Dalby Toogoolawah Kilcoy Caloundra
St George Pittsworth Oakey Crows Nest Caboolture
Bollon Millmerran Clifton Gatton Redcliffe Moreton I.
Dirranbandi Talwood Mt Domville 642 Allora Ipswich Brisbane N. Stradbroke I.
Hebel Thallon Inglewood Warwick Boonah Beenleigh
Mungindi Goondiwindi Killarney Beaudesert Gold Coast Tweed Heads
Goodooga Boggabilla Stanthorpe Texas Kyogle Murwillumbah Mullumbimby C. Byron
New Angledool Yetman Croppa Ck Ashford Lismore Casino Ballina
Lightning Ridge Garah Woodburn
Collarenebri Moree Warialda Deepwater Yamba Maclean
Pokataroo Gravesend Bingara Glen Innes Grafton
Narran L. Bellata Dorrigo Coff's Harbour
Walgett Burren Jcn Wee Waa Bundarra Guyra Round Mtn 1615 Bellingen Nambucca Heads
Narrabri Kaputar 1508 Barraba Uralla Armidale Macksville
Gwabegar Boggabri Manilla Walcha Kempsey Smoky C.
Baradine Gunnedah Mullaley Tamworth Wauchope Port Macquarie
Coonabarabran Werris Creek Black Sugarloaf 1494 Kendall Wingham
Gulargambone Quirindi Murrurundi Gloucester Taree C. Hawke
Nyngan Gilgandra Coolah Scone Forster Sugarloaf Pt
Warren Merriwa Gulgong Muswellbrook Dungog Raymond Terrace
Nevertire Trangie Dunedoo Mudgee Singleton Maitland Port Stephens
Nymagee Narromine Dubbo Kandos Kurri Kurri Newcastle L. Macquarie
Tottenham Wellington Mt Canicudgy 1274 Cessnock Morisset
Trundle Peak Hill Yeoval Kurri Kurri Wyong Tuggerah L.
Condobolin Molong Portland Lithgow Richmond Windsor
Cargelligo Forbes Parkes Orange Bathurst Katoomba Parramatta
Burcher L. Cowal Blayney Camden Sydney
West Wyalong Grenfell Cowra Canowindra L. Burragorang Port Jackson
Ardlethan Young Crookwell Campbelltown Wollongong
Temora Boorowa Bowral Picton Port Kembla
Coolamon Junee Murrumburrah Goulburn Shellharbour
Wagga Wagga Cootamundra Burrinjuck Resr Nowra Shoalhaven R.
Gundagai Yass Jervis B.
Tumut L. George Canberra A.C.T. Queanbeyan Ulladulla
Holbrook Batlow Tumbarumba Hume L. Eucumbene Cooma Batemans Bay
Wodonga Corryong Moruya
Beechworth Mt Kosciusko 2230 Cobargo
Bright Mt Bogong 1986 Nimmitabel Bega Merimbula
Bombala Eden
Delegate Genoa C. Howe
Orbost Cann River
Bairnsdale Lakes Entrance Pt Hicks
Sale Ninety Mile Beach

Darling Downs

Moonie R.

Maranoa Balonne Neabul Moonie Condamine

Great Dividing Range

New England Range

Nandewar Ra Mooki Ra Liverpool Ra

Macquarie Castlereagh Namoi Gwydir Barwon Pian Bogan

Blue Mts Snowy Mts Australian Alps

NEW SOUTH WALES

PACIFIC OCEAN

155 30 155 35

TASMANIA (inset)

145E Wilson's Promontory ©
Bass Strait C. Frankland Furneaux Flinders I.
C. Wickham King I. Naracoopa Whitemark Lady Barron 40S
Currie Grassy Cape Barren I.
Stokes Pt Hunter Is Stanley Banks Strait C. Portland Gladstone
C. Grim Smithton Wynyard Burnie Ulverstone George Town Scottsdale Bridport Eddystone Pt
Marrawah Ulverstone Latrobe St Helens
Waratah Devonport Deloraine Launceston Ben Lomond 1573 St Marys
Rosebery Longford Great L.
Queenstown Mt Ossa 1617 Strahan Frenchmans Cap 1444 Derwent Br. Oatlands Freycinet Peninsula
Macquarie Har Tarraleah Oyster Bay Maria I.
New Norfolk Sorell C. Pillar
Maydena Hobart Huonville Tasman Pen.
Port Davey Geeveston Storm Bay Bruny I.
S.W. Cape S.E. Cape

at the same scale

150

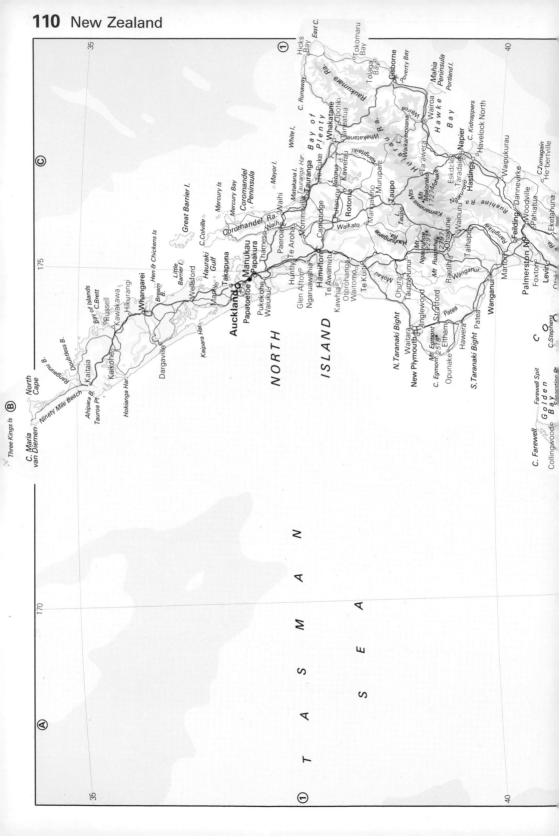

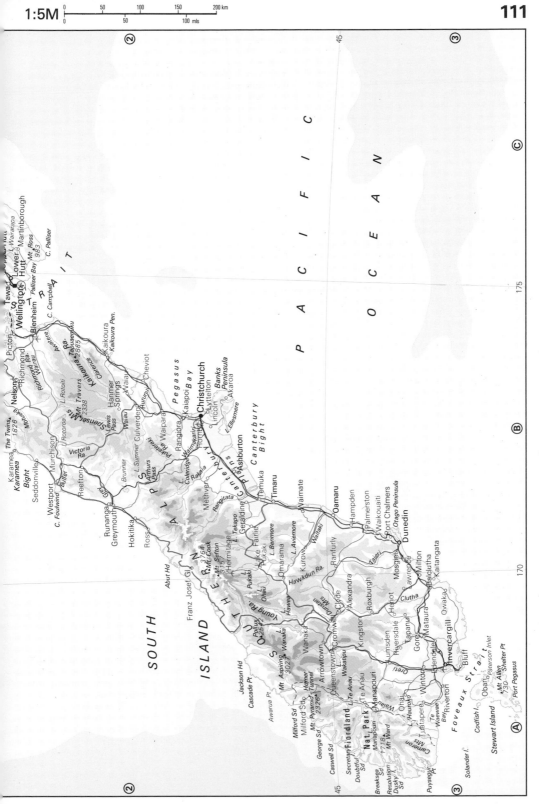

0   50   100   150   200 km
0   50   100 mls

P A C I F I C   O C E A N

SOUTH

ISLAND

SOUTHERN ALPS

Canterbury Plains

Canterbury Bight

Pegasus Bay

Banks Peninsula

Wellington
Lower Hutt
Upper Hutt
Wairarapa
Martinborough
Mt Ross 983
C. Palliser
Palliser Bay

Picton
Nelson
Richmond
Blenheim
C. Campbell
Waitohi

Tawa
Porirua

Karamea
The Twins 1826
Karamea Bight
Seddonville
Westport
C. Foulwind
Runanga
Greymouth
Hokitika
Ross
Abut Hd
Murchison
Reefton
Buller
Grey
Brunner
Victoria Ra.
L. Rotoroa
L. Rotoiti
Mou
Richmond Ra.
St. Arnaud Ra.
Spenser Mts.
Mt Travers 2885
Lewis Pass
Hanmer Springs
Kaikoura
Kaikoura Pen.
Clarence
Waiau
Cheviot
Aunui
Waipara
Rangiora
Arthurs Pass
L. Sumner
Culverden
Waimakariri
Kaiapoi
Christchurch
Lyttelton
Lincoln
Akaroa
L. Ellesmere
Puketeraki Ra.
Mt Cook 3764
Mt Sefton 3151
Hermitage
Franz Josef Gl.
Jackson Hd
Cascade Pt
Awarua Pt
Milford Sd
Mt Aspiring 3027
Pollux 2541
Young Ra.
L. Wanaka
L. Hawea
Hawea
Wanaka
Cromwell
Clyde
Alexandra
Queenstown
Arrowtown
Kingston
L. Wakatipu
Te Anau
L. Te Anau
Manapouri
L. Manapouri
Fiordland Nat. Park
Cameron Mts.
Mt Ward 1718
George Sd
Doubtful Sd
Dusky Sd
Breaksea Sd
Resolution I.
Caswell Sd
Secretary I.
Mt Pyramid Tunnel 2326
Homer Tunnel
Puysegur Pt
Waewae Bay
Te Waewae
L. Hauroko
L. Poteriteri
Tuatapere
Riverton
Winton
Otautau
Oreti
Ohai
Nightcaps
Lumsden
Mossburn
Athol
Garston
Mataura
Gore
Wyndham
Edendale
Invercargill
Bluff
Foveaux Strait
Codfish I.
Stewart Island
Oban
Paterson Inlet
Mt Allen 730
Shelter Pt
Port Pegasus
Solander I.
Waiau
Hanmer
Waipara
Amberley
Darfield
Coleridge
L. Coleridge
Methven
Rangitata
Geraldine
Fairlie
L. Tekapo
L. Pukaki
Pukaki
L. Ohau
Ohau
Twizel
L. Benmore
Omarama
L. Aviemore
L. Waitaki
Kurow
Hakataramea
Hawkdun Ra.
Ranfurly
Naseby
Ngapara
Palmerston
Waikouaiti
Port Chalmers
Otago Peninsula
Dunedin
Mosgiel
Taieri
Lawrence
Milton
Balclutha
Clutha
Kaitangata
Owaka
Catlins
Clinton
Tapanui
Heriot
Roxburgh
Ranfurly
Clyde
Waipiata
Temuka
Timaru
Waimate
Oamaru
Hampden
Ashburton
Rakaia
Dunstan Mts.
Old Man Ra.
Garvie Mts.

170

175

45

S T R A I T

2

2

3

3

A

B

C

1:40M

| 0 | 400 | 800 | 1200 | 1600 km |
| 0 | 400 | 800 mls | | |

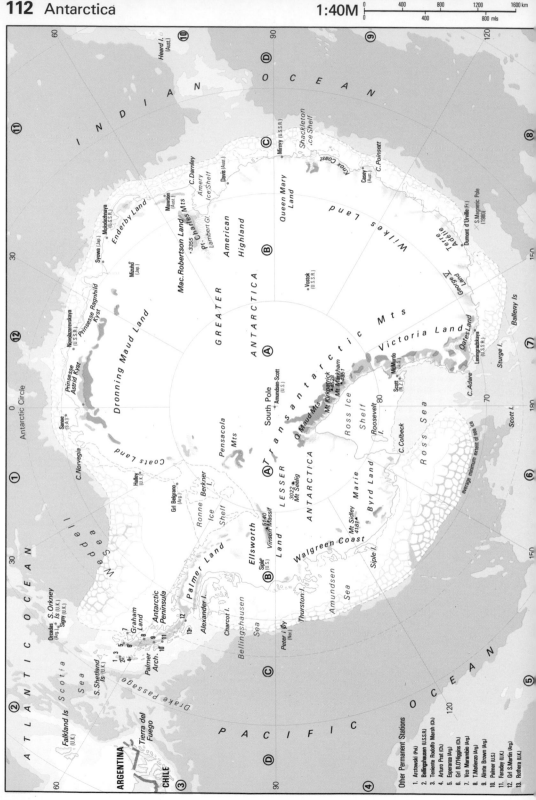

Other Permanent Stations

1. Arctowski (Pol.)
2. Bellingshausen (U.S.S.R.)
3. Teniente Rodolfo Marsh (Ch.)
4. Arturo Prat (Ch.)
5. Esperanza (Arg.)
6. Grl B.O'Higgins (Ch.)
7. Vco Marambio (Arg.)
8. T.Marienzo (Arg.)
9. Almte Brown (Arg.)
10. Palmer (U.S.)
11. Faraday (U.K.)
12. Grl S.Martin (Arg.)
13. Rothera (U.K.)

Index

In the index, the first number refers to the page, and the following letter and number to the section of the map in which the index entry can be found. For example, Paris 48C2 means that Paris can be found on page 48 where column C and row 2 meet.

Abbreviations used in the index

Afghan	Afghanistan	Hung	Hungary
Alb	Albania	Ind	Indonesia
Alg	Algeria	Irish Rep	Ireland
Ant	Antarctica	N Ire	Ireland, Northern
Arg	Argentina	Leb	Lebanon
Aust	Australia	Lib	Liberia
Bang	Bangladesh	Liech	Liechtenstein
Belg	Belgium	Lux	Luxembourg
Bol˙	Bolivia	Madag	Madagascar
Bulg	Bulgaria	Malay	Malaysia
Camb	Cambodia	Maur	Mauritania
Can	Canada	Mor	Morocco
CAR	Central African Republic	Mozam	Mozambique
Czech	Czechoslovakia	Neth	Netherlands
Den	Denmark	NZ	New Zealand
Dom Rep	Dominican Republic	Nic	Nicaragua
E Germ	East Germany	Nig	Nigeria
El Sal	El Salvador	Nor	Norway
Eng	England	Pak	Pakistan
Eq Guinea	Equatorial Guinea	PNG	Papua New Guinea
Eth	Ethiopia	Par	Paraguay
Fin	Finland	Phil	Philippines
Pol	Poland	Arch	Archipelago
Port	Portugal	B	Bay
Rom	Romania	C	Cape
S Arabia	Saudi Arabia	Chan	Channel
Scot	Scotland	Gl	Glacier
Sen	Senegal	I(s)	Island(s)
S Africa	South Africa	Lg	Lagoon
S Yemen	South Yemen	L	Lake
Switz	Switzerland	Mt(s)	Mountain(s)
Tanz	Tanzania	O	Ocean
Thai	Thailand	P	Pass
Turk	Turkey	Pass	Passage
USSR	Union of Soviet Socialist Republics	Pen	Peninsula
USA	United States of America	Plat	Plateau
U Volta	Upper Volta	Pt	Point
Urug	Uruguay	Res	Reservoir
Ven	Venezuela	R	River
Viet	Vietnam	S	Sea
W Germ	West Germany	Sd	Sound
Yugos	Yugoslavia	Str	Strait
Zim	Zimbabwe	V	Valley

Adré

2

Algonquin Park Can	15C1	Al Līth S Arabia	81C3	Altape PNG	71F4	Ambovombe Madag	101D3
Al Hadd Oman	91C5	Al Liwā, Region UAE	91B5	Altata Mexico	24B2	Ambriz Angola	98B3
Al Hadithah Iraq	93D3	Allora Aust	109D1	Altay China	63A3	Am Dam Chad	98C1
Al Hadithah S Arabia	92C3	Alma, Michigan USA	14B2	Altay Mongolia	63B3	Amderma USSR	64H3
Al Haḑr Iraq	93D2	Alma Ata USSR	82B1	Altay, Mts USSR	63A2	Ameca Mexico	24B2
Al Hajar al Gharbī, Mts Oman	91C5	Almada Port	50A2	Altdorf Switz	47C1	Amecacameca Mexico	23B2
Al Hajar ash Sharqī, Mts Oman	91C5	Almagan, I Pacific O	71F2	Altenkirchen W Germ	46D1	Ameghino Arg	34C2
Al Hamad, Desert Region Jordan/S Arabia	93C3	Al Manāmah Bahrain	91B4	Altiplanicie del Payún, Plat Arg	34B3	Ameland, I Neth	56B2
Al Haniyah, Desert Region Iraq	93E4	Al Ma'nīyah Iraq	93D3	Altkirch France	47B1	Amenia USA	16C2
Al Harīq S Arabia	91A5	Almanor,L USA	21A1	Alto Molócue Mozam	101C2	American Highland, Upland Ant	112B10
Al Harrah, Desert Region S Arabia	93C3	Almansa Spain	51B2	Alton USA	10A3	American Samoa, Is Pacific O	105H4
Al Harūj al Aswad, Upland Libya	95A2	Alma Peak, Mt Can	13B1	Altoona USA	15C2	Americus USA	17B1
Al Hasa, Region S Arabia	91A4	Al Māriyyah UAE	91B5	Alto Pencoso, Mts Arg	34B2	Amersfoort S Africa	101G1
Al Hasakah Syria	93D2	Al Marj Libya	95B1	Alto Sucuriú Brazil	35A1	Amery Ice Shelf Ant	112C10
Al Hawjā' S Arabia	93C4	Almazán Spain	50B1	Altotonga Mexico	23B2	Amfilokhía Greece	55B3
Al Hayy Iraq	93E3	Almenara Brazil	35C1	Altoyac de Alvarez Mexico	23A2	Amfissa Greece	55B3
Al Hījānah Syria	94C2	Almeria Spain	50B2	Altun Shan, Mts China	82C2	Amga USSR	63F1
Al Hillah Iraq	93D3	Al'met'yevsk USSR	61H3	Alturas USA	20B2	Amgal, R USSR	63F1
Al Hillah S Arabia	91A5	Älmhult Sweden	56C1	Altus USA	9D3	Amgu USSR	69F2
Al Hoceima Mor	96B1	Al Miqdādīyah Iraq	93E3	Al'Ubaylah S Arabia	91B5	Amgun', R USSR	69F1
Al Hufūf S Arabia	91A4	Almirante Brown, Base Ant	112C3	Alula Somalia	99F1	Amhara, Region Eth	99D1
Al Humrah, Region UAE	91B5	Almirante Latorre Chile	34A1	Al Urayq, Desert Region S Arabia	93C4	Amherst Can	7D5
Al Huwatsah Oman	91C5	Almirós Greece	55B3	Al'Uruq al Mu'taridah, Region S Arabia	91B5	Amherst, Massachusetts USA	16C1
Aliābad Iran	90A2	Al Mish'ab A Arabia	91A4	Alva USA	9D2	Amiens France	48C2
Aliabad Iran	91C4	Almodôvar Port	50A2	Alvarado Mexico	23B2	Amino Japan	75B1
Aliákmon, R Greece	55B2	Almora India	84D3	Alvarado USA	19A3	Amioune Leb	94B1
Alī al Gharbī Iraq	93E3	Al Mubarraz S Arabia	91A4	Älvdalen Sweden	39G6	Amirante Is Indian O	89K8
Alībāg India	87A1	Al Mudawwara Jordan	92C4	Alvin USA	19A4	Amlekhgan Nepal	86B1
Alicante Spain	51B2	Al Mudaybi Oman	91C5	Alvsbyn Sweden	38J5	Amman Jordan	92C3
Alice USA	9D4	Al Muharraq Bahrain	91B4	Al Wajh S Arabia	80B3	Ämmänsaario Fin	38K6
Alice Springs Aust	106C3	Al Mukallā S Yemen	81C4	Alwar India	85D3	Ammersfoort Neth	56B2
Alicudi, I Italy	53B3	Al Mukhā Yemen	81C4	Al Widyān, Desert Region Iraq/S Arabia	93D3	Amoda'ya, R USSR	80E1
Aligarh India	84D3	Al Musayyib Iraq	93D3	Alxa Yougi China	72A2	Amol Iran	90B2
Aligüdarz Iran	90A3	Alness Scot	44B3	Alyat USSR	93E2	Amos Can	7C5
Ali-Khel Afghan	84B2	Al Nu'mānīyah Iraq	93E3	Alytus USSR	39J8	Ampanihy Madag	101D3
Alimniá, I Greece	55C3	Alnwick Eng	42D2	Alzey W Germ	46E2	Amparo Brazil	35B2
Alīpur Duār India	86B1	Alor, I Indon	71D4	Amacuzac, R Mexico	23B2	Amposta Spain	51C1
Aliquippa USA	14B2	Alor Setar Malay	77C4	Amadi Sudan	99D2	Amrāvati India	85D4
Alisal USA	22B2	Alotau PNG	107E2	Amādīyah Iraq	93D2	Amreli India	85C4
Al' Īsawiyah S Arabia	93C3	Aloysius,Mt Aust	106B3	Amadjuak L Can	6C3	Amritsar India	84C2
Aliwal N Africa	100B4	Alpachiri Arg	34C3	Amakusa-shotō, I Japan	74B4	Amsterdam Neth	56A2
Al Jaghbūb Libya	95B2	Alpena USA	14B1	Åmål Sweden	39G7	Amsterdam S Africa	101H1
Al Jālamīd S Arabia	93D3	Alpes du Valais, Mts Switz	47B2	Amalat, R USSR	63D2	Amsterdam USA	15D2
Al Jawf Libya	95B2	Alpi Dolomitiche, Mts Italy	52B1	Amaliás Greece	55B3	Am Timan Chad	98C1
Al Jawf S Arabia	93C4	Alpi Graie, Mts Italy	47B2	Amalner India	85D4	Amu Darya, R USSR	88L3
Al Jazīrah, Desert Region Syria/Iraq	93D2	Alpine, Texas USA	9C3	Amami, I Japan	69E4	Amund Ringes I Can	6A2
Aljezur Port	50A2	Alpi Orobie, Mts Italy	47C1	Amami gunto, Arch Japan	69E4	Amundsen G Can	4F2
Al Jubayl S Arabia	91A4	Alpi Pennine, Mts Italy	47B2	Amanzimtoti S Africa	100C4	Amundsen S Ant	112B4
Al Kāmil Oman	91C5	Alpi Retiche, Mts Switz	47C1	Amapá Brazil	33G3	Amundsen-Scott, Base Ant	80E
Al Khābūr, R Syria	93D2	Alpi Venoste, Mts Italy	47D1	Amapá, State Brazil	33G3	Amuntai Indon	78D3
Al Khābūrah Oman	91C5	Alps, Mts Europe	52A1	Amarillo USA	9C3	Amur, R USSR	63E2
Al Khālis Iraq	93D3	Al Qaddāhiyah Libya	95A1	Amasya Turk	60E5	Anaco Ven	33E2
Al Khasab Oman	91C4	Al Qadmūs Syria	94C1	Amatitan Mexico	23A1	Anaconda USA	8B2
Al Khawr Qatar	91B4	Al Qā'im Iraq	93D3	Amazonas Brazil	33G4	Anacortes USA	20B1
Al Khums Libya	95A1	Al Qalībah S Arabia	93C4	Amazonas, State Brazil	32D4	Anáfi, I Greece	55C3
Al Kidan, Region S Arabia	91B5	Al Qāmishlī Syria	93D2	Amazonas, R Brazil	28C3	'Ānah Iraq	93D3
Al Kiswah Syria	94C2	Al Qaryah Ash Sharqiyah Libya	95A1	Ambala India	84D2	Anaheim USA	21B3
Alkmaar Neth	56A2	Al Qaryatayn Syria	92C3	Ambalangoda Sri Lanka	87C3	Anaimalai Hills India	87B2
Al Kufrah Oasis Libya	95B2	Al Qātif S Arabia	91A4	Ambalavao Madag	101D3	Anakapalle India	83C4
Al Kūt Iraq	93E3	Al Qatrūn Libya	95A2	Ambam Cam	98B2	Anaktuvuk P USA	12E1
Al Lādhiqīyah Syria	92C2	Al Qayşāmah S Arabia	91A4	Ambanja Madag	101D2	Analalava Madag	101D2
Allahābād India	86A1	Al Quatayfah Syria	94C2	Ambarchik USSR	1C7	Anamur Turk	92B2
Al Lajāh, Mt Syria	94C2	Al Qunaytirah Syria	92C3	Ambato Ecuador	32B4	Anan Japan	75A2
Allakaket USA	12D1	Al Qunfidhah S Arabia	81C4	Ambato-Boeny Madag	101D2	Anantapur India	87B2
Allanmyo Burma	76B2	Al Qurnah Iraq	93E3	Ambatolampy Madag	101D2	Anantnag India	84D2
'Allaqi, Watercourse Egypt	95C2	Al Quşayr Syria	94C1	Ambatondrazaka Madag	101D2	Anápolis Brazil	31B5
Allatoona L USA	17B1	Al Qutayfah Syria	92C3	Amberg W Germ	57C3	Anār Iran	90C3
Allegheny, R USA	15C2	Als, I Den	56B1	Ambergris Cay, I Belize	25D3	Anārak Iran	90B3
Allegheny Mts USA	10C3	Alsace, Region France	49D2	Ambikāpur India	86A2	Anatahan, I Pacific O	71F2
Allendale USA	17B1	Alsfeld W Germ	57B2	Ambilobe Madag	101D2	Añatuya Arg	30D4
Allen,Mt NZ	111A3	Alston Eng	42C2	Amboasary Madag	101D3	Anbyŏn N Korea	74B3
Allentown USA	15C2	Alta Nor	38J5	Ambodifototra Madag	101D2	Ancapa Is USA	22C4
Alleppey India	87B3	Alta Gracia Arg	29D2	Ambohimahasoa Madag	101D3	Anchorage USA	4D3
Aller, R France	49C2	Altagracia de Orituco Ven	27D5	Ambon Indon	71D4	Ancohuma, Mt Bol	30C2
Allgäu, Mts W Germ	47D1	Altai, Mts Mongolia	68A2	Ambositra Madag	101D3	Ancón Peru	32B6
Alliance USA	8C2	Altamaha, R USA	17B1			Ancona Italy	52B2
		Altamira Brazil	33G4			Ancram USA	16C1
		Altamira Mexico	23B1			Ancud Chile	29B4
		Altamura Italy	53C2			Anda China	69E2
		Altanbulag Mongolia	68C1			Andacollo Arg	34A3
						Andado Aust	108A1
						Andahuaylas Peru	32C6
						Andalsnes Nor	38F6

Andalucia

4

Argyle,L Aust	106B2
Århus Den	56C1
Ariamsvlei Namibia	100A3
Arian zón, R Spain	50B1
Arias Arg	34C2
Aribinda Upper Volta	97B3
Arica Chile	30B2
Arifwala Pak	84C2
Arima Trinidad	27L1
Arinos Brazil	35B1
Arinos, R Brazil	33F6
Ario de Rosales Mexico	23A2
Aripo,Mt Trinidad	27L1
Aripuana Brazil	33E5
Aripuaná, R Brazil	33E5
Arisaig Scot	44B3
Ariskere India	87B2
Aristazabal I Can	13B2
Arizona Arg	34B3
Arizona, State USA	9B3
Ärjäng Sweden	39G7
Arkadak USSR	61F3
Arkadelphia USA	19B3
Arkalya USSR	65H4
Arkansas, State USA	11A3
Arkansas, R USA	11A3
Arkansas City USA	18A2
Arkhangel'sk USSR	64F3
Arklow Irish Rep	41B3
Arlberg P Austria	47D1
Arles France	49C3
Arlington, Texas USA	19A3
Arlington, Virginia USA	15C3
Arlington, Washington USA	20B1
Arlit Niger	97C3
Arlon Belg	57B3
Armagh, County N Ire	45C1
Armagh N Ire	45C1
Armagós, I Greece	55C3
Armavir USSR	61F5
Armena Mexico	23A2
Armenia Colombia	32B3
Armidale Aust	107E4
Armstrong Can	13D2
Armyanskaya SSR, Republic USSR	65F5
Arnaud, R Can	7C3
Arnauti, C Cyprus	92B2
Arnhem Neth	56B2
Arnhem,C Aust	106C2
Arnhem Land Aust	106C2
Arnold USA	22B1
Arnprior Can	15C1
Arnsberg W Germ	46E1
Aroab Namibia	100A3
Arona Italy	47C2
Aropuk L USA	12B2
Arosa Switz	52A1
Arquipélago dos Bijagós, Arch Guinea-Bissau	97A3
Ar Ramādī Iraq	93D3
Arran, I Scot	42B2
Ar Raqqah Syria	93C2
Arras France	49C1
Arrecife Canary Is	96A2
Arrecifes Arg	34C2
Arriaga Mexico	23A1
Ar Rifā't Iraq	93E3
Ar Rihāb, Desert Region Iraq	93E3
Arrochar Scot	44B3
Arrowtown NZ	111A2
Arroyo Seco Mexico	23B1
Ar Ru'ays Qatar	91B4
Ar Rustaq Oman	91C5
Ar Rutbah Iraq	93D3
Arsiero Italy	47D2
Arsizio Italy	49D2
Arsk USSR	61G2
Árta Greece	55B3
Arteaga Mexico	23A2
Artemovsk USSR	63B2
Artemovskiy USSR	63D2
Artesia USA	9C3
Arthurs P NZ	111B2
Artic Bay Can	6B2
Artigas Urug	29E2
Artillery L Can	4H3
Artois, Region France	48C1
Arturo Prat, Base Ant	112C2
Artvin Turk	93D1
Aru Zaïre	99D2
Aruanã Brazil	33G6
Aruba, I Caribbean	27C4
Arun, R Nepal	86B1
Arunāchal Pradesh, Union Territory India	86C1
Aruppukkottai India	87B3
Arusha Tanz	99D3
Aruwimi, R Zaïre	98C2
Arvayheer Mongolia	68C2
Arve, R France	47B2
Arvida Can	7C5
Arvidsjaur Sweden	38H5
Arvika Sweden	39G7
Arvin USA	21B2
Arwad, I Syria	94B1
Arzamas USSR	61F2
Asadabad Afghan	84C2
Asahi, R Japan	75A2
Asahi dake, Mt Japan	74E2
Asahikawa Japan	74E2
Asansol India	86B2
Asawanwah, Well Libya	95A2
Asbest USSR	61K2
Asbury Park USA	15D2
Ascension, I Atlantic O	103H5
Aschaffenburg W Germ	57B3
Aschersleben E Germ	56C2
Ascoli Piceno Italy	52B2
Ascona Switz	47C1
Asedjirad, Upland Alg	96C2
Åsele Sweden	38H6
Aselle Eth	99D2
Asenovgrad Bulg	54B2
Asfeld France	46C2
Asha USSR	61J2
Ashburn USA	17B1
Ashburton NZ	111B2
Ashburton, R Aust	106A3
Ashdod Israel	92B3
Ashdown USA	19B3
Asheville USA	11B3
Ashford Aust	109D1
Ashford Eng	43E4
Ashikaga Japan	74D3
Ashizuri-misaki, Pt Japan	75A2
Ashkhabad USSR	65G6
Ashland, Kentucky USA	10B3
Ashland, Nebraska USA	18A1
Ashland, Ohio USA	14B2
Ashland, Oregon USA	8A2
Ashley Aust	109C1
Ashokan Res USA	16B2
Ashqelon Israel	94B3
Ash Shabakh Iraq	93D3
Ash Sha'm UAE	91C4
Ash Sharqāt Iraq	93D2
Ash Shatrah Iraq	93E3
Ash Shihr S Yemen	81C4
Ash Shumlul S Arabia	91A4
Ashtabula USA	14B2
Ashuanipi L Can	7D4
Asi, R Syria	92C3
Asiago Italy	47D2
Asinara, I Medit S	53A2
Asino USSR	65K4
Aşkale Turk	93D2
Askersund Sweden	39G7
Asmar Afghan	84C1
Asmara Eth	95C3
Aso Japan	75A2
Asosa Eth	99D1
Aspiring,Mt NZ	111A2
Assab Eth	99E1
As Sabkhah Syria	93C2
As Salamiyah S Arabia	91A5
As Salamīyah Syria	92C2
As Salmañ Iraq	93D3
Assam, State India	86C1
As Samāwah Iraq	93E3
As Şanām, Region S Arabia	91B5
As Sanamayn Syria	94C2
Assen Neth	56B2
Assens Den	56B1
As Sidrah Libya	95A1
Assiniboia Can	5H5
Assiniboine,Mt Can	5G4
Assis Brazil	30F3
As Sukhnah Syria	93C3
As Summan, Region S Arabia	91A5
Assumption, I Seychelles	99E3
As Suwaydā' Syria	92C3
As Suwayrah Iraq	93D3
Astara USSR	93E2
Asti Italy	52A2
Astipálaia, I Greece	55C3
Astorga Spain	50A1
Astoria USA	8A2
Astrakhan' USSR	61G4
Asturias, Region Spain	50A1
Asunción Par	30E4
Aswa, R Uganda	99D2
Aswân Egypt	80B3
Aswân High Dam Egypt	95C2
Asyût Egypt	95C2
As Zilaf Syria	92C3
Atakpamé Togo	97C4
Atambua Indon	71D4
Atangmik Greenland	6E3
Atar Maur	96A2
Atasu USSR	65J5
Atbara Sudan	95C3
Atbasar USSR	65H4
Atchafalaya B USA	11A4
Atchison USA	10A3
Atco USA	16B3
Atenguillo Mexico	23A1
Atessa Italy	52B2
Ath Belg	46B1
Athabasca Can	13E2
Athabasca, R Can	5G4
Athabasca L Can	5H4
Athenry Irish Rep	45B2
Athens, Georgia USA	11B3
Athens, Ohio USA	14B3
Athens, Texas USA	19A3
Athínai Greece	55B3
Athlone Irish Rep	41B3
Athol USA	16C1
Áthos, Mt Greece	55B2
Athy Irish Rep	45C2
Ati Chad	98B1
Atikoken Can	7A5
Atkarsk USSR	61F3
Atkins USA	18B2
Atlacomulco Mexico	23B2
Atlanta, Georgia USA	11B3
Atlanta, Michigan USA	14B2
Atlantic USA	18A1
Atlantic City USA	10C3
Atlantic Highlands USA	16B2
Atlantic Indian Basin Atlantic O	103H8
Atlantic Indian Ridge Atlantic O	103H7
Atlas Saharien, Mts Alg	96C1
Atlin Can	4E4
Atlin L Can	4E4
'Atlit Israel	94D2
Allixco Mexico	23B2
Atmore USA	11B3
Atofinandrahana Madag	101D3
Atognak I USA	12D3
Atoka USA	19A3
Atotonilco Mexico	23A1
Atoyac, R Mexico	23B2
Atrato, R Colombia	32B2
Attaf, Region UAE	91B5
At Tā'if S Arabia	81C3
At Tall Syria	94C2
Attalla USA	17A1
Attauapiskat Can	7B4
Attauapiskat, R Can	7B4
At Taysīyah, Desert Region S Arabia	93D3
Attica, Indiana USA	14A2
Attigny France	46C2
Attleboro, Massachusetts USA	15D2
Attopeu Laos	76D3
At Tubayq, Upland S Arabia	92C4
Atuel, R Arg	34B3
Atvidaberg Sweden	39H7
Atwater USA	22B2
Aubagne France	49D3
Aube, Department France	46C2
Aubenas France	49C3
Auburn, Alabama USA	17A1
Auburn, California USA	21A2
Auburn, Indiana USA	14A2
Auburn, Nebraska USA	18A1
Auburn, New York USA	15C2
Auburn, Washington USA	20B1
Auch France	48C3
Auckland NZ	110B1
Auckland Is NZ	105G6
Aude, R France	48C3
Auden Can	7B4
Audincourt France	47B1
Augathella Aust	109C1
Augsburg W Germ	57C3
Augusta Aust	106A4
Augusta, Georgia USA	11B3
Augusta, Kansas USA	18A2
Augusta, Maine USA	10D2
Augustine I Can	12D3
Augustow Pol	58C2
Augustus,Mt Aust	106A3
Aumale France	46A2
Auraiya India	85D3
Aurangābād India	85D5
Aurès, Mts Alg	96C1
Aurillac France	48C3
Aurora, Colorado USA	8C3
Aurora, Illinois USA	10B2
Aurora, Indiana USA	14B3
Aurora, Mississippi USA	18B2
Aus Namibia	100A3
Au Sable USA	14B2
Ausert, Well Mor	96A2
Austin, Minnesota USA	10A2
Austin, Nevada USA	21B2
Austin, Texas USA	9D3
Australian Alps, Mts Aust	107D4
Austria, Fed Republic Europe	37E4
Authie, R France	46A1
Autlán Mexico	24B3
Autun France	49C2
Auvergne, Region France	49C2
Auxerre France	49C2
Auxi-le-Châteaux France	46B1
Avallon France	49C2
Avalon USA	22C4
Avalon Pen Can	7E5
Avaré Brazil	35B2
Avaz Iran	90D3
Avedat, Hist Site Israel	94B3
Aveiro Brazil	33F4
Aveiro Port	50A1
Avellaneda Arg	29E2

Avellino

Avellino *Italy*	53B2
Avesnes-sur-Helpe *France*	46B1
Avesta *Sweden*	39H6
Avezzano *Italy*	52B2
Aviemore *Scot*	44C3
Aviemore,L *NZ*	111B2
Avigliana *Italy*	47B2
Avignon *France*	49C3
Avila *Spain*	50B1
Aviles *Spain*	50A1
Avisio, R *Italy*	47D1
Avoca, R *Aust*	108B3
Avon, County *Eng*	43C4
Avon, R, Dorset *Eng*	43D4
Avon, R, Warwick *Eng*	43D3
Avonmouth *Wales*	43C4
Avon Park *USA*	17B2
Avre, R *France*	46B2
Avtovac *Yugos*	54A2
A'waj, R *Syria*	94C2
Awaji-shima, B *Japan*	74D4
Awarem *Eth*	99E2
Awarua Pt *NZ*	111A2
Awash *Eth*	99E2
Awash, R *Eth*	99E2
Awa-shima, I *Japan*	75B1
Awatere, R *NZ*	111B2
Awbārī *Libya*	95A2
Aweil *Sudan*	98C2
Awjilan *Libya*	95B2
Axel Heiburg I *Can*	6A2
Axminster *Eng*	43C4
Ayabe *Japan*	75B1
Ayacucho *Arg*	29E3
Ayacucho *Peru*	32C6
Ayaguz *USSR*	65K5
Ayakkum Hu, L *China*	82C2
Ayamonte *Spain*	50A2
Ayan *USSR*	63F2
Ayauiri *Peru*	32C6
Aydin *Turk*	92A2
Áyios Evstrátios, I *Greece*	55C3
Aylesbury *Eng*	43D4
Aylmer,Mt *Can*	13D2
'Ayn al Fijah *Syria*	94C2
Ayn Zālah *Iraq*	93D2
Ayn Zuwayyah, Well *Libya*	95B2
Ayod *Sudan*	99D2
Ayr *Aust*	107D2
Ayr *Scot*	42B2
Ayr, R *Scot*	42B2
Ayre,Pt of *Eng*	42B2
Aytthaya *Thai*	76C3
Ayutla *Mexico*	23A1
Ayvacik *Turk*	55C3
Ayvalik *Turk*	55C3
Äzamgarh *India*	86A1
Azaouad, Desert Region *Mali*	97B3
Azare *Nig*	97D3
A'Zāz *Syria*	92C2
Azeffal, Watercourse *Maur*	96A2
Azerbaydzhanskaya SSR, Republic *USSR*	65F5
Azogues *Ecuador*	32B4
Azoum, R *Chad*	98C1
Azovskoye More, S *USSR*	60E4
Azrou *Mor*	96B1
Azucena *Arg*	34D3
Azuero,Pen de *Panama*	32A2
Azúl *Arg*	29E3
Az-Zabdāni *Syria*	94C2
Az Zāhirah, Mts *Oman*	91C5
Az Zubayr *Iraq*	93E3

B

Ba'abda *Leb*	94B2
Ba'albek *Leb*	92C3
Ba'al Hazor, Mt *Israel*	94B3
Baardheere *Somalia*	99E2
Babadag *Rom*	54C2
Babaeski *Turk*	92A1
Babahoyo *Ecuador*	32B4
Bāb al Mandab, Str *Djibouti/S Yemen*	81C4
Babar, I *Indon*	71D4
Babati *Tanz*	99D3
Babayevo *USSR*	60E2
Baberton *USA*	14B2
Babine, R *Can*	13B1
Babine L *Can*	5F4
Bäbol *Iran*	90B2
Babuyan Chan *Phil*	79B2
Babuyan Is *Phil*	79B2
Bacabal *Brazil*	31C2
Bacan, I *Indon*	71D4
Bačau *Rom*	60C4
Bac Can *Viet*	76D1
Baccchus Marsh *Aust*	108B3
Bachu *China*	82B2
Back, R *Can*	4J3
Backbone Ranges, Mts *Can*	12J2
Bac Ninh *Viet*	76D1
Bacolod *Phil*	79B3
Baco,Mt *Phil*	79B3
Badagara *India*	87B2
Badain Jaran Shamo, Desert *China*	72A1
Badajoz *Spain*	50A2
Badalona *Spain*	51C1
Badanah *S Arabia*	93D3
Bad Bergzabern *W Germ*	46D2
Bad Ems *W Germ*	46D1
Baden *Switz*	47C1
Baden-Baden *W Germ*	57B3
Baden-Württemberg, State *W Germ*	57B3
Badgastein *Austria*	57C3
Badger *USA*	22C2
Bad-Godesberg *W Germ*	57B2
Bad Hersfeld *W Germ*	57B2
Bad Honnef *W Germ*	46D1
Badin *Pak*	85B4
Bad Ischl *Austria*	52B1
Badiyat ash Sham, Desert Region *Jordan/Iraq*	93C3
Bad-Kreuznach *W Germ*	57B3
Bad Nevenahr-Ahrweiler *W Germ*	46D1
Bad Ragaz *Switz*	47C1
Bad Tolz *W Germ*	57C3
Badulla *Sri Lanka*	87C3
Baena *Spain*	50B2
Bafatá *Guinea-Bissau*	97A3
Baffin B *Greenland/Can*	6C2
Baffin I *Can*	6C2
Bafia *Cam*	98B2
Bafing, R *Mali*	97A3
Bafoulabé *Mali*	97A3
Bafoussam *Cam*	98B2
Bāfq *Iran*	90C3
Bafra Burun, Pt *Turk*	60E5
Bāft *Iran*	91C4
Bafwasende *Zaïre*	98C2
Bagaha *India*	86A1
Bāgalkot *India*	87B1
Bagamoyo *Tanz*	99D3
Bagé *Brazil*	29F2
Baghdād *Iraq*	93D3
Bagherhat *Bang*	86B2
Bāghīn *Iran*	91C3
Baghlan *Afghan*	84B1
Bagnoa *Ivory Coast*	97B4
Bagnols-sur-Cèze *France*	49C3
Bagoé, R *Mali*	97B3
Baguio *Phil*	79B2
Bāhādurābād *India*	86B1
Bahamas,The, Is *Caribbean*	11C4
Baharampur *India*	86B2
Bahar Dar *Eth*	99D1
Baharīya Oasis *Egypt*	92A4
Bahawahpur, Province *Pak*	85C3
Bahawalpur *Pak*	84C3
Bahawathagar *Pak*	85C3
Bahia, State *Brazil*	31C4
Bahía Blanca *Arg*	29D3
Bahia Blanca, B *Arg*	29D3
Bahia Concepción, B *Chile*	34A3
Bahia da Ilha Grande, B *Brazil*	35C2
Bahia de Banderas, B *Mexico*	24B2
Bahia de Campeche, B *Mexico*	24C2
Bahia de la Ascension, B *Mexico*	25D3
Bahia de Petacalco, B *Mexico*	24B3
Bahia de Rio de Oro, B *Mor*	96A2
Bahia de Sepetiba, B *Brazil*	35C2
Bahía Grande, B *Arg*	29C6
Bahía Kino *Mexico*	9B4
Bahia Magdalena, B *Mexico*	24A2
Bahia Sebastia Vizcaino, B *Mexico*	24A2
Bahraich *India*	86A1
Bahrain, Sheikdom *Arabian Pen*	80D3
Bahr al Milh, L *Iraq*	93D3
Bahr Aouk, R *Chad/CAR*	98C2
Bahr el Arab, Watercourse *Sudan*	98C2
Bahr el Ghazal, R *Sudan*	99D2
Bahr el Ghazal, Watercourse *Chad*	98B1
Baia de Maputo, B *Mozam*	101H1
Baia de Marajó, B *Brazil*	31B2
Baiá de Pemba, B *Mozam*	101D2
Baia de São Marcos, B *Brazil*	31C2
Baia de Setúbal, B *Port*	50A2
Baia de Todos os Santos, B *Brazil*	31D4
Baia dos Tigres *Angola*	100A2
Baia Mare *Rom*	60B4
Baïbokoum *Chad*	98B2
Baicheng *China*	69E2
Baie Antongila, B *Madag*	101E2
Baie-Comeau *Can*	7D5
Baie de Bombetoka, B *Madag*	101D2
Baie de Mahajamba, B *Madag*	101D2
Baie de St Augustin, B *Madag*	101D3
Baie de St Georges, B *Leb*	94B2
Baie des Chaleurs, B *Can*	10D2
Baie-du-Poste *Can*	7C4
Baihe *China*	72B3
Bai He, R *China*	72C3
Ba'ijī *Iraq*	93D3
Baikunthpur *India*	86A2
Bāilesti *Rom*	54B2
Bailleul *France*	46B1
Baima *China*	72A3
Bainbridge *USA*	17B1
Baird Inlet *USA*	12B2
Baird Mts *USA*	4B3
Bairin Youqi *China*	72D1
Bairin Zuoqi *China*	72D1
Bairnsdale *Aust*	107D4
Bais *Phil*	79B4
Baja *Hung*	54A1
Baja California, State *Mexico*	9B3
Baja California, Pen *Mexico*	24A1
Bakal *USSR*	61J2
Bakala *CAR*	98C2
Bakel *Sen*	97A3
Baker, Montana *USA*	8C2
Baker, Oregon *USA*	8B2
Baker Foreland, Pt *Can*	6A3
Baker L *Can*	4J3
Baker Lake *Can*	4J3
Baker,Mt *USA*	8A2
Bakersfield *USA*	9B3
Bakharden *USSR*	90C2
Bakhardok *USSR*	90C2
Bakhmach *USSR*	60D3
Bakkaflói, B *Iceland*	38C1
Bako *Eth*	99D2
Bakouma *CAR*	98C2
Baku *USSR*	65F5
Balâ *Turk*	92B2
Balabac, I *Phil*	79A4
Balabac, Str *Malay*	70C3
Balaikarangan *Indon*	78C2
Balaklava *Aust*	108A2
Balakovo *USSR*	61G3
Balāngīr *India*	86A2
Balashov *USSR*	61F3
Balasore *India*	86B2
Balāt *Egypt*	80A3
Balaton, L *Hung*	52C1
Balbniggan *Irish Rep*	45C2
Balcarce *Arg*	29E3
Balchik *Bulg*	54C2
Balclutha *NZ*	111B3
Bald Knob *USA*	18B2
Baldwin *USA*	17B1
Baldy Peak, Mt *USA*	9C3
Baleh, R *Malay*	78C2
Baler *Phil*	79B2
Balezino *USSR*	61H2
Bali, I *Indon*	106A1
Balikesir *Turk*	92A2
Balīkh, R *Syria*	93C2
Balikpapan *Indon*	78D3
Balintang Chan *Phil*	79B2
Bali S *Indon*	78C4
Baliza *Brazil*	35A1
Balkh *Afghan*	84B1
Balkhash *USSR*	65J5
Ballachulish *Scot*	44B3
Ballaghaderreen *Irish Rep*	45B2
Ballantrae *Scot*	42B2
Ballantyne Str *Can*	4G2
Ballapur *India*	87B2
Ballarat *Aust*	107D4
Ballater *Scot*	44C3
Balleny Is *Ant*	112C7
Ballia *India*	86A1
Ballina *Aust*	109D1
Ballina *Irish Rep*	41B3
Ballinasloe *Irish Rep*	45B2
Ballinrobe *Irish Rep*	45B2
Ballycastle *Irish Rep*	45B1
Ballycastle *N Ire*	45C1
Ballymena *N Ire*	45C1
Ballymoney *N Ire*	45C1
Ballyshannon *Irish Rep*	45B1
Ballyvaghan *Irish Rep*	45B2
Balmoral *Aust*	108B3
Balnearia *Arg*	34C2
Balombo *Angola*	100A2
Balonn, R *Aust*	109C1
Balotra *India*	85C3
Balrāmpur *India*	86A1
Balranald *Aust*	107D4
Balsas *Brazil*	31B3
Balsas *Mexico*	23B2
Balsas, R *Mexico*	24B3
Balta *USSR*	60C4
Baltic S *N Europe*	39H7
Baltîm *Egypt*	92B3
Baltimore *Irish Rep*	45B3
Baltimore *USA*	10C3

Baluchistan, Region Pak	84B3
Bālurghāt India	86B1
Balykshi USSR	61H4
Bam Iran	91C4
Bama Nig	98B1
Bamako Mali	97B3
Bambari CAR	98C2
Bamberg USA	17B1
Bamberg W Germ	57C3
Bambili Zaïre	98C2
Bambui Brazil	35B2
Bamenda Cam	98B2
Bamfield Can	13C3
Bamingui, R CAR	98B2
Bamingui Bangoran, National Park CAR	98B2
Bamiyan Afghan	84B2
Bampur Iran	91D4
Bampur, R Iran	91D4
Banalia Zaïre	98C2
Banamba Mali	97B3
Ban Aranyaprathet Thai	76C3
Ban Ban Laos	76C2
Ban Betong Thai	77C4
Banbridge N Ire	45C1
Banbury Eng	43D3
Banchory Scot	44C3
Banco Chinchorro, Is Mexico	25D3
Bancroft Can	15C1
Bända India	86A1
Banda Aceh Indon	70A3
Bandama, R Ivory Coast	97B4
Bandar Abbās Iran	91C4
Bandar Anzalī Iran	90A2
Bandar-e Daylam Iran	91B4
Bandar-e Lengheh Iran	91B4
Bandar-e Māqām Iran	91B4
Bandar-e Rig Iran	91B4
Bandar-e Torkoman Iran	90B2
Bandar Khomeynī Iran	91A3
Bandar Seri Begawan Brunei	78C2
Banda S Indon	71D4
Band Bont Iran	91C4
Bandeira, Mt Brazil	35C2
Bandiagara Mali	97B3
Bandirma Turk	60C5
Bandon Irish Rep	45B3
Bandundu Zaïre	98B3
Bandung Indon	78B4
Banes Cuba	25E2
Banff Can	13D2
Banff Scot	44C3
Banff, R Can	5G4
Banff Nat Pk Can	13D2
Bangalore India	87B2
Bangassou CAR	98C2
Banggi, I Malay	70C3
Bang Hieng, R Laos	76D2
Bangka, I Indon	78B3
Bangko Indon	78A3
Bangkok Thai	76C3
Bangladesh, Republic Asia	82C3
Bangong Co, L China	84D2
Bangor, Maine USA	10D2
Bangor N Ire	45D1
Bangor, Pennsylvania USA	16B2
Bangor Wales	42B3
Bangsalsembera Indon	78D3
Bang Saphan Yai Thai	76B3
Bangued Phil	79B2
Bangui CAR	98B2
Bangweulu, L Zambia	100C2
Ban Hat Yai Thai	77C4
Ban Hin Heup Laos	76C2
Ban Houei Sai Laos	76C1
Ban Hua Hin Thai	76B3
Bani, R Mali	97B3
Bani Bangou Niger	97C3
Banī Walīd Libya	95A1
Bāniyās Syria	92C2
Baniyas Syria	94B2
Banja Luka Yugos	52C2
Banjarmasin Indon	78C3
Banjul The Gambia	97A3
Ban Kantang Thai	77B4
Ban Khemmarat Laos	76D2
Ban Khok Kloi Thai	77B4
Banks I Aust	71F5
Banks I, British Columbia Can	5E4
Banks I, Northwest Territories Can	4F2
Banks L USA	20C1
Banks Pen NZ	111B2
Banks Str Aust	109C4
Bankura India	86B2
Ban Mae Sariang Thai	76B2
Ban Mae Sot Thai	76B2
Ban Me Thuot Viet	76D3
Bann, R N Ire	45C1
Ban Na San Thai	77B4
Bannu Pak	84C2
Baños Maule Chile	34A3
Ban Pak Neun Laos	76C2
Ban Pak Phanang Thai	77C4
Ban Ru Kroy Camb	76D3
Ban Sai Yok Thai	76B3
Ban Sattahip Thai	76C3
Banská Bystrica Czech	59B3
Bänswära India	85C4
Ban Tha Kham Thai	77B4
Ban Thateng Laos	76D2
Ban Tha Tum Thai	76C2
Bantry Irish Rep	41B3
Bantry, B Irish Rep	41A3
Ban Ya Soup Viet	76D3
Banyuwangi Indon	78C4
Baofeng China	72C3
Bao Ha Viet	76C1
Baoji China	72B3
Bao Loc Viet	76D3
Baoshan China	68B4
Baotou China	72C1
Bäpatla India	87C1
Bapaume France	46B1
Ba'Qūbah Iraq	93D3
Baquerizo Morena Ecuador	32J7
Bar Yugos	54A2
Bara Sudan	99D1
Baraawe Somalia	99E2
Barabai Indon	78D3
Bära Banki India	86A1
Barabinsk USSR	65J4
Barabinskaya Step, Steppe USSR	65J4
Baracaldo Spain	50B1
Baracoa Cuba	26C2
Baradá, R Syria	94C2
Baradine Aust	109C2
Bärämati India	87A1
Baramula Pak	84C2
Bärän India	85D3
Barangas Phil	79B3
Baranof I USA	4E4
Baranovichi USSR	60C3
Baratta Aust	108A2
Barauni India	86B1
Barbacena Brazil	31C6
Barbados, I Caribbean	27F4
Barbastro Spain	51C1
Barberton S Africa	101H1
Barbezieux France	48B2
Barbosa Colombia	32C2
Barbuda, I Caribbean	27E3
Barcaldine Aust	107D3
Barcellona Italy	53C3
Barcelona Spain	51C1
Barcelona Ven	33E1
Barcoo, R Aust	107D3
Barda del Medio Arg	34B3
Bardai Chad	95A2
Bardas Blancas Arg	29C3
Barddhamän India	86B2
Bardejov Czech	59C3
Bardi Italy	47C2
Bardonecchia Italy	47B2
Bardsey, I Wales	43B3
Bareilly India	84D3
Barentsøya, I Barents S	64D2
Barentu Eth	95C3
Bargarh India	86A2
Barge Italy	47B2
Barguzin USSR	63D2
Barguzin, R USSR	63D2
Barhi India	86B2
Bari Italy	53C2
Barika Alg	51D2
Barinas Ven	32C2
Baripäda India	86B2
Bari Sädri India	85C4
Barisal Bang	86C2
Barito, R Indon	78C3
Barjuj, Watercourse Libya	95A2
Barkam China	73A3
Barkley,L USA	18C2
Barkley Sd Can	13B3
Barkly East S Africa	100B4
Barkly Tableland, Mts Aust	106C2
Bar-le-Duc France	46C2
Barlee,L Aust	106A3
Barlee Range, Mts Aust	106A3
Barletta Italy	53C2
Barmer India	85C3
Barmera Aust	108B2
Barmouth Wales	43B3
Barnard Castle Eng	42D2
Barnaul USSR	65K4
Barnegat USA	16B3
Barnegat B USA	16B3
Barnes Icecap Can	6C2
Barnesville, Georgia USA	17B1
Barnesville, Ohio USA	14B3
Barnsley Eng	42D3
Barnstaple Eng	43B4
Baro Nig	97C4
Barpeta India	86C1
Barquisimeto Ven	32D1
Barra Brazil	31C4
Barra, I Scot	44A3
Barraba Aust	109D2
Barra de Navidad Mexico	23A2
Barra de Piraí Brazil	35C2
Barra do Garças Brazil	35A1
Barragem do Castelo do Bode, Res Port	50A2
Barragem do Maranhão Port	50A2
Barra Head, Pt Scot	44A3
Barra Mansa Brazil	31C6
Barranca Peru	32B6
Barrancabermeja Colombia	32C2
Barrancas Ven	33E2
Barranqueras Arg	30E4
Barranquilla Colombia	32C1
Barra,Sound of, Chan Scot	44A3
Barre USA	16C1
Barreal Arg	34B2
Barreiras Brazil	31C4
Barreiro Port	50A2
Barreiros Brazil	31D3
Barren,C Aust	107D5
Barren Is USA	12D3
Barretos Brazil	31B6
Barrhead Can	13E2
Barrie Can	14C2
Barrière Can	13C2
Barrier Range, Mts Aust	108B2
Barrington,Mt Aust	107E4
Barrouaillie St Vincent	27N2
Barrow USA	4C2
Barrow, R Irish Rep	45C2
Barrow Creek Aust	106C3
Barrow I Aust	106A3
Barrow-in-Furness Eng	42C2
Barrow,Pt USA	4C2
Barrow Str Can	6A2
Barry's Bay Can	15C1
Barsi India	87B1
Barstow USA	9B3
Bar-sur-Aube France	49C2
Bartica Guyana	33F2
Bartın Turk	92B1
Bartle Frere,Mt Aust	107D2
Bartlesville USA	9D3
Bartolomeu Dias Mozam	101C3
Bartoszyce Pol	58C2
Barung, I Indon	78C4
Barwäh India	85D4
Barwäni India	85D4
Barwon, R Aust	109C1
Barysh USSR	61G3
Basankusu Zaïre	98B2
Basavilbas Arg	34D2
Basco Phil	79B1
Basel Switz	52A1
Basento, R Italy	53C2
Bashaw Can	13E2
Bashi Chan Phil	79B1
Bashkirskaya ASSR, Republic USSR	61H3
Basilan, I Phil	79B4
Basildon Eng	43E4
Basingstoke Eng	43D4
Basin Region USA	8B2
Basra Iraq	93E3
Bas-Rhin, Department France	46D2
Bassac, R Camb	76D3
Bassano Can	13E2
Bassano Italy	52B1
Bassano del Grappa Italy	47D2
Bassari Togo	97C4
Bassas da India, I Mozam Chan	101C3
Bassein Burma	76A2
Basse Terre Guadeloupe	27E3
Bassila Benin	97C4
Bass Lake USA	22C2
Bass Str Aust	107D4
Båstad Sweden	39G7
Bastak Iran	91B4
Basti India	86A1
Bastia Corse	52A2
Bastogne Belg	57B3
Bastrop, Louisiana USA	19B3
Bastrop, Texas USA	19A3
Bata Eq Guinea	98A2
Batakan Indon	78C3
Batala India	84D2
Batang China	68B3
Batangafo CAR	98B2
Batan Is Phil	79B1
Batatais Brazil	35B2
Batavia USA	15C2
Batemans Bay Aust	109D3
Batesburg USA	17B1
Batesville, Arkansas USA	18B2
Batesville, Mississippi USA	19C3
Bath Eng	43C4
Bath, New York USA	15C2
Batha, R Chad	98B1
Bathurst Aust	107D4
Bathurst Can	7D5
Bathurst,C Can	4F2
Bathurst I Aust	106C2
Bathurst I Can	4H2
Bathurst Inlet, B Can	4H3
Bätläq-e-Gavkhūnī, Salt Flat Iran	90B3
Batlow Aust	109C3
Batman Turk	93D2
Batna Alg	96C1
Baton Rouge USA	11A3
Batroun Leb	94B1
Battambang Camb	76C3
Batticaloa Sri Lanka	87C3
Battle, R Can	13F2
Battle Creek USA	10B2

Battle Harbour

8

Berner Orberland, Mts	
Switz	47B1
Bernier B Can	6B2
Berounka, R Czech	57C3
Berri Aust	108B2
Berriane Alg	96C1
Berry, Region France	48C2
Berryessa,L USA	22A1
Berry Is Bahamas	11C4
Bertoua Cam	98B2
Bertraghboy B Irish	
Rep	45B2
Berwick USA	15C2
Berwick-upon-Tweed	
Eng	42C2
Berwyn, Mts Wales	43C3
Besalampy Madag	101D2
Besançon France	49D2
Beskidy Zachodnie,	
Mts Pol	59C3
Besni Turk	93C2
Besor, R Israel	94B3
Bessemer USA	11B3
Betafo Madag	101D2
Betanzos Spain	50A1
Bet Guvrin Israel	94B3
Bethal S Africa	101G1
Bethanie Namibia	100A3
Bethany, Missouri	
USA	18B1
Bethany, Oklahoma	
USA	18A2
Bethel, Alaska USA	4B3
Bethel, Connecticut	
USA	16C2
Bethel Park USA	14B2
Bethesda USA	15C3
Bethlehem Israel	94B3
Bethlehem S Africa	101G1
Bethlehem USA	15C2
Bethune France	48C1
Betioky Madag	101D3
Betoota Aust	108B1
Betou Congo	98B2
Betpak Dala, Steppe	
USSR	82A1
Betroka Madag	101D3
Betsiamites Can	7D5
Bettiah India	86A1
Bettles USA	12D1
Béttola Italy	47C2
Bétul India	85D4
Betwa, R India	85D3
Betzdorf W Germ	46D1
Beverley,L USA	12C3
Beverly USA	16D1
Beverly Hills USA	21B3
Beyla Guinea	97B4
Beypore India	87B2
Beyşehir Turk	92B2
Beyşehir Gölü, L Turk	92B2
Beyt Shean Israel	94B2
Bezau Austria	47C1
Bezhetsk USSR	60E2
Béziers France	49C3
Bezmein USSR	90C2
Beznosova USSR	63C2
Bhadgaon Nepal	86B1
Bhadrachalam India	87C1
Bhadrakh India	86B2
Bhadra Res India	87B2
Bhadrāvati India	87B2
Bhag Pak	84B3
Bhāgalpur India	86B1
Bhakkar Pak	84C2
Bhamo Burma	82D3
Bhandāra India	85D4
Bharatpur India	85D3
Bharūch India	85C4
Bhātiāpāra Ghat Bang	86B2
Bhatinda India	84C2
Bhatkal India	87A2
Bhātpāra India	86B2
Bhāvnagar India	85C4
Bhera Pak	84C2
Bheri, R Nepal	86A1
Bhilai India	86A2
Bhilwāra India	85C3

Bhīmavaram India	87C1
Bhind India	85D3
Bhiwāni India	84D3
Bhongir India	87B1
Bhopāl India	85D4
Bhubaneshwar India	86B2
Bhuj India	85B4
Bhusāwal India	85D4
Bhutan, Kingdom Asia	82C3
Biak, I Indon	71E4
Biala Podlaska Pol	58C2
Bialograd Pol	58B2
Bialystok Pol	58C2
Biargtangar, C Iceland	38A1
Biarjmand Iran	90C2
Biarritz France	48B3
Biasca Switz	47C1
Biba Egypt	92B4
Bibai Japan	74E2
Bibala Angola	100A2
Biberach W Germ	57B3
Bibiani Ghana	97B4
Bicaz Rom	54C1
Bida Nig	97C4
Bidar India	87B1
Bidbid Oman	91C5
Bideford Eng	43B4
Bideford B Eng	43B4
Bidon 5 Alg	96C2
Bié Angola	100A2
Biebrza Pol	58C2
Biel Switz	52A1
Bielawa Pol	59B2
Bielefeld W Germ	56B2
Bieler See, L Switz	47B1
Biella Italy	52A1
Bielsk Podlaski Pol	58C2
Bien Hoa Viet	76D3
Biferno, R Italy	53B2
Biga Turk	92A1
Bigadiç Turk	55C3
Big Black, R USA	19C3
Big Blue, R USA	18A1
Big Cypress Swamp	
USA	17B2
Big Delta USA	4D3
Bigent W Germ	49D2
Biggar Can	13F2
Biggar Kindersley Can	5H4
Biggenden Aust	109D1
Bigger,Mt Can	12G3
Bighorn, R USA	8C2
Bight of Bangkok, B	
Thai	76C3
Bight of Benin, B W	
Africa	97C4
Bight of Biafra, B Cam	97C4
Big I Can	6C3
Bignasco Switz	47C1
Bignona Sen	97A3
Big Pine USA	21B2
Big Pine Key USA	17B2
Big Pine Mt USA	22C3
Big Rapids USA	14A2
Big River Can	5H4
Big Spring USA	9C3
Big Trout L Can	7A4
Big Trout Lake Can	7B4
Bihać Yugos	52C2
Bihār India	86B1
Bihar, State India	86B2
Biharamulo Tanz	99D3
Bihor, Mt Rom	60B4
Bijāpur India	87B1
Bijāpur India	87C1
Bījār Iran	90A2
Bijauri Nepal	86A1
Bijeljina Yugos	54A2
Bijie China	73B4
Bijnor India	84D3
Bijnot Pak	84C3
Bikāner India	84C3
Bikfaya Leb	94B2
Bikin USSR	69F2
Bikoro Zaïre	98B3
Bilara India	85C3
Bilaspur India	84D2
Biläspur India	86A2

Bilauktaung Range,	
Mts Thai	76B3
Bilbao Spain	50B1
Bilé, R Czech	59B3
Bileća Yugos	54A2
Bilecik Turk	92B1
Bili, R Zaïre	98C2
Biliran, I Phil	79B3
Billings USA	8C2
Bilma Niger	95A3
Biloxi USA	11B3
Biltine Chad	98C1
Bina-Etawa India	85D4
Binalbagan Phil	79B3
Bindura Zim	101C2
Binga Zim	100B2
Binga, Mt Zim	101C2
Bingara Aust	109D1
Bingen W Germ	57B3
Binghamton USA	10C2
Bingkor Malay	78D1
Bingöl Turk	93D2
Binhai China	72D3
Bintan, I Indon	78A2
Bintuhan Indon	78A3
Bintulu Malay	78C2
Bió Bió, R Chile	29B3
Bioko, I Atlantic O	102J4
Bir India	87B1
Bîr Abu Husein, Well	
Egypt	95B2
Bi'r al Harash, Well	
Libya	95B2
Birao CAR	98C1
Biratnagar Nepal	86B1
Birch Creek USA	12E1
Birchip Aust	108B3
Birch Mts Can	5G4
Bird Can	7A4
Birdsville Aust	106C3
Birdum Aust	106C2
Birganj Nepal	86A1
Bîr Gifgâfa, Well	
Egypt	94A3
Bîr Hasana, Well	
Egypt	94A3
Birigui Brazil	35A2
Birjand Iran	90C3
Birkat Qarun, L Egypt	92B4
Birkenfeld W Germ	46D2
Birkenhead Eng	42C3
Bîrlad Rom	60C4
Bir Lahfân, Well Egypt	94A3
Birmingham Eng	43C3
Birmingham USA	11B3
Bîr Misâha, Well	
Egypt	95B2
Bir Moghrein Maur	96A2
Birnin Kebbi Nig	97C3
Birni N'Konni Nig	97C3
Birobidzhan USSR	69F2
Birr Irish Rep	45C2
Bir Rabalou Alg	51C2
Birrie, R Aust	109C1
Birsay Scot	44C2
Birsk USSR	61J2
Bîr Tarfâwi, Well	
Egypt	95B2
Biryusa USSR	63B2
Birzai USSR	39J7
Bir Zreigat, Well Maur	96B2
Biscay,B of Spain/	
France	48A2
Biscayne B USA	17B2
Bischwiller France	46D2
Bishan China	73B4
Bishop USA	8B3
Bishop Auckland Eng	42D2
Bishop's Stortford Eng	43E4
Bishrāmpur India	86A2
Biskra Alg	96C1
Bislig Phil	79C4
Bismarck USA	8C2
Bisotün Iran	90A3
Bissau Guinea-Bissau	97A3
Bissett Can	10A1
Bistcho L Can	5G4
Bistrita, R Rom	54C1

Bitam Gabon	98B2
Bitburg W Germ	57B3
Bitche France	46D2
Bitlis Turk	93D2
Bitola Yugos	55B2
Bitterfeld E Germ	56C2
Bitterfontein S Africa	100A4
Bitter Lakes Egypt	92B3
Bitteroot Range, Mts	
USA	8B2
Biwa-ko, L Japan	74D3
Biyo Kaboba Eth	99E1
Biysk USSR	65K4
Bizerte Tunisia	96C1
Bj bou Arréridj Alg	51C2
Bjelovar Yugos	52C1
Bj Flye Ste Marie Alg	96B2
Bjørnøya, I Barents S	64C2
Black, R USA	12F1
Black, R USA	18B2
Blackall Aust	107D3
Blackburn Eng	42C3
Blackburn,Mt USA	4D3
Black Diamond Can	13E2
Black Hills USA	5H5
Black Isle, Pen Scot	44B3
Blackman's Barbados	27R3
Black Mts Wales	43C4
Blackpool Eng	43C3
Black Rivor Jamaica	27H1
Black Rock Desert	
USA	8B2
Black S USSR/Europe	65E5
Blacksod B Irish Rep	45A1
Black Sugarloaf, Mt	
Aust	109D2
Black Volta, R Ghana	97B3
Blackwater, R Irish	
Rep	41B3
Blackwell USA	18A2
Blagoevgrad Bulg	54B2
Blagoveshchensk	
USSR	63E2
Blaine USA	20B1
Blair Atholl Scot	44C3
Blairgowrie Scot	44C3
Blakely USA	17B1
Blanche,L Aust	108A1
Blanco, R Arg	34A2
Blanco, R Arg	34B1
Blanco,C USA	8A2
Blanc Sablon Can	7E4
Blandford Forum Eng	43C4
Blangy-sur-Bresle	
France	46A2
Blankenberge Belg	46B1
Blantyre Malawi	101C2
Blaye France	48B2
Blayney Aust	109C2
Blenheim NZ	111B2
Blida Alg	96C1
Blind River Can	14B1
Blinman Aust	108A2
Blitar Indon	78C4
Block I USA	15D2
Block Island Sd USA	16D2
Bloemfontein S Africa	101G1
Bloemhof S Africa	101G1
Bloemhof Dam, Res S	
Africa	101G1
Blommesteinmeer, L	
Surinam	33F3
Blonduós Iceland	38A1
Bloody Foreland, C	
Irish Rep	45B1
Bloomfield, Indiana	
USA	14A3
Bloomfield, Iowa USA	18B1
Bloomington, Illinois	
USA	10B2
Bloomington, Indiana	
USA	14A3
Bloomsburg USA	16A2
Blora Indon	78C4
Blosseville Kyst, Mts	
Greenland	6H3
Bludenz Austria	57B3
Bluefield USA	11B3

Bluefields

Bluefields *Nic*	32A1
Blue Mountain Peak, Mt *Jamaica*	26B3
Blue Mt *USA*	16A2
Blue Mts *Aust*	109D2
Blue Mts *Jamaica*	27J1
Blue Mts *USA*	8A2
Blue Nile, R *Sudan*	99D1
Bluenose L *Can*	4G3
Blue Ridge Mts *USA*	11B3
Blue River *Can*	13D2
Blue Stack, Mt *Irish Rep*	45B1
Bluff *NZ*	111A3
Bluff Knoll, Mt *Aust*	106A4
Blumenau *Brazil*	30G4
Blundez *Austria*	49D2
Bly *USA*	20B2
Blying Sd *USA*	12E3
Blyth *Eng*	42D2
Blythe *USA*	9B3
Blytheville *USA*	11B3
Bo *Sierra Leone*	97A4
Boac *Phil*	79B3
Boading *China*	72D2
Boardman *USA*	14B2
Boatou *China*	63C3
Boa Vista *Brazil*	33E3
Boa Vista, I *Cape Verde*	97A4
Bobai *China*	76E1
Bóbbio *Italy*	47C2
Bobo Dioulasso *U Volta*	97B3
Bobruysk *USSR*	60C3
Boca Chica Key, I *USA*	17B2
Bôca do Acre *Brazil*	32D5
Bocaiúva *Brazil*	35C1
Bocaranga *CAR*	98B2
Boca Raton *USA*	17B2
Bochnia *Pol*	59C3
Bocholt *W Germ*	56B2
Bochum *W Germ*	46D1
Bocoio *Angola*	100A2
Boda *CAR*	98B2
Bodaybo *USSR*	63D2
Bodega Head, Pt *USA*	21A2
Bodélé, Region *Chad*	95A3
Boden *Sweden*	38J5
Bodensee, L *Switz/W Germ*	47C1
Bodhan *India*	87B1
Bodināyakkanūr *India*	87B2
Bodmin *Eng*	43B4
Bodmin Moor, Upland *Eng*	43B4
Bodø *Nor*	38G5
Bodorodskoye *USSR*	63G2
Bodrum *Turk*	55C3
Boende *Zaïre*	98C3
Boffa *Guinea*	97A3
Bogale *Burma*	76B2
Bogalusa *USA*	19C3
Bogan, R *Aust*	109C2
Bogandé *U Volta*	97B3
Bogarnes *Iceland*	6H3
Boğazlıyan *Turk*	92C2
Bogdanovich *USSR*	61K2
Bogda Shan, Mt *China*	68A2
Bogenfels *Namibia*	100A3
Boggabilla *Aust*	109D1
Boggabri *Aust*	109C2
Boggeragh Mts *Irish Rep*	45B2
Bogo *Phil*	79B3
Bogong,Mt *Aust*	109C3
Bogor *Indon*	78B4
Bogorodskoye *USSR*	61H2
Bogotá *Colombia*	32C3
Bogotol *USSR*	63A2
Bogra *Bang*	86B2
Bo Hai, B *China*	72D2
Bohain-en-Vermandois *France*	46B2
Bohai Wan, B *China*	72D2
Böhmer-Wald, Upland *W Germ*	57C3
Bohol, I *Phil*	79B4
Bohol S *Phil*	79B4
Bois, R *Brazil*	35A1
Bois Blanc I *USA*	14B1
Boise *USA*	8B2
Bojador,C *Mor*	96A2
Bojeador,C *Phil*	79B2
Bojnürd *Iran*	90C2
Boké *Guinea*	97A3
Bokhara, R *Aust*	109C1
Boknafjord, Inlet *Nor*	39F7
Boko *Congo*	98B3
Bokor *Camb*	76C3
Bokungu *Zaïre*	98C3
Bol *Chad*	98B1
Bolaänos *Mexico*	23A1
Bolama *Guinea-Bissau*	97A3
Bolanos, R *Mexico*	23A1
Bolbec *France*	48C2
Bole *Ghana*	97B4
Boleslawiec *Pol*	59B2
Bolgatanga *Ghana*	97B3
Bolgrad *USSR*	60C4
Bolívar *Arg*	34C3
Bolivar, Missouri *USA*	18B2
Bolivar, Tennessee *USA*	18C2
Bolivia, Republic *S America*	30C2
Bollnas *Sweden*	38H6
Bollon *Aust*	109C1
Bollvar, Mt *Ven*	32C2
Bologna *Italy*	52B2
Bologoye *USSR*	60D2
Bolon *USSR*	69F2
Bol'shoy Irgiz, R *USSR*	61G3
Bol'shoy Kamen *USSR*	74C2
Bol'shoy Kavkaz, Mts *USSR*	65F5
Bol'shoy Uzen, R *USSR*	61G4
Bolson de Mapimi, Desert *Mexico*	9C4
Bolton *Eng*	43C3
Bolu *Turk*	92B1
Bolungarvik *Iceland*	38A1
Bolvadin *Turk*	92B2
Bolzano *Italy*	52B1
Boma *Zaïre*	98B3
Bombala *Aust*	107D4
Bombay *India*	87A1
Bombo *Uganda*	99D2
Bom Despacho *Brazil*	35B1
Bomdila *India*	86C1
Bomi Hills *Lib*	97A4
Bom Jesus da Lapa *Brazil*	31C4
Bomnak *USSR*	63E2
Bomokandi, R *Zaïre*	99C2
Bomu, R *CAR/Zaïre*	98C2
Bonaire, I *Caribbean*	27D4
Bona,Mt *USA*	12F2
Bonanza *Nic*	25D3
Bonavista *Can*	7E5
Bon Bon *Aust*	108A2
Bondo *Zaïre*	98C2
Bondoukou *Ivory Coast*	97B4
Bonfim *Guyana*	33E3
Bongandanga *Zaïre*	98C2
Bongor *Chad*	98B1
Bonham *USA*	19A3
Bonifacio *Corse*	53A2
Bonifacio,Str of, Chan *Medit S*	52A2
Bonita Springs *USA*	17B2
Bonn *W Germ*	57B2
Bonners Ferry *USA*	20C1
Bonnet Plume, R *Can*	12H1
Bonnyville *Can*	13E2
Bonthe *Sierra Leone*	97A4
Booaaso *Somalia*	99E1
Booligal *Aust*	108B2
Boonah *Aust*	109D1
Boonville *USA*	15C2
Boorowa *Aust*	109C2
Boothia,G of *Can*	6A2
Boothia Pen *Can*	6A2
Booué *Gabon*	98B3
Bopeechee *Aust*	108A1
Bor *Sudan*	99D2
Bor *Turk*	92B2
Bor *Yugos*	54B2
Borah Peak, Mt *USA*	8B2
Borås *Sweden*	39G7
Borãzjän *Iran*	91B4
Borda,C *Aust*	108A3
Bordeaux *France*	48B3
Borden I *Can*	4G2
Borden Pen *Can*	6B2
Bordentown *USA*	16B2
Borders, Region *Scot*	42C2
Bordertown *Aust*	108B3
Bordi Omar Dris *Alg*	96C2
Borens River *Can*	8D1
Borgå *Fin*	39K6
Borgarnes *Iceland*	38A2
Borger *USA*	9C3
Borgholm *Sweden*	39H7
Borgosia *Italy*	47C2
Borgo Valsugana *Italy*	47D1
Borislav *USSR*	59C3
Borisoglebsk *USSR*	61F3
Borisov *USSR*	60C3
Borisovka *USSR*	60E3
Borkou, Region *Chad*	95A3
Borlänge *Sweden*	39H6
Bormida *Italy*	47C2
Bormio *Italy*	47D1
Borneo, I *Malaysia/Indon*	67F5
Bornholm, I *Den*	39H7
Bornova *Turk*	55C3
Boro, R *Sudan*	98C2
Boromo *U Volta*	97B3
Borovichi *USSR*	60D2
Borroloola *Aust*	106C2
Borsa *Rom*	54B1
Borüjed *Iran*	90A3
Borüjen *Iran*	90B3
Bory Tucholskie, Region *Pol*	58B2
Borzya *USSR*	63D2
Bose *China*	73B5
Boshof *S Africa*	101G1
Bosna, R *Yugos*	54A2
Bôsõ-hantõ, B *Japan*	75C1
Bosquet *Alg*	51C2
Bossangoa *CAR*	98B2
Bossèmbélé *CAR*	98B2
Bossier City *USA*	19B3
Bosten Hu, L *China*	65K5
Boston *Eng*	43D3
Boston *USA*	10C2
Boston Mts *USA*	11A3
Botãd *India*	85C4
Botevgrad *Bulg*	54B2
Bothaville *S Africa*	101G1
Bothnia,G of *Sweden/Fin*	64C3
Botletli, R *Botswana*	100B3
Botosani *Rom*	60C4
Botswana, Republic *Africa*	100B3
Botte Donato, Mt *Italy*	53C3
Bottrop *W Germ*	46D1
Botucatu *Brazil*	35B2
Botwood *Can*	7E5
Bouaflé *Ivory Coast*	97B4
Bouaké *Ivory Coast*	89D7
Bouar *CAR*	98B2
Bouârfa *Mor*	96B1
Bouca *CAR*	98B2
Boufarik *Alg*	51C2
Bougouni *Mali*	97B3
Bouillon *France*	46C2
Bou Izakarn *Mor*	96B2
Boulay-Moselle *France*	46D2
Boulder, Colorado *USA*	8C2
Boulder City *USA*	9B3
Boulder Creek *USA*	22A2
Boulogne *France*	48C1
Boumba, R *CAR*	98B2
Bouna *Ivory Coast*	97B4
Boundary Peak, Mt *USA*	8B3
Boundiali *Ivory Coast*	97B4
Bourail *Nouvelle Calédonie*	107F3
Bourem *Mali*	97B3
Bourg *France*	49D2
Bourg de Péage *France*	49D2
Bourges *France*	48C2
Bourg-Madame *France*	48C3
Bourgogne, Region *France*	49C2
Bourg-St-Maurice *France*	47B2
Bourke *Aust*	108C2
Bournemouth *Eng*	43D4
Bou Saâda *Alg*	96C1
Bousso *Chad*	98B1
Boutilimit *Maur*	97A3
Bouvet I *Atlantic O*	103J7
Bovril *Arg*	34D2
Bow, R *Can*	13E2
Bowen *Aust*	107D2
Bowie, Texas *USA*	19A3
Bow Island *Can*	13E2
Bowling Green, Kentucky *USA*	11B3
Bowling Green, Missouri *USA*	18B2
Bowling Green, Ohio *USA*	14B2
Bowling Green, Virginia *USA*	15C3
Bowmanville *Can*	15C2
Bowral *Aust*	109D2
Bowron, R *Can*	13C2
Bo Xian *China*	72D3
Boxing *China*	72D2
Boyabat *Turk*	92B1
Boyali *CAR*	98B2
Boyd *Can*	5J4
Boyertown *USA*	16B2
Boyle *Can*	13E2
Boyle *Irish Rep*	41B3
Boyne, R *Irish Rep*	45C2
Boynoton Beach *USA*	17B2
Boyoma Falls *Zaïre*	98C2
Bozcaada, I *Turk*	55C3
Boz Dağlari, Mts *Turk*	55C3
Bozeman *USA*	8B2
Bozene *Zaïre*	98B2
Bozoum *CAR*	98B2
Bra *Italy*	47B2
Brač, I *Yugos*	52C2
Bracebridge *Can*	15C1
Brach *Libya*	95A2
Bräcke *Sweden*	38H6
Bradenton *USA*	17B2
Bradford *Eng*	42D3
Brae *Scot*	44E1
Braemar *Scot*	44C3
Braga *Port*	50A1
Bragado *Arg*	34C3
Bragana *Port*	50A1
Bragança *Brazil*	31B2
Bragança Paulista *Brazil*	35B2
Brahman-Baria *Bang*	86C2
Brãhmani, R *India*	86B2
Brahmaputra, R *India*	86C1
Braie Verte *Can*	7E5
Brãila *Rom*	60C4
Brainerd *USA*	10A2
Brakna, Region *Maur*	97A3
Bralorne *Can*	5F4
Brampton *Can*	14C2
Branco, R *Brazil*	33E3
Brandberg, Mt *Namibia*	100A3
Brandenburg *E Germ*	56C2
Brandfort *S Africa*	101G1
Brandon *Can*	8D2
Brandvlei *S Africa*	100B4
Brandys nad Lebem *Czech*	57C2
Braniewo *Pol*	58B2
Brantford *Can*	10B2

Branxholme *Aust*	108B3
Bras D'Or L *Can*	7D5
Brasíla de Minas *Brazil*	35C1
Brasiléia *Brazil*	32D6
Brasilia *Brazil*	31B5
Brasov *Rom*	54C1
Brassay Range, Mts *Malay*	78D1
Bratislava *Czech*	59B3
Bratsk *USSR*	63C2
Brattleboro *USA*	15D2
Braunschweig *W Germ*	56C2
Brava, I *Cape Verde*	97A4
Brawley *USA*	9B3
Bray *Irish Rep*	45C2
Bray I *Can*	6C3
Brazeau, R *Can*	13D2
Brazeau,Mt *Can*	13D2
Brazil, Republic *S America*	28D4
Brazil Basin *Atlantic O*	103G5
Brazos, R *USA*	9D3
Brazzaville *Congo*	98B3
Brdy, Upland *Czech*	57C3
Breaksea Sd *NZ*	111A3
Bream B *NZ*	110B1
Brebes *Indon*	78B4
Brechin *Scot*	44C3
Brecht *Belg*	46C1
Břeclav *Czech*	59B3
Brecon *Wales*	43C4
Brecon Beacons, Mts *Wales*	43C4
Brecon Beacons Nat Pk *Wales*	43B3
Breda *Neth*	56A2
Bredasdorp *S Africa*	100B4
Bredbyn *Sweden*	38H6
Bredy *USSR*	61J3
Breezewood *USA*	15C2
Bregenz *Austria*	47C1
Bregenzer Ache, R *Austria*	47C1
Breiðafjörður, B *Iceland*	38A1
Brembo, R *Italy*	47C2
Bremen *USA*	17A1
Bremen *W Germ*	56B2
Bremerhaven *W Germ*	56B2
Bremerton *USA*	20B1
Brenham *USA*	19A3
Brenner, P *Austria/Italy*	57C3
Breno *Italy*	47D2
Brenta, R *Italy*	47D2
Brentwood *USA*	22B2
Brescia *Italy*	52B1
Bressanone *Italy*	47D1
Bressay, I *Scot*	44D1
Bressuire *France*	48B2
Brest *France*	48B2
Brest *USSR*	58C2
Bretagne, Region *France*	48B2
Breteuil *France*	46B2
Breton Woods *USA*	16B2
Brett,C *NZ*	110B1
Brewarrina *Aust*	109C1
Brewster, New York *USA*	16C2
Brewster, Washington *USA*	20C1
Breyten *S Africa*	101G1
Brezhnev *USSR*	61H2
Brežice *Yugos*	52C1
Bria *CAR*	98C2
Briancon *France*	49D3
Briare *France*	49C2
Bridgeport, California *USA*	21B2
Bridgeport, Connecticut *USA*	15D2
Bridgeport, Texas *USA*	19A3
Bridgeport Res *USA*	22C1
Bridgeton *USA*	16B3
Bridgetown *Barbados*	27F4
Bridgewater *Can*	7D5
Bridgewater *USA*	16D2
Bridgwater *Eng*	43C4
Bridgwater B *Eng*	43C4
Bridlington *Eng*	42D2
Bridport *Aust*	109C4
Brienzer See, L *Switz*	47B1
Briey *France*	46C2
Brig *Switz*	52A1
Brigham City *USA*	8B2
Bright *Aust*	109C3
Brighton *Eng*	43D4
Brilon *W Germ*	46E1
Brindisi *Italy*	55A2
Brinkley *USA*	19B3
Brisbane *Aust*	107E3
Bristol, Connecticut *USA*	15D2
Bristol *Eng*	43C4
Bristol, Pennsylvania *USA*	15D2
Bristol, Rhode Island *USA*	16D2
Bristol, Tennessee *USA*	11B3
Bristol B *USA*	12B3
Bristol Chan *Eng/Wales*	43B4
British, Mts *USA*	4D3
British Columbia, Province *Can*	5F4
British Empire Range, Mts *Can*	6B1
Brits *S Africa*	101G1
Britstown *S Africa*	100B4
Brive *France*	48C2
Brno *Czech*	59B3
Broad, R *USA*	17B1
Broadback, R *Can*	7C4
Broad Bay, Inlet *Scot*	44A2
Broadford *Scot*	44B3
Brochet *Can*	5H4
Brock I *Can*	4G2
Brockport *USA*	15C2
Brockton *USA*	16D1
Brockville *Can*	15C2
Brodeur Pen *Can*	6B2
Brodick *Scot*	42B2
Brodnica *Pol*	58B2
Brody *USSR*	60C3
Broken Bow, Oklahoma *USA*	19B3
Broken Bow L *USA*	19B3
Broken Hill *Aust*	107D4
Broni *Italy*	47C2
Brønnøysund *Nor*	38G5
Bronx, Borough, New York *USA*	16C2
Brooke's Point *Phil*	79A4
Brookfield, Missouri *USA*	18B2
Brookhaven *USA*	11A3
Brookings, Oregon *USA*	20B2
Brookings, South Dakota *USA*	8D2
Brookline *USA*	16D1
Brooklyn, Borough, New York *USA*	16C2
Brooks *Can*	5G4
Brooks,L *USA*	12C3
Brooks Mt *USA*	12A1
Brooks Range, Mts *USA*	4C3
Brooksville *USA*	17B2
Brooloo *Aust*	109D1
Broome *Aust*	106B2
Brora *Scot*	44C2
Brothers *USA*	20B2
Broulkou *Chad*	95A3
Browning *USA*	13E3
Brownsville *USA*	9D4
Brownwood *USA*	9D3
Bruay-en-Artois *France*	46B1
Bruce,Mt *Aust*	106A3
Bruce Pen *Can*	14B1
Bruck an der Mur *Austria*	59B3
Brugge *Belg*	46B1
Brühl *W Germ*	46D1
Brunei, Sultanate *S E Asia*	78C2
Brunico *Italy*	52B1
Brunner,L *NZ*	111B2
Brunswick, Georgia *USA*	11B3
Brunswick, Mississippi *USA*	18B2
Brunswick,Pen de *Chile*	29B6
Bruny I *Aust*	109C4
Brusenets *USSR*	61F1
Brus Laguna *Honduras*	26A3
Bruxelles *Belg*	56A2
Bryan *USA*	9D3
Bryan,Mt *Aust*	108A2
Bryansk *USSR*	60D3
Bryant *USA*	19B3
Brzeg *Pol*	59B2
Būbiyan, I *Kuwait/Iraq*	93E4
Bubu, R *Tanz*	99D3
Bucaramanga *Colombia*	32C2
Buchan, Oilfield *N Sea*	44D3
Buchanan *Lib*	97A4
Buchan Deep *N Sea*	44D3
Buchan G *Can*	6C2
Buchan Ness, Pen *Scot*	40C2
Buchans *Can*	7E5
Buchardo *Arg*	34C2
Buchs *Switz*	47C1
Buckingham *Eng*	43D3
Buckland *USA*	12B1
Buckland, R *USA*	12B1
Buckleboo *Aust*	108A2
Buco Zau *Congo*	98B3
Bucureşti *Rom*	54C2
Budapest *Hung*	59B3
Budaun *India*	84D3
Bude *Eng*	43B4
Bude *USA*	19B3
Budennovsk *USSR*	61F5
Budva *Yugos*	54A2
Buéa *Cam*	98A2
Buellton *USA*	22B3
Buena Esperanza *Arg*	34B2
Buenaventura *Colombia*	32B3
Buenavista *Mexico*	23A2
Buenos Aires *Arg*	29E2
Buenos Aires, State *Arg*	29D3
Buffalo, Mississipi *USA*	18B2
Buffalo, New York *USA*	10C2
Buffalo, South Dakota *USA*	8C2
Buffalo, Texas *USA*	19A3
Buffalo, Wyoming *USA*	8C2
Buffalo, R *S Africa*	101H1
Buffalo L, Alberta *Can*	13E2
Buffalo L, Northwest Territories *Can*	5G3
Buffalo Narrows *Can*	5H4
Buford *USA*	17B1
Buftea *Rom*	54C2
Bug, R *USSR/Pol*	59C2
Buga *Colombia*	32B3
Bugdayli *USSR*	90B2
Bugulma *USSR*	61H3
Buguruslan *USSR*	61H3
Buhayrat al Asad, Res *Syria*	93C2
Builth Wells *Wales*	41C3
Buin *Chile*	34A2
Bujumbura *Burundi*	99C3
Bukama *Zaïre*	98C3
Bukavu *Zaïre*	99C3
Bukhara *USSR*	80E2
Bukit Batubrok, Mt *Indon*	78C2
Bukittinggi *Indon*	70B4
Bukoba *Tanz*	99D3
Buku Gandadiwata, Mt *Indon*	78D3
Bula *Indon*	71E4
Bulan *Phil*	79B3
Bulandshahr *India*	84D3
Bulawayo *Zim*	100B3
Buldan *Turk*	55C3
Buldāna *India*	85D4
Bulgan *Mongolia*	68C2
Bulgaria, Republic *Europe*	54B2
Bulle *Switz*	47B1
Buller, R *NZ*	111B2
Buller,Mt *Aust*	109C3
Bullfinch *Aust*	106A4
Bulloo, R *Aust*	108B1
Bulloo Downs *Aust*	108B1
Bulloo L *Aust*	108B1
Bull Shoals Res *USA*	18B2
Bulnes *Chile*	34A3
Bultfontein *S Africa*	101G1
Bumpa *Zaïre*	98C2
Bumphal Dam *Thai*	76B2
Buna *Kenya*	99D2
Bunbury *Aust*	106A4
Buncrana *Irish Rep*	45C1
Bundaberg *Aust*	107E3
Bundarra *Aust*	109D2
Būndi *India*	85D3
Bundoran *Irish Rep*	45B1
Bungil, R *Aust*	109C1
Bungo *Angola*	98B3
Bungo-suidō, Str *Japan*	75A2
Bunguran, I *Ind*	70B3
Bunia *Zaïre*	99D2
Bunker *USA*	18B2
Bunkie *USA*	19B3
Bunnell *USA*	17B2
Buntok *Indon*	78C3
Buol *Indon*	71D3
Burāg *Syria*	94C2
Buram *Sudan*	98C1
Burauen *Phil*	79B3
Buraydah *S Arabia*	80C3
Burbank *USA*	21B3
Burcher *Aust*	109C2
Burco *Somalia*	99E2
Burdur *Turk*	92B2
Bureinskiy Khrebet, Mts *USSR*	63F3
Burg *E Germ*	56C2
Burgas *Bulg*	54C2
Burgaw *USA*	17C1
Burgdorf *Switz*	47B1
Burgersdorp *S Africa*	100B4
Burgin *USSR*	65K5
Burgos *Spain*	50B1
Burgsvik *Sweden*	58B1
Burhaniye *Turk*	55C3
Burhānpur *India*	85D4
Burias, I *Phil*	79B3
Buriram *Thai*	76C2
Buritis *Brazil*	35B1
Burke Chan *Can*	13B2
Burkina, Republic *Africa*	97B3
Burks Falls *Can*	15C1
Burley *USA*	8B2
Burlington, Iowa *USA*	10A2
Burlington, New Jersey *USA*	16B2
Burlington, Vermont *USA*	10C2
Burlington, Washington *USA*	20B1
Burma, Republic *Asia*	83D3
Burney *USA*	20B2
Burnham *USA*	16A2
Burnie *Aust*	107D5
Burnley *Eng*	42C3
Burns *USA*	20C2
Burns Lake *Can*	5F4
Burqin *China*	82C1
Burra *Aust*	108A2
Burragorang,L *USA*	109D2
Burray, I *Scot*	44C2
Burren Junction *Aust*	109C2

Burrinjuck Res

Burrinjuck Res *Aust*	109C2
Bursa *Turk*	60C5
Bur Safâga *Egypt*	80B3
Burton *USA*	14B2
Burton upon Trent *Eng*	43D3
Burtrask *Sweden*	38J6
Burtundy *Aust*	108B2
Buru *Indon*	71D4
Burundi, Republic *Africa*	99C3
Burung *Indon*	78A2
Buryatskaya ASSR, Republic *USSR*	63D2
Burye *Eth*	99D1
Burynshik *USSR*	61H4
Bury St Edmunds *Eng*	43E3
Büshehr *Iran*	91B4
Busira, R *Zaïre*	98B3
Buskozdroj *Pol*	58C2
Busrä ash Shäm *Syria*	94C2
Busselton *Aust*	106A4
Busto *Italy*	49D2
Busto Arsizio *Italy*	52A1
Busuanga, I *Phil*	79A3
Buta *Zaïre*	98C2
Buta Ranquil *Arg*	34B3
Butare *Rwanda*	99C3
Bute, I *Scot*	42B2
Butha Qi *China*	69E2
Butler *USA*	14C2
Butte *USA*	8B2
Butterworth *Malay*	77C4
Butt of Lewis, C *Scot*	40B2
Button Is *Can*	6D3
Butuan *Phil*	79C4
Butung, I *Indon*	71D4
Buturlinovka *USSR*	61F3
Butwal *Nepal*	86A1
Buulo Barde *Somalia*	99E2
Buur Hakaba *Somalia*	99E2
Buy *USSR*	61F2
Buyant Ovvo *Mongolia*	72B1
Buynaksk *USSR*	61G5
Buyr Nuur, L *Mongolia*	63D3
Büyük Ağri, Mt *Turk*	93D2
Büyük Menderes, R *Turk*	92A2
Buzău *Rom*	54C1
Buzau, R *Rom*	54C1
Buzuluk *USSR*	61H3
Buzzards B *USA*	16D2
Byala *Bulg*	54C2
Byala Slatina *Bulg*	54B2
Byam Martin, Chan *Can*	4H2
Byam Martin I *Can*	4H2
Bydgoszcz *Pol*	58B2
Bygland *Nor*	39F7
Bylot I *Can*	6C2
Byrock *Aust*	109C2
Byron *USA*	22B2
Byron,C *Aust*	109D1
Bytom *Pol*	59B2

C

Caacupé *Par*	30E4
Caála *Angola*	100A2
Caamano Sd *Can*	13B2
Caazapá *Par*	30E4
Cabanatuan *Phil*	79B2
Cabedelo *Brazil*	31E3
Cabeza del Buey *Spain*	50A2
Cabildo *Arg*	34C3
Cabildo *Chile*	34A2
Cabimas *Ven*	32C1
Cabinda *Angola*	98B3
Cabinda, Province *Angola*	98B3
Cabo Beata *Dom Rep*	27C3
Cabo Binibeca, C *Spain*	51C2
Cabo Carbonara, C *Sardegna*	53A3
Cabo Carranza, C *Chile*	34A3
Cabo Carvoeiro, C *Port*	50A2
Cabo Colnett, C *Mexico*	9B3
Cabo Corrientes, C *Colombia*	32B2
Cabo Corrientes, C *Mexico*	24B2
Cabo Cruz, C *Cuba*	26B3
Cabo de Ajo, C *Spain*	50B1
Cabo de Caballeria, C *Spain*	51C1
Cabo de Creus, C *Spain*	51C1
Cabo de Gata, C *Spain*	50B2
Cabo de Hornos, C *Chile*	29C7
Cabo de la Nao, C *Spain*	51C2
Cabo de Peñas, C *Spain*	50A1
Cabo de Roca, C *Port*	50A2
Cabo de Salinas, C *Spain*	51C2
Cabo de São Tomé, C *Brazil*	35C2
Cabo de São Vicente, C *Port*	50A2
Cabo de Sines, C *Port*	50A2
Cabo de Tortosa, C *Spain*	51C1
Cabo Dos Bahias, C *Arg*	29C4
Cabo Espichel, C *Port*	50A2
Cabo Falso, C *Mexico*	9B4
Cabo Ferrat, C *Alg*	51B2
Cabo Finisterre, C *Spain*	50A1
Cabo Formentor, C *Spain*	51C1
Cabo Frio *Brazil*	35C2
Cabo Frio, C *Brazil*	35C2
Cabo Gracias à Dios *Honduras*	26A4
Cabo Maguarinho, C *Brazil*	31B2
Cabo Negro, C *Mor*	50A2
Cabonga,Résr *Can*	10C2
Caboolture *Aust*	109D1
Cabo Orange, C *Brazil*	33G3
Cabo Punta Banda, C *Mexico*	21B3
Cabora Bassa Dam *Mozam*	101C2
Caborca *Mexico*	24A1
Cabo Rojo, C *Mexico*	24C2
Cabos *Mexico*	23B1
Cabo San Diego, C *Arg*	29C6
Cabo San Lorenzo, C *Ecuador*	32A4
Cabo Teulada, C *Sardegna*	53A3
Cabo Trafalgar, C *Spain*	50A2
Cabo Tres Forcas, C *Mor*	50B2
Cabo Tres Puntas, C *Arg*	29C5
Cabot Str *Can*	7D5
Cabra *Spain*	50B2
Cabreira, Mt *Port*	50A1
Cabrera, I *Spain*	51C2
Cabrero *Chile*	34A3
Cabriel, R *Spain*	51B2
Cacahuamilpa *Mexico*	23B2
Čačak *Yugos*	54B2
C A Carillo *Mexico*	23B2
Cáceres *Brazil*	30E2
Caceres *Spain*	50A2
Cache, R *USA*	18B2
Cache Creek *Can*	13C2
Cachi *Arg*	30C4
Cachimbo *Brazil*	33G5
Cachoeira *Brazil*	31D4
Cachoeira Alta *Brazil*	35A1
Cachoeira de Paulo Alfonso, Waterfall *Brazil*	31D3
Cachoeira do Sul *Brazil*	29F2
Cachoeiro de Itapemirim *Brazil*	31C6
Cachuma,L *USA*	22C3
Cacolo *Angola*	100A2
Caconda *Angola*	100A2
Caçu *Brazil*	35A1
Caculuvar, R *Angola*	100A2
Čadca *Czech*	59B3
Cader Idris, Mts *Wales*	43C3
Cadillac *USA*	10B2
Cadiz *Phil*	79B3
Cadiz *Spain*	50A2
Caen *France*	48B2
Caernarfon *Wales*	42B3
Caernarfon B *Wales*	43B3
Caesarea, Hist Site *Israel*	94B2
Caetité *Brazil*	31C4
Cafayate *Arg*	30C4
Caga Tepe *Turk*	92B2
Cagayan, R *Phil*	79B2
Cagayan de Oro *Phil*	79B4
Cagayan Is *Phil*	79B4
Cagayan Sulu, I *Phil*	79A4
Cagliari *Sardegna*	53A3
Caguas *Puerto Rico*	27D3
Caha Mts *Irish Rep*	45B3
Cahersiveen *Irish Rep*	45A3
Cahir *Irish Rep*	45C2
Cahone Pt *Irish Rep*	45C2
Cahors *France*	48C3
Caia *Mozam*	101C2
Caianda *Angola*	100B2
Caiapó, R *Brazil*	35A1
Caiapônia *Brazil*	35A1
Caicó *Brazil*	31D3
Caicos Is *Caribbean*	26C2
Caicos Pass *Bahamas*	11C4
Cairn Mt *USA*	12C2
Cairngorms, Mts *Scot*	44C3
Cairns *Aust*	107D2
Cairo *Egypt*	92B3
Cairo *USA*	11B3
Caiwarro *Aust*	108B1
Cajabamba *Peru*	32B5
Cajamarca *Peru*	32B5
Calabozo *Ven*	27D5
Calafat *Rom*	54B2
Calafate *Arg*	29B6
Calagua Is *Phil*	79B3
Calahorra *Spain*	51B1
Calais *France*	48C1
Calama *Chile*	30C3
Calamar *Colombia*	32C3
Calamian Group, Is *Phil*	79A3
Calang *Indon*	70A3
Calanscio Sand Sea *Libya*	95B2
Calapan *Phil*	79B3
Calarasi *Rom*	54C2
Calatayud *Spain*	51B1
Calaveras Res *USA*	22B2
Calbayog *Phil*	79B3
Calcasieu L *USA*	19B4
Calcutta *India*	86B2
Caldas da Rainha *Port*	50A2
Caldas Novas *Brazil*	31B5
Caldera *Chile*	30B4
Caldwell *USA*	8B2
Caleta Olivia *Arg*	29C5
Calexico *USA*	9B3
Calgary *Can*	5G4
Calhoun *USA*	17B1
Calhoun Falls *USA*	17B1
Cali *Colombia*	32B3
Calicut *India*	87B2
Caliente, Nevada *USA*	8B3
California, State *USA*	8A3
California Aqueduct *USA*	22C3
Calimera,Pt *India*	87B2
Calingasta *Arg*	34B2
Calistoga *USA*	22A1
Callabonna, R *Aust*	108B1
Callabonna,L *Aust*	108A1
Callander *Can*	15C1
Callander *Scot*	44B3
Callanna *Aust*	108A1
Callao *Peru*	32B6
Calling L *Can*	13E1
Calnali *Mexico*	23B1
Caloosahatchee, R *USA*	17B2
Caloundra *Aust*	109D1
Calpulalpan *Mexico*	23B2
Caltanissetta *Italy*	53B3
Caluango *Angola*	98B3
Calulo *Angola*	100A2
Caluquembe *Angola*	100A2
Calvert I *Can*	13B2
Calvi *Corse*	52A2
Calvillo *Mexico*	23A1
Calvinia *S Africa*	100A4
Camagüey *Cuba*	25E2
Camagüey,Arch de, Is *Cuba*	25E2
Camaná *Peru*	30B2
Camargo *Bol*	30C3
Camarillo *USA*	22C3
Camarones *Arg*	29C4
Camas *USA*	20B1
Camaxilo *Angola*	98B3
Cambatela *Angola*	98B3
Cambodia, Republic S E ASia	76C3
Camborne *Eng*	43B4
Cambrai *France*	49C1
Cambrian Mts *Wales*	43C3
Cambridge *Can*	14B2
Cambridge, County *Eng*	43D3
Cambridge *Eng*	43E3
Cambridge *Jamaica*	27H1
Cambridge, Maryland *USA*	15C3
Cambridge, Massachussets *USA*	15D2
Cambridge *NZ*	110C1
Cambridge, Ohio *USA*	14B2
Cambridge Bay *Can*	4H3
Cam Burun, Pt *Turk*	60E5
Camden, Arkansas *USA*	11A3
Camden *Aust*	109D2
Camden, New Jersey *USA*	15D3
Camden, South Carolina *USA*	17B1
Cameron, Missouri *USA*	18B2
Cameron, Texas *USA*	19A3
Cameron I *Can*	4H2
Cameron Mts *NZ*	111A3
Cameroon, Federal Republic *Africa*	98A2
Cameroun, Mt *Cam*	98A2
Cametá *Brazil*	31B2
Camiguin, I *Phil*	79B4
Camiling *Phil*	79B2
Camilla *USA*	17B1
Camino *USA*	22B1
Camiri *Bol*	30D3
Camocim *Brazil*	31C2
Camooweal *Aust*	106C2
Campana *Arg*	34D2
Campana, I *Chile*	29A5
Campania I *Can*	13B2
Campbell,C *NZ*	111B2
Campbell I *Can*	13B2
Campbell I *NZ*	105G6
Campbell,Mt *Can*	4E3
Campbellpore *Pak*	84C2
Campbell River *Can*	5F5
Campbellton *Can*	7D5
Campbelltown *Aust*	109D2
Campbeltown *Scot*	42B2
Campeche *Mexico*	25C3
Camperdown *Aust*	108B3

Campina Grande *Brazil*	31D3
Campinas *Brazil*	31B6
Campina Verde *Brazil*	35B1
Campo *Cam*	98A2
Campobasso *Italy*	53B2
Campo Belo *Brazil*	35B2
Campo Florido *Brazil*	35B1
Campo Gallo *Arg*	30D4
Campo Grande *Brazil*	30F3
Campo Maior *Brazil*	31C2
Campo Mourão *Brazil*	30F3
Campos *Brazil*	35C2
Campos Altos *Brazil*	35B1
Campo Tures *Italy*	47D1
Cam Ranh *Viet*	76D3
Camrose *Can*	5G4
Camucuio *Angola*	100A2
Canaan *Tobago*	27K1
Canaan *USA*	16C1
Canacupa *Angola*	100A2
Canada, Dominion *N America*	2F3
Cañada de Gomez *Arg*	29D2
Canadian, R *USA*	9C3
Canakkale *Turk*	60C5
Canalejas *Arg*	34B3
Canal Flats *Can*	13D2
Cananea *Mexico*	24A1
Canary Basin *Atlantic O*	102G3
Canas *Mexico*	23A2
Canatlán *Mexico*	24B2
Canaveral,C *USA*	11B4
Canavieiras *Brazil*	31D5
Canberra *Aust*	107D4
Canby, California *USA*	20B2
Candala *Somalia*	99F1
Candlewood,L *USA*	16C2
Canelones *Urug*	29E2
Caney *USA*	18A2
Cangamba *Angola*	100A2
Cangombe *Angola*	100B2
Cangzhou *China*	72D2
Caniapiscau, R *Can*	7D4
Caniapiscau,L *Can*	7D4
Canicatti *Italy*	53B3
Canindé *Brazil*	31D2
Çankırı *Turk*	92B1
Canmore *Can*	13D2
Canna, I *Scot*	44A3
Cannanore *India*	87B2
Cannes *France*	49D3
Cann River *Aust*	109C3
Canõas *Brazil*	30F4
Canoe L *Can*	13F1
Canon City *USA*	9C3
Canopus *Aust*	108B2
Canora *Can*	5H4
Canowindra *Aust*	109C2
Cansore Pt *Irish Rep*	45C2
Canterbury *Eng*	43E4
Canterbury Bight, B *NZ*	111B2
Canterbury Plains *NZ*	111B2
Can Tho *Viet*	77D4
Canton, Mississippi *USA*	19C3
Canton, Missouri *USA*	18B1
Canton, Ohio *USA*	10B2
Cantwell *USA*	12E2
Canyon City *USA*	20C2
Canyon Range, Mts *Can*	12J2
Canyonville *USA*	20B2
Canzar *Angola*	98C3
Cao Bang *Viet*	76D1
Capanema *Brazil*	31B2
Capão Bonito *Brazil*	35B2
Capbreton *France*	48B3
Cap Corrientes, C *Mexico*	24B2
Cap Corse *C Corse*	52A2
Cap d'Ambre, C *Madag*	101D2
Cap de la Hague, C *France*	48B2
Cap-de-la-Madeleine *Can*	15D1
Cap de Nouvelle-France, C *Can*	6C3
Capdepera *Spain*	51C2
Cap de Tancitiario, C *Mexico*	23A2
Cape Barren I *Aust*	109C4
Cape Basin *Atlantic O*	103J6
Cape Breton I *Can*	7E5
Cape Coast *Ghana*	97B4
Cape Cod B *USA*	15D2
Cape Dorset *Can*	6C3
Cape Fear, R *USA*	17C1
Cape Girardeau *USA*	18C2
Cape Henrietta Maria *Can*	6B3
Cape Johnston Depth *Pacific O*	104E3
Capelinha *Brazil*	35C1
Cape Lisburne *USA*	4B3
Capelongo *Angola*	100A2
Cape May *USA*	15D3
Cape Mendocino *USA*	5F5
Capenda Camulemba *Angola*	98B3
Cape Perry *Can*	4F2
Cape Province *S Africa*	100B4
Cape Tatnam *Can*	7A4
Cape Town *S Africa*	100A4
Cape Verde, Is *Atlantic O*	102G4
Cape Verde Basin *Atlantic O*	102G4
Cape Yakataga *USA*	12F3
Cape York Pen *Aust*	107D2
Cap Gris Nez, C *France*	46A1
Cap-Haitien *Haiti*	26C3
Capim, R *Brazil*	31B2
Cap Moule à Chique, C *St Lucia*	27P2
Capo Isola di Correnti C *Italy*	53C3
Capo Rizzuto, C *Italy*	53C3
Capo Santa Maria di Leuca, C *Italy*	55A3
Capo San Vito *Italy*	53B3
Capo Spartivento, C *Italy*	53C3
Cap Pt *St Lucia*	27P2
Capri, I *Italy*	53B2
Caprivi Strip, Region *Namibia*	100B2
Cap Rosso, C *Corse*	52A2
Cap Vert, C *Sen*	97A3
Caquetá, R *Colombia*	32C4
Caracal *Rom*	54B2
Caracaraí *Brazil*	33E3
Caracas *Ven*	32D1
Caraguatatuba *Brazil*	35B2
Carahue *Chile*	29B3
Caraí *Brazil*	35C1
Carandaí *Brazil*	35C2
Carangola *Brazil*	31C6
Caransebeş *Rom*	54B1
Carappee Hill, Mt *Aust*	108A2
Caratasca *Honduras*	26A3
Caratinga *Brazil*	35C1
Caravaca *Spain*	51B2
Caravelas *Brazil*	35D1
Carbondale, Illinois *USA*	18C2
Carbonia *Sardegna*	53A3
Carborear *Can*	7E5
Carcaion *Can*	5G4
Carcar Mts *Somalia*	99E1
Carcassonne *France*	48C3
Carcross *Can*	4E3
Cardel *Mexico*	23B2
Cardenas *Cuba*	25D2
Cárdenas *Mexico*	23B1
Cardiff *Wales*	43C4
Cardigan *Wales*	43B3
Cardigan B *Wales*	43B3
Cardston *Can*	13E2
Carei *Rom*	54B1
Careiro *Brazil*	33F4
Carén *Chile*	34A2
Carey *USA*	14B2
Carhaix-Plouguer *France*	48B2
Carhué *Arg*	29D3
Cariacica *Brazil*	31C6
Caribou *Can*	5J4
Caribou Mts, Alberta *Can*	5G4
Caribou Mts, British Columbia *Can*	5F4
Carigara *Phil*	79B3
Carignan *France*	46C2
Caripito *Ven*	33E1
Carleton Place *Can*	15C1
Carletonville *S Africa*	101G1
Carlinville *USA*	18C2
Carlisle *Eng*	42C2
Carlisle *USA*	15C2
Carlos *Arg*	34C3
Carlos Chagas *Brazil*	35C1
Carlow, County *Irish Rep*	45C2
Carlow *Irish Rep*	45C2
Carlsbad, California *USA*	21B3
Carlsbad, New Mexico *USA*	9C3
Carlyle *Can*	5H5
Carmacks *Can*	12G2
Carmagnola *Italy*	47B2
Carmarthen *Wales*	43B4
Carmarthen B *Wales*	43B4
Carmel, California *USA*	22B2
Carmel, New York *USA*	16C2
Carmel,Mt *Israel*	94B2
Carmelo *Urug*	34D2
Carmel Valley *USA*	22B2
Carmen, I *Mexico*	9B4
Carmen de Patagones *Arg*	29D4
Carmi *USA*	18C2
Carmichael *USA*	21A2
Carmo do Paranaiba *Brazil*	35B1
Carmona *Spain*	50A2
Carnarvon *Aust*	106A3
Carnarvon *S Africa*	100B4
Carncacá *Brazil*	35D1
Carndonagh *Irish Rep*	45C1
Carnegi,L *Aust*	106B3
Carnot *CAR*	98B2
Carnot,C *Aust*	108A2
Carol City *USA*	17B2
Carolina *Brazil*	31B3
Carolina *S Africa*	101H1
Carolina Beach *USA*	17C1
Caroline Is *Pacific O*	104F3
Carpathians, Mts *E Europe*	60B4
Carpatii Orientali, Mts *Rom*	59D3
Carpentaria,G of *Aust*	106C2
Carpenter Ridge *Indian O*	83C5
Carpentras *France*	49D3
Carpi *Italy*	52B2
Carpinteria *USA*	22C3
Carrabelle *USA*	17B2
Carrara *Italy*	52B2
Carrauntoohill, Mt *Irish Rep*	41B3
Carrickmacross *Irish Rep*	45C2
Carrick on Shannon *Irish Rep*	45B2
Carrick-on-Suir *Irish Rep*	45C2
Carrieton *Aust*	108A2
Carrington *USA*	8D2
Carrión, R *Spain*	50B1
Carroll *USA*	10A2
Carrollton, Georgia *USA*	17A1
Carrollton, Kentucky *USA*	14A3
Carrollton, Missouri *USA*	18B2
Carruthersville *USA*	18C2
Carsamba *Turk*	60E5
Carsamba, R *Turk*	92B2
Carson City *USA*	8B3
Carsonville *USA*	14B2
Cartagena *Colombia*	26B4
Cartagena *Spain*	51B2
Cartago *Colombia*	32B3
Cartago *Costa Rica*	25D4
Carterton *NZ*	111C2
Carthage, Missouri *USA*	18B2
Carthage, New York *USA*	15C2
Carthage, Texas *USA*	19B3
Cartier I *Timor S*	106B2
Cartwright *Can*	7E4
Caruaru *Brazil*	31D3
Carúpano *Ven*	33E1
Carvin *France*	46B1
Casablanca *Chile*	34A2
Casablanca *Mor*	96B1
Casa Branca *Brazil*	35B2
Casa Grande *USA*	9B3
Casale Monferrato *Italy*	52A1
Casalmaggiore *Italy*	47D2
Casares *Arg*	34C3
Casino *Aust*	107E3
Casma *Peru*	32B5
Caspe *Spain*	51B1
Casper *USA*	8C2
Caspian S *USSR*	65G6
Cass *USA*	14C3
Cascade Mts *Can/USA*	13C3
Cascade Pt *NZ*	111A2
Cascade Range, Mts *USA*	8A2
Cascavel *Brazil*	30F3
Caserta *Italy*	53B2
Casey, Base *Ant*	112C9
Cashel *Irish Rep*	45C2
Casilda *Arg*	34C2
Cassamba *Angola*	100B2
Cassel *France*	46B1
Cassiar *Can*	12J3
Cassiar Mts *Can*	4E3
Cassilândia *Brazil*	35A1
Cassino *Italy*	53B2
Castaic *USA*	22C3
Castaño, R *Arg*	34B2
Castelfranco *Italy*	47D2
Castellane *France*	49D3
Castelli *Arg*	34D3
Castellon de la Plana *Spain*	51B2
Castelo *Brazil*	31C3
Castelo Branco *Port*	50A2
Castelsarrasin *France*	48C3
Castelvetrano *Italy*	53B3
Casterton *Aust*	108B3
Castilla La Nueva, Region *Spain*	50B2
Castilla La Vieja, Region *Spain*	50B1
Castlebar *Irish Rep*	41B3
Castlebay *Scot*	44A3
Castle Douglas *Scot*	42C2
Castlegar *Can*	20C1
Castleisland *Irish Rep*	45B2
Castlemain *Aust*	108B3
Castlerea *Irish Rep*	45B2
Castlereagh *Aust*	109C2
Castres-sur-l'Agout *France*	48C3
Castries *St Lucia*	27E4
Castro *Arg*	29B4
Castro *Brazil*	30F3
Castro Alves *Brazil*	31D4
Castrovillari *Italy*	53C3
Castroville *USA*	22B2

Caswell Sd

14

Chattanooga USA	11B3
Chauk Burma	76A1
Chaumont France	49D2
Chauny France	46B2
Chau Phu Viet	77D3
Chaves Port	50A1
Chazaouet Alg	50B2
Chazón Arg	34C2
Chcontá Colombia	32C2
Cheb Czech	57C2
Cheboksary USSR	65F4
Cheboygan USA	10B2
Chech'on S Korea	74B3
Chechro Pak	85C3
Checotah USA	18A2
Cheduba, I Burma	76A2
Cheepie Aust	108B1
Chegga Maur	96B2
Chegutu Zim	100C2
Chehalis USA	20B1
Cheju S Korea	74B4
Cheju do, I S Korea	74B4
Cheju-haehyŏp, Str S Korea	74B4
Chekunda USSR	63F2
Chelan,L USA	20B1
Cheleken USSR	90B2
Chelforo Arg	34B3
Chelkar USSR	80D1
Chelm Pol	59C2
Chelmno Pol	58B2
Chelmsford Eng	43E4
Cheltenham Eng	43C4
Chelyabinsk USSR	65H4
Chemba Mozam	101C2
Chenab, R India/Pak	84D2
Chenachen Alg	96B2
Cheney USA	20C1
Cheney Res USA	18A2
Chengda China	72D1
Chengdu China	73A3
Chengshan Jiao, Pt China	72E2
Chenxi China	73C4
Chen Xian China	73C4
Cheo Xian China	73D3
Chepén Peru	32B5
Chepes Arg	34B2
Cher, R France	48C2
Cheran Mexico	23A2
Cheraw USA	17C1
Cherbourg France	48B2
Cherchell Alg	96C1
Cheremkhovo USSR	63C2
Cherepovets USSR	60E2
Cherkassy USSR	60D4
Cherkessk USSR	61F5
Chernigov USSR	60D3
Chernobyl USSR	60D2
Chernovtsy USSR	60C4
Chernushka USSR	61J2
Chernyakhovsk USSR	60B3
Chernyye Zemli, Region USSR	61G4
Cherokees,L o'the USA	18A2
Cherquenco Chile	34A3
Cherrapunji India	86C1
Cherven' USSR	60C3
Chervonograd USSR	59C2
Chesapeake, B USA	10C3
Cheshire, County Eng	42C3
Cheshire USA	16C1
Chëshskaya Guba, B USSR	64F3
Chester, California USA	21A1
Chester Eng	42C3
Chester, Illinois USA	18C2
Chester, Massachusets USA	16C1
Chester, Pennsylvania USA	15C3
Chester, S Carolina USA	17B1
Chester, R USA	16A3
Chesterfield Eng	42D3
Chesterfield Inlet Can	6A3
Chestertown USA	16A3
Chetumal Mexico	25D3
Chetwynd Can	13C1
Chevak USA	12A2
Cheviot NZ	111B2
Cheviots, Hills Eng/ Scot	40C2
Chewelah USA	13D3
Cheyenne USA	8C2
Chhapra India	86A1
Chhatak Bang	86C1
Chhatarpur India	85D4
Chhindwāra India	85D4
Chhuka Bhutan	86B1
Chia'i Taiwan	73E5
Chiange Angola	100A2
Chiang Kham Thai	76C2
Chiang Mai Thai	76B2
Chiavenna Italy	47C1
Chiba Japan	74E3
Chibāsa India	86B2
Chibia Angola	100A2
Chibougamou Can	7C4
Chiburi-jima, I Japan	75A1
Chibuto Mozam	101C3
Chicago USA	10B2
Chicago Heights USA	14A2
Chichagof I USA	12G3
Chichester Eng	43D4
Chichibu Japan	75B1
Chichi-jima, I Japan	69G4
Chickamauga L USA	11B3
Chickasawhay, R USA	19C3
Chickasha USA	9D3
Chicken USA	12F2
Chiclayo Peru	32A5
Chico USA	8A3
Chico, R Arg	29C4
Chicoa Mozam	101C2
Chicopee USA	15D2
Chicoutimi Can	7C5
Chicualacuala Mozam	101C3
Chidambaram India	87B2
Chidley,C Can	6D3
Chiefland USA	17B2
Chiehn Lib	97B4
Chiengi Zambia	99C3
Chieri Italy	47B2
Chiers, R France	46C2
Chiesa, R Italy	47C1
Chiese, R Italy	47D2
Chieti Italy	52B2
Chifeng China	72D1
Chiginigak,Mt USA	12C3
Chigmit Mts USA	4C3
Chignahuapán Mexico	23B2
Chignik USA	12C3
Chihuahua Mexico	24B2
Chik Ballāpur India	87B2
Chikmagalūr India	87B2
Chikuminuk L USA	12C2
Chikwawa Malawi	101C2
Chi-kyaw Burma	76A1
Chilakalūrupet India	87C1
Chilapa Mexico	23B2
Chilaw Sri Lanka	87B3
Chile, Republic	28B6
Chilecito, Mendoza Arg	34B2
Chililabombwe Zambia	100B2
Chilka, L India	86B2
Chilko, R Can	13C2
Chilko L Can	5F4
Chilkotin, R Can	13C2
Chillán Chile	34A3
Chillar Arg	34D3
Chillicothe, Missouri USA	18B2
Chillicothe, Ohio USA	14B3
Chilliwack Can	13C3
Chilmari India	86B1
Chilongozi Zambia	101C2
Chiloquin USA	20B2
Chilpancingo Mexico	24C3
Chiltern Hills, Upland Eng	43D4
Chilton USA	14A2
Chilumba Malawi	101C2
Chi-lung Taiwan	69E4
Chilwa, L Malawi	101C2
Chimay Belg	46C1
Chimbay USSR	65G5
Chimborazo, Mt Ecuador	32B4
Chimbote Peru	32B5
Chimkent USSR	65H5
Chimoio Mozam	101C2
China, Republic Asia	67E3
Chinandega Nic	25D3
Chincha Alta Peru	32B6
Chinchilla Aust	109D1
Chinde Mozam	101C2
Chindwin, R Burma	86C2
Chingola Zambia	100B2
Chinguar Angola	100A2
Chinguetti Maur	96A2
Chinhae S Korea	74B3
Chinhoyi Zim	100C2
Chiniak,C USA	12D3
Chiniot Pak	84C2
Chinju S Korea	74B3
Chinko, R CAR	98C2
Chino Japan	75B1
Chinsali Zambia	101C2
Chioggia Italy	52B1
Chipata Zambia	101C2
Chipinge Zim	101C3
Chiplūn India	87A1
Chippenham Eng	43C4
Chippewa Falls USA	10A2
Chipuriro Zim	100C2
Chira, R Peru	32A4
Chīrāla India	87C1
Chiredzi Zim	101C3
Chirfa Niger	95A2
Chiriqui, Mt Panama	32A2
Chirpan Bulg	54C2
Chirrīpo Grande, Mt Costa Rica	32A2
Chirundu Zim	100B2
Chisamba Zambia	100B2
Chishui He, R China	73B4
Chisone, R Italy	47B2
Chita USSR	68D1
Chitado Angola	100A2
Chitembo Angola	100A2
Chitina USA	12F2
Chitina, R USA	12F2
Chitradurga India	87B2
Chitral Pak	84C1
Chitré Panama	32A2
Chittagong Bang	86C2
Chittaurgarh India	85C4
Chittoor India	87B2
Chiume Angola	100B2
Chiusa Italy	47D1
Chivasso Italy	47B2
Chivilcoy Arg	29D2
Chivu Zim	100C2
Chizu Japan	75A1
Choele Choel Arg	29C3
Choique Arg	34C3
Choix Mexico	24B2
Chojnice Pol	58B2
Choke, Mts Eth	99D1
Cholet France	48B2
Cholula Mexico	23B2
Choma Zambia	100B2
Chomo Yummo, Mt China/India	86B1
Chomutov Czech	57C2
Chona, R USSR	63C1
Ch'ŏnan S Korea	74B3
Chon Buri Thai	76C3
Chone Ecuador	32A4
Ch'ŏngjin N Korea	74B2
Chongju N Korea	74B3
Ch'ŏngju S Korea	74B3
Chongoroi Angola	100A2
Chongqing China	73B4
Chŏngŭp S Korea	74B3
Chŏnju S Korea	74B3
Chooyu, Mt China/ Nepal	86B1
Chortkov USSR	59D3
Ch'ŏrwŏn N Korea	74B3
Chorzow Pol	59B2
Choshi Japan	74E3
Chos-Malal Arg	34A3
Choszczno Pol	58B2
Chotanāgpur, Region India	86A2
Chott Melrhir Alg	96C1
Chowchilla USA	22B2
Choybalsan Mongolia	63D3
Chrantrey Inlet, B Can	6A3
Chraykovskiy USSR	61H2
Christchurch NZ	111B2
Christiana S Africa	101G1
Christian,C Can	6D2
Christian Sd USA	12H3
Christianshab Greenland	6E3
Christmas I Indian O	104D4
Christopol USSR	61G2
Chu USSR	65J5
Chu, R USSR	65J5
Chubut, State Arg	29C4
Chubut, R Arg	29C4
Chudovo USSR	60D2
Chudskoye Ozer, L USSR	64D4
Chugach Mts USA	4D3
Chugiak USA	12E2
Chūgoku-sanchi, Mts Japan	75A1
Chuí Brazil	29F2
Chuillán Chile	29B3
Chukai Malay	77C5
Chu Lai Viet	76D2
Chula Vista USA	21B3
Chulitna USA	12E2
Chulman USSR	63E2
Chulucanas Peru	32A5
Chulumani Bol	30C2
Chulym USSR	65K4
Chulym, R USSR	63A2
Chuma, R USSR	63B2
Chumar India	84D2
Chumikan USSR	63F2
Chumphon Thai	77B3
Chunchura India	86B2
Ch'unch'ŏn S Korea	74B3
Ch'ungju S Korea	74B3
Chunya Tanz	99D3
Chunya, R USSR	63C1
Chupara Pt Trinidad	27L1
Chuquicamata Chile	30C3
Chur Switz	52A1
Churāchāndpur India	86C2
Churchill Can	7A4
Churchill, R, Labrador Can	7D4
Churchill, R, Manitoba Can	7A4
Churchill,C Can	7A4
Churchill Falls Can	7D4
Churchill L Can	5H4
Chūru India	84C3
Churumuco Mexico	23A2
Chusovoy USSR	61J2
Chuvashskaya ASSR, Republic USSR	61G2
Chuxiong China	68B4
Chu Yang Sin, Mt Viet	76D3
Cianjur Indon	78B4
Ciano d'Enza Italy	47D2
Cianorte Brazil	35A2
Ciechanow Pol	58C2
Ciego de Avila Cuba	25E2
Ciénaga Colombia	32C1
Cienfuegos Cuba	25D2
Cieszyn Pol	59B3
Cieza Spain	51B2
Cihanbeyli Turk	92B2
Cihuatlán Mexico	23A2
Cijulang Indon	78B4
Cilacap Indon	78B4
Cîmpina Rom	54C1
Cinca, R Spain	51C1
Cinčer, Mt Yugos	52C2
Cincinnati USA	10B3
Cindrelu, Mt Rom	54B1
Cine, R Turk	55C3

15

Ciney

16

Crooked

Comeragh, Mts *Irish Rep*	45C2
Comilla *Bang*	86C2
Comitán *Mexico*	25C3
Commercy *France*	46C2
Committees B *Can*	6B3
Como *Italy*	52A1
Comodoro Rivadavia *Arg*	29C5
Comonfort *Mexico*	23A1
Comorin,C *India*	87B3
Comoros, Is *Indian O*	101D2
Compiègne *France*	49C2
Compostela *Mexico*	23A1
Comte Salas *Arg*	34B2
Cona *China*	86C1
Conakry *Guinea*	97A4
Concarán *Arg*	34B2
Concarneau *France*	48B2
Conceiçao da Barra *Brazil*	35D1
Conceição do Araguaia *Brazil*	31B3
Conceiçao do Mato Dentro *Brazil*	35C1
Concepción *Chile*	29B3
Concepción *Par*	30E3
Concepción, R *Arg*	29E2
Concepcion del Oro *Mexico*	24B2
Concepcion del Uruguay *Arg*	34D2
Conception,Pt *USA*	9A3
Conchas *Brazil*	35B2
Conchos, R *Mexico*	9C4
Concord, California *USA*	21A2
Concord, New Hampshire *USA*	10C2
Concordia *Arg*	29E2
Concordia *USA*	8D3
Concrete *USA*	20B1
Condamine *Aust*	109D1
Condobolin *Aust*	107D4
Condon *USA*	20B1
Condroz, Mts *Belg*	46C1
Conecuh, R *USA*	17A1
Conegliano *Italy*	47E2
Congo, Republic *Africa*	89F8
Congo, R *Congo*	89F8
Coniston *Can*	14B1
Connaught, Region *Irish Rep*	45B2
Conneaut *USA*	14B2
Connecticut, State *USA*	10C2
Connecticut, R *USA*	15D2
Connellsville *USA*	15C2
Connemara,Mts of *Irish Rep*	45B2
Connersville *USA*	14A3
Conoble *Aust*	108B2
Conroe *USA*	19A3
Conselheiro Lafaiete *Brazil*	35C2
Con Son, Is *Viet*	77D4
Constanta *Rom*	60C5
Constantine *Alg*	96C1
Constantine,C *USA*	12C3
Constitución *Chile*	29B3
Consul *Can*	13F3
Contarina *Italy*	47E2
Contas, R *Brazil*	31C4
Contreras *Mexico*	23B2
Contuoyto L *Can*	4H3
Conway, Arkansas *USA*	11A3
Conway, New Hampshire *USA*	15D2
Conway, South Carolina *USA*	17C1
Conway,L *Aust*	108A1
Conwy *Wales*	42C3
Coober Pedy *Aust*	106C3
Cook *Str NZ*	110B2
Cook,C *Can*	13B2
Cook Inlet, B *USA*	4C3

Cook Is *Pacific O*	105H4
Cook,Mt *NZ*	111B2
Cooktown *Aust*	107D2
Coolabah *Aust*	109C2
Cooladdi *Aust*	108C1
Coolah *Aust*	109C2
Coolamon *Aust*	109C2
Coolgardie *Aust*	106B4
Cooma *Aust*	109C3
Coonabarabran *Aust*	109C2
Coonambie *Aust*	109C2
Coonbah *Aust*	108B2
Coondambo *Aust*	108A2
Coondapoor *India*	87A2
Coongoola *Aust*	108C1
Coonoor *India*	87B2
Cooper Basin *Aust*	108B1
Cooper Creek *Aust*	106C3
Cooper Creek, R *Aust*	108B1
Coorong,The *Aust*	108A3
Cooroy *Aust*	109D1
Coos B *USA*	20B2
Coos Bay *USA*	20B2
Cootamundra *Aust*	107D4
Cootehill *Irish Rep*	45C1
Copala *Mexico*	23B2
Copalillo *Mexico*	23B2
Copiapó *Chile*	30B4
Copparo *Italy*	47D2
Copper, R *USA*	12F2
Copper Centre *USA*	4D3
Copper Cliff *Can*	14B1
Coppermine *Can*	4G3
Coppermine, R *Can*	4G3
Coquimbo *Chile*	30B4
Corabia *Rom*	54B2
Coral Gables *USA*	17B2
Coral Harbour *Can*	6B3
Coral S *Aust/PNG*	107D2
Coral Sea Basin *Pacific O*	104F4
Coral Sea Island Territories *Aust*	107E2
Corangamite,L *Aust*	108B3
Corantijn, R *Surinam/ Guyana*	33F3
Corbeil-Essonnes *France*	46B2
Corcubíon *Spain*	50A1
Cordele *USA*	11B3
Cordillera Cantabrica, Mts *Spain*	50A1
Cordillera Central, Mts *Dom Rep*	26C3
Cordillera Central, Mts *Phil*	79B2
Cordillera de Ansita, Mts *Arg*	34B2
Cordillera de los Andes, Mts *Peru*	32B5
Cordillera del Toro, Mt *Arg*	30C4
Cordillera de Mérida *Ven*	32C2
Cordillera de Viento, Mts *Arg*	34A3
Cordillera Isabelia, Mts *Nicaragua*	25D3
Cordillera Occidental, Mts *Colombia*	32B3
Cordillera Oriental, Mts *Colombia*	32B3
Cordillo Downs *Aust*	108B1
Córdoba *Arg*	29D2
Córdoba *Mexico*	24C3
Córdoba *Spain*	50B2
Córdoba, State *Arg*	29D2
Cordova *USA*	4D3
Coricudgy,Mt *Aust*	109D2
Corigliano Calabro *Italy*	53C3
Corinth, Mississippi *USA*	11B3
Corinto *Brazil*	31C5
Cork, County *Irish Rep*	45B2
Cork *Irish Rep*	41B3
Çorlu *Turk*	92A1

Cornel Fabriciano *Brazil*	31C5
Cornelio Procópio *Brazil*	35A2
Corner Brook *Can*	7E5
Corner Inlet, B *Aust*	109C3
Corning *USA*	15C2
Cornwall *Can*	7C5
Cornwall, County *Eng*	43B4
Cornwall,C *Eng*	43B4
Cornwall I *Can*	4H2
Cornwallis I *Can*	6A2
Coro *Ven*	32D1
Coroatá *Brazil*	31C2
Coroico *Bol*	30C2
Coromandel *Brazil*	35B1
Coromandel Coast *India*	87C2
Coromandel Pen *NZ*	110C1
Coromandel Range, Mts *NZ*	110C1
Corona, California *USA*	22D4
Coronation *Can*	13E2
Coronation G *Can*	4G3
Coronda *Arg*	34C2
Coronel *Chile*	29B3
Coronel Brandsen *Arg*	34D3
Coronel Dorrego *Arg*	34C3
Coronel Fabriciano *Brazil*	35C1
Coronel Oviedo *Par*	30E4
Coronel Pringles *Arg*	29D3
Coronel Suárez *Arg*	34C3
Coronel Vidal *Arg*	34D3
Coropuna, Mt *Peru*	30B2
Corowa *Aust*	109C3
Corps *France*	49D3
Corpus Christi *USA*	9D4
Corpus Christi,L *USA*	9D4
Corregidor, I *Phil*	79B3
Corrente, R, Mato Grosso *Brazil*	35A1
Corrientes *Arg*	30E4
Corrientes, State *Arg*	30E4
Corrigan *USA*	19B3
Corrigin *Aust*	106A4
Corringe Is *Aust*	107E2
Corryong *Aust*	109C3
Corse, I *Medit S*	52A2
Corsewall, Pt *Scot*	42B2
Corsicana *USA*	9D3
Corte *Corse*	52A2
Cortez *USA*	9C3
Cortina d'Ampezzo *Italy*	52B1
Cortland *USA*	15C2
Coruca de Catalan *Mexico*	23A2
Çoruh, R *Turk*	93D1
Çorum *Turk*	60E5
Corumbá *Brazil*	30E2
Corumba, R *Brazil*	35B1
Corumbaiba *Brazil*	35B1
Corvallis *USA*	20B2
Corvo, I *Açores*	96A1
Corwen *Wales*	43C3
Coscomatopec *Mexico*	23B2
Cosenza *Italy*	53C3
Cosmoledo, Is *Seychelles*	101D1
Cosquín *Arg*	34C2
Costa Blanca, Region *Spain*	51B2
Costa Brava, Region *Spain*	51C1
Costa de la Luz, Region *Spain*	50B2
Costa del Sol, Region *Spain*	50B2
Costa Mesa *USA*	22D4
Costa Rica, Republic *C America*	25D3
Cotabato *Phil*	79B4
Cotagaita *Bol*	30C3
Côte d'Azur, Region *France*	49D3

Côtes de Meuse, Mts *France*	46C2
Cotonou *Benin*	97C4
Cotopaxi, Mt *Ecuador*	32B4
Cotswold Hills, Upland *Eng*	43C4
Cottage Grove *USA*	20B2
Cottbus *E Germ*	56C2
Couedic,C du *Aust*	108A3
Couer d'Alene L *USA*	20C1
Coulommiers *France*	46B2
Coulonge, R *Can*	15C1
Coulterville *USA*	22B2
Council *USA*	4B3
Council Bluffs *USA*	8D2
Courmayeur *Italy*	47B2
Courtenay *Can*	13B3
Coutances *France*	48B2
Coventry *Eng*	43D3
Covilhã *Spain*	50A1
Covington, Georgia *USA*	17B1
Covington, Louisiana *USA*	19B3
Cowal,L *Aust*	109C2
Cowangie *Aust*	108B3
Cowansville *Can*	15D1
Coward Springs *Aust*	108A1
Cowell *Aust*	108A2
Cowes *Aust*	108C3
Cowichan L *Can*	20B1
Cowiltz, R *USA*	20B1
Cowra *Aust*	109C2
Coxim *Brazil*	30F2
Coxsackie *USA*	16C1
Cox's Bazar *Bang*	86C2
Coyote *USA*	22B2
Coyuca de Benitez *Mexico*	23A2
Cradock *S Africa*	100B4
Craig *USA*	8C2
Crailsheim *W Germ*	57C3
Craiova *Rom*	54B2
Cranberry L *USA*	15D2
Cranbrook *Can*	5G5
Crane, Oregon *USA*	20C2
Cranston *USA*	16D2
Crater L *USA*	20B2
Crater Lake Nat Pk *USA*	20B2
Crateus *Brazil*	31C3
Crato *Brazil*	31D3
Crawfordsville *USA*	14A2
Crawfordville *USA*	17B1
Crawley *Eng*	43D4
Cree L *Can*	5H4
Creil *France*	46B2
Crema *Italy*	47C2
Cremona *Italy*	52B1
Crépy-en-Valois *France*	46B2
Cres, I *Yugos*	52B2
Crescent City *USA*	20B2
Crespo *Arg*	34C2
Creston *Can*	13D3
Creston *USA*	18B1
Crestview *USA*	17A1
Creswick *Aust*	108B3
Crêt de la Neige, Mt *France*	47A1
Crete *USA*	18A1
Crete,S of *Greece*	55B3
Creuse, R *France*	48C2
Crewe *Eng*	43C3
Crianlarich *Scot*	44B3
Criciuma *Brazil*	30G4
Crieff *Scot*	44C3
Crillon,Mt *USA*	12G3
Cristalina *Brazil*	35B1
Croatia, Region *Yugos*	52C1
Crocker Range, Mts *Malay*	78D1
Crockett *USA*	19A3
Croker I *Aust*	106C2
Cromarty *Scot*	44C3
Cromer *Eng*	43E3
Cromwell *NZ*	111A3
Crooked, I *Bahamas*	11C4

17

Crooked

Crooked, R *Can*	13C2	Curicó *Chile*	29B2
Crookston *USA*	8D2	Curitiba *Brazil*	30G4
Crookwell *Aust*	109C2	Curnamona *Aust*	108A2
Croppa Creek *Aust*	109D1	Curoca, R *Angola*	100A2
Crossett *USA*	11A3	Curvelo *Brazil*	31C5
Cross Sd *USA*	12G3	Cushing *USA*	18A2
Crotone *Italy*	53C3	Cuthbert *USA*	17B1
Crowley *USA*	19B3	Cutral-Có *Arg*	34B3
Crown Pt *Tobago*	27K1	Cuttack *India*	86B2
Crows Nest *Aust*	109D1	Cuvelai *Angola*	100A2
Croydon *Aust*	107D2	Cuxhaven *W Germ*	56B2
Croydon *Eng*	43D4	Cuyahoga Falls *USA*	14B2
Crozet Basin *Indian O*	104B5	Cuyo Is *Phil*	79B3
Crozier Chan *Can*	4F2	Cuzco *Peru*	32C6
Cruz Alta *Brazil*	30F4	Cyangugu *Zaïre*	99C3
Cruz,C *Cuba*	25E3	Cypress Hills, Mts *Can*	13F3
Cruz del Eje *Arg*	29D2	Cyprus, Republic	
Cruzeiro *Brazil*	35C2	Medit S	92B3
Cruzeiro do Sul *Brazil*	32C5	Cyrus Field B *Can*	6D3
Crysdale,Mt *Can*	13C1	Czechoslovakia,	
Crystal Brook *Aust*	108A2	Republic *Europe*	59B3
Crystal City, Missouri		Częstochowa *Pol*	59B2
USA	18B2		
Crystal Falls *USA*	14A1	**D**	
Cuamba *Mozam*	101C2		
Cuando, R *Angola*	100B2	Da, R *Viet*	76C1
Cuangar *Angola*	100A2	Da'an *China*	69E2
Cuarto, R *Arg*	34C2	Dab'a *Jordan*	94C3
Cuauhtémoc *Mexico*	24B2	Dabajuro *Ven*	27C4
Cuautla *Mexico*	23B2	Dabaro *Somalia*	99E2
Cuba, Republic		Daba Shan, Mts *China*	73B3
Caribbean	25D2	Dabat *Eth*	99D1
Cubango, R *Angola*	100A2	Dabhoi *India*	85C4
Cuchi *Angola*	100A2	Dabie Shan, U *China*	73C3
Cuchi, R *Angola*	100A2	Dabola *Guinea*	97A3
Cuchillo Có *Arg*	34C3	Dabou *Ivory Coast*	97B4
Cucui *Brazil*	32D3	Dabrowa Gorn *Pol*	59B2
Cúcuta *Colombia*	32C2	Dachau *W Germ*	57C3
Cuddalore *India*	87B2	Dachstein, Mt *Austria*	52B1
Cuddapah *India*	87B2	Dada He, R *China*	73A3
Cue *Aust*	106A3	Dade City *USA*	17B2
Cuenca *Ecuador*	32B4	Dadhar *Pak*	84B3
Cuenca *Spain*	51B1	Dadu *Pak*	85B3
Cuernavaca *Mexico*	24C3	Dadu He, R *China*	68C3
Cuero *USA*	19A4	Daet *Phil*	79B3
Cuiabá *Brazil*	30E2	Dafang *China*	73B4
Cuiabá, R *Brazil*	30E2	Daga, R *Burma*	76B2
Cuicatlan *Mexico*	23B2	Dagabur *Eth*	99E2
Cuieté, R *Brazil*	35C1	Dagana *Sen*	97A3
Cuillin Hills, Mts *Scot*	44A3	Dagestanskaya ASSR,	
Cuilo, R *Angola*	98B3	Republic *USSR*	65F5
Cuito, R *Angola*	100A2	Dagupan *Phil*	79B2
Cuito Cunavale		Dahab *Egypt*	92B4
Angola	100A2	Da Hinggan Ling, Mts	
Cuitzeo *Mexico*	23A2	*China*	63E3
Cu Lao Hon, I *Viet*	77D3	Dahlonega *USA*	17B1
Culcairn *Aust*	109C3	Dahod *India*	85C4
Culgoa, R *Aust*	109C1	Dahra *Libya*	95A2
Culiacán *Mexico*	24B2	Dahra, Region *Alg*	51C2
Culion, I *Phil*	79A3	Dailekh *Nepal*	86A1
Cullman *USA*	17A1	Daireaux *Arg*	34C3
Culoz *France*	47A2	Daitō, Is *Pacific Oc*	69F4
Culpeper *USA*	15C3	Dajarra *Aust*	106C3
Culpepper, I *Ecuador*	32J7	Dakar *Sen*	97A3
Culter Ridge *USA*	17B2	Dakhla *Mor*	96A2
Culverden *NZ*	111B2	Dakhla Oasis *Egypt*	95B2
Cumaná *Ven*	33E1	Dakoro *Niger*	97C3
Cumberland, Maryland		Dakovica *Yugos*	54B2
USA	10C3	Dakovo *Yugos*	54A1
Cumberland, R *USA*	11B3	Dala *Angola*	100B2
Cumberland Pen *Can*	6D3	Dalaba *Guinea*	97A3
Cumbernauld Sd *Can*	6D3	Dalai Nur, L *China*	72D1
Cumbria *Eng*	42C2	Dalandzadgad	
Cummings *USA*	21A2	*Mongolia*	68C2
Cummins *Aust*	108A2	Dalanganem Is *Phil*	79B3
Cumnock *Scot*	42B2	Dalanjargalan	
Cunco *Chile*	34A3	*Mongolia*	68C2
Cunene, R *Angola/*		Da Lat *Viet*	76D3
Namibia	100A2	Dalby *Aust*	107E3
Cuneo *Italy*	52A2	Dalen *Nor*	39F7
Cunnamulla *Aust*	107D3	Dales,The, Upland *Eng*	42C2
Cupar *Scot*	44C3	Daleville *USA*	17A1
Ćuprija *Yugos*	54B2	Dalhart *USA*	9C3
Curaçao, I *Caribbean*	27D4	Dalhousie,C *Can*	4E2
Curacautin *Chile*	34A3	Dallas *USA*	9D3
Curaco, R *Arg*	34B3	Dalles,The *USA*	20B1
Curanilahue *Chile*	34A3	Dall I *USA*	5E4
Curepto *Chile*	34A3		

Dalli Rajhara *India*	86A2	Darnley,C *Ant*	112C10
Dallol, R *Niger*	97C3	Daroca *Spain*	51B1
Dallol Bosso, R *Niger*	97C3	Dar Rounga, Region	
Dalmatia, Region		*CAR*	98C2
Yugos	52C2	Dart, R *Eng*	43C4
Dal'nerechensk *USSR*	69F2	Dartmoor, Moorland	
Daloa *Ivory Coast*	97B4	*Eng*	41C3
Dalou Shan, Mts		Dartmoor Nat Pk *Eng*	43C4
China	73B4	Dartmouth *Can*	7D5
Dāltenganj *India*	86A2	Dartmouth *Eng*	43C4
Dalton, Georgia *USA*	17B1	Daru *PNG*	107D1
Dalton, Massachusetts		Daruvar *Yugos*	52C1
USA	16C1	Darwin *Aust*	106C2
Daly, R *Aust*	106C2	Daryācheh-ye	
Daly City *USA*	21A2	Bakhtegan, L *Iran*	91B4
Daly Waters *Aust*	106C2	Daryācheh-ye Mahārlū	
Damaguete *Phil*	79B4	L *Iran*	91B4
Damān *India*	85C4	Daryācheh-ye Namak,	
Damanhûr *Egypt*	92B3	Salt Flat *Iran*	90B3
Damar, I *Indon*	71D4	Daryācheh-ye-Sistan,	
Damara *CAR*	98B2	Salt Lake *Iran/*	
Damascus *Syria*	92C3	*Afghan*	90D3
Damascus *USA*	16A3	Daryācheh-ye Tashk, L	
Damaturu *Nig*	97D3	*Iran*	91B4
Damavand *Iran*	90B2	Daryācheh-ye	
Damba *Angola*	98B3	Urumīyeh, L *Iran*	65F6
Dambulla *Sri Lanka*	87C3	Dārzīn *Iran*	91C4
Damghan *Iran*	90B2	Das, I *UAE*	91B4
Damoh *India*	85D4	Dashennonglia, Mt	
Damot *Eth*	99E2	*China*	73C3
Damour *Leb*	94B2	Dasht *Iran*	90C2
Dampier *Aust*	106A3	Dasht-e-Kavir, Salt	
Danā *Jordan*	94B3	Desert *Iran*	90B3
Dana,Mt *USA*	22C2	Dasht-e Lut, Salt	
Danané *Lib*	97B4	Desert *Iran*	90C3
Da Nang *Viet*	76D2	Dasht-e Naomid,	
Danao *Phil*	79B3	Desert Region *Iran*	90D3
Danau Tobu, L *Indon*	70A3	Datia *India*	85D3
Danau Tuwuti, L		Datong *China*	72A2
Indon	71D4	Datong *China*	72C1
Danbu *China*	73A3	Datong He, R *China*	72A2
Danbury *USA*	15D2	Datu Piang *Phil*	79B4
Dandeldhura *Nepal*	86A1	Daugava, R *USSR*	39K7
Dandeli *India*	87A1	Daugavpils *USSR*	60C2
Dandenong *Aust*	108C3	Dauguard Jensen	
Dandong *China*	74A2	Land *Greenland*	6D1
Danger Pt *S Africa*	100A4	Daulatabad *Afghan*	84A1
Dangila *Eth*	99D1	Daulpur *India*	85D3
Danguard Jenson		Daun *W Germ*	46D1
Land, Region *Can*	6D1	Daund *India*	87A1
Daniels Harbour *Can*	7E4	Dauphin *Can*	5H4
Dannebrogs Øy, I		Dauphin *USA*	16A2
Greenland	6G3	Dauphiné, Region	
Dannevirke *NZ*	110C2	*France*	49D2
Dantewāra *India*	87C1	Daura *Nig*	97C3
Danville, Illinois *USA*	10B2	Dausa *India*	85D3
Danville, Kentucky		Dāvangere *India*	87B2
USA	11B3	Davao *Phil*	79C4
Danville, Pennsylvania		Davao G *Phil*	79C4
USA	16A2	Davenport, California	
Danville, Virginia *USA*	11C3	*USA*	22A2
Dao Xian *China*	73C4	Davenport, Iowa *USA*	10A2
Daozhen *China*	73B4	David *Panama*	32A2
Dapiak,Mt *Phil*	79B4	Davidson Mts *USA*	4D3
Dapitan *Phil*	79B4	Davis *USA*	21A2
Da Qaidam *China*	68B3	Davis, Base *Ant*	112C10
Dar'a *Syria*	94C2	Davis Inlet *Can*	7D4
Dārāb *Iran*	91B4	Davis Str *Greenland/*	
Daraj *Libya*	95A1	*Can*	6E3
Dārān *Iran*	90B3	Davlekanovo *USSR*	61J3
Dar'ā Salkhad *Syria*	92C3	Davos *Switz*	47C1
Darbhanga *India*	86B1	Dawa, R *Eth*	99E2
Dardanelle *USA*	22C1	Dawan *China*	73A4
Dardanelle,L *USA*	18B2	Dawat Yar *Afghan*	84B2
Dar es Salaam *Tanz*	99D3	Dawḥat Salwah, B	
Dargaville *NZ*	110B1	*Qatar/S Arabia*	91B4
Darien *USA*	17B1	Dawna Range, Mts	
Dārjiling *India*	86B1	*Burma*	76B2
Darling, R *Aust*	107D4	Dawson *Can*	4E3
Darling Downs *Aust*	109C1	Dawson, Georgia *USA*	17B1
Darling Pen *Can*	6C1	Dawson, R *Aust*	107D3
Darlington *Aust*	108B2	Dawson Creek *Can*	5F4
Darlington *Eng*	42D2	Dawson,Mt *Can*	13D2
Darlington *USA*	17C1	Dawson Range, Mts	
Darmstadt *W Germ*	57B3	*Can*	12G2
Darnah *Libya*	95B1	Dawu *China*	73A3
Darnick *Aust*	108B2	Dawu *China*	73C3
Darnley B *Can*	4F3	Dax *France*	48B3

Daxian *China*	73B3
Daxin *China*	73B5
Daxue Shan, Mts *China*	73A3
Dayong *China*	73C4
Dayr'Ali *Syria*	94C2
Dayr'Atïyah *Syria*	94C1
Dayr az Zawr *Syria*	93D2
Dayton, Ohio *USA*	10B3
Dayton, Texas *USA*	19B4
Dayton, Washington *USA*	20C1
Daytona Beach *USA*	11B4
Dayu *China*	73C4
Dayu *Indon*	78D3
Da Yunhe, R *China*	72D2
Dayville *USA*	20C2
Dazhu *China*	73B3
De Aar *S Africa*	100B4
Deadman's Cay *Bahamas*	26C2
Dead S *Israel/Jordan*	92C3
Deal *Eng*	46A1
Dealesville *S Africa*	101G1
Dean, R *Can*	13B2
Dean Chan *Can*	13B2
Deán Funes *Arg*	34C2
Dearborn *USA*	14B2
Dease Arm, B *Can*	4F3
Dease Lake *Can*	4E4
Death V *USA*	9B3
Deauville *France*	48C2
Debakala *Ivory Coast*	97B4
Debauch Mt *USA*	12B2
Débé *Trinidad*	27L1
Debica *Pol*	59C2
Deblin *Pol*	58C2
Débo,L *Mali*	97B3
Debra Birhan *Eth*	99D2
Debra Markos *Eth*	99D1
Debra Tabor *Eth*	99D1
Debrecen *Hung*	59C3
Decatur, Alabama *USA*	11B3
Decatur, Georgia *USA*	17B1
Decatur, Illinois *USA*	10B3
Decatur, Indiana *USA*	14B2
Decazeville *France*	48C3
Dechang *China*	73A4
Dedza *Malawi*	101C2
Dee, R, Dumfries and Galloway *Scot*	42B2
Dee, R *Eng/Wales*	42C3
Dee, R, Grampian *Scot*	44C3
Deep River *Can*	15C1
Deep River *USA*	16C2
Deepwater *Aust*	109D1
Deer Lake *Can*	7E5
Deer Lodge *USA*	8B2
Defferrari *Arg*	34D3
De Funiak Springs *USA*	17A1
Dêgê *China*	68B3
De Grey, R *Aust*	106A3
Deh Bïd *Iran*	91B3
Dehi *Afghan*	84B1
Dehibat *Tunisia*	96D1
Dehiwala-Mt Lavinia *Sri Lanka*	87B3
Dehlorän *Iran*	90A3
Dehra Dün *India*	84D2
Dehri *India*	86A2
Deim Zubeir *Sudan*	98C2
Deir Abu Sa'id *Jordan*	94B2
Deir el Ahmar *Leb*	94C1
Dej *Rom*	60B4
De Kalb, Texas *USA*	19B3
De Kastri *USSR*	63G2
Dekese *Zaïre*	98C3
Dekoa *CAR*	98B2
Delano *USA*	9B3
Delaware, State *USA*	10C3
Delaware *USA*	14B2
Delaware, R *USA*	15C2
Delaware B *USA*	10C3
Delegate *Aust*	109C3
Delemont *Switz*	47B1
Delgado, C *Mozam*	101D2
Delhi *India*	84D3
Delhi, New York *USA*	15D2
Delice *Turk*	92B1
Delicias *Mexico*	24B2
Delïjän *Iran*	90B3
Delle *France*	47B1
Del Mar *USA*	22D4
Delmenhorst *W Germ*	39F8
De Long, Mts *USA*	4B3
Deloraine *Aust*	109C4
Deloraine *Can*	5H5
Delray Beach *USA*	17B2
Del Rio *USA*	9C4
Delta *USA*	8B3
Delta, R *USA*	12E2
Delta Junction *USA*	12E2
Dembidollo *Eth*	99D2
Demer, R *Belg*	46C1
Deming *USA*	9C3
Demirköy *Turk*	54C2
Denain *France*	49C1
Denau *USSR*	82A2
Denbigh *Wales*	42C3
Denbigh,C *USA*	12B2
Dendang *Indon*	78B3
Dendermond *Belg*	46C1
Dendi, Mt *Eth*	99D2
Dèndre, R *Belg*	46B1
Dengkou *China*	72B1
Deng Xian *China*	72C3
Denham,Mt *Jamaica*	27H1
Den Helder *Neth*	56A2
Denia *Spain*	51C2
Deniliquin *Aust*	107D4
Denio *USA*	20C2
Denison, Texas *USA*	9D3
Denison,Mt *USA*	12D3
Denizli *Turk*	92A2
Denmark, Kingdom *Europe*	39F7
Denmark Str *Greenland/Iceland*	1C1
Dennery *St Lucia*	27P2
Denpasar *Indon*	78D4
Denton, Maryland *USA*	16B3
Denton, Texas *USA*	9D3
D'Entrecasteaux Is *PNG*	107E1
Dents du Midi, Mt *Switz*	47B1
Denver *USA*	8C3
Déo, R *Cam*	98B2
Deoghar *India*	86B2
Deolāli *India*	85C5
Deosai Plain *India*	84D1
Dépression du Mourdi *Chad*	95B3
De Queen *USA*	19B3
Dera *Pak*	84C3
Dera Bugti *Pak*	84B3
Dera Ismail Khan *Pak*	84C2
Derby *Aust*	106B2
Derby, Connecticut *USA*	16C2
Derby, County *Eng*	43D3
Derby *Eng*	43D3
Derby, Kansas *USA*	18A2
Dergachi *USSR*	60E3
De Ridder *USA*	19B3
Derna *Libya*	95B1
Derudeb *Sudan*	95C3
Derwent Bridge *Aust*	109C4
Desaguadero *Arg*	34B2
Desaguadero, R *Arg*	34B2
Désaguadero, R *Bol*	30C2
Descanso *Mexico*	21B3
Deschutes, R *USA*	20B2
Deseado *Arg*	29C5
Deseado, R *Arg*	29C5
Desenzano *Italy*	47D2
Deserta Grande, I *Medeira*	96A1
Desierto de Atacama, Desert *Chile*	30C4
Desloge *USA*	18B2
Des Moines, Iowa *USA*	10A2
Desna, R *USSR*	60D3
Desolación, I *Chile*	29B6
Des Plaines *USA*	14A2
Dessau *E Germ*	56C2
Dessye *Eth*	99D1
Destruction Bay *Can*	12G2
Desvres *France*	46A1
Deta *Rom*	54B1
Dete *Zim*	100B2
Detroit *USA*	10B2
Det Udom *Thai*	76D3
Deva *Rom*	54B1
Deventer *Neth*	56B2
Deveron, R *Scot*	44C3
Devikot *India*	85C3
Devil Postpile Nat Mon *USA*	22C2
Devils Gate, P *USA*	22C1
Devils Lake *USA*	8D2
Devils Paw, Mt *Can*	12H3
Devizes *Eng*	43D4
Devli *India*	85D3
Devoll, R *Alb*	55B2
Devon, County *Eng*	43B4
Devon I *Can*	6A2
Devonport *Aust*	107D5
Dewangiri *Bhutan*	86C1
Dewàs *India*	85D4
Dewctsdorp *S Africa*	101G1
Dewey Res *USA*	11B3
De Witt *USA*	19B3
Dexter, Missouri *USA*	18C2
Deyang *China*	73A3
Deyhuk *Iran*	90C3
Dezfül *Iran*	90A3
Dezhou *China*	72D2
Dezh Shāhpür *Iran*	90A2
Dhahran *S Arabia*	91B4
Dhākā *Bang*	86C2
Dhamavaram *India*	87B2
Dhamtari *India*	86A2
Dhanbād *India*	86B2
Dhangarhi *Nepal*	86A1
Dhankuta *Nepal*	86B1
Dhār *India*	85D4
Dharmapuri *India*	87B2
Dharmsāla *India*	84D2
Dhar Oualata, Desert Region *Maur*	97B3
Dhaulagiri, Mt *Nepal*	86A1
Dhenkānāi *India*	86B2
Dhibah *Jordan*	94B3
Dhíkti Óri, Mt *Greece*	55C3
Dhomokós *Greece*	55B3
Dhone *India*	87B1
Dhoraji *India*	85C4
Dhrängadhra *India*	85C4
Dhuburi *India*	86B1
Dhule *India*	85C4
Diablo,Mt *USA*	22B2
Diablo Range, Mts *USA*	21A2
Diamante *Arg*	34C2
Diamante, R *Arg*	34B2
Diamantina *Brazil*	31C5
Diamantina, R *Aust*	107D3
Diamond Harbours *India*	86B2
Diamond Springs *USA*	22B1
Dibā *UAE*	91C4
Dibaya *Zaïre*	98C3
Dibrugarh *India*	86C1
Dickinson *USA*	8C2
Dickson *USSR*	1B10
Dickson City *USA*	15C2
Dicle, R *Turk*	93D2
Didsbury *Can*	13E2
Dïdwāna *India*	85C3
Diebougou *U Volta*	97B3
Diekirch *Lux*	46D2
Diéma *Mali*	97B3
Dien Bien Phu *Viet*	76C1
Diepholz *W Germ*	56B2
Dieppe *France*	48C2
Diest *Belg*	46C1
Dieuze *France*	46D2
Digby *Can*	7D5
Digne *France*	49D3
Digoin *France*	49C2
Digos *Phil*	79C4
Digul, R *Indon*	71E4
Dihang, R *India*	86C1
Dijon *France*	49C2
Dik *Chad*	98B2
Dikhil *Djibouti*	99E1
Diksmuide *Belg*	46B1
Dilaram *Afghan*	82A2
Dili *Indon*	106B1
Di Linh *Viet*	76D3
Dillenburg *W Germ*	46E1
Dilling *Sudan*	99C1
Dillingham *USA*	12C3
Dillon *USA*	8B2
Dillsburg *USA*	16A2
Dilolo *Zaïre*	100B2
Dimbelenge *Zaïre*	98C3
Dimbokro *Ivory Coast*	97B4
Dimitrovgrad *Bulg*	54C2
Dimitrovgrad *USSR*	61G3
Dimona *Israel*	94B3
Dïmäpur *India*	86C1
Dinagat, I *Phil*	79C3
Dinajpur *India*	86B1
Dinan *France*	48B2
Dinant *Belg*	46C1
Dinar *Turk*	92B2
Dinder, R *Sudan*	99D1
Dindigul *India*	87B2
Dingbian *China*	72B2
Dinggyê *China*	86B1
Dingle *Irish Rep*	41A3
Dingle, B *Irish Rep*	41A3
Dinguiraye *Guinea*	97A3
Dingwall *Scot*	44B3
Dingxi *China*	72A2
Ding Xian *China*	72D2
Dinh Lap *Viet*	76D1
Dinuba *USA*	22C2
Diouloulou *Sen*	97A3
Diphu *India*	86C1
Diredawa *Eth*	99E2
Dirk Hartog, I *Aust*	106A3
Dirkou *Niger*	95A3
Dirranbandi *Aust*	109C1
Dirri *Somalia*	99E2
Disappointment,C *South Georgia*	29G8
Disappointment,C *USA*	20B1
Disappointment,L *Aust*	106B3
Discovery B *Aust*	108B3
Discovery Tablemount *Atlantic O*	103J7
Disentis Muster *Switz*	47C1
Disko *Greenland*	6E3
Disko Bugt, B *Greenland*	6E3
Diskorjord *Greenland*	6E3
Disna, R *USSR*	58D1
Distrito Federal, Federal District *Brazil*	35B1
Diu *India*	85C4
Diuat Mts *Phil*	79C4
Divinópolis *Brazil*	31C6
Divnoye *USSR*	61F4
Divriği *Turk*	93C2
Dixon, California *USA*	22B1
Dixon Entrance, Sd *Can/USA*	5E4
Dixonville *Can*	13D1
Diyālā, R *Iraq*	93E3
Diyarbakir *Turk*	65F6
Diz, R *Iran*	90A3
Dja, R *Cam*	98B2
Djadi, R *Alg*	96C1
Djado,Plat du *Niger*	95A2
Djambala *Congo*	98B3
Djanet *Alg*	96C2
Djebel Bouhalla, Mt *Mor*	50A2
Djelfa *Alg*	96C1
Djéma *CAR*	98C2

Djenné

Embalse de Mequinenza

Embalse de Mequinenza, Res *Spain*	51B1
Embalse de Ricobayo, Res *Spain*	50A1
Embalse de Rio Negro Res *Urug*	29E2
Embalse El Chocón, L *Arg*	29C3
Embalse Florentine Ameghino, L *Arg*	29C4
Embalse Gabriel y Galan, Res *Spain*	50A1
Embarcación *Arg*	30D3
Embarras Portage *Can*	5G4
Embrun *France*	47B2
Embu *Kenya*	99D3
Emden *W Germ*	56B2
Emei *China*	73A4
Emerald *Aust*	107D3
Emeri *Can*	7D4
Emerson *Can*	5J5
Emigrant P *USA*	21B1
Emi Koussi, Mt *Chad*	95A3
Emilo Mitre *Arg*	34B3
Emirdağ *Turk*	92B2
Emmaus *USA*	16B2
Emmen *Neth*	56B2
Emmett *USA*	20C2
Emmitsburg *USA*	16A3
Emmonak *USA*	12B2
Emory Peak, Mt *USA*	9C4
Empalme *Mexico*	24A2
Empangeni *S Africa*	101H1
Empedrado *Arg*	30E4
Emperor Seamount Chain *Pacific O*	105G1
Emporia, Kansas *USA*	18A2
Ems, R *W Germ*	56B2
Enard, B *Scot*	44B2
Encarnacion *Mexico*	23A1
Encarnación *Par*	30E4
Enchi *Ghana*	97B4
Encinitas *USA*	22D4
Encruzilhada *Brazil*	35C1
Ende *Indon*	106B1
Enderby *Can*	13D2
Enderby Land, Region *Ant*	112C11
Endicott *USA*	15C2
Endicott Mts *USA*	12D1
Engadin, Mts *Switz*	47D1
Engaño,C *Phil*	79B2
En Gedi *Israel*	94B3
Engelberg *Switz*	47C1
Engel's *USSR*	61G3
Enggano, I *Indon*	78A4
England, Country *UK*	41C3
Englee *Can*	7E4
English Channel *Eng/France*	41C3
Enji, Well *Maur*	97B3
Enkoping *Sweden*	39H7
Enna *Italy*	53B3
En Nahud *Sudan*	99C1
Ennedi, Region *Chad*	95B3
Enngonia *Aust*	109C1
Ennis *Irish Rep*	41B3
Ennis, Texas *USA*	19A3
Enniscorthy *Irish Rep*	45C2
Enniskillen *N Ire*	45C1
Ennistimon *Irish Rep*	45B2
Enn Nâqoûra *Leb*	94B2
Enns, R *Austria*	57C3
Enschede *Neth*	39F8
Ensenada *Mexico*	24A1
Enshi *China*	73B3
Entebbe *Uganda*	99D2
Enterprise, Alabama *USA*	17A1
Enterprise, Oregon *USA*	20C1
Enugu *Nig*	97C4
Enzan *Japan*	75B1
Epernay *France*	49C2
Ephrata, Pennsylvania *USA*	16A2
Ephrata, Washington *USA*	20C1
Épinal *France*	49D2
Epte, R *France*	46A2
Epukiro *Namibia*	100A3
Epu pel *Arg*	34C3
Eqlid *Iran*	90B3
Equator	89D7
Equatorial Guinea, Republic *Africa*	98A2
Erba *Italy*	47C2
Erbeskopf, Mt *W Germ*	46D2
Ercilla *Chile*	34A3
Erciş *Turk*	93D2
Erciyas Daglari, Mt *Turk*	92C2
Erdaobaihe *China*	74B2
Erdene *Mongolia*	72C1
Erdenet *Mongolia*	68C2
Erdi, Region *Chad*	95B3
Erechim *Brazil*	30F4
Ereğlï *Turk*	92B1
Ereğlï *Turk*	92B2
Erenhot *China*	68D2
Eresma, R *Spain*	50B1
Erft, R *W Germ*	46D1
Erfurt *E Germ*	57C2
Ergani *Turk*	93C2
Erg Chech, Desert Region *Alg*	96B2
Erg du Djourab, Desert *Chad*	95A3
Erg Du Ténéré, Desert Region *Niger*	97D3
Ergene, R *Turk*	92A1
Erg Iguidi, Region *Alg*	96B2
Ergli *USSR*	58D1
Erguig, R *Chad*	98B1
Ergun' *USSR*	63D2
Ergun, R *USSR*	68D1
Ergun Zuoqi *China*	63E2
Eriba *Sudan*	95C3
Erie *USA*	10C2
Erie,L *USA/Can*	10B2
Erin Port *Eng*	42B2
Eriskay, I *Scot*	44A3
Erkelenz *W Germ*	46D1
Erlangen *W Germ*	57C3
Erling,L *USA*	19B3
Ermelo *S Africa*	101G1
Ernäkulam *India*	87B3
Erode *India*	87B2
Eromanga *Aust*	108B1
Er Rachidia *Mor*	96B1
Er Rahad *Sudan*	99D1
Errego *Mozam*	101C2
Errigal, Mt *Irish Rep*	40B2
Erris Head, Pt *Irish Rep*	41A3
Er Roseires *Sudan*	99D1
Er Rummän *Jordan*	94B2
Erzgebirge, Upland *E Germ*	57C2
Erzincan *Turk*	93C2
Erzurum *Turk*	65F6
Esara, R *Spain*	48C3
Esbjerg *Den*	56B1
Escalón *Mexico*	9C4
Escanaba *USA*	10B2
Escárcega *Mexico*	25C3
Esch *Luxembourg*	46C2
Escondido *USA*	21B3
Escuinapa *Mexico*	24B2
Escuintla *Guatemala*	25C3
Eséka *Cam*	98B2
Esera, R *Spain*	51C1
Eşfahān *Iran*	90B3
Eshowe *S Africa*	101H1
Eskdale *NZ*	110C1
Eskifjörður *Iceland*	38C1
Eskilstuna *Sweden*	39H7
Eskimo L *Can*	4E3
Eskimo Point *Can*	7A3
Eskisehir *Turk*	92B2
Esla, R *Spain*	50A1
Esmeralda, I *Chile*	29A5
Esmeraldas *Ecuador*	32B3
Esmerelda *Cuba*	26B2
Espalion *France*	49C3
Espanola *Can*	14B1
Española, I *Ecuador*	32J7
Esperance *Aust*	106B4
Esperanza *Arg*	34C2
Esperanza, Base *Ant*	112C2
Espírito Santo, State *Brazil*	35C1
Espungabera *Mozam*	101C3
Esquel *Arg*	29B4
Esquimalt *Can*	20B1
Esquina *Arg*	34D2
Es Samra *Jordan*	94C2
Essaouira *Mor*	96B1
Essen *W Germ*	56B2
Essequibo, R *Guyana*	33F3
Essex, County *Eng*	43E4
Essexville *USA*	14B2
Esslingen *W Germ*	57B3
Essonne *France*	46B2
Estância *Brazil*	31D4
Estcourt *S Africa*	101G1
Este *Italy*	47D2
Esternay *France*	46B2
Esteros *Par*	30D3
Estevan *Can*	5H5
Estill *USA*	17B1
Estonskaya SSR, Republic *USSR*	60B2
Estrecho de Magallanes, Str *Chile*	29B6
Estremoz *Port*	50A2
Esztergom *Hung*	59B3
Etadunna *Aust*	108A1
Etam *France*	46C2
Etampes *France*	48C2
Etamunbanie,L *Aust*	108A1
Etaples *France*	46A1
Etäwah *India*	85D3
Ethiopia, Republic *Africa*	99D2
Etla *Mexico*	23B2
Etna, Mt *Italy*	53B3
Etolin I *USA*	12H3
Etolin Str *USA*	12A2
Eton *Can*	6C2
Etosha Nat Pk *Namibia*	100A2
Etosha Pan, Salt L *Namibia*	100A2
Etowah, R *USA*	17B1
Ettelbruck *Lux*	46D2
Euabalong *Aust*	109C2
Euclid *USA*	14B2
Eucumbene,L *Aust*	109C3
Eudunda *Aust*	108A2
Eufala L *USA*	19A2
Eufaula *USA*	17A1
Eugene *USA*	8A2
Eulo *Aust*	108C1
Eunice, Louisiana *USA*	19B3
Eupen *W Germ*	46D1
Euphrates, R *Iraq*	93D3
Eupora *USA*	19C3
Eure, R *France*	48C2
Eureka, California *USA*	20B2
Eureka *Can*	6B1
Eureka, Nevada *USA*	8B3
Eureka, Sd *Can*	6B2
Euroa *Aust*	108C3
Eurombah, R *Aust*	109C1
Europa, I *Mozam Chan*	101D3
Euskirchen *W Germ*	57B2
Eutsuk L *Can*	13B2
Evansburg *Can*	13D2
Evans,C *Can*	6B1
Evans,L *Can*	7C4
Evans Str *Can*	6B3
Evanston, Illinois *USA*	14A2
Evanston, Wyoming *USA*	8B2
Evansville, Indiana *USA*	11B3
Evaton *S Africa*	101G1
Everard,L *Aust*	106C4
Everest,Mt *Nepal/China*	82C3
Everett, Washington *USA*	8A2
Everett,Mt *USA*	16C1
Everglades,The, Swamp *USA*	11B4
Evesham *Eng*	43D3
Evinayong *Eq Guinea*	98B2
Evje *Nor*	39F7
Evolène *Switz*	47B1
Évora *Port*	50A2
Evreux *France*	48C2
Évvoia, I *Greece*	55B3
Ewo *Congo*	98B3
Excelsior Mt *USA*	22C1
Excelsior Springs *USA*	18B2
Exeter, California *USA*	21B2
Exeter *Eng*	43C4
Exeter, New Hampshire *USA*	15D2
Exmoor Nat Pk *Eng*	43C4
Exmouth *Eng*	43C4
Extremadura, Region *Spain*	50A2
Exuma Sd *Bahamas*	25E2
Eyasi, L *Tanz*	99D3
Eyemouth *Scot*	42C2
Eyl *Somalia*	99E2
Eyre *Aust*	106B4
Eyre Creek, R *Aust*	106C3
Eyre,L *Aust*	106C3
Eyre Pen *Aust*	106C4
Eyte, I *Phil*	79B3
Ezatlan *Mexico*	23A1
Ezine *Turk*	55C3

F

Faber L *Can*	4G3
Fåborg *Den*	39G7
Fabriano *Italy*	52B2
Fachi *Niger*	95A3
Fada *Chad*	95B3
Fada N'Gourma *U Volta*	97C3
Faenza *Italy*	52B2
Faeringehavn *Greenland*	6E3
Faeroerne, Is *N Atlantic*	36C2
Fafa, R *CAR*	98B2
Fafan, R *Eth*	99E2
Făgăras *Rom*	54B1
Fagnes, Region *Belg*	46C1
Faguibine,L, L *Mali*	97B3
Fahud *Oman*	91C5
Faiol, I *Açores*	96A1
Fairbanks *USA*	4D3
Fairbault *USA*	7A5
Fairborn *USA*	14B3
Fairbury *USA*	8D2
Fairfax *USA*	16A3
Fairfield, California *USA*	21A2
Fairfield, Connecticut *USA*	16C2
Fairfield, Ohio *USA*	14B3
Fair Head, Pt *N Ire*	45C1
Fair Isle, I *Scot*	40C2
Fairlie *NZ*	111B2
Fairmont, W Virginia *USA*	14B3
Fairview *Can*	13D1
Fairweather,Mt *USA*	4E4
Fais, I *Pacific O*	71F3
Faisalabad *Pak*	84C2
Faith *USA*	8C2
Faither,The, Pen *Scot*	44D1
Faizabad *Afghan*	84C1
Faizābād *India*	86A1
Fakenham *Eng*	43E3
Faköping *Sweden*	39G7
Falam *Burma*	86C2
Falcon Res *USA/Mexico*	24C2
Falémé, R *Mali/Sen*	97A3

Fort Rupert

Golconda

Greater Antilles, Is *Caribbean*	26B2
Greater London, Metropolitan County *Eng*	43D4
Greater Manchester, Metropolitan County *Eng*	43C3
Great Exuma, I *Bahamas*	25E2
Great Falls *USA*	8B2
Great Glen, V *Scot*	44B3
Great Himalayan Range, Mts *Asia*	86B1
Great Inagua, I *Bahamas*	11C4
Great Karroo, Mts *S Africa*	100B4
Great L *Aust*	109C4
Great Namaland, Region *Namibia*	100A3
Great Ormes Head, C *Wales*	42C3
Great Ragged, I *Bahamas*	11C4
Great Ruaha, R *Tanz*	99D3
Great Sacandaga L *USA*	15D2
Great Salt L *USA*	8B2
Great Sand Sea *Libya/ Egypt*	95B2
Great Sandy Desert *Aust*	106B3
Great Sandy Desert *USA*	8A2
Great Slave L *Can*	4G3
Great South B *USA*	16C2
Great Victoria Desert *Aust*	106B3
Great Wall *China*	72B2
Great Yarmouth *Eng*	43E3
Greco,C *Cyprus*	94B1
Greece, Republic *Europe*	55B3
Greece *USA*	15C2
Greeley *USA*	8C2
Greely Fjord *Can*	6B1
Green B *USA*	14A1
Green Bay *USA*	14A2
Greencastle, Indiana *USA*	14A3
Greenfield, Massachusetts *USA*	16C1
Greenfield, Wisconsin *USA*	14A2
Green Lake *Can*	13F2
Greenland, Dependency *N Atlantic*	6F2
Greenland Basin *Greenland S*	102H1
Greenland S *Greenland*	1B1
Greenock *Scot*	42B2
Greenport *USA*	16C2
Greensboro, Maryland *USA*	16B3
Greensboro, N Carolina *USA*	11C3
Greensburg, Pennsylvania *USA*	15C2
Greenstone, Pt *Scot*	44B3
Greenup *USA*	18C2
Greenville, Alabama *USA*	17A1
Greenville *Lib*	97B4
Greenville, Mississippi *USA*	19B3
Greenville, N Hampshire *USA*	16D1
Greenville, Ohio *USA*	14B2
Greenville, S Carolina *USA*	17B1
Greenville, Texas *USA*	19A3
Greenwich *Eng*	43E4
Greenwich *USA*	16C2
Greenwood, Delaware *USA*	16B3

Greenwood, Mississippi *USA*	19B3
Greenwood, S Carolina *USA*	17B1
Greers Ferry L *USA*	18B2
Gregory,L *Aust*	108A1
Gregory Range, Mts *Aust*	107D2
Greifswald *E Germ*	56C2
Gremikha *USSR*	64F3
Grenå *Den*	56C1
Grenada *USA*	19C3
Grenada, I *Caribbean*	27E4
Grenadines,The, Is *Caribbean*	27E4
Grenfell *Aust*	109C2
Grenoble *France*	49D2
Grenville *Grenada*	27M2
Grenville,C *Aust*	107D2
Gresham *USA*	20B1
Gresik, Jawa *Indon*	78C4
Gresik, Sumatera *Indon*	78A3
Gretna *USA*	19B4
Grey, R *NZ*	111B2
Grey Hunter Pk, Mt *Can*	12G2
Grey Is *Can*	7E4
Greylock,Mt *USA*	16C1
Greymouth *NZ*	111B2
Grey Range, Mts *Aust*	107D3
Greystones *Irish Rep*	45C2
Greytown *S Africa*	101H1
Griekwastad *S Africa*	101F1
Griffin *USA*	17B1
Griffith *Aust*	108C2
Grim,C *Aust*	107D5
Grimsby *Can*	15C2
Grimsby *Eng*	42D3
Grimsey, I *Iceland*	38B1
Grimshaw *Can*	13D1
Grimstad *Nor*	39F7
Grindelwald *Switz*	47C1
Grinnell Pen *Can*	6A2
Grise Fjord *Can*	6B2
Griva *USSR*	61H1
Grobina *USSR*	39J7
Grodno *USSR*	58C2
Gromati, R *India*	86A1
Groningen *Neth*	56B2
Groote Eylandt, I *Aust*	106C2
Grootfontein *Namibia*	100A2
Grootvloer, Salt L *S Africa*	100B3
Gros Islet *St Lucia*	27P2
Grosser Feldberg, Mt *W Germ*	46E1
Grosseto *Italy*	52B2
Gross-Gerau *W Germ*	46E2
Grossglockner, Mt *Austria*	57C3
Gross Venediger, Mt *Austria*	47E1
Grosvenor,L *USA*	12C3
Groveland *USA*	22B2
Grover City *USA*	21A2
Groveton *USA*	15D2
Groznyy *USSR*	61G5
Grudziadz *Pol*	58B2
Grünau *Namibia*	100A3
Grutness *Scot*	44D2
Gruzinskaya SSR, Republic *USSR*	65F5
Gryazi *USSR*	61F3
Gryazovets *USSR*	61E2
Grytviken *South Georgia*	29G8
Gt Blasket, I *Irish Rep*	45A2
Guaçuí *Brazil*	35C2
Guadalajara *Mexico*	23A1
Guadalajara *Spain*	50B1
Guadalcanal, I *Solomon Is*	107E1
Guadalimar, R *Spain*	50B2
Guadalope, R *Spain*	51B1
Guadalqivir, R *Spain*	50B2
Guadalupe *Mexico*	24B2
Guadalupe, I *Mexico*	3G6

Guadeloupe, I *Caribbean*	27E3
Guadian, R *Spain*	50B2
Guadiana, R *Port*	50A2
Guadix *Spain*	50B2
Guajará Mirim *Brazil*	32D6
Guajira,Pen de *Colombia*	32C1
Gualaceo *Ecuador*	32B4
Gualeguay *Arg*	34D2
Gualeguaychú *Arg*	34D2
Guam, I *Pacific O*	71F2
Guamini *Arg*	34C3
Gua Musang *Malay*	77C5
Guanajuato *Mexico*	23A1
Guanajuato, State *Mexico*	23A1
Guanare *Ven*	32D2
Guane *Cuba*	25D2
Guangdong, Province *China*	73C5
Guanghan *China*	73A3
Guanghua *China*	72C3
Guangmao Shan, Mt *China*	73A4
Guangnan *China*	73B5
Guangyuan *China*	72B3
Guangze *China*	73D4
Guangzhou *China*	67F3
Guanhães *Brazil*	35C1
Guania, R *Colombia*	32D3
Guanipa, R *Ven*	27E5
Guantánamo *Cuba*	26B2
Guanting Shuiku, Res *China*	72D1
Guanxi, Province *China*	73B5
Guan Xian *China*	73A3
Guapa *Colombia*	32B2
Guaporé, R *Brazil/Bol*	33E6
Guaquí *Bol*	30C2
Guaranda *Ecuador*	32B4
Guarapuava *Brazil*	30F4
Guaratinguetá *Brazil*	35B2
Guarda *Port*	50A1
Guardafui,C *Somalia*	99F1
Guarda Mor *Brazil*	35B1
Guasave *Mexico*	9C4
Guastalla *Italy*	47D2
Guatemala *Guatemala*	25C3
Guatemala, Republic *C America*	25C3
Guatraché *Arg*	34C3
Guavrare, R *Colombia*	32C3
Guaxupé *Brazil*	35B2
Guayaguayare *Trinidad*	27L1
Guayaquil *Ecuador*	32A4
Guaymas *Mexico*	24A2
Guayquiraro, R *Arg*	34D2
Guba *Eth*	99D2
Guba *Zaïre*	100B2
Guban, Region *Somalia*	99E2
Gubat *Phil*	79B3
Gubin *Pol*	56C2
Gūdūr *India*	87B2
Guelpho *Can*	14B2
Guelta Zemmur *Mor*	96A2
Guenabacoa *Cuba*	26A2
Guéréda *Chad*	98C1
Guéret *France*	48C2
Guernsey, I *UK*	48B2
Guerrero, State *Mexico*	23A2
Gughe, Mt *Eth*	99D2
Gugigu *China*	63E2
Guguan, I *Pacific O*	71F2
Guidong *China*	73C4
Guiglo *Ivory Coast*	97B4
Gui Jiang, R *China*	73C5
Guildford *Eng*	43D4
Guilin *China*	73C4
Guillestre *France*	47B2
Guinan *China*	72A2
Guinea, Republic *Africa*	97A3

Guinea Basin *Atlantic O*	102H4
Guinea-Bissau, Republic *Africa*	97A3
Guinea,G of *W Africa*	97C4
Güines *Cuba*	26A2
Guir, Well *Mali*	97B3
Guiranwala *Pak*	84C2
Güiria *Ven*	33E1
Guise *France*	46B2
Guiuan *Phil*	79C3
Gui Xian *China*	73B5
Guiyang *China*	73B4
Guizhou, Province *China*	73B4
Gujarāt, State *India*	85C4
Gujrat *Pak*	84C2
Gulbarga *India*	87B1
Gulbene *USSR*	58D1
Guledagudda *India*	87B1
Gulf,The *S W Asia*	80D3
Gulgong *Aust*	109C2
Gulin *China*	73B4
Gulkana *USA*	12E2
Gulkana, R *USA*	12E2
Gull L *Can*	13E2
Gull Lake *Can*	13F2
Gulu *Uganda*	99D2
Guluguba *Aust*	109C1
Gumel *Nig*	97C3
Gummersbach *W Germ*	46D1
Gumpla *India*	86A2
Gümüşhane *Turk*	93C1
Guna *India*	85D4
Guna, Mt *Eth*	99D1
Gundagai *Aust*	109C3
Gunnedah *Aust*	109D2
Guntakal *India*	87B1
Guntersville *USA*	17A1
Guntersville L *USA*	17A1
Guntūr *India*	87C1
Gunung Batu Putch, Mt *Malay*	77C5
Gunung Besar, Mt *Indon*	78D3
Gunung Bulu, Mt *Indon*	78D2
Gunung Gedang, Mt *Indon*	78A3
Gunung Lawit, Mt *Malay*	78C2
Gunung Lawu, Mt *Indon*	78C4
Gunung Menyapa, Mt *Indon*	78D2
Gunung Niapa, Mt *Indon*	78D2
Gunung Patah, Mt *Indon*	78A3
Gunung Raung, Mt *Indon*	78C4
Gunung Resag, Mt *Indon*	78A3
Gunung Sarempaka, Mt *Indon*	78D3
Gunung Sumbing, Mt *Indon*	78C4
Gunung Tahan, Mt *Malay*	77C5
Gunung Talakmau, Mt *Indon*	78A2
Gunza *Angola*	100A2
Guoyang *China*	72D3
Gurdāspur *India*	84D2
Gurgaon *India*	84D3
Gurkha *Nepal*	86A1
Gürün *Turk*	92C2
Gurupi, R *Brazil*	31B2
Gurvan Sayhan Uul, Upland *Mongolia*	72A1
Gur'yev *USSR*	61H4
Gurzinskaya, Republic *USSR*	65F5
Gusau *Nig*	97C3
Gusev *USSR*	58C2
Gushan *China*	74A3

Gus'khrustalnyy

Gus'khrustalnyy USSR	61F2
Gustavus USA	12G3
Gustine USA	22B2
Guston USA	11B3
Gütersloh W Germ	56B2
Guthrie, Kentucky USA	18C2
Guthrie, Oklahoma USA	18A2
Gutiérrez Zamora Mexico	23B1
Guyana, Republic S America	33F3
Guyana Basin Atlantic O	102F4
Guyang China	72C1
Guyenne, Region France	48B3
Guymon USA	9C3
Guyra Aust	109D2
Guyuan China	72B2
Gwabegar Aust	109C2
Gwalior India	85D3
Gwanda Zim	100B3
Gwane Zaïre	98C2
Gwardar Pak	82A3
Gweebarra B Irish Rep	45B1
Gwelo Zim	89G9
Gwent, County Wales	43C4
Gweru Zim	100B2
Gwydir, R Aust	109C1
Gwynedd Wales	43C3
Gyangzê China	86B1
Gyaring Hu, L China	68B3
Gydanskiy Poluostrov, Pen USSR	64J2
Gyirong China	86B1
Gyldenløues Greenland	6F3
Gympie Aust	109D1
Gyöngyös Hung	59B3
Györ Hung	59B3

H

Haapajärvi Fin	38K6
Haapsalu USSR	60B2
Haarlem Neth	56A2
Haarstrang, Region W Germ	46D1
Habana Cuba	25D2
Habiganj Bang	86C2
Hachijō-jima, I Japan	74D4
Hachiman Japan	75B1
Hachinohe Japan	74E2
Hachioji Japan	75B1
Hackettstown USA	16B2
Hack,Mt, Mt Aust	108A2
Haddington Scot	42C2
Haddon Corner Aust	108B1
Haddon Downs Aust	108B1
Hadejia Nig	97D3
Hadejia, R Nig	97C3
Hadera Israel	94B2
Haderslev Den	56B1
Hadiboh Socotra	81D4
Hadley B Can	4H2
Hadong Vietnam	73B5
Hadramawt, Region S Yemen	81C4
Hadsund Den	56C1
Haeju N Korea	74B3
Hafar al Bâtin S Arabia	91A4
Haffners Bjerg, Mt Greenland	6D2
Hafizabad Pak	84C2
Haflong India	86C1
Hafnafjörður Iceland	38A2
Hagemeister, I USA	12B3
Hagen W Germ	56B2
Hagerstown USA	15C3
Hagi Japan	75A2
Ha Giang Vietnam	73A5
Hagondange France	46D2
Hags Hd, C Irish Rep	45B2
Haguenan France	46D2
Hagunia, Well Mor	96A2

Haha-jima, I Japan	69G4
Hah Xil Hu, L China	68B3
Haicheng China	74A2
Hai Duong Viet	76D1
Haifa Israel	94B2
Haifa,B of Israel	94B2
Hai He, R China	72D2
Haikang China	73C5
Haikou China	76E1
Ha'il S Arabia	80C3
Hailākāndi India	86C2
Hailar China	63D3
Hailong China	74B2
Hoilun China	69E2
Hailuoto, I Fin	38J5
Hainan, I China	76D2
Haines USA	12G3
Haines Junction Can	12G2
Hainfeld Austria	59B3
Haiphong Vietnam	73B5
Haiti, Republic Caribbean	26C3
Haiya Sudan	95C3
Haiyan China	72A2
Haiyuan China	72B2
Haizhou Wan, B China	72D3
Hajdúböszörmény Hung	59C3
Hajiki-saki, Pt Japan	75B1
Haka Burma	86C2
Hakalau Hawaiian Is	21C4
Hakkâri Turk	93D2
Hakodate Japan	74E2
Hakui Japan	75B1
Haku-san, Mt Japan	75B1
Halab Syria	92C2
Halabja Iraq	93E3
Halaib Sudan	95C2
Halba Leb	94C1
Halberstadt E Germ	56C2
Halcon,Mt Phil	79B3
Halden Nor	39G7
Haldia India	86B2
Haldwāni India	84D3
Halfway, R Can	13C1
Halifax Can	7D5
Halifax Eng	42D3
Hall Basin, Sd Can	6D1
Hall Beach Can	6B3
Halle Belg	46C1
Halle E Germ	56C2
Halley, Base Ant	112B1
Hallingdal, R Nor	39F6
Hall Pen Can	6D3
Hall's Creek Aust	106B2
Halmahera, I Indon	71D3
Halmstad Sweden	39G7
Haltern W Germ	56B2
Haltia, Mt Nor	38J5
Haltwhistle Eng	42C2
Halul, I Qatar	91B4
Haluza, Hist Site Israel	94B3
Hamada Japan	75A2
Hamada de Tinrhert, Desert Region Alg	96C2
Hamada du Dra, Upland Alg	96B2
Hamadān Iran	90A3
Hamada Tounassine, Region Alg	96B2
Hamāh Syria	92C2
Hamamatsu Japan	75B2
Hamar Nor	39G6
Hambantota Sri Lanka	87C3
Hamburg, Arkansas USA	19B3
Hamburg, Iowa USA	18A1
Hamburg, Pennsylvania USA	16B2
Hamburg W Germ	56B2
Hamden USA	16C2
Hämeeninna Fin	39J6
Hamersley Range, Mts Aust	106A3
Hamgyong Sanmaek, Mts N Korea	74B2
Hamhŭng N Korea	74B2
Hami China	68B2

Hamīdīyah Syria	94B1
Hamilton Aust	108B3
Hamilton Can	14C2
Hamilton NZ	110C1
Hamilton, Ohio USA	14B3
Hamilton Scot	42B2
Hamilton Inlet, B Can	7E4
Hamilton,Mt USA	22B2
Hamina Fin	38K6
Hamirpur India	86A1
Hamm W Germ	56B2
Hammādāh al Hamra, Upland Libya	95A2
Hammerdal Sweden	38H6
Hammerfest Nor	38J4
Hammond, Illinois USA	14A2
Hammond, Louisiana USA	19B3
Hammonton USA	16B3
Hampden NZ	111B3
Hampshire, County Eng	43D4
Hampton, Arkansas USA	19B3
Hāmūn-e Jaz Mūriān, L Iran	91C4
Hamun-i-Lora, Salt L Pak	84B3
Hana Hawaiian Is	21C4
Hanalei Hawaiian Is	21C4
Hanamaki Japan	74E3
Hancheng China	72C2
Hanchuan China	73C3
Hancock, Maryland USA	15C3
Hancock, Michigan USA	10B2
Handa Japan	75B2
Handan China	72C2
Handeni Tanz	99D3
Hanggin Qi China	72B2
Hangö Fin	39J7
Hangzhou China	73E3
Hangzhou Wan, B China	73E3
Hanmer Springs NZ	111B2
Hanna Can	13E2
Hannibal USA	18B2
Hannover W Germ	56B2
Hanöbukten, B Sweden	39G7
Hanoi Viet	76D1
Hanover USA	16A3
Hanover, I Chile	29B6
Han Shui China	72B3
Han Shui, R China	73C3
Hānsi India	85D3
Hantay Mongolia	68C2
Hanzhong China	72B3
Hāora India	86B2
Haparanda Sweden	38J5
Hāpoli India	86C1
Haql S Arabia	92C4
Haradh S Arabia	91A5
Hara Fanna Eth	99E2
Haramachi Japan	75C1
Harar Eth	99E2
Harare Zim	101C2
Harazé Chad	98C1
Harbor Beach USA	14B2
Harda India	85D4
Hardangerfjord, Inlet Nor	39F6
Hardt, Region W Germ	46D2
Hardwicke B Aust	108A2
Hardy USA	18B2
Hargeysa Somalia	99E2
Har Hakippa, Mt Israel	94B3
Harhu, L China	68B3
Hari, R Indon	78A3
Harima-nada, B Japan	75A2
Harlingen Neth	56B2
Harlingen USA	9D4
Harlow Eng	43E4
Har Meron, Mt Israel	94B2
Harney Basin USA	20C2

Harney L USA	20C2
Härnösand Sweden	38H6
Har Nuur, L Mongolia	63B3
Harper Lib	97B4
Harper,Mt USA	12F2
Harpers Ferry USA	15C3
Har Ramon, Mt Israel	94B3
Harricanaw, R Can	7C4
Harrington India	16B3
Harrington Harbour Can	7E4
Harris, District Scot	44A3
Harrisburg, Illinois USA	18C2
Harrisburg, Pennsylvania USA	16A2
Harrismith S Africa	101G1
Harrison USA	18B2
Harrisonburg USA	15C3
Harrison,C Can	7E4
Harrison L Can	13C3
Harrisonville USA	18B2
Harris,Sound of, Chan Scot	44A3
Harrisville USA	14B2
Harrogate Eng	42D3
Har Saggi, Mt Israel	94B3
Harstad Nor	38H5
Hart, R Can	12G2
Hårteigen, Mt Nor	39F6
Hartford, Connecticut USA	16C2
Hartford, Michigan USA	14A2
Hartkjølen, Mt Nor	38G6
Hart,L Aust	108A2
Hartland Pt Eng	43B4
Hartlepool Eng	42D2
Hartshorne USA	19A3
Hartwell Res USA	17B1
Hartz, R S Africa	101F1
Har Us Nuur, L Mongolia	68B2
Harwich Eng	43E4
Haryāna, State India	84D3
Hāsā Jordan	94B3
Häsbaiya Leb	94B2
Haselmere Eng	43D4
Hashimoto Japan	75B2
Hashtpar Iran	90A2
Hashtrūd Iran	90A2
Hassan India	87B2
Hasselt Belg	56B2
Hassi Inifel Alg	96C2
Hassi Mdakane, Well Alg	96B2
Hassi Messaoud Alg	96C1
Hastings Aust	108C3
Hastings Eng	43E4
Hastings, Nebraska USA	8D2
Hastings NZ	110C1
Hatfield Aust	108B2
Hatham Inlet USA	12B1
Hāthras India	85D3
Ha Tinh Viet	76D2
Hattah Aust	108B2
Hatteras,C USA	11C3
Hattiesburg USA	19C3
Hatvan Hung	59B3
Hau Bon Viet	76D3
Haud, Region Eth	99E2
Haugesund Nor	39F7
Hauhungaroa Range, Mts NZ	110C1
Haultain, R Can	13F1
Hauraki G NZ	110B1
Hauroko,L NZ	111A3
Hausstock, Mt Switz	47C1
Haut Atlas, Mts Mor	96B1
Haute Kotto, Region CAR	98C2
Hautes Fagnes, Mts Belg	46C1
Hautmont Belg	46B1
Hauts Plateaux, Mts Alg	96B1
Hauzdar Iran	90D3

Homerville

Isla Puná

Jebel esh Sharqi, Mts	
Leb/Syria	92C3
Jebel Ithrīyat, Mt	
Jordan	94C3
Jebel Ja'lan, Mt Oman	91C5
Jebel Liban, Mts Leb	94B2
Jebel Ma'lūlā, Mt	
Syria	94C2
Jebel Marra, Mt	
Sudan	98C1
Jebel Mudeisisat, Mt	
Jordan	94C3
Jebel Oda, Mt Sudan	95C2
Jebel Qasr ed Deir,	
Mt Jordan	94B3
Jebel Um ed Daraj,	
Mt Jordan	94B2
Jebel Uweinat, Mt	
Sudan	95B2
Jedburgh Scot	42C2
Jedrzejów Pol	59C2
Jefferson, Texas USA	19B3
Jefferson City USA	11A3
Jefferson,Mt USA	8B3
Jeffersonville USA	14A3
Jekabpils USSR	60C2
Jelena Gora Pol	59B2
Jelgava USSR	60B2
Jember Indon	78C4
Jena E Germ	57C2
Jenaja, I Indon	78B2
Jenbach Austria	47D1
Jenin Israel	94B2
Jennings USA	19B3
Jenseniky, Upland	
Czech	59B2
Jensen Nunatakker,	
Mt Greenland	6F3
Jens Munk, I Can	6B3
Jeparit Aust	108B3
Jequié Brazil	31D4
Jequital, R Brazil	35C1
Jequitinhonha Brazil	35C1
Jequitinhonha, R	
Brazil	31C5
Jerez de la Frontera	
Spain	50A2
Jerez de los	
Caballeros Spain	50A2
Jericho Israel	94B3
Jerilderie Aust	108C3
Jersey, I UK	48B2
Jersey City USA	10C2
Jersey Shore USA	15C2
Jerseyville USA	18B2
Jerusalem Israel	92C3
Jervis B Aust	109D3
Jervis Inlet, Sd Can	13C2
Jesenice Yugos	52B1
Jessore Bang	86B2
Jesup USA	11B3
Jesus Maria Arg	34C2
Jewett City USA	16D2
Jezerce, Mt Alb	54A2
Jezioro Mamry, L Pol	58C2
Jezioro Śniardwy, L	
Pol	58C2
Jezzine Leb	94B2
Jhābua India	85C4
Jhālāwār India	85D4
Jhang Maghiana Pak	84C2
Jhānsi India	85D3
Jhārsuguda India	86A2
Jhelum Pak	84C2
Jhelum, R Pak	84C2
J H Kerr L USA	11C3
Jhunjhunūn India	84D3
Jiamusi China	69F2
Ji'an, Jiangxi China	73C4
Ji'an, Jilin China	74B2
Jiande China	73D4
Jiang'an China	73B4
Jiangbiancun China	73D4
Jiangcheng China	73A5
Jiang Jiang, R China	73B3
Jiangmen China	73C5
Jiangsu, Province	
China	72D3
Jiangxi, Province	
China	73C4
Jiangyou China	73A3
Jianping China	72D1
Jianshui China	73A5
Jian Xi, R China	73D4
Jianyang China	73D4
Jiaonan China	72E2
Jiao Xian China	72E2
Jiaozhou Wan, B	
China	72E2
Jiaozuo China	72C2
Jiaxiang China	73E3
Jiayuguan China	68B3
Jiddah S Arabia	81B3
Jieshou China	72D3
Jiexiu China	72C2
Jigzhi China	72A3
Jihlava Czech	59B3
Jilib Somalia	99E2
Jilin China	69E2
Jiloca, R Spain	51B1
Jiménez, Coahuila	
Mexico	9C4
Jimma Eth	99D2
Jinan China	72D2
Jind India	84D3
Jingbian China	72B2
Jingdezhen China	73D4
Jinghong China	76C1
Jingmen China	73C3
Jingning China	72B2
Jing Xiang China	73B4
Jinhua China	73D4
Jining, Nei Monggol	
China	72C1
Jining, Shandong	
China	72D2
Jinja Uganda	99D2
Jinping China	76C1
Jinsha Jiang, R China	73A4
Jinshi China	73C4
Jinxi China	72E1
Jin Xian China	72E2
Jinzhou China	72E1
Jiparaná, R Brazil	33E5
Jipijapa Ecuador	32A4
Jiquilpan Mexico	23A2
Jīroft Iran	91C4
Jishou China	73B4
Jisr ash Shughūr Syria	92C2
Jiu, R Rom	54B2
Jiujiang China	73D4
Jiulong China	73A4
Jiulong Jiang, R China	73D4
Jixi China	69F2
Jiza Jordan	94B3
Jīzan S Arabia	81C4
Joal Sen	97A3
João Monlevade Brazil	35C1
João Pessoa Brazil	31E3
João Pirheiro Brazil	35B1
Jocoli Arg	34B2
Jodhpur India	85C3
Joensuu Fin	38K6
Joeuf France	46C2
Joffre,Mt Can	13D2
Jogbani India	86B1
Jog Falls India	87A2
Johannesburg S Africa	101G1
Johannesburg USA	21B2
Johan Pen Can	6C2
John, R USA	12D1
John Day USA	20C2
John Day, R USA	20B1
John O'Groats Scot	44C2
John Redmond Res	
USA	18A2
Johnson City,	
Tennessee USA	11B3
Johnston USA	17B1
Johnston Pt St	
Vincent	27N2
Johnstown,	
Pennsylvania USA	15C2
Johor Bharu Malay	77C5
Joigny France	49C2
Joinville Brazil	30G4
Jok, R USSR	61H3
Jokkmokk Sweden	38H5
Jolfa Iran	93E2
Joliet USA	10B2
Joliette Can	7C5
Jolo Phil	79B4
Jolo, I Phil	79B4
Joma, Mt China	82D2
Jonava USSR	58C1
Jonê China	72A3
Jonesboro, Arkansas	
USA	11A3
Jonesboro, Louisiana	
USA	19B3
Jones Sd Can	6B2
Joniškis USSR	58C1
Jönköping Sweden	39G7
Joplin USA	11A3
Jordan, Kingdom S W	
Asia	92C3
Jordan, R Israel	94B2
Jordan Valley USA	20C2
Jorhāt India	86C1
Jörn Sweden	38J5
Jorong Indon	78C3
Jørpeland Nor	39F7
Jose Pañganiban Phil	79B3
Joseph Bonaparte G	
Aust	106B2
Jotunheimen, Mt Nor	64B3
Jouai'ya Leb	94B2
Jounié Leb	94B2
Jowal India	86C1
Jowhar Somalia	99E2
Joy,Mt Can	12H2
Juan de Fuca,Str of	
USA/Can	5F5
Juan de Nova, I	
Mozam Chan	101D2
Juárez Arg	34D3
Juàzeiro Brazil	31C3
Juazeiro do Norte	
Brazil	31D3
Juba Sudan	99D2
Juba, R Somalia	99E2
Jubail Leb	94B1
Jubbah S Arabia	93D3
Jucar, R Spain	51B2
Juchatengo Mexico	23B2
Juchipila, R Mexico	23A1
Juchitlan Mexico	23A1
Judenburg Austria	57C3
Juilaca Peru	30B2
Juiling Shan, Hills	
China	73C4
Juiz de Fora Brazil	31C6
Jujuy, State Arg	30C3
Juli Peru	30C2
Julianatop, Mt	
Surinam	33F3
Julianehab Greenland	6F3
Jülich W Germ	46D1
Jullundur India	84D2
Jumla Nepal	86A1
Jum Suwwāna, Mt	
Jordan	94B3
Jūnāgadh India	85C4
Junan China	72D2
Junction City USA	9D3
Jundiaí Brazil	31B6
Juneau USA	4E4
Junee Aust	107D4
June Lake USA	22C2
Jungfrau, Mt Switz	52A1
Juniata, R USA	16A2
Junín Arg	29D2
Junlian China	73A4
Juquiá Brazil	31B6
Jur, R Sudan	99C2
Jura, I Scot	42B2
Jura, Mts France	49D2
Jura,Sound of, Chan	
Scot	44B3
Jurf ed Darāwīsh	
Jordan	94B3
Jūrmala USSR	60B2
Juruá, R Brazil	32D4
Juruena, R Brazil	33F6
Jūsīyah Syria	94C1
Justo Daract Arg	34B2
Jutai, R Brazil	32D4
Juticalpa Honduras	25D3
Jüymand Iran	90C3
Jylland, Pen Den	56B1
Jyväskyla Fin	38K6

K

K2, Mt China/India	82B2
Kaakhka USSR	90C2
Kaapmuiden S Africa	101H1
Kabaena, I Indon	71D4
Kabala Sierra Leone	97A4
Kabale Rwanda	99D3
Kabalo Zaïre	98C3
Kabambare Zaïre	98C3
Kabarole Uganda	99D2
Kabinda Zaïre	98C3
Kabir Kuh, Mts Iran	90A3
Kabompo Zambia	100B2
Kabompo, R Zambia	100B2
Kabongo Zaïre	98C3
Kabul Afghan	84B2
Kachchh,G of India	85B4
Kachkanar USSR	61J2
Kachug USSR	63C2
Kadan Burma	76B3
Kadapongan, I Indon	78D3
Kadi India	85C4
Kadina Aust	108A2
Kadınhanı Turk	92B2
Kadiri India	87B2
Kadiyevka USSR	60E4
Kadoma Zim	100B2
Kadugli Sudan	99C1
Kaduna Nig	97C3
Kaduna, R Nig	97C3
Kadūr India	87B2
Kaédi Maur	97A3
Kaena Pt Hawaiian Is	21C4
Kaesöng N Korea	74B3
Kafanchan Nig	97C4
Kaffrine Sen	97A3
Kafrün Bashür Syria	94C1
Kafue Zambia	100B2
Kafue, R Zambia	100B2
Kafue Nat Pk Zambia	100B2
Kaga Japan	74D3
Kagan USSR	65H6
Kağizman Turk	93D1
Kagoshima Japan	74C4
Kãhak Iran	90C2
Kahama Tanz	99D3
Kahan Pak	84B3
Kahayan, R Indon	78C3
Kahemba Zaïre	98B3
Kahler Asten, Mt W	
Germ	46E1
Kahnūj Iran	91C4
Kahoka USA	18B1
Kahoolawe, I	
Hawaiian Is	21C4
Kahramanmaraş Turk	92C2
Kahuku Pt Hawaiian Is	21C4
Kaiapoi NZ	111B2
Kaieteur Fall Guyana	33F2
Kaifeng China	72C3
Kaikohe NZ	110B1
Kaikoura NZ	111B2
Kaikoura Pen NZ	111B2
Kaikoura Range, Mts	
NZ	111B2
Kaili China	73B4
Kailua Hawaiian Is	21C4
Kaimana Indon	71E4
Kainan Japan	75B2
Kainji Res Nig	97C3
Kaipara Harbour, B NZ	110B1
Kaiping China	73C5
Kairouan Tunisia	96D1
Kaiser Peak, Mt USA	22C2
Kaiserslautern W	
Germ	57B3
Kaishantun China	74B2
Kaisiadorys USSR	58D2
Kaitaia NZ	110B1

Kastamonou *Turk*	92B1	Kecskemet *Hung*	59B3	Kenya, Republic *Africa*	99D2	Kettle River Range,
Kastélli *Greece*	55B3	Kedainiai *USSR*	58C1	Kenya,Mt *Kenya*	99D3	Mts *USA*	20C1
Kastellorizon, I *Greece*	92A2	Kédougou *Sen*	97A3	Keokuk *USA*	18B1	Kettlestone B *Can*	7C3
Kastoría *Greece*	55B2	Keele, R *Can*	12J2	Keonchi *India*	86A2	Kevir-i Namak, Salt
Kástron *Greece*	55C3	Keele Pk, Mt *Can*	12H2	Keonjhargarh *India*	86B2	Flat *Iran*	90C3
Kasugai *Japan*	74D3	Keeler *USA*	21B2	Kepaluan Tanimbar,		Kewaunee *USA*	14A2
Kasumi *Japan*	75A1	Keene, New		Arch *Indon*	71E4	Key Harbour *Can*	14B1
Kasungu *Malawi*	101C2	Hampshire *USA*	15D2	Keplavik *Iceland*	6H3	Key Largo *USA*	17B2
Kasur *Pak*	84C2	Keetmanshoop		Kepno *Pol*	59B2	Key West *USA*	11B4
Kataba *Zambia*	100B2	Namibia	100A3	Kepulauan Anambas,		Kezhma *USSR*	63C2
Katako-kombe *Zaïre*	98C3	Keewanee *USA*	18C1	Arch *Indon*	78B2	K'féleghāza *Hung*	54A1
Katalla *USA*	4D3	Keewatin, Region *Can*	6A3	Kepulauan Aru, Arch		Kgun L *USA*	12B2
Katangli *USSR*	63G2	Kefallinía, I *Greece*	55B3	*Indon*	71E4	Khabab *Syria*	94C2
Katanning *Aust*	106A4	Kefar Sava *Israel*	94B2	Kepulauan Badas, Is		Khabarovsk *USSR*	62H3
Kateríni *Greece*	55B2	Keffi *Nig*	97C4	*Indon*	78B2	Khairpur *Pak*	85B3
Kates Needle, Mt		Keflavik *Iceland*	38A2	Kepulauan Banda,		Khairpur, Region *Pak*	85B3
Can/USA	5E4	Keg River *Can*	5G4	Arch *Indon*	71E4	Khakhea *Botswana*	100B3
Katha *Burma*	82D3	Kehsi Mansam *Burma*	76B1	Kepulauan Banggai, I		Khálki, I *Greece*	55C3
Katherine *Aust*	106C2	Keith *Aust*	108B3	*Indon*	71D4	Khalkidhíki, Pen
Käthiäwär, Pen *India*	85C4	Keith *Scot*	44C3	Kepulauan Bunguran		*Greece*	55B2
Kathua *India*	84D2	Keith Arm, B *Can*	4F3	Seletan, Arch *Indon*	78B2	Khalkís *Greece*	55B3
Kathmandu *Nepal*	86B1	Kekertuk *Can*	6D3	Kepulauan Kai, Arch		Khalturin *USSR*	61G2
Katihär *India*	86B1	Kekri *India*	85D3	*Indon*	71E4	Khambhät,G of *India*	85C4
Katima Mulilo *Namibia*	100B2	Kelang *Malay*	77C5	Kepulauan Leti, I		Khämgaon *India*	85D4
Katmai,Mt *USA*	4C4	Kelantan, R *Malay*	77C4	*Indon*	71D4	Kham Keut *Laos*	76C2
Katmai Nat Mon *USA*	12D3	Kelif *USSR*	84B1	Kepulauan Lingga, Is		Khammam *India*	87C1
Katni *India*	86A2	Kelkit, R *Turk*	92C1	*Indon*	78A3	Khamseh, Mts *Iran*	90A2
Katoomba *Aust*	109D2	Kellé *Congo*	98B3	Kepulauan Mentawi,		Khan, R *Laos*	76C2
Katowice *Pol*	59B2	Kellet,C *Can*	4F2	Arch *Indon*	70A4	Khanabad *Afghan*	84B1
Katrineholm *Sweden*	39H7	Kellogg *USA*	20C1	Kepulauan Riau, Arch		Khanaqin *Iraq*	93E3
Katsina *Nig*	97C3	Kelloselka *Fin*	64D3	*Indon*	78A2	Khandwa *India*	85D4
Katsina Ala *Nig*	97C4	Kells *Irish Rep*	45C2	Kepulauan Sabalana,		Khanewal *Pak*	84C2
Katsuta *Japan*	75C1	Kells Range, Hills *Scot*	42B2	Arch *Indon*	78D4	Khan ez Zabib *Jordan*	94C3
Katsuura *Japan*	75C1	Kelme *USSR*	58C1	Kepulauan Sangihe,		Khanh Hung *Viet*	77D4
Katsuy *Japan*	75B1	Kelowna *Can*	5G5	Arch *Indon*	71D3	Khaniá *Greece*	55B3
Kattakurgan *USSR*	65H6	Kelsey Bay *Can*	5F4	Kepulauan Sula, I		Khanpur *Pak*	84C3
Kattegat, Str		Kelso *Scot*	42C2	*Indon*	71D4	Khanty-Mansiysk
Denmark/Sweden	39G7	Kelso *USA*	20B1	Kepulauan Talaud,		*USSR*	65H3
Kauai, I *Hawaiian Is*	21C4	Kem' *USSR*	64E3	Arch *Indon*	71D3	Khan Yunis *Egypt*	94B3
Kauai Chan *Hawaiian*		Kem', R *USSR*	38L6	Kepulauan Tambelan,		Khapalu *India*	84D1
Is	21C4	Ke Macina *Mali*	97B3	Is *Indon*	78B2	Khapcheranga *USSR*	68C2
Kaulakahi Chan		Kemano *Can*	13B2	Kepulauan Tanimbar, I		Kharabali *USSR*	61G4
Hawaiian Is	21C4	Kemerovo *USSR*	65K4	*Indon*	71E4	Kharagpur *India*	86B2
Kaunakaki *Hawaiian Is*	21C4	Kemi *Fin*	38J5	Kepulauan Togian, I		Khäran *Iran*	91C4
Kaunas *USSR*	60B3	Kemi, R *Fin*	38K5	*Indon*	71D4	Kharan *Pak*	84B3
Kaura Namoda *Nig*	97C3	Kemijärvi *Fin*	38K5	Kepulauan Tukambesi,		Kharänaq *Iran*	90B3
Kautokeino *Nor*	38J5	Kempen, Region *Belg*	46C1	Is *Indon*	71D4	Khärg, Is *Iran*	91B4
Kavadarci *Yugos*	55B2	Kemps Bay *Bahamas*	26B2	Kerala, State *India*	87B2	Khârga Oasis *Egypt*	95C2
Kavajë *Alb*	55A2	Kempsey *Aust*	109D2	Kerang *Aust*	108B3	Khargon *India*	85D4
Kavali *India*	87B2	Kempten *W Germ*	57C3	Kerava *Fin*	39K6	Khar'Kov *USSR*	60E4
Kaválla *Greece*	55B2	Kenai *USA*	12D2	Kerch' *USSR*	60E4	Kharmanli *Bulg*	54C2
Kävda *India*	85B4	Kenai Mts *USA*	12D3	Kerema *PNG*	71F4	Kharovsk *USSR*	61F2
Kawagoe *Japan*	75B1	Kenai Pen *USA*	12D2	Keremeps *Can*	20C1	Khartoum *Sudan*	95C3
Kawaguchi *Japan*	75B1	Kenamuke Swamp		Keren *Eth*	95C3	Khartoum North
Kawakawa *NZ*	110B1	*Sudan*	99D2	Kerguelen Ridge		*Sudan*	95C3
Kawambwa *Zambia*	99C3	Kendal *Eng*	42C2	*Indian O*	104B6	Khasan *USSR*	74C2
Kawardha *India*	86A2	Kendall *Aust*	109D2	Kericho *Kenya*	99D3	Khashm el Girba
Kawartha Lakes *Can*	15C2	Kendari *Indon*	71D4	Kerinci, Mt *Indon*	70B4	*Sudan*	95C3
Kawasaki *Japan*	74D3	Kendawangan *Indon*	78C3	Kerio, R *Kenya*	99D2	Khasi-Jaîntia Hills
Kawerau *NZ*	110C1	Kendräpära *India*	86B2	Kerki *USSR*	80E2	*India*	86C1
Kawhia *NZ*	110B1	Kendrick *USA*	20C1	Kérkira *Greece*	55A3	Khaskovo *Bulg*	54C2
Kaya *U Volta*	97B3	Kenema *Sierra Leone*	97A4	Kérkira, I *Greece*	55A3	Khatanga *USSR*	1B9
Kayak I *USA*	12F3	Kenge *Zaïre*	98B3	Kerman *Iran*	91C3	Khawsa *Burma*	76B3
Kayan, R *Indon*	78D2	Kengtung *Burma*	76B1	Kerman *USA*	22B2	Khe Bo *Viet*	76C2
Käyankulam *India*	87B3	Kenhardt *S Africa*	100B3	Kermänshäh *Iran*	90A3	Khed Brahma *India*	85C4
Kayes *Mali*	97A3	Kéniéba *Mali*	97A3	Kerme Körfezi, B *Turk*	55C3	Khemis *Alg*	51C2
Kayseri *Turk*	92C2	Kenitra *Mor*	96B1	Kern, R *USA*	21B2	Kherrata *Alg*	51D2
Kazach'ye *USSR*	1B8	Kenmare *Irish Rep*	45B3	Kerrobert *Can*	13F2	Kherson *USSR*	60D4
Kazakh *USSR*	93E1	Kenmare, R *Irish Rep*	45B3	Kerry, County *Irish*		Khilok *USSR*	63D2
Kazakhskaya SSR,		Kenner *USA*	19B4	*Rep*	45B2	Khíos *Greece*	55C3
Republic *USSR*	65G5	Kennett *USA*	18C2	Kershaw *USA*	17B1	Khíos, I *Greece*	55C3
Kazan' *USSR*	61G2	Kennett Square *USA*	16B3	Kertamulia *Indon*	78B3	Khmel'nitskiy *USSR*	60C4
Kazanlŭk *Bulg*	54C2	Kennewick *USA*	20C1	Kerulen, R *Mongolia*	63D3	Khodorov *USSR*	59C3
Kazan Retto, Is *Japan*	69G4	Kenny Dam *Can*	5F4	Kerzaz *Alg*	96B2	Kholm *Afghan*	84B1
Käzerün *Iran*	91B4	Kenora *Can*	7A5	Keşan *Turk*	55C2	Khong *Laos*	76D3
Kazhim *USSR*	61H1	Kenosha *USA*	10B2	Kesennuma *Japan*	74E3	Khonj *Iran*	91B4
Kazi Magomed *USSR*	93E1	Kent, County *Eng*	43E4	Kestenga *USSR*	38L5	Khor *USSR*	69F2
Kazincbarcika *Hung*	59C3	Kent, Washington		Keswick *Eng*	42C2	Khoramshahr *Iran*	91A3
Kéa, I *Greece*	55B3	*USA*	20B1	Kéta *Ghana*	97C4	Khôr Duwayhin, B
Kealaikahiki Chan		Kentland *USA*	14A2	Ketapang *Indon*	78C3	*UAE*	91B5
Hawaiian Is	21C4	Kenton *USA*	14B2	Ketchikan *USA*	5E4	Khorog *USSR*	84C1
Kearney *USA*	8D2	Kent Pen *Can*	4H3	Ketia *Niger*	97C3	Khorramäbad *Iran*	90A3
Keban Baraji, Res *Turk*	93C2	Kentucky, State *USA*	11B3	Keti Bandar *Pak*	85B4	Khosf *Iran*	90C3
Kébémer *Sen*	97A3	Kentucky L *USA*	11B3	Ketrzyn *Pol*	58C2	Khost *Pak*	84B2
Kebili *Tunisia*	96C1	Kentwood, Louisiana		Kettering *Eng*	43D3	Khotin *USSR*	60C4
Kebîr, R *Syria/Leb*	94C1	*USA*	19B3	Kettering *USA*	14B3	Khotol, Mt *USA*	12C2
Kebrekaise, Mt		Kentwood, Michigan		Kettle, R *Can*	20C1	Khoyniku *USSR*	60C3
Sweden	38H5	*USA*	14A2				

Khrebet Dzhugdzhur, Mts USSR	63F2
Khrebet Kopet Dag, Mts USSR	90C2
Khrebet Pay-khoy, Mts USSR	64H3
Khrebet Tarbagatay, Mts USSR	82C1
Khrebet Tukuringra, Mts USSR	63E2
Khulna Bang	86B2
Khunjerab, P China/India	84D1
Khunsar Iran	90B3
Khurays S Arabia	91A4
Khurda India	86B2
Khurja India	84D3
Khushab Pak	84C2
Khushnīyah Syria	94B2
Khust USSR	59C3
Khuwei Sudan	99C1
Khuzdar Pak	85B3
Khvāf Iran	90D3
Khvalynsk USSR	61G3
Khvor Iran	90C3
Khvormūj Iran	91B4
Khvoy Iran	93D2
Khwaja Muhammad, Mts Afghan	84C1
Khyber P Afghan/Pak	84C2
Kiambi Zaïre	99C3
Kiamichi, R USA	19A3
Kiana USA	12B1
Kibangou Congo	98B3
Kibaya Tanz	99D3
Kibombo Zaïre	98C3
Kibondo Tanz	99D3
Kibungu Rwanda	99D3
Kičevo Yugos	55B2
Kicking Horse P Can	5G4
Kidal Mali	97C2
Kidderminster Eng	43C3
Kidira Sen	97A3
Kidnappers,C NZ	110C1
Kiel W Germ	56C2
Kielce Pol	59C2
Kieler Bucht, B W Germ	56C2
Kifab USSR	80E2
Kiffa Maur	97A3
Kigali Rwanda	89H8
Kigluaik Mts USA	12A2
Kigoma Tanz	99C3
Kii-sanchi, Mts Japan	75B2
Kii-suido, B Japan	74C4
Kikinda Yugos	54B1
Kikládhes, Is Greece	55B3
Kikori PNG	71F4
Kikwit Zaïre	98B3
Kilauea Crater, Mt Hawaiian Is	21C4
Kilbuck Mts USA	4C3
Kilchu N Korea	74B2
Kilcoy Aust	109D1
Kildare, County Irish Rep	45C2
Kildare Irish Rep	45C2
Kilgore USA	19B3
Kilifi Kenya	99D3
Kilimanjaro, Mt Tanz	99D3
Kilindoni Tanz	99D3
Kilis Turk	92C2
Kilkee Irish Rep	45B2
Kilkenny, County Irish Rep	45C2
Kilkenny Irish Rep	45C2
Kilkieran B Irish Rep	45B2
Kilkís Greece	55B2
Killala B Irish Rep	45B1
Killaloe Irish Rep	45B2
Killarney Aust	109D1
Killarney Irish Rep	41B3
Killeen USA	19A3
Killik, R USA	12D1
Killin Scot	44B3
Killíni, Mt Greece	55B3
Killybegs Irish Rep	45B1
Kilmarnock Scot	42B2
Kil'mez USSR	61H2
Kilosa Tanz	99D3
Kilrush Irish Rep	41B3
Kilwa Zaïre	99C3
Kilwa Kisiwani Tanz	99D3
Kilwa Kivinje Tanz	99D3
Kimba Aust	108A2
Kimball,Mt USA	12F2
Kimberley Can	13D3
Kimberley S Africa	101F1
Kimberley Plat Aust	106B2
Kimch'aek N Korea	74B2
Kimch'ŏn S Korea	74B3
Kími Greece	55B3
Kimry USSR	60E2
Kinabalu, Mt Malay	70C3
Kinabatangan, R Malay	78D1
Kincardine Can	14B2
Kincolith Can	13B1
Kinder USA	19B3
Kindersley Can	13F2
Kindia Guinea	97A3
Kindu Zaïre	98C3
Kinel' USSR	61H3
Kineshma USSR	61F2
Kingaroy Aust	109D1
King City USA	21A2
Kingcome Inlet Can	5F4
King George Is Can	7C4
King I Aust	107D4
King I Can	13B2
Kingissepp USSR	60B2
King Leopold Range, Mts Aust	106B2
Kingman USA	9B3
Kingombe Zaïre	98C3
Kingoonya Aust	108A2
Kingsburg USA	22C2
Kings Canyon Nat Pk USA	21B2
Kingscote Aust	108A3
King Sd Aust	106B2
Kingsford USA	14A1
Kingsland USA	17B1
King's Lynn Eng	43E3
Kings Park USA	16C2
Kings Peak, Mt USA	8B2
Kingston Aust	107C4
Kingston Can	7C5
Kingston Jamaica	25E3
Kingston, New York USA	15D2
Kingston NZ	111A3
Kingstown St Vincent	27E4
Kingsville USA	9D4
Kingussie Scot	44B3
King William I Can	4J3
King William's Town S Africa	100B4
Kinkala Congo	98B3
Kinna Sweden	39G7
Kinnairds Head, Pt Scot	44D3
Kinomoto Japan	75B1
Kinross Scot	44C3
Kinsale Irish Rep	45B3
Kinshasa Zaïre	98B3
Kintap Indon	78D3
Kintyre, Pen Scot	42B2
Kinuso Can	13D1
Kinyeti, Mt Sudan	99D2
Kiparissía Greece	55B3
Kiparissiakós Kólpos, G Greece	55B3
Kipawa,L Can	15C1
Kipili Tanz	99D3
Kipnuk USA	12B3
Kippure, Mt Irish Rep	45C2
Kipushi Zaïre	100B2
Kirensk USSR	63C2
Kirgizskaya SSR, Republic USSR	65J5
Kirgizskiy Khrebet, Mts USSR	82B1
Kiri Zaïre	98B3
Kiribati, Is Pacific O	105G4
Kırıkkale Turk	92B2
Kirishi USSR	60D2
Kirithar Range, Mts Pak	85B3
Kirkağaç Turk	55C3
Kirk Bulāg Dāgh, Mt Iran	90A2
Kirkby Eng	42C2
Kirkcaldy Scot	44C3
Kirkcudbright Scot	42B2
Kirkenes Nor	38K5
Kirkland Lake Can	7B5
Kirkpatrick,Mt Ant	80E
Kirksville USA	10A2
Kirkūk Iraq	93D2
Kirkwall Scot	44C2
Kirkwood USA	18B2
Kirov USSR	60D3
Kirov USSR	61G2
Kirovabad USSR	65F5
Kirovakan USSR	93D1
Kirovgrad USSR	61J2
Kirovograd USSR	60D4
Kirovsk USSR	64E3
Kirs USSR	61H2
Kirşehir Turk	92B2
Kiruna Sweden	56C2
Kiryū Japan	75B1
Kisangani Zaïre	98C2
Kisarazu Japan	75B1
Kishanganj India	86B1
Kishangarh India	85C3
Kishinev USSR	60C4
Kishiwada Japan	75B2
Kisii Kenya	99D3
Kisiju Tanz	99D3
Kiskunhalas Hung	59B3
Kislovodsk USSR	65F5
Kismaayo Somalia	99E3
Kiso-sammyaku, Mts Japan	75B1
Kissidougou Guinea	97A4
Kissimmee,L USA	17B2
Kisumu Kenya	99D3
Kisvárda Hung	59C3
Kita Mali	97B3
Kitab USSR	65H6
Kitakata Japan	75C1
Kita-Kyūshū Japan	74C4
Kitale Kenya	99D2
Kitalo, I Japan	69G4
Kitami Japan	74E2
Kitchener Can	7B5
Kitgum Uganda	99D2
Kithira, I Greece	55B3
Kíthnos, I Greece	55B3
Kiti,C Cyprus	94A1
Kitimat Can	5F4
Kitnen, R Fin	38K5
Kitsuki Japan	75A2
Kittanning USA	15C2
Kittilä Fin	38J5
Kitunda Tanz	99D3
Kitwanga Can	13B1
Kitwe Zambia	100B2
Kitzbühel Austria	57C3
Kitzbühel Alpen, Mts Austria	47E1
Kitzingen W Germ	57C3
Kiumbi Zaïre	98C3
Kivalina USA	12B1
Kivercy USSR	59D2
Kivu,L Zaïre/Rwanda	99C3
Kiwalik USA	4B3
Kiyev USSR	60D3
Kizel USSR	61J2
Kizil, R Turk	92C2
Kizyl-Arvat USSR	80D2
Kizyl-Atrek USSR	90B2
Kladno Czech	57C2
Klagenfurt Austria	57C3
Klaipēda USSR	60B2
Klamath USA	8A2
Klamath, R USA	20B2
Klamath Falls USA	8A2
Klamath Mts USA	20B2
Klatovy Czech	57C3
Klawak USA	12H3
Kleiat Leb	94B1
Klerksdorp S Africa	101G1
Klin USSR	60E2
Klintehamn Sweden	58B1
Klintsy USSR	60D3
Ključ Yugos	52C2
Kłodzko Pol	59B2
Klondike, R USA/Can	12G2
Klondike Plat USA/Can	4D3
Klosterneuburg Austria	59B3
Kluane, R Can	12G2
Kluane L Can	12G2
Kluane Nat Pk Can	12G2
Kluczbork Pol	59B2
Klukwan USA	12G3
Klutina L USA	12E2
Knight I USA	12E2
Knighton Wales	43C3
Knin Yugos	52C2
Knob,C Aust	106A4
Knokke-Heist Belg	46B1
Knox Coast Ant	112C9
Knoxville, Tennessee USA	11B3
Knud Ramsussens Land, Region Greenland	6H3
Koba Indon	78B3
Kobbermirebugt Greenland	6F3
Kobe Japan	74D4
København Den	56C1
Koblenz W Germ	57B2
Kobrin USSR	60B3
Kobroör, I Indon	71E4
Kobuk, R USA	12C1
Kočani Yugos	54B2
Ko Chang, I Thai	76C3
Koch Bihar India	86B1
Kochel W Germ	47D1
Koch I Can	6C3
Kōchi Japan	74C4
Kodiak USA	12D3
Kodiak I USA	12D3
Kodikkarai India	87B2
Kodok Sudan	99D2
Koes Namibia	100A3
Koffiefontein S Africa	101G1
Koforidua Ghana	97B4
Kōfu Japan	74D3
Koga Japan	75B1
Køge Den	39G7
Kohat Pak	84C2
Koh-i-Baba, Mts Afghan	84B2
Koh-i-Hisar, Mts Afghan	84B1
Koh-i-Khurd, Mt Afghan	84B2
Kohīma India	86C1
Koh-i-Mazar, Mt Afghan	84B1
Kohlu Pak	84B3
Kohtla Järve USSR	60C2
Koide Japan	75B1
Koidern Can	12F2
Koihoa, Is Nicobar Is	77A4
Kŏje-do, I S Korea	74B4
Kokchetav USSR	65H4
Kokemaki, L Fin	39J6
Kokkola Fin	38J6
Kokoda PNG	107D1
Kokomo USA	14A2
Kokonau Indon	71E4
Kokpekty USSR	65K5
Koksoak, R Can	7D4
Kokstad S Africa	100B4
Ko Kut, I Thai	76C3
Kola USSR	38L5
Kolaka Indon	71D4
Ko Lanta, I Thai	77B4
Kolār India	87B2
Kolār Gold Fields India	87B2
Kolda Sen	97A3
Kolding Den	39F7
Kolhāpur India	87A1
Koliganek USA	12C3

Kolín *Czech*	59B2	Korčula, I *Yugos*	52C2	Kowt-e-Ashrow		Kuala Kubu Baharu	
Köln *W Germ*	57B2	Korea B *China/Korea*	72E2	*Afghan*	84B2	*Malay*	77C5
Kolo *Pol*	58B2	Korea Str *S Korea/*		Köyceğğiz *Turk*	92A2	Kuala Lipis *Malay*	77C5
Kolobrzeg *Pol*	58B2	*Japan*	74B4	Koydor *USSR*	38L5	Kuala Lumpur *Malay*	77C5
Kolokani *Mali*	97B3	Korec *USSR*	59D2	Koyna Res *India*	87A1	Kuala Trengganu	
Kolomna *USSR*	60E2	Körğlu Tepesi, Mt		Koyuk *USA*	12B2	*Malay*	77C4
Kolomyya *USSR*	60C4	*Turk*	92B1	Koyuk, R *USA*	12B1	Kuamut *Malay*	78D1
Kolpashevo *USSR*	65K4	Korhogo *Ivory Coast*	97B4	Koyukuk *USA*	12C2	Kuandian *China*	74A2
Kolpekty *USSR*	68A2	Kori Creek *India*	85B4	Koyukuk, R *USA*	12C1	Kuantan *Malay*	77C5
Kólpos Merabéllou, B		Korinthiakós Kólpos, G		Kozan *Turk*	92C2	Kuba *USSR*	93E1
Greece	55C3	*Greece*	55B3	Kozańi *Greece*	55B2	Kubar *PNG*	71F4
Kólpos Singitikós, G		Kórinthos *Greece*	55B3	Koz'modemyansk		Kuching *Malay*	78C2
Greece	55B2	Kōriyama *Japan*	74E3	*USSR*	61G2	Kudat *Malay*	70C3
Kólpos Strimonikós, G		Korkino *USSR*	61K3	Koztroma *USSR*	61F2	Kudus *Indon*	78C4
Greece	55B2	Korkuteli *Turk*	92B2	Kōzu-shima, I *Japan*	75B2	Kudymkar *USSR*	61H2
Kólpos Toronaíos, G		Korla *China*	82C1	Kragerø *Nor*	39F7	Kufstein *Austria*	57C3
Greece	55B2	Kornat, I *Yugos*	52C2	Kragujevac *Yugos*	54B2	Kuh Duren, Upland	
Kol'skiy Poluostrov,		Köroğlu Tepesi, Mt		Kra,Isthmus of *Burma/*		*Iran*	90C3
Pen *USSR*	38L5	*Turk*	60D5	*Malay*	77B3	Kūh e Bazmān, Mt	
Kolvereid *Nor*	38G6	Korogwe *Tanz*	99D3	Krak des Chevaliers,		*Iran*	91C4
Kolwezi *Zaïre*	100B2	Koroit *Aust*	108B3	Hist Site *Syria*	94C1	Kūh-e Dinar, Mt *Iran*	90B3
Kolyma, R *USSR*	1C7	Koror, Palau Is *Pacific*		Kraków *Pol*	59B2	Kūh-e-Hazār Masjed,	
Kom, Mt *Bulg/Yugos*	54B2	*O*	71E3	Kraljevo *Yugos*	54B2	Mts *Iran*	90C2
Koma *Eth*	99D2	Körös, R *Hung*	59C3	Kramatorsk *USSR*	60E4	Kūh-e Jebāl Barez,	
Komaduga Gana, R		Korosten *USSR*	60C3	Kramfors *Sweden*	38H6	Mts *Iran*	91C4
Nig	97D3	Koro Toro *Chad*	95A3	Kranj *Yugos*	52B1	Kūh-e Karkas, Mts *Iran*	90B3
Komárno *Czech*	59B3	Korovin, I *USA*	12B3	Krapotkin *USSR*	61F4	Kuh-e Laleh Zar, Mt	
Komati, R *S Africa*	101H1	Korsakov *USSR*	69G2	Krasavino *USSR*	61G1	*Iran*	91C4
Komatsu *Japan*	74D3	Korsør *Den*	39G7	Krashnokamsk *USSR*	61J2	Kūh-e Sahand, Mt *Iran*	90A2
Komatsushima *Japan*	75A2	Kortrijk *Belg*	56A2	Krasino *USSR*	64G2	Kuh e Taftān, Mt *Iran*	91D4
Komi, Republic *USSR*	64G3	Kós, I *Greece*	55C3	Kraśnik *Pol*	59C2	Kūhhaye Sabalan, Mts	
Komodo, I *Indon*	70C4	Ko Samui, I *Thai*	77C4	Krasnoarmeysk *USSR*	61G3	*Iran*	90A2
Komoran, I *Indon*	71E4	Koscierzyna *Pol*	58B2	Krasnodar *USSR*	60E5	Kūhjä-ye Zāgros, Mts	
Komoro *Japan*	75B1	Kosciusko, Mt *Aust*	107D4	Krasnotur'insk *USSR*	61K2	*Iran*	90A3
Komotiní *Greece*	55C2	Kosciusko I *USA*	12H3	Krasnoufimsk *USSR*	61J2	Kuhmo *Fin*	38K6
Kompong Cham *Camb*	76D3	Koshikijima-retto, I		Krasnousol'-skiy *USSR*	61J3	Kühpäyeh *Iran*	90B3
Kompong Chhnang,		*Japan*	74B4	Krasnovishersk *USSR*	65G3	Kühpäyeh, Mt *Iran*	90C3
Mts *Camb*	76C3	Košice *Czech*	59C3	Krasnovodsk *USSR*	65G5	Kūh ye Bashäkerd,	
Kompong Som *Camb*	77C3	Kosong *N Korea*	74B3	Krasnoyarsk *USSR*	63B2	Mts *Iran*	91C4
Kompong Thom *Camb*	76C3	Kosovska Mitrovica		Krasnystaw *Pol*	59C2	Kūh ye Sabalan, Mt	
Kompong Trabek		*Yugos*	54B2	Krasnyy Kut *USSR*	61G3	*Iran*	90A2
Camb	76D3	Kossou, L *Ivory Coast*	97B4	Krasnyy Luch *USSR*	60E4	Kuibis *Namibia*	100A3
Komsomol'sk na		Koster *S Africa*	101G1	Krasnyy Yar *USSR*	61G4	Kuigillingok *USA*	4B4
Amure *USSR*	63F2	Kosti *Sudan*	99D1	Kratie *Camb*	76D3	Kuiu I *USA*	12H3
Konda, R *USSR*	65H4	Kostopol' *USSR*	59D2	Kraulshavn *Greenland*	6E2	Kuji *Japan*	74E2
Kondoa *Tanz*	99D3	Kostroma *USSR*	61F2	Krefeld *W Germ*	56B2	Kuju-san, Mt *Japan*	75A2
Kondukūr *India*	87B1	Kostrzyn *Pol*	56C2	Kremenchug *USSR*	60D4	Kukaklek L *USA*	12C3
Kong Christian IX		Koszalin *Pol*	39H8	Kremenchugskoye		Kukës *Alb*	54B2
Land, Region		Kota *India*	85D3	Vodokhranilische,		Kukup *Malay*	77C5
Greenland	6G3	Kotaagung *Indon*	78A4	Res *USSR*	60D4	Kūl, R *Iran*	91C4
Kong Frederik VI Kyst,		Kotabaharu *Indon*	78C3	Kremenets *USSR*	59D2	Kula *Turk*	55C3
Mts *Greenland*	6F3	Kotabaru *Indon*	78D3	Kribi *Cam*	98A2	Kulakshi *USSR*	61J4
Kong Karls Land, Is		Kota Bharu *Malay*	77C4	Krichev *USSR*	60D3	Kulal,Mt *Kenya*	99D2
Barents S	64C2	Kotabum *Indon*	78A3	Krimml *Austria*	47E1	Kulata *Bulg*	55B2
Kongkemul, Mt *Indon*	78D2	Kot Addu *Pak*	84C2	Krinstinestad *Fin*	38J6	Kuldīga *USSR*	60B2
Kongolo *Zaïre*	98C3	Kota Kinabulu *Malay*	78D1	Krishna, R *India*	87B1	Kul'sary *USSR*	61H4
Kongsberg *Den*	39F7	Kotapad *India*	87C1	Krishnagiri *India*	87B2	Kulu *India*	84D2
Kongsvinger *Nor*	39G6	Kotel'nich *USSR*	61G2	Krishnangar *India*	86B2	Kulu *Turk*	92B2
Konin *Pol*	58B2	Kotel'nikovo *USSR*	61F4	Kristiansand *Nor*	39F7	Kulunda *USSR*	65J4
Konjic *Yugos*	54A2	Kotka *Fin*	39K6	Kristianstad *Sweden*	39G7	Kulwin *Aust*	108B2
Konosha *USSR*	61F1	Kotlas *USSR*	64F3	Kristiansund *Nor*	64B3	Kuma, R *USSR*	61G5
Konosu *Japan*	75B1	Kotlik *USA*	12B2	Kristinehamn *Sweden*	39G7	Kumagaya *Japan*	75B1
Konotop *USSR*	60D3	Kotor *Yugos*	54A2	Kríti, I *Greece*	55B3	Kumai *Indon*	78C3
Konsk *USSR*	63B2	Kotovsk *USSR*	60C4	Krivoy Rog *USSR*	60D4	Kumamoto *Japan*	74C4
Końskie *Pol*	59C2	Kotri *Pak*	85B3	Krk, I *Yugos*	52B1	Kumano *Japan*	75B2
Konstanz *W Germ*	49D2	Kottagūdem *India*	87C1	Kronpris Frederik		Kumanovo *Yugos*	54B2
Kontagora *Nig*	97C3	Kottayam *India*	87B3	Bjerge, Mts		Kumara *China*	63E2
Kontum *Viet*	76D3	Kotto, R *CAR*	98C2	*Greenland*	6G3	Kumasi *Ghana*	97B4
Konya *Turk*	92B2	Kottüru *India*	87B2	Kronshtadt *USSR*	39K7	Kumba *Cam*	98A2
Kootenay, R *Can*	13D3	Kotzebue *USA*	12B1	Kroonstad *S Africa*	101G1	Kumbakonam *India*	87B2
Kopargaon *India*	85C5	Kotzebue Sd *USA*	4B3	Kropotkin *USSR*	65F5	Kumertau *USSR*	61J3
Kópasker *Iceland*	6J3	Kouande *Benin*	97C3	Krugersdorp *S Africa*	101G1	Kŭmhwa *S Korea*	74B3
Kópavogur *Iceland*	38A2	Kouango *CAR*	98C2	Krui *Indon*	78A4	Kumla *Sweden*	39H7
Koper *Yugos*	52B1	Koudougou *U Volta*	97B3	Kruje *Alb*	55A2	Kumta *India*	87A2
Kopet Dag, Mts *Iran/*		Koulamoutou *Gabon*	98B3	Krupki *USSR*	58D2	Kümüx *China*	82C1
USSR	80D2	Koulikoro *Mali*	97B3	Krusenstern,C *USA*	12B1	Kunar, R *Afghan*	84C2
Kopeysk *USSR*	61K2	Koupéla *U Volta*	97B3	Kruševac *Yugos*	54B2	Kunda *USSR*	39K7
Ko Phangan, I *Thai*	77C4	Kourou *French Guiana*	33G2	Krustpils *USSR*	39K7	Kundla *India*	85C4
Ko Phuket, I *Thai*	77B4	Kouroussa *Guinea*	97B3	Kruzof I *USA*	12G3	Kunduz *Afghan*	84B1
Köping *Sweden*	39H7	Kousséri *Cam*	98B1	Krym, Pen *USSR*	65E5	Kunene, R *Angola*	89F9
Koppal *India*	87B1	Kouvola *Fin*	39K6	Krym, R *USSR*	60D5	Kungsbacka *Sweden*	39G7
Koprivnica *Yugos*	52C1	Kovel *USSR*	60B3	Krymsk *USSR*	60E5	Kungur *USSR*	61J2
Korangi *Pak*	85B4	Kovrov *USSR*	61F2	Krzyz *Pol*	58B2	Kunhing *Burma*	76B1
Koraput *India*	87C1	Kovvlkino *USSR*	61F3	Ksar El Boukhari *Alg*	96C1	Kunlun Shan, Mts	
Korba *India*	86A2	Kovzha, R *USSR*	60E1	Ksar el Kebir *Mor*	96B1	*China*	82B2
Korbach *W Germ*	57B2	Ko Way, I *Thai*	77C4	Kuala *Indon*	70A3	Kunming *China*	73A4
Korbuk, R *USA*	4B3	Kowloon *Hong Kong*	73C5	Kuala Dungun *Malay*	77C5	Kunsan *S Korea*	74B3
Korçë *Alb*	55B2			Kuala Kerai *Malay*	77C4	Kuopio *Fin*	38K6

Kupa

Lake City, S Carolina USA	17C1
Lake District, Region Eng	42C2
Lake Elsinore USA	22D4
Lake Eyre Basin Aust	106C3
Lakefield Can	15C2
Lake Harbour Can	6D3
Lake Hughes USA	22C3
Lakehurst USA	16B2
Lake Jackson USA	19A4
Lake la Biche Can	13E2
Lakeland USA	17B2
Lake of the Woods Can	7A5
Lake Oswego USA	20B1
Lakeport USA	21A2
Lake Providence USA	19B3
Lake Pukaki NZ	111B2
Lakes Entrance Aust	109C3
Lakeshore USA	22C2
Lake Stewart Aust	108B1
Lake Traverse Can	15C1
Lakeview USA	8A2
Lakeview Mt Can	20B1
Lake Village USA	19B3
Lake Wales USA	17B2
Lakewood, California USA	22C4
Lakewood, New Jersey USA	16B2
Lakewood, Ohio USA	14B2
Lake Worth USA	17B2
Lakhīmpur India	86A1
Lakhpat India	85B4
Lakki Pak	84C2
Lakonikós Kólpos, G Greece	55B3
Lakota Ivory Coast	97B4
Laksefjord, Inlet Nor	38K4
Lakselv Nor	38K4
La Laguna Arg	34C2
La Libertad Ecuador	32A4
La Ligua Chile	34A2
La Linea Spain	50A2
Lalitpur India	85D4
La Loche Can	5H4
la Loche,L Can	13F1
La Louvière Belg	46C1
La Luz Nic	26A4
La Malbaie Can	7C5
La Malinche, Mt Mexico	23B2
La Mancha, Region Spain	50B2
Lamar, Colorado USA	9C3
Lamar, Missouri USA	18B2
La Marque USA	19A4
Lambaréné Gabon	98B3
Lambayeque Peru	32A5
Lambert Gl Ant	112B10
Lambertville USA	16B2
Lamblon,C Can	4F2
Lambro, R Italy	47C2
Lam Chi, R Thai	76C2
Lamego Port	50A1
La Meije, Mt France	47B2
La Merced Peru	32B6
La Mesa USA	21B3
Lamía Greece	55B3
Lammermuir Hills Scot	42C2
Lammhult Sweden	39G7
Lamon B Phil	79B3
Lamoni USA	18B1
Lamotrek, I Pacific O	71F3
Lampeter Wales	43B3
Lamu Kenya	99E3
Lana Italy	47D1
Lanai, I Hawaiian Is	21C4
Lanai City Hawaiian Is	21C4
Lanark Scot	42C2
Lanbi I, Burma	76B3
Lancang, R China	76C1
Lancashire, County Eng	42C3
Lancaster, California USA	21B3
Lancaster Eng	42C2
Lancaster, Mississippi USA	18B1
Lancaster, New Hampshire USA	15D2
Lancaster, Ohio USA	14B3
Lancaster, Pennsylvania USA	10C3
Lancaster, S Carolina USA	17B1
Lancaster Sd Can	6B2
Landak, R Indon	78B3
Landan W Germ	46E2
Landeck Austria	57C3
Lander USA	8C2
Landeta Arg	34C2
Landsberg W Germ	57C3
Lands End, C Can	4F2
Land's End, Pt Eng	43B4
Landshut W Germ	57C3
Làndskrona Sweden	39G7
Lanett USA	17A1
Langenhagen W Germ	56B2
Langenthal Switz	47B1
Langholm Scot	42C2
Langjökull, Mts Iceland	38A2
Langkawi, I Malay	77B4
Langley Can	13C3
Langlo, R Aust	108C1
Langnau Switz	47B1
Langres France	49D2
langsa Indon	70A3
Lang Shan, Mts China	68C2
Lang Son Viet	76D1
Languedoc, Region France	48C3
Lanin, Mt Arg	29B3
Lanoa,L, L Phil	79B4
Lansdale USA	16B2
Lansdowne House Can	7B4
Lansford USA	16B2
Lansing USA	10B2
Lanslebourg France	47B2
Lanzarote, I Canary Is	96A2
Lanzhou China	72A2
Lanzo Torinese Italy	47B2
Laoag Phil	79B2
Lao Cai Viet	76C1
Laoha He, R China	72D1
Laois, County Irish Rep	45C2
Laon France	46B2
La Oroya Peru	32B6
Laos, Republic S E Asia	76C2
Lapalisse France	49C2
La Palma Panama	32A2
La Palma, I Canary Is	96A2
La Pampa, State Arg	34B3
La Paragua Ven	33E2
La Paz Arg	29E2
La Paz Arg	34B2
La Paz Bol	30C2
La Paz Mexico	24A2
La Perouse, Str USSR/Japan	69G2
La Piedad Mexico	23A1
La Pine USA	20B2
Laplace USA	19B3
la Placita Mexico	23A2
La Plata Arg	29E2
La Plonge,L Can	13F1
La Porte USA	14A2
Lappeenranta Fin	39K6
Lappland, Region Sweden/Fin	38H5
Laprida Arg	34C3
Laptev S USSR	1B8
Lapua Fin	38J6
Lapu-Lapu Phil	79B3
La Purisma Mexico	9B4
Laqiya Arba'in, Well Sudan	95B2
La Quiaca Arg	30C3
L'Aquila Italy	52B2
Làr Iran	91B4
Larache Mor	96B1
Laramie USA	8C2
Laramie Range, Mts USA	8C2
Larca Spain	50B2
Laredo USA	9D4
Larestan, Region Iran	91B4
L'Argentière France	47B2
Largo USA	17B2
Largs Scot	42B2
Lāri Iran	90A2
La Rioja Arg	30C4
La Rioja, State Arg	30C4
Lárisa Greece	55B3
Larkana Pak	85B3
Larnaca Cyprus	92B3
Larnaca B Cyprus	94A1
Larne N Ire	45D1
La Robla Spain	50A1
La Roche-en-Ardenne Belg	46C1
La Rochelle France	48B2
La Roche-sur-Foron France	47B1
La Roche-sur-Yon France	48B2
La Roda Spain	51B2
La Romana Dom Rep	27D3
La Ronge Can	5H4
La Ronge,L Can	5H4
Larvik Nor	39F7
Lar'yak USSR	65J3
La Sagra, Mt Spain	50B2
La Salle Can	15D1
La Salle USA	18C1
La Sarre Can	7C5
Las Avispas Arg	34C1
Las Cabras Chile	34A2
Lascombe Can	5G4
Las Cruces USA	9C3
La Selle, Mt Haiti	26C3
Lasengmia China	72B2
La Serena Chile	30B4
Las Flores Arg	29E3
Lashio Burma	76B1
La Sila, Mts Italy	53C3
Lāsjerd Iran	90B2
Las Lajas Chile	34A3
Las Marismas, Marshland Spain	50A2
Las Palmas de Gran Canaria Canary Is	96A2
La Spezia Italy	52A2
Las Plumas Arg	29C4
Las Rosas Arg	34C2
Lassen Peak, Mt USA	20B2
Lassen Volcanic Nat Pk USA	20B2
las Tinai Mexico	23B2
Lastoursville Gabon	98B3
Lastovo, I Yugos	52C2
Las Tres Marias, Is Mexico	24B2
Las Varillas Arg	34C2
Las Vegas USA	9C3
Latina Italy	53B2
La Toma Arg	34B2
La Tortuga, I Ven	32D1
La Trinidad Phil	79B2
Latrobe Aust	109C4
Latrun Israel	94B3
La Tuque Can	7C5
Lātūr India	87B1
Latviyskaya SSR, Republic USSR	60B2
Launceston Aust	107D5
Launceston Eng	43B4
La Unión Chile	29B4
La Union El Salvador	25D3
La Unión Mexico	23A2
La Unión Peru	32B5
Laura Aust	107D2
Laurel, Delaware USA	15C3
Laurel, Maryland USA	16A3
Laurel, Mississippi USA	11B3
Laurens USA	17B1
Laurinburg USA	17C1
Lausanne Switz	52A1
Laut, I Indon	78D3
Lautaro, Mt Chile	29B5
Lauterecken W Germ	46D2
Laval Can	15D1
Laval France	48B2
Laveaga Peak, Mt USA	22B2
Laveno Italy	47C2
Lavras Brazil	31B6
Lavrentiya USSR	4A3
Lavumisa Swaziland	101H1
Lawas Malay	78D1
Lawksawk Burma	76B1
Lawrence, Kansas USA	18A2
Lawrence, Massachusetts USA	15D2
Lawrence NZ	111A3
Lawrenceville, Illinois USA	14A3
Lawton USA	9D3
Layla S Arabia	91A5
Laylo Sudan	99D2
La'youn Mor	96A2
Lázaro Cárdenas Mexico	23A2
Laz Daua Somalia	99E1
Lazi Phil	79B4
Lead USA	8C2
Loader Can	13F2
Leavenworth USA	18A2
Leba Pol	58B2
Lebanon, Missouri USA	18B2
Lebanon, Oregon USA	20B2
Lebanon, Pennsylvania USA	15C2
Lebanon, Republic S W Asia	92C3
Lebombo, Mts Mozam/S Africa/Swaziland	101C3
Lebork Pol	58B2
Le Bourg-d'Oisans France	47A2
Le Brassus Switz	47B1
Lebu Chile	29B3
Le Buet, Mt France	47B1
Le Cateau France	46B1
Lecce Italy	55A2
Lecco Italy	52A1
Lech, R Austria	47D1
Lechtaler Alpen, Mts Austria	47D1
Le Creusot France	49C2
Ledbury Eng	43C3
Leduc Can	13E2
Lee USA	16C1
Lee, R Irish Rep	45B3
Leeds Eng	41C3
Leek Eng	43C3
Leer W Germ	56B2
Leesburg, Florida USA	17B2
Leesburg, Virginia USA	16A3
Leesville USA	19B3
Leeton Aust	109C2
Leeuwarden Neth	56B2
Leeuwin,C Aust	106A4
Lee Vining USA	22C2
Leeward Is Caribbean	27E3
Lefkara Cyprus	94A1
Legazpi Phil	79B3
Legnago Italy	47D2
Legnica Pol	59B2
Leguan Inlet Guyana	33F2
Leguizamo Colombia	32C4
Leh India	84D2
Le Harve France	48C2
Lehigh, R USA	16B2
Lehighton USA	16B2
Leiah Pak	84C2
Leibnitz Austria	59B3
Leicester, County Eng	43D3
Leicester Eng	43D3
Leichhardt, R Aust	107C2
Leiden Neth	56A2
Leie, R Belg	46B1

Leigh Creek

Leigh Creek *Aust*	106C4	Lesser Antilles, Is		
Leighton Buzzard *Eng*	43D4	Caribbean	27D4	
Leine, R *W Germ*	56B2	Lesser Slave L *Can*	13E1	
Leinster, Region *Irish*		Lésvos, I *Greece*	55C3	
Rep	45C2	Leszno *Pol*	58B2	
Leipzig *E Germ*	57C2	Letha Range, Mts		
Leiria *Port*	50A2	Burma	86C2	
Leirvik *Nor*	39F7	Lethbridge *Can*	5G5	
Leitrim, County *Irish*		Lethem *Guyana*	33F3	
Rep	45B1	Letichev *USSR*	59D3	
Leiyang *China*	73C4	Let Oktyobr'ya *USSR*	63D2	
Leizhou Bandao, Pen		Letong *Indon*	78B2	
China	73B5	Le Touquet-Paris-		
Leizhou Wan, B *China*	73C5	Plage *France*	46A1	
Lek, R *Neth*	56A2	Letpadan *Burma*	76B2	
Lekemti *Eth*	99D2	Le Tréport *France*	48C1	
Leland *USA*	19B3	Leuk *Switz*	47B1	
Lelija, Mt *Yugos*	54A2	Leuven *Belg*	57A2	
Le Locle *France*	47B1	Levádhia *Greece*	55B3	
Le Mans *France*	48C2	Levanger *Nor*	38G6	
Lemicux Is *Can*	6D3	Levanna, Mt *Italy*	47B2	
Lemmon *USA*	8C2	Lévêque,C *Aust*	71D5	
Lemoore *USA*	21B2	Leverkusen *W Germ*	46D1	
Lempdes *France*	49C2	Levice *Czech*	59B3	
Lemro, R *Burma*	86C2	Levico *Italy*	47D1	
Le Murge, Region		Levin *NZ*	110C2	
Italy	52C2	Lévis *Can*	7C5	
Lena, R *USSR*	63C2	Levittown *USA*	15D2	
Lendery *USSR*	38L6	Lévka Óri, Mt *Greece*	55B3	
Lengshujiang *China*	73C4	Levkás *Greece*	55B3	
Leninabad *USSR*	82A1	Levkás, I *Greece*	55B3	
Leninakan *USSR*	65F5	Lévque,C *Aust*	106B2	
Leningrad *USSR*	60D2	Levski *Bulg*	54C2	
Leningradskaya, Base		Lewes *Eng*	43E4	
Ant	112B7	Lewis, I *Scot*	40B2	
Leninogorsk, Tatar		Lewisburg *USA*	16A2	
ASSR *USSR*	61H3	Lewis P *NZ*	111B2	
Leninogorsk *USSR*	68A1	Lewis Range, Mts		
Leninsk-Kuznetskiy		USA	8B2	
USSR	65K4	Lewiston, Idaho *USA*	8B2	
Leninskoye *USSR*	69F2	Lewiston, Maine *USA*	10C2	
Lenkoran' *USSR*	65F6	Lewistown, Montana		
Lenne, R *W Germ*	46E1	USA	8C2	
Lenox *USA*	16C1	Lewistown,		
Lens *France*	46B1	Pennsylvania *USA*	15C2	
Lensk *USSR*	63D1	Lewisville *USA*	19B3	
Lentini *Italy*	53B3	Lexington, Kentucky		
Lenya, R *Burma*	76B3	USA	11B3	
Leoben *Austria*	52B1	Lexington, Missouri		
Leominster *Eng*	43C3	USA	18B2	
Leominster *USA*	16D1	Lexington Park *USA*	15C3	
Leon *Mexico*	24B2	Leyte G *Phil*	79C3	
León *Nic*	25D3	Lezhe *Alb*	54A2	
Leon, Region *Spain*	50A1	Lhasa *China*	82D3	
León *Spain*	50A1	Lhazê *China*	86B1	
Leonardville *Namibia*	100A3	Lhokseumawe *Indon*	70A3	
Leonora *Aust*	106B3	Lhozhag *China*	86C1	
Leopoldina *Brazil*	35C2	Lhunze *China*	68B4	
Lepel *USSR*	60C3	Lianga *Phil*	79C4	
Leping *China*	73D4	Liangdang *China*	72B3	
Le Puy *France*	49C2	Lianjiang *China*	73C5	
Léré *Chad*	98B2	Lianping *China*	73C5	
Leribe *Lesotho*	101G1	Lian Xian *China*	73C5	
Lerici *Italy*	47C2	Lianyungang *China*	72D3	
Lérida *Spain*	51C1	Liaoding Bandao, Pen		
Lerma, R *Mexico*	23A1	China	72E1	
Lermoos *Austria*	47D1	Liaodong Wan, B		
Léros, I *Greece*	55C3	China	72E1	
Lerwick *Scot*	40C1	Liao He, R *China*	72E1	
Les Andelys *France*	46A2	Liaoning, Province		
Les Cayes *Haiti*	26C3	China	72E1	
Les Ecrins, Mt		Liaoyang *China*	72E1	
France	47B2	Liaoyuan *China*	72E1	
Leshan *China*	73A4	Liaoyuan *China*	74B2	
Leskovac *Yugos*	54B2	Liard, R *Can*	4F3	
Les Landes, Region		Liard River *Can*	4F4	
France	48B3	Liart *France*	46C2	
Leslie *S Africa*	101G1	Libenge *Zaïre*	98B2	
Lesnoy *USSR*	61H2	Liberal *USA*	9C3	
Lesosibirsk *USSR*	63B2	Liberec *Czech*	57C2	
Lesotho, Kingdom *S*		Liberia, Republic		
Africa	101G1	Africa	97A4	
Lesozavodsk *USSR*	69F2	Liberty, Missouri *USA*	18B2	
Les Sables-d'Olonne		Liberty, New York		
France	48B2	USA	15D2	
Lesser Antarctica,		Liberty, Texas *USA*	19B3	
Region *Ant*	80E	Libourne *France*	48B3	
		libres *Mexico*	23B2	

Libreville *Gabon*	98A2	Linden *Guyana*	33F2
Libya, Republic *Africa*	95A2	Lindesnes, C *Nor*	39F7
Libyan Desert *Libya*	95B2	Lindi *Tanz*	99D3
Libyan Plat *Egypt*	95B1	Lindi, R *Zaïre*	98C2
Licata *Italy*	53B3	Lindley *S Africa*	101G1
Lichfield *Eng*	43D3	Lindos *Greece*	55C3
Lichinga *Mozam*	101C2	Lindsay *Can*	15C2
Lichtenburg *S Africa*	101G1	Line Is *Pacific O*	105J3
Licking, R *USA*	14B3	Linfen *China*	72C2
Lick Observatory *USA*	22B2	Lingao *China*	76D2
Lida *USSR*	60C3	Lingayen *Phil*	79B2
Lidköping *Sweden*	39G7	Lingen *W Germ*	56B2
Lido di Ostia *Italy*	53B2	Lingling *China*	73C4
Liechtenstein,		Lingshan *China*	73B5
Principality *Europe*	52A1	Lingshi *China*	72C2
Liège *Belg*	57B2	Linguère *Sen*	97A3
Lielupe, R *USSR*	58C1	Linhai, Rhejiang *China*	73E4
Lienart *Zaïre*	98C2	Linhares *Brazil*	31D5
Lienz *Austria*	57C3	Linhe *China*	72B1
Liepāja *USSR*	60B2	Linjiang *China*	74B2
Lier *Belg*	46C1	Linköping *Sweden*	39H7
Liestal *Switz*	47B1	Linqing *China*	72D2
Liévre, R *Can*	15C1	Lins *Brazil*	35B2
Liezen *Austria*	57C3	Lintao *China*	72A2
Liffey, R *Irish Rep*	45C2	Linthal *Switz*	47C1
Lifford *Irish Rep*	45C1	Linxi *China*	68D2
Lifu, I *Nouvelle*		Linxia *China*	72A2
Calédonie	107F3	Linz *Austria*	57C3
Lightning Ridge *Aust*	109C1	Lipa *Phil*	79B3
Ligny-en-Barrois		Lipari, I *Italy*	53B3
France	46C2	Lipetsk *USSR*	61E3
Ligonha, R *Mozam*	101C2	Lipova *Rom*	54B1
Liguria, Region *Italy*	47C2	Lippe, R *W Germ*	56B2
Ligurian, S *Italy*	52A2	Lippstadt *W Germ*	46E1
Lihue *Hawaiian Is*	21C4	Lira *Uganda*	99D2
Likasi *Zaïre*	100B2	Liranga *Congo*	98B3
Lille *France*	49C1	Lisala *Zaïre*	98C2
Lillehammer *Nor*	39G6	Lisboa *Port*	50A2
Lillers *France*	46B1	Lisburn *N Ire*	45C1
Lillestøm *Nor*	39G7	Liscannor B *Irish Rep*	45B2
Lil/ Lilooet *Can*	13C2	Lishui *China*	73D4
Lillooet, R *Can*	13C2	Li Shui, R *China*	73C4
Lilongwe *Malawi*	101C2	Lisichansk *USSR*	60E4
Liloy *Phil*	79B4	Lisieux *France*	48C2
Lim, R *Yugos*	54A2	L'Isle-Adam *France*	46B2
Lima *Peru*	32B6	L'Isle-sur-le-Doubs	
Lima *Spain*	50A1	France	47B1
Lima *USA*	10B2	Lismore *Aust*	107E3
Limassol *Cyprus*	92B3	Listowel *Irish Rep*	45B2
Limavady *N Ire*	45C1	Litang *China*	73B5
Limay, R *Arg*	34B3	Litani, R *Leb*	94B2
Limay Mahuida *Arg*	34B3	Litani, R *Suriname*	33G3
Limbe *Malawi*	101C2	Litchfield *USA*	18C2
Limburg *W Gem*	57B2	Lithgow *Aust*	107E4
Limeira *Brazil*	31B6	Lititz *USA*	16A2
Limerick, County *Irish*		Litovko *USSR*	69F2
Rep	45B2	Litovskaya SSR,	
Limerick *Irish Rep*	41B3	Republic *USSR*	60B2
Limfjorden, L *Den*	56B1	Little, R *USA*	19A3
Limmen Bight, B *Aust*	106C2	Little Abaco, I	
Límnos, I *Greece*	55C3	Bahamas	11C4
Limoeiro *Brazil*	31D3	Little Barrier I *NZ*	110C1
Limoges *France*	48C2	Little Bow, R *Can*	13E2
Limón *Costa Rica*	25D4	Little Cayman, I	
Limon *USA*	8C3	Caribbean	25D3
Limousin, Region		Little Egg Harbor, B	
France	48C2	USA	16B3
Linapacan Str *Phil*	79A3	Little Inagua, I	
Linares *Chile*	29B3	Caribbean	26C2
Linares *Mexico*	9D4	Little Nicobar, I	
Linares *Spain*	50B2	Nicobar Is	77A4
Lincang *China*	68B4	Little Rock *USA*	11A3
Lincoln *Arg*	29D2	Littlerock *USA*	22D3
Lincoln, California		Little Smoky *Can*	13D2
USA	18A1	Little Smoky, R *Can*	13D2
Lincoln, County *Eng*	42D3	Littlestown *USA*	16A3
Lincoln *Eng*	42D3	Littleton, New	
Lincoln, Illinois *USA*	18C1	Hampshire *USA*	15D2
Lincoln, Nebraska		Liuhe *China*	74B2
USA	8D2	Liuzhou *China*	73B5
Lincoln, New		Livanátais *Greece*	55B3
Hampshire *USA*	15D2	Līvāni *USSR*	58D1
Lincoln *NZ*	111B2	Livengood *USA*	12E1
Lincoln, S *Greenland*	80A	Live Oak *USA*	17B1
Lincoln City *USA*	20B2	Livermore *USA*	21A2
Lincoln Park *USA*	14B2	Liverpool *Can*	7D5
L'Incudina, Mt *Corse*	52A2	Liverpool *Eng*	42C3
Lindau *W Germ*	57B3	Liverpool B *Can*	4E2

Lübeck

Liverpool B *Eng*	42C3	Loch Torridon, Inlet		Longford *Irish Rep*	45C2	Lough Conn, L *Irish*
Liverpool,C *Can*	6C2	*Scot*	44B3	Long Forties, Region		*Rep* 41B3
Liverpool Range, Mts		Lockerbie *Scot*	108A2	*N Sea*	44D3	Lough Corrib, L *Irish*
Aust	109D2	Lock Aust	42C2	Longhua *China*	72D1	*Rep* 41B3
Livingston, Montana		Lock Haven *USA*	15C2	Long I *Can*	7C4	Lough Derg, L *Irish*
USA	8B2	Lockport *USA*	15C2	Long I *USA*	10C2	*Rep* 41B3
Livingston, Texas *USA*	19B3	Loc Ninh *Viet*	76D3	Long Island Sd *USA*	16C2	Lough Derravaragh, L
Livingston *UK*	44C4	Locri *Italy*	53C3	Longlac *Can*	7B4	*Irish Rep* 45C2
Livingston,L *USA*	19A3	Lod *Israel*	94B3	Longlin *China*	73B5	Loughead I *Can* 4H2
Livno *Yugos*	52C2	Loddon, R *Aust*	108B3	Longmont *USA*	8C2	Lough Ennell, L *Irish*
Livny *USSR*	60E3	Lodeynoye Pole *USSR*	60D1	Longnawan *Indon*	78D2	*Rep* 45C2
Livonia *USA*	14B2	Lodhran *Pak*	84C3	Longquimay *Chile*	29B3	Lough Erne, L *N Ire* 41B3
Livorno *Italy*	52B2	Lodi *Italy*	52A1	Longreach *Aust*	107D3	Lough Foyle, Estuary
Liwale *Tanz*	99D3	Lodi *USA*	21A2	Longshou Shan,		*N Ire/Irish Rep* 40B2
Ljubljana *Yugos*	52B1	Lodja *Zaïre*	98C3	Upland *China*	72A2	Lough Neagh, L *N Ire* 40B3
Ljungan, R *Sweden*	38G6	Lods *France*	47B1	Longtown *Eng*	42C2	Lough Oughter, L *Irish*
Ljungby *Sweden*	39G7	Lodwar *Kenya*	99D2	Longueuil *Can*	15D1	*Rep* 45C1
Ljusdal *Sweden*	39H6	Łódź *Pol*	58B2	Longuimay *Chile*	34A3	Loughrea *Irish Rep* 45B2
Ljusnan, R *Sweden*	38H6	Lofoten, Is *Nor*	38G5	Longuyon *France*	46C2	Lough Ree, L *Irish*
Llandeilo *Wales*	43C4	Logan, Utah *USA*	8B2	Longview, Texas *USA*	11A3	*Rep* 45C2
Llandovery *Wales*	43C4	Logan,Mt *Can*	4D3	Longview, Washington		Lough Sheelin, L *Irish*
Llandrindod Wells		Logansport, Indiana		*USA*	8A2	*Rep* 45C2
Wales	43C3	*USA*	14A2	Longwy *France*	46C2	Lough Strangford, L
Llandudno *Wales*	42C3	Logansport, Louisiana		Longxi *China*	72A3	*Irish Rep* 42B2
Llanelli *Wales*	43B4	*USA*	19B3	Long Xuyen *Viet*	77D3	Lough Swilly, Estuary
Llangollen *Wales*	43C3	Logroño *Spain*	50B1	Longyan *China*	73D4	*Irish Rep* 45C1
Llano Estacado, Plat		Lohārdaga *India*	86A2	Longzhou *China*	73B5	Louisa *USA* 14B3
USA	9C3	Lohja *Fin*	39J6	Lonigo *Italy*	47D2	Louisa Reef, I *S E*
Llanos, Region		Loikaw *Burma*	76B2	Lons-le-Saunier *France*	49D2	*Asia* 70C3
Colombia/Ven	Z4D2	Loimaa *Fin*	39J6	Lookout,C *USA*	11C3	Louise,L *USA* 12E2
Llanos de Chiquitos,		Loir, R *France*	48C2	Loolmalasin, Mt *Tanz*	99D3	Louisiade Arch
Region *Bol*	30D2	Loire, R *France*	49C2	Loon, R *Can*	13D1	*Solomon Is* 107E2
Llerena *Spain*	50A2	Loja *Ecuador*	32B4	Loop Hd, C *Irish Rep*	45B2	Louisiana, State *USA* 11A3
Lleyn, Pen *Wales*	43B3	Loja *Spain*	50B2	Lop Buri *Thai*	76C3	Louisville, Georgia
Llimsk *USSR*	63C2	Lokan Tekojärvi, Res		Lopez, C *Gabon*	98A3	*USA* 17B1
Llin *USSR*	63C2	*Fin*	38K5	Lop Nur, L *China*	68B2	Louisville, Kentucky
Llorin *Nigeria*	89E7	Lokeren *Belg*	46B1	Lora del Rio *Spain*	50A2	*USA* 11B3
Lloydminster *Can*	5H4	Lokitaung *Kenya*	99D2	Lorain *USA*	10B2	Loukhi *USSR* 38L5
Llullaillaco, Mt *Chile/*		Loknya *USSR*	58D1	Loralai *Pak*	84B2	Lourdes *France* 48B3
Arg	30C3	Lokolo, R *Zaïre*	98C3	Lordegán *Iran*	90B3	Louth *Aust* 108C2
Loa, R *Chile*	30C3	Lokoro, R *Zaïre*	98C3	Lord Howe, I *Aust*	107E4	Louth, County *Irish*
Loan *France*	49C2	Loks Land, I *Can*	6D3	Lord Howe Rise		*Rep* 45C2
Loange, R *Zaïre*	98B3	Lolland, I *Den*	56C2	Pacific O	105G5	Louth *Eng* 42D3
Lobatse *Botswana*	100B3	Lom *Bulg*	54B2	Lord Mayor B *Can*	6A3	Louviers *France* 48C2
Lobaye, R *CAR*	98B2	Lomami, R *Zaïre*	98C3	Lordsburg *USA*	9C3	Lovat, R *USSR* 60D2
Loberia *Arg*	34D3	Loma Mts *Sierra*		Lorena *Brazil*	35B2	Lovech *Bulg* 54B2
Lobito *Angola*	100A2	*Leone/Guinea*	97A4	Loreo *Italy*	47E2	Lovelock *USA* 21B1
Lobos *Arg*	34D3	Lombardia, Region		Loreto *Mexico*	23A1	Lóvere *Italy* 52B1
Locano *Italy*	47B2	*Italy*	47C2	Lorient *France*	48B2	Lovington *USA* 9C3
Locarno *Switz*	47C1	Lomblen, I *Indon*	71D4	Lorne *Aust*	108B3	Lovozero *USSR* 38L5
Loch Awe, L *Scot*	44B3	Lombok, I *Indon*	78D4	Lörrach *W Germ*	57B3	Low,C *Can* 6B3
Lochboisdale *Scot*	44A3	Lomé *Togo*	97C4	Lorraine, Region		Lowell, Massachusetts
Loch Bracadale, Inlet		Lomela *Zaïre*	98C3	*France*	49D2	*USA* 10C2
Scot	44A3	Lomela, R *Zaïre*	98C3	Los Alamos *USA*	9C3	Lowell, Oregon *USA* 20B2
Loch Broom, Estuary		Lomonosov *USSR*	60C2	Los Andes *Chile*	34A2	Lowell *USA* 16D1
Scot	44B3	Lomont, Region		Los Angeles *Chile*	29B3	Lower Hutt *NZ* 111B2
Loch Doon, L *Scot*	42B2	*France*	47B1	Los Angeles *USA*	9B3	Lower Seal,L *Can* 7C4
Loch Earn, L *Scot*	44B3	Lompoc *USA*	21A3	Los Banos *USA*	21A2	Lowestoft *Eng* 43E3
Loch Eriboll, Inlet *Scot*	44B2	Łomza *Pol*	58C2	Los Cerrillos *Arg*	34B2	Łowicz *Pol* 58B2
Loch Ericht, L *Scot*	44B3	Lonāvale *India*	87A1	Los Gatos *USA*	21A2	Loxton *Aust* 108B2
Loches *France*	48C2	Loncoche *Chile*	29B3	Lošinj, I *Yugos*	52B2	Loyd George,Mt *Can* 5F4
Loch Etive, Inlet *Scot*	44B3	London *Can*	7B5	Los Lagos *Chile*	29B3	Loznica *Yugos* 54A2
Loch Ewe, Inlet *Scot*	44B3	London *Eng*	43D4	Los Mochis *Mexico*	24B2	loz Reyes *Mexico* 23A2
Loch Fyne, Inlet *Scot*	44B3	Londonderry, County		Los Olivos *USA*	22B3	Lozva, R *USSR* 65H3
Loch Hourn, Inlet *Scot*	44B3	*N Ire*	45C1	Los Sauces *Chile*	34A3	Luacano *Angola* 100B2
Lochinver *Scot*	44B2	Londonderry *N Ire*	45C1	Lossiemouth *Scot*	44C3	Luachimo *Angola* 98C3
Loch Katrine, L *Scot*	44B3	Londonderry, I *Chile*	29B7	Los Testigos, Is *Ven*	27E4	Lualaba, R *Zaïre* 98C3
Loch Leven, L *Scot*	44C3	Londonderry,C *Aust*	106B2	Los Vilos *Chile*	29B2	Luampa *Zambia* 100B2
Loch Linnhe, Inlet		Londres *Arg*	30C4	Lot, R *France*	48C3	Luân *Angola* 100B2
Scot	44B3	Londrina *Brazil*	30F3	Lota *Chile*	34A3	Lu'an *China* 73D3
Loch Lochy, L *Scot*	44B3	Lone Pine *USA*	21B2	Lothian, Region *Scot*	42C2	Luanda *Angola* 98B3
Loch Lomond, L *Scot*	44B3	Long, I *Bahamas*	11C4	Lotikipi Plain *Sudan/*		Luando, R *Angola* 100A2
Loch Long, Inlet *Scot*	44B3	Long, I *PNG*	71F4	*Kenya*	99D2	Luanginga, R *Angola* 100B2
Lochmaddy *Scot*	44A3	Long Akah *Malay*	78C2	Loto *Zaïre*	98C3	Luang Namtha *Laos* 76C1
Loch Maree, L *Scot*	44B3	Longarone *Italy*	47E1	Lötschberg Tunnel		Luang Prabang *Laos* 76C2
Loch Morar, L *Scot*	44B3	Longavi, Mt *Chile*	34A3	*Switz*	47B1	Luangue, R *Angola* 98B3
Lochnagar, Mt *Scot*	44C3	Long B *Jamaica*	27H2	Lotta, R *Fin/USSR*	38K5	Luangwa, R *Zambia* 100C2
Loch Noss, L *Scot*	44B3	Long B *USA*	17C1	Loudéac *France*	48B2	Luan He, R *China* 72D1
Loch Rannoch, L *Scot*	44B3	Long Beach, California		Louga *Sen*	97A3	Luanping *China* 72D1
Loch Roag, Inlet *Scot*	44A2	*USA*	9B3	Lough Allen, L *Irish*		Luanshya *Zambia* 100B2
Loch Sheil, L *Scot*	44B3	Long Beach, New		*Rep*	41B3	Luapula, R *Zaïre* 100B2
Loch Shin, L *Scot*	44B2	York *USA*	15D2	Lough Boderg, L *Irish*		Luarca *Spain* 50A1
Loch Snizort, Inlet		Long Branch *USA*	15D2	*Rep*	45C2	Lubalo *Angola* 98B3
Scot	44A3	Longchuan *China*	73D5	Loughborough *Eng*	43D3	L'uban *USSR* 58D2
Loch Sunart, Inlet		Long Creek *USA*	20C2	Lough Bowna, L *Irish*		Lubang Is *Phil* 79B3
Scot	44B3	Longford *Aust*	109C4	*Rep*	45C2	Lubango *Angola* 100A2
Loch Tay, L *Scot*	44B3	Longford, County *Irish*		Lough Carlingford, L		Lubbock *USA* 9C3
		Rep	45C2	*N Ire*	45C1	Lübeck *W Germ* 56C2

Lubefu

Magdalena *Mexico*	24A1
Magdalena, R *Colombia*	26C4
Magdalena,Mt *Malay*	78D1
Magdalen Is *Can*	7D5
Magdeburg *E Germ*	56C2
Magé *Brazil*	31C6
Magelang *Indon*	78C4
Maggia, R *Switz*	47C1
Maghâgha *Egypt*	92B4
Magherafelt *N Ire*	45C1
Maglie *Italy*	55A2
Magnitogorsk *USSR*	61J3
Magnolia *USA*	19B3
Magoé *Mozam*	101C2
Magog *Can*	15D1
Magosal *Mexico*	23B1
Magrath *Can*	13E2
Maguse River *Can*	7A3
Magwe *Burma*	76B1
Mahābād *Iran*	90A2
Mahabharat Range, Mts *Nepal*	86B1
Mahād *Iran*	87A1
Mahadeo Hills *India*	85D4
Mahajanga *Madag*	101D2
Mahalapye *Botswana*	100B3
Mahānadi, R *India*	86A2
Mahanoro *Madag*	101D2
Mahanoy City *USA*	16A2
Maharashtra, State *India*	87A1
Māhāsamund *India*	86A2
Maha Sarakham *Thai*	76C2
Mahavavy, R *Madag*	101D2
Mahbūbnagar *India*	87B1
Mahdia *Tunisia*	96D1
Mahe *India*	87B2
Mahekar *India*	85D4
Mahéli, I *Comoros*	101D2
Mahendragarh *India*	86A2
Mahenge *Tanz*	99D3
Mahesāna *India*	85C4
Mahia Pen *NZ*	110C1
Mahoba *India*	85D3
Mahón *Spain*	51C2
Mahony L *Can*	12J1
Mahrès *Tunisia*	96D1
Mahuva *India*	85C4
Maicao *Colombia*	32C1
Maîche *France*	47B1
Maidstone *Eng*	43E4
Maiduguri *Nig*	98B1
Maihar *India*	86A2
Maijdi *Bang*	86C2
Mail Kyun, I *Burma*	76B3
Maimana *Afghan*	84A1
Main Chan *Can*	14B1
Mai-Ndombe, L *Zaïre*	98B3
Maine, State *USA*	10D2
Maine, Region *France*	48B2
Mainland, I *Scot*	44C2
Mainpuri *India*	85D3
Maintenon *France*	46A2
Maintirano *Madag*	101D2
Mainz *W Germ*	57B2
Maio, I *Cape Verde*	97A4
Maipó, Mt *Arg/Chile*	29C2
Maipú *Arg*	34D3
Maiquetía *Ven*	32D1
Maira, R *Italy*	47B2
Mairābāri *India*	86C1
Maiskhal I *Bang*	86C2
Maitland, New South Wales *Aust*	107E4
Maitland, S Australia *Aust*	108A2
Maizuru *Japan*	74D3
Majene *Indon*	70C4
Majes, R *Peru*	30B2
Maji *Eth*	99D2
Majia He, R *China*	72D2
Makale *Eth*	99D1
Makale *Indon*	70C4
Makalu, Mt *China/Nepal*	86B1
Makarska *Yugos*	52C2
Makaryev *USSR*	61F2
Makassar Str *Indon*	78D3
Makat *USSR*	61H4
Makeni *Sierra Leone*	97A4
Makeyevka *USSR*	60E4
Makgadikgadi, Salt Pan *Botswana*	100B3
Makhachkala *USSR*	61G5
Makindu *Kenya*	99D3
Makkovik *Can*	7E4
Makó *Hung*	59C3
Makokou *Gabon*	98B2
Makorako,Mt *NZ*	110C1
Makoua *Congo*	98B2
Makrāna *India*	85C3
Makran Coast Range, Mts *Pak*	85A3
Maktar *Tunisia*	96C1
Mākü *Iran*	93D2
Makumbi *Zaïre*	98C3
Makurazaki *Japan*	74C4
Makurdi *Nig*	97C4
Malabang *Phil*	79B4
Malabar Coast *India*	87A2
Malabo *Bioko*	89E7
Malacca,Str of *S E Asia*	77C5
Málaga *Colombia*	32C2
Malaga *Spain*	50B2
Malaimbandy *Madag*	101D3
Malaita, I *Solomon Is*	107F1
Malakal *Sudan*	99D2
Malakand *Pak*	84C2
Malang *Indon*	78C4
Malange *Angola*	98B3
Malanville *Benin*	97C3
Malargüe *Arg*	34B3
Malaspina Gl *USA*	12F3
Malatya *Turk*	93C2
Malawi, Republic *Africa*	101C2
Malaybalay *Phil*	79C4
Malāyer *Iran*	90A3
Malaysia, Federation *S E Asia*	70B3
Malazgirt *Turk*	93D2
Malbork *Pol*	58B2
Malchin *E Germ*	56C2
Malden *USA*	18C2
Maldives Is *Indian O*	83B5
Maldives Ridge *Indian O*	104B4
Maldonado *Urug*	29F2
Male *Italy*	47D1
Malegaon *India*	85C4
Malé Karpaty, Upland *Czech*	59B3
Malema *Mozam*	101C2
Mālestān *Afghan*	84B2
Maleuz *USSR*	61J3
Malgomaj, L *Sweden*	38H5
Malha, Well *Sudan*	95B3
Malheur L *USA*	20C2
Mali, Republic *Africa*	97B3
Malinau *Indon*	78D1
Malindi *Kenya*	99E3
Malin Head, Pt *Irish Rep*	40B2
Malkala Range, Mts *India*	86A2
Malkāpur *India*	85D4
Malkara *Turk*	55C2
Malko Türnovo *Bulg*	54C2
Mallaig *Scot*	44B3
Mallawi *Egypt*	95C2
Málles Venosta *Italy*	47D1
Mallorca, I *Spain*	51C2
Mallow *Irish Rep*	45B2
Malm *Nor*	38G6
Malmberget *Sweden*	38J5
Malmédy *W Germ*	46D1
Malmesbury *Eng*	43C4
Malmesbury *S Africa*	100A4
Malmö *Sweden*	39G7
Malmyzh *USSR*	61G2
Malolos *Phil*	79B3
Malone *USA*	15D2
Maloti Mts *Lesotho*	101G1
Mâloy *Nor*	38F6
Malpelo, I *Colombia*	28A2
Malpo, R *Chile*	34A2
Mālpura *India*	85D3
Malta, Montana *USA*	8C2
Malta, Chan *Malta/Italy*	53B3
Malta, I *Medit S*	53B3
Maltahöhe *Namibia*	100A3
Malton *Eng*	42D2
Malung *Sweden*	39G6
Mālvan *India*	87A1
Malvern *USA*	19B3
Malwa Plat *India*	85D4
Malyy Kavkaz, Mts *USSR*	65F5
Malyy Uzen', R *USSR*	H006
Mama *USSR*	63D2
Mamadysh *USSR*	61H2
Mambasa *Zaïre*	99C2
Mamberamo, R *Indon*	71E4
Mambéré, R *CAR*	98B2
Mamfé *Cam*	98A2
Mamoré, R *Bol*	33D6
Mamou *Guinea*	97A3
Mampikony *Madag*	101D2
Mampong *Ghana*	97B4
Mamshit, Hist Site *Israel*	94B3
Mamuno *Botswana*	100B3
Man *Ivory Coast*	97B4
Mana *Hawaiian Is*	21C4
Manabo *Madag*	101D3
Manacapuru *Brazil*	33E4
Manacor *Spain*	51C2
Manado *Indon*	71D3
Managua *Nic*	25D3
Manakara *Madag*	101D3
Mananara *Madag*	101D2
Mananjary *Madag*	101D3
Manapouri *NZ*	111A3
Manapouri,L *NZ*	111A3
Manas *Bhutan*	86C1
Manas *China*	82C1
Manas Hu, L *China*	65K5
Manaslu, Mt *Nepal*	86A1
Manasquan *USA*	16B2
Manaus *Brazil*	33F4
Manavgat *Turk*	92B2
Manbij *Syria*	93C2
Man,Calf of, I *Eng*	42B2
Mancheral *India*	87B1
Manchester, Connecticut *USA*	15D2
Manchester *Eng*	42C3
Manchester, New Hampshire *USA*	10C2
Manchester, Pennsylvania *USA*	16A2
Manchuria, Hist Region *China*	69E2
Mand, R *Iran*	91B4
Manda *Tanz*	101C2
Mandaguari *Brazil*	35A2
Mandal *Nor*	39F7
Mandalay *Burma*	76B1
Mandalgovi *Mongolia*	68C2
Mandal Ovoo *Mongolia*	72A1
Mandalya Körfezi, B *Turk*	55C3
Mandan *USA*	8C2
Mandelona *USA*	14A2
Mandera *Eth*	99E2
Mandeville *Jamaica*	26B3
Mandidzudzure *Zim*	100C2
Mandimba *Mozam*	101C2
Mandla *India*	86A2
Mandritsara *Madag*	101D2
Mandsaur *India*	85D4
Manduria *Italy*	53C2
Māndvi *India*	85B4
Mandya *India*	87B2
Manevichi *USSR*	58D2
Manfield *Eng*	42D3
Manfredonia *Italy*	53C2
Manga, Desert Region *Niger*	98B1
Mangakino *NZ*	110C1
Mangalia *Rom*	54C2
Mangalmé *Chad*	98B1
Mangalore *India*	87A2
Manggar *Indon*	78B3
Mangnia *China*	68B3
Mangoche *Malawi*	101C2
Mangoky, R *Madag*	101D3
Mangole, I *Indon*	71D4
Māngral *India*	85B4
Mangui *China*	63E2
Manhattan *USA*	8D3
Manhuacu *Brazil*	31C6
Mania, R *Madag*	101D2
Manica *Mozam*	101C2
Manicouagan, R *Can*	7D5
Manicouagan Res *Can*	7D4
Manifah *S Arabia*	91A4
Manila *Phil*	79B3
Manilla *Aust*	109D2
Maninian *Ivory Coast*	97B3
Manipur, State *India*	86C2
Manipur, R *Burma*	86C2
Manisa *Turk*	92A2
Man,Isle of *Irish Sea*	41C3
Manistee *USA*	14A2
Manistee, R *USA*	14A2
Manistique *USA*	14A1
Manitoba, Province *Can*	5H4
Manitoba,L *Can*	5J4
Manito L *Can*	13F2
Manitou Is *USA*	14A1
Manitoulin, I *Can*	7B5
Manitowoc *USA*	14A2
Maniwaki *Can*	15C1
Manizales *Colombia*	32B2
Manja *Madag*	101D3
Manjimup *Aust*	106A4
Mānjra, R *India*	87B1
Mankato *USA*	10A2
Mankono *Ivory Coast*	97B4
Manley Hot Springs *USA*	12D2
Manly *NZ*	110B1
Manmād *India*	85C4
Manna *Indon*	78A3
Mannahill *Aust*	108A2
Mannar *Sri Lanka*	87B3
Mannār,G of *India*	87B3
Mannārgudi *India*	87B2
Mannheim *W Germ*	57B3
Manning *Can*	13D1
Manning *USA*	17B1
Mannum *Aust*	108A2
Mano *Sierra Leone*	97A4
Manokwari *Indon*	71E4
Manono *Zaïre*	98C3
Manoron *Burma*	76B3
Mano-wan, B *Japan*	75B1
Manp'o *N Korea*	74B2
Mānsa *India*	84D3
Mansa *Zambia*	100B2
Mansel I *Can*	6B3
Mansfield, Arkansas *USA*	19B2
Mansfield *Aust*	108C3
Mansfield, Louisiana *USA*	19B3
Mansfield, Massachusetts *USA*	16D1
Mansfield, Ohio *USA*	10B2
Mansfield, Pennsylvania *USA*	15C2
Mansyu Deep *Pacific O*	71E2
Manta *Ecuador*	32A4
Mantalingajan,Mt *Phil*	79A4
Mantaro, R *Peru*	32B6
Manteca *USA*	22B2
Mantes *France*	48C2
Mantova *Italy*	52B1
Mantta *Fin*	38J6
Manturovo *USSR*	61F2
Manuel Ribas *Brazil*	35A2
Manukan *Phil*	79B4
Manukau *NZ*	110B1
Manus, I *Pacific O*	71F4

Manzanares

44

Mayaguana, I Bahamas	11C4
Mayagüez Puerto Rico	27D3
Mayahi Niger	97C3
Mayama Congo	98B3
Mayamey Iran	90C2
Maybole Scot	42B2
May,C USA	10C3
Maydena Aust	109C4
Mayen W Germ	46D1
Mayenne France	48B2
Mayerthorpe Can	13D2
Mayfield USA	18C2
Maykop USSR	61E5
Maymaneh Afghan	65H6
Maymyo Burma	76B1
Mayo Can	4E3
Mayo, County Irish Rep	45B2
Mayo USA	16A3
Mayo,Mts of Irish Rep	45B1
Mayon, Mt Phil	79B3
Mayor, Mt Spain	51C2
Mayor Buratovich Arg	34C3
Mayor I NZ	110C1
Mayor P Lagerenza Par	30D2
Mayotte, I Indian O	101D2
May Pen Jamaica	27H2
May Point,C USA	16B3
Mayrhofen Austria	47D1
Mays Landing USA	16B3
Maysville USA	14B3
Mayumba Gabon	98B3
Mazabuka Zambia	100B2
Mazar China	84D1
Mazār Jordan	94B3
Mazara del Vallo Italy	53B3
Mazar-i-Sharif Afghan	84B1
Mazatlán Mexico	24B2
Mazeikiai USSR	60B2
Mazra Jordan	94B3
Mbabane Swaziland	101C3
Mbaïki CAR	98B2
Mbala Zambia	99D3
Mbalabala Zim	100B3
Mbale Uganda	99D2
Mbalmayo Cam	98B2
Mbam, R Cam	98B2
Mbamba Bay Tanz	101C2
Mbandaka Zaïre	98B2
Mbanza Congo Angola	98B3
Mbanza-Ngungu Zaïre	98B3
Mbarara Uganda	99D3
Mbènza Congo	98B2
Mbére, R Cam	98B2
Mbeya Tanz	99D3
Mbinda Congo	98B3
Mbout Maur	97A3
Mbuji-Mayi Zaïre	98C3
Mbulu Tanz	99D3
Mcherrah, Region Alg	96B2
Mchinji Malawi	101C2
Mdrak Viet	76D3
Mead,L USA	9B3
Meadow Lake Can	5H4
Meadville USA	14B2
Mealy Mts Can	7E4
Meandarra Aust	109C1
Meander River Can	5G4
Meath, County Irish Rep	45C2
Meaux France	49C2
Mechanicville USA	16C1
Mechelen Belg	56A2
Mecheria Alg	96B1
Mecklenburger Bucht, B E Germ	56C2
Meconta Mozam	101C2
Mecuburi Mozam	101C2
Mecufi Mozam	101D2
Mecula Mozam	101C2
Medan Indon	70A3
Medanos Arg	34C3
Médanos Arg	34D2
Medecine Hat Can	13E2
Medellin Colombia	32B2
Medenine Tunisia	96D1
Medford USA	8A2
Medgidia Rom	54C2
Media Agua Arg	34B2
Mediaş Rom	54B1
Medical Lake USA	20C1
Medicine Hat Can	5G5
Medina Brazil	35C1
Medina S Arabia	80B3
Medinaceli Spain	50B1
Medina del Campo Spain	50B1
Medina de Rio Seco Spain	50A1
Medinīpur India	86B2
Mediterranean S Europe	88E4
Medley Can	13F2
Mednogorsk USSR	61J3
Mêdog China	86D1
Medouneu Gabon	98B2
Medvedista, R USSR	61F3
Medvezh'yegorsk USSR	64E3
Meekatharra Aust	106A3
Meerut India	84D3
Mega Eth	99D2
Megalópolis Greece	55B3
Mégara Greece	55B3
Meghālaya, State India	86C1
Meghna, R Bang	86C2
Megido, Hist Site Israel	94B2
Mehran, R Iran	91B4
Mehriz Iran	90B3
Meia Ponte, R Brazil	35B1
Meiganga Cam	98B2
Meiktila Burma	76B1
Meiringen Switz	47C1
Meishan China	73A4
Meissen E Germ	57C2
Mei Xian China	73D5
Meizhou China	73D5
Mejillones Chile	30B3
Mekambo Gabon	98B2
Meknès Mor	96B1
Mekong, R Camb	76D3
Mekrou, R Benin	97C3
Melaka Malay	77C5
Melanesia, Region Pacific O	104F4
Melawi, R Indon	78C3
Melbourne Aust	107D4
Melbourne USA	11B4
Melchor Muźguiz Mexico	9C4
Melfi Chad	98B1
Melfort Can	5H4
Melilla N W Africa	96B1
Melimoyu, Mt Chile	29B4
Melincué Arg	34C2
Melipilla Chile	34A2
Melitopol' USSR	60E4
Meliville Bugt, B Greenland	6D2
Melmoth S Africa	101H1
Melo Arg	34C2
Melo Urug	29F2
Melones Res USA	22B2
Melozitna, R USA	12D1
Mels Switz	47C1
Melton Mowbray Eng	43D3
Melun France	49C2
Melville Can	5H4
Melville,C Dominica	27Q2
Melville Hills, Mts Can	4F3
Melville I Aust	106C2
Melville I Can	4G2
Melville,L Can	7E4
Melville Pen Can	6B3
Melvin,L Irish Rep	45B1
Memba Mozam	101D2
Memboro Indon	106A1
Memmingen W Germ	57C3
Mempawan Indon	78B2
Memphis, Tennessee USA	11B3
Mena USA	19B3
Menai Str Wales	43B3
Ménaka Mali	97C3
Menasha USA	14A2
Mendawai, R Indon	78C3
Mende France	49C3
Mendebo, Mts Eth	99D2
Mendip Hills, Upland Eng	43C4
Mendocino,C USA	20B2
Mendocino Seascarp Pacific O	105J2
Mendota, California USA	22B2
Mendoza Arg	29C2
Mendoza, State Arg	29C3
Menemen Turk	55C3
Menen Belg	46B1
Mengcheng China	72D3
Menggala Indon	78B3
Menghai China	76B1
Mengla China	73A5
Menglian China	76B1
Mengzi China	73A5
Menindee Aust	107D4
Menindee L Aust	108B2
Meningie Aust	108A3
Menominee USA	14A1
Menomonee Falls USA	14A2
Menongue Angola	100A2
Menorca, I Spain	51C1
Mentasta Mts USA	12F2
Mentok Indon	78B3
Mentor USA	14B2
Ménu France	46B2
Menyuan China	72A2
Menzelinsk USSR	61H2
Meppen W Germ	56B2
Merah Indon	78D2
Meramec, R USA	18B2
Merano Italy	52B1
Merauke Indon	71F4
Merced USA	8A3
Merced, R USA	22B2
Mercedario, Mt Chile	29B2
Mercedes Arg	29C2
Mercedes, Buenos Aires Arg	29E2
Mercedes, Corrientes Arg	30E4
Mercedes Urug	29E2
Mercury B NZ	110C1
Mercury Is NZ	110C1
Mercy B Can	4F2
Mercy,C Can	6D3
Meregh Somalia	99E2
Mergui Burma	76B3
Mergui Arch Burma	76B3
Mérida Mexico	25D2
Mérida Spain	50A2
Mérida Ven	32C2
Meridian USA	11B3
Merimbula Aust	109C3
Meringur Aust	108B2
Merowe Sudan	95C3
Merredin Aust	106A4
Merrick, Mt Scot	42B2
Merrillville USA	14A2
Merritt Can	13C2
Merritt Island USA	17B2
Merriwa Aust	109D2
Mersa Fatma Eth	99E1
Mers el Kebir Alg	51B2
Mersey, R Eng	42C3
Merseyside, Metropolitan County Eng	42C3
Mersin Turk	92B2
Mersing Malay	77C5
Merta India	85C3
Merthyr Tydfil Wales	43C4
Mertola Port	50A2
Meru, Mt Tanz	99D3
Merzifon Turk	60E5
Merzig W Germ	46D2
Mesa USA	9B3
Meschede W Germ	46E1
Mescit Dağ, Mt Turk	93D1
Meshik USA	12C3
Meshra Er Req Sudan	99C2
Mesocco Switz	47C1
Mesolóngion Greece	55B3
Mesquite, Texas USA	19A3
Messalo, R Mozam	101C2
Messina Italy	53C3
Messina S Africa	100B3
Messíni Greece	55B3
Messiniakós Kólpos, G Greece	55B3
Mesta, R Bulg	54B2
Mestre Italy	52B1
Meta, R Colombia	32C3
Meta, R USSR	60D2
Meta, R Ven	32D2
Meta Incognito Pen Can	6C3
Metairie USA	19B4
Metaline Falls USA	20C1
Metán Arg	30D4
Metangula Mozam	101C2
Metaponto Italy	53C2
Methil Scot	44C3
Methuen USA	16D1
Methven NZ	111B2
Metlakatla USA	12H3
Metropolis USA	18C2
Mettür India	87B2
Metz France	49D2
Meulaboh Indon	70A3
Meulan France	46A2
Meuse, Department France	46C2
Meuse, R France	49D2
Mexia USA	19A3
Mexicali Mexico	24A1
Mexico, Federal Republic Central America	24B2
México Mexico	24C3
México, State Mexico	23A2
Mexico USA	18B2
Mexico,G of C America	24C2
Mezada, Hist Site Israel	94B3
Mezcala Mexico	23B2
Mezen' USSR	64F3
Mezhdusharskiy, I USSR	64G3
Mhow India	85D4
Miahuatlán Mexico	23B2
Miami, Florida USA	11B4
Miami, Oklahoma USA	18B2
Miami Beach USA	11B4
Miandowāb Iran	90A2
Miandrivazo Madag	101D2
Miāneh Iran	90A2
Mianwali Pak	84C2
Mianyang China	73A3
Mianyang China	73C3
Mianzhu China	73A3
Miaodao Qundao, Arch China	72E2
Miao Ling, Upland China	73B4
Miass USSR	61K3
Michalovce Czech	59C3
Miches Dom Rep	27D3
Michigan, State USA	10B2
Michigan City USA	14A2
Michigan,L USA	10B2
Michipicoten I Can	7B5
Michoacan, State Mexico	23A2
Michunnsk USSR	65F4
Michurin Bulg	54C2
Michurinsk USSR	61F3
Micronesia, Region Pacific O	104F3
Midai, I Indon	78B2
Mid Atlantic Ridge Atlantic O	102F4
Middelburg Neth	46B1

Moudon

Mys Kanin Nos, C *USSR*	64F3
Myślenice *Pol*	59B3
Mys Lopatka, C *USSR*	69H1
Mysore *India*	87B2
Mys Sarych, C *USSR*	60D5
Mystic *USA*	16D2
Mys Tyub-Karagan, Pt *USSR*	61H5
Mys Yelizavety, C *USSR*	63G2
Mys Zhelaniya, C *USSR*	64H2
My Tho *Viet*	77D3
Mytle Point *USA*	20B2
Mzimba *Malawi*	101C2
Mzuzú *Malawi*	101C2

N

Naalehu *Hawaiian Is*	21C4
Naantali *Fin*	39J6
Naas *Irish Rep*	45C2
Nabari *Japan*	75B2
Nabesna, R *USA*	12F2
Nabeul *Tunisia*	96D1
Nablus *Israel*	94B2
Nacala *Mozam*	101D2
Naches *USA*	20B1
Nachingwea *Tanz*	101C2
Nacogdoches *USA*	19B3
Nacondam, I *Indian O*	76A3
Nacozari *Mexico*	24B1
Nadiād *India*	85C4
Nador *Mor*	50B2
Nadūshan *Iran*	90B3
Nadvornaya *USSR*	59C3
Naestved *Den*	56C1
Nafoora *Libya*	95B2
Nagahama *Japan*	75A2
Naga Hills *Burma*	82D3
Nagai *Japan*	75B1
Nāgāland, State *India*	86C1
Nagano *Japan*	74D3
Nagaoka *Japan*	74D3
Nāgappattinam *India*	87B2
Nagar Parkar *Pak*	85C4
Nagasaki *Japan*	74B4
Nagashima *Japan*	75B2
Nagato *Japan*	75A2
Nāgaur *India*	85C3
Nāgercoil *India*	87B3
Nagha Kalat *Pak*	85B3
Nagīna *India*	84D3
Nagoya *Japan*	74D3
Nāgpur *India*	85D4
Nagqu *China*	82D2
Nagykanizsa *Hung*	59B3
Nagykörös *Hung*	59B3
Naha *Japan*	69E4
Nahaimo *Can*	8A2
Nāhan *India*	84D2
Nahanni Butte *Can*	4F3
Nahariya *Israel*	94B2
Nahāvand *Iran*	90A3
Nahe, R *W Germ*	46D2
Nahpu *China*	72D2
Naimen Qi *China*	72E1
Nain *Can*	7D4
Nā'īn *Iran*	90B3
Naini Tai *India*	84D3
Nairn *Scot*	44C3
Nairobi *Kenya*	99D3
Najafābād *Iran*	90B3
Najin *N Korea*	74C2
Nakama *Japan*	75A2
Nakaminato *Japan*	74E3
Nakamura *Japan*	75A2
Nakano *Japan*	75B1
Nakano-shima, I *Japan*	75A1
Nakatsu *Japan*	74C4
Nakatsu-gawa *Japan*	75B1
Nakfa *Eth*	95C3
Nakhichevan *USSR*	93E2
Nakhl *Egypt*	92B4
Nakhodka *USSR*	74C2
Nakhon Pathom *Thai*	76C3

Nakhon Ratchasima *Thai*	76C3
Nakhon Si Thammarat *Thai*	77C4
Nakina *Can*	12H3
Nakina, Ontario *Can*	7B4
Naknek *USA*	12C3
Naknek L *USA*	12C3
Nakrek *USA*	4C4
Nakskov *Den*	39G8
Nakuru *Kenya*	99D3
Nakusp *Can*	13D2
Nal'chik *USSR*	61F5
Nalgonda *India*	87B1
Nallamala Range, Mts *India*	87B1
Namaacha *Mozam*	101H1
Namak, L *Iran*	65G6
Namakzar-e Shadad, Salt Flat *Iran*	90C3
Namangan *USSR*	65J5
Namapa *Mozam*	101C2
Namaqualand, Region *S Africa*	100A4
Nambour *Aust*	109D1
Nambucca Heads *Aust*	109D2
Nam Can *Viet*	77D4
Namcha Barwa, Mt *China*	82D3
Nam Co, L *China*	82D2
Nam Dinh *Viet*	76D1
Nametil *Mozam*	101C2
Namhae-do, I *S Korea*	74B4
Namib Desert *Namibia*	100A2
Namibe *Angola*	100A2
Namibia, Dependency *Africa*	100A3
Namlea *Indon*	71D4
Namoi, R *Aust*	109C2
Nampa *Can*	13D1
Nampa *USA*	20C2
Nampala *Mali*	97B3
Nam Phong *Thai*	76C2
Namp'o *N Korea*	74B3
Nampula *Mozam*	101C2
Namsos *Nor*	38G6
Namton *Burma*	76B1
Namtu *Burma*	86D2
Namu *Can*	13B2
Namuno *Mozam*	101C2
Namur *Belg*	46C1
Namutoni *Namibia*	100A2
Namwŏn *S Korea*	74B3
Nanaimo *Can*	13C3
Nanam *N Korea*	74B2
Nanango *Aust*	109D1
Nanao *Japan*	74D3
Nanatsu-jima, I *Japan*	75B1
Nanbu *China*	73B3
Nanchang *China*	73D4
Nanchong *China*	73B3
Nancy *France*	49D2
Nānded *India*	87B1
Nandewar Range, Mts *Aust*	109D2
Nandurbar *India*	85C4
Nandyāl *India*	87B1
Nanga Eboko *Cam*	98B2
Nanga Parbat, Mt *Pak*	84C1
Nangapinoh *Indon*	78C3
Nangatayap *Indon*	78C3
Nangnim Sanmaek, Mts *N Korea*	74B2
Nang Xian *China*	86C1
Nangzhou *China*	67F3
Nanjangüd *India*	87B2
Nanjing *China*	72D3
Nankoku *Japan*	75A2
Nan Ling, Region *China*	73C4
Nanliu, R *China*	76D1
Nanning *China*	73B5
Nanortalik *Greenland*	6F3
Nanpan Jiang, R *China*	73A5
Nānpāra *India*	86A1

Nanping *China*	73D4
Nansen Sd *Can*	6A1
Nansio *Tanz*	99D3
Nantes *France*	48B2
Nanton *Can*	13E2
Nantong *China*	72E3
Nantucket, I *USA*	10C2
Nanuque *Brazil*	35C1
Nanyang *China*	72C3
Nanyang Hu, L *China*	72D2
Nanyuki *Kenya*	99D2
Naoetsu *Japan*	74D3
Naokot *Pak*	85B4
Napa *USA*	22A1
Napaiskak *USA*	12B2
Napanee *Can*	15C2
Napas *USSR*	65K4
Napassoq *Greenland*	6E3
Nape *Laos*	76D2
Napier *NZ*	110C1
Naples, Florida *USA*	17B2
Naples, Texas *USA*	19B3
Napo *China*	73B5
Napo, R *Peru/Ecuador*	32C4
Napoli *Italy*	53B2
Naqadeh *Iran*	90A2
Naqb Ishtar *Jordan*	92C4
Nara *Japan*	75B2
Nara *Mali*	97B3
Naracoorte *Aust*	107D4
Naranjos *Mexico*	23B1
Narasarãopet *India*	87C1
Narathiwat *Thai*	77C4
Narayanganj *Bang*	86C2
Nārāyenpet *India*	87B1
Narbonne *France*	49C3
Narendranagar *India*	84D2
Nares Str *Can*	6C2
Narew, R *Pol*	58C2
Narita *Japan*	75C1
Narmada, R *India*	85C4
Närnaul *India*	84D3
Naro Fominsk *USSR*	60E2
Narok *Kenya*	99D3
Narowal *Pak*	84C2
Narrabri *Aust*	107D4
Narran, L *Aust*	109C1
Narran, R *Aust*	109C1
Narrandera *Aust*	109C2
Narrogin *Aust*	106A4
Narromine *Aust*	109C2
Narsimhapur *India*	85D4
Narsīpatnam *India*	87C1
Narssalik *Greenland*	6F3
Narssaq *Greenland*	6F3
Narssarssuaq *Greenland*	6F3
Narugo *Japan*	75C1
Naruto *Japan*	75A2
Narva *USSR*	60C2
Narvik *Nor*	38H5
Narwāna *India*	84D3
Nar'yan Mar *USSR*	64G3
Narylico *Aust*	108B1
Naryn *USSR*	65J5
Nasarawa *Nig*	97C4
Nasca Ridge *Pacific O*	103D5
Nashua *USA*	16D1
Nashville, Arkansas *USA*	19B3
Nashville, Tennessee *USA*	11B3
Našice *Yugos*	54A1
Nāsik *India*	85D4
Nasir *Sudan*	99D2
Nass, R *Can*	13B1
Nassau *Bahamas*	26B1
Nassau *USA*	16C1
Nasser,L *Egypt*	95C2
Nässjö *Sweden*	39G7
Nastapoka Is *Can*	7C4
Nata *Botswana*	100B3
Natal *Brazil*	31D3
Natal *Indon*	70A3
Natal, Province *S Africa*	101H1
Natanz *Iran*	90B3
Natashquan *Can*	7D4

Natashquan, R *Can*	7D4
Natchez *USA*	19B3
Natchitoches *USA*	19B3
Nathalia *Aust*	108C3
Nathorsts Land, Region *Greenland*	6H2
Nation, R *Can*	13C1
National City *USA*	21B3
Natori *Japan*	75C1
Natovl'a *USSR*	58D2
Natron, L *Tanz*	99D3
Naturaliste,C *Aust*	106A4
Nauders *Austria*	47D1
Nauen *E Germ*	56C2
Naugatuck *USA*	16C2
Naumburg *E Germ*	57C2
Naur *Jordan*	94B3
Nauru, I *Pacifio O*	105G4
Naushki *USSR*	63C2
Nautla *Mexico*	23B1
Navajo Res *USA*	9C3
Navalmoral de la Mata *Spain*	50A2
Navarino, I *Chile*	29C7
Navarra, Province *Spain*	51B1
Navarro *Arg*	34D3
Navasota *USA*	19A3
Navasota, R *USA*	19A3
Navia, R *Spain*	50A1
Navidad *Chile*	34A2
Navlakhi *India*	85C4
Navlya *USSR*	60D3
Navojoa *Mexico*	24B2
Návpaktos *Greece*	55B3
Návplion *Greece*	55B3
Navsāri *India*	85C4
Nawá *Syria*	94C2
Nawāda *India*	86B2
Nawah *Afghan*	84B2
Nawrabshah *Pak*	85B3
Naxi *China*	73B4
Náxos, I *Greece*	55C3
Nayar *Mexico*	23A1
Nay Band *Iran*	90C3
Nāy Band *Iran*	91B4
Nayoro *Japan*	74E2
Nazareth *Israel*	94B2
Nazay *France*	48B2
Nazca *Peru*	32C6
Nazilli *Turk*	92A2
Nazimovo *USSR*	63B2
Nazko, R *Can*	13C2
Nazwa *Oman*	91C5
Nazyvayevsk *USSR*	65J4
Ndalatando *Angola*	98B3
Ndélé *CAR*	98C2
Ndendé *Gabon*	98B3
Ndjamena *Chad*	98B1
Ndjolé *Gabon*	98B3
Ndola *Zambia*	100B2
Neabul *Aust*	109C1
Neales, R *Aust*	108A1
Neápolis *Greece*	55B3
Neath *Wales*	43C4
Nebine, R *Aust*	109C1
Nebit Dag *USSR*	65G6
Nebraska, State *USA*	8C2
Nebraska City *USA*	18A1
Nechako, R *Can*	13C2
Neches, R *USA*	19A3
Necochea *Arg*	34D3
Nêdong *China*	86C1
Needles *USA*	9B3
Neenah *USA*	14A2
Neepawa *Can*	5J4
Neerpelt *Belg*	46C1
Neftelensk *USSR*	63C2
Negelli *Eth*	99D2
Negev, Desert *Israel*	94B3
Negolu, Mt *Rom*	60B4
Negombo *Sri Lanka*	87B3
Negrais,C *Burma*	76A2
Negritos *Peru*	32A4
Negro, R, Amazonas *Brazil*	33E4
Negro, R *Arg*	29C4
Negro, R *Urug*	34D2

Negros

Nuristan

Padova

Padova Italy	47D2
Padre I USA	9D4
Padstow Eng	43B4
Padthaway Aust	108B3
Paducah, Kentucky USA	14A3
Paducah USA	11B3
Padunskoye More, L USSR	38L5
Paengnyŏng-do, I S Korea	74A3
Paeroa NZ	110C1
Pafuri Mozam	100C3
Pag, I Yugos	52B2
Pagadian Phil	79B4
Pagai Selatan, I Indon	70B4
Pagai Utara, I Indon	70B4
Pagan, I Pacific O	71F2
Pagatan Indon	78D3
Pagondhas Greece	55C3
Pahiatua NZ	110C2
Pahoa Hawaiian Is	21C4
Pahokee USA	17B2
Päijänna, L Fin	39K6
Pailola Chan Hawaiian Is	21C4
Painesville USA	14B2
Painted Desert USA	9B3
Paisley Scot	42B2
Paita Peru	32A5
Pajala Sweden	38J5
Pakistan, Republic Asia	80E3
Pak Lay Laos	76C2
Pakokku Burma	86D2
Pakowki L Can	13E2
Pakrac Yugos	52C1
Paks Hung	54A1
Pak Sane Laos	76C2
Pakse Laos	76D2
Pakwach Uganda	99D2
Pala Chad	98B2
Palagruža, I Yugos	52C2
Palaiseau France	46B2
Palangkaraya Indon	78C3
Palani India	87B2
Palanpur India	85C4
Palapye Botswana	100B3
Palatka USA	17B2
Palau Is Pacific O	71E3
Palaw Burma	76B3
Palawan, I Phil	79A4
Palawan Pass Phil	79A4
Palayankottai India	87B3
Paldiski USSR	39J7
Palembang Indon	78A3
Palencia Spain	50B1
Paleokhorio Cyprus	94A1
Palermo Italy	53B3
Palestine, Region Israel	94B3
Palestine USA	19A3
Paletwa Burma	86C2
Pālghāt India	87B2
Pāli India	85C3
Pālitāna India	85C4
Palk Str India/Sri Lanka	87B3
Pallasovka USSR	61G3
Pallastunturi, Mt Fin	38J5
Palliser B NZ	111B2
Palliser,C NZ	111C2
Palma Mozam	101D2
Palma de Mallorca Spain	51C2
Palmares Brazil	31D3
Palmar Sur Costa Rica	26A5
Palmas,C Lib	97B4
Palma Soriano Cuba	26B2
Palm Bay USA	17B2
Palm Beach USA	17B2
Palmdale USA	22C3
Palmeira dos Indos Brazil	31D3
Palmer USA	12E2
Palmer, Base Ant	112C3
Palmer Arch Ant	112C3
Palmer Land, Region Ant	112B3
Palmerston NZ	111B3
Palmerston North NZ	110C2
Palmerton USA	16B2
Palmetto USA	17B2
Palmi Italy	53C3
Palmira Colombia	32B3
Palm Is Aust	107D2
Palm Springs USA	21B3
Palmyra, Missouri USA	18B2
Palmyra, Pennsylvania USA	16A2
Palmyras Pt India	86B2
Palo Alto USA	22A2
Paloh Indon	78B2
Paloích Sudan	99D1
Palomar Mt USA	21B3
Palopo Indon	70D4
Palu Indon	70C4
Palu Turk	93C2
Palwal India	84D3
Pama U Volta	97C3
Pamekasan Indon	78C4
Pameungpeuk Indon	78B4
Pamiers France	48C3
Pamir, Mts China	82B2
Pamir, R USSR	65J6
Pamlico Sd USA	11C3
Pampa USA	9C3
Pampa de la Salinas, Salt pan Arg	34B2
Pampa de la Varita, Plain Arg	34B3
Pamplona Colombia	32C2
Pamplona Spain	50B1
Pana USA	18C2
Panagyurishte Bulg	54B2
Panaji India	87A1
Panamá Panama	32B2
Panama, Republic C America	32A2
Panama Canal Panama	26B5
Panama City USA	17A1
Panamint Range, Mts USA	21B2
Panamint V USA	21B2
Panaro, R Italy	47D2
Panay, I Phil	79B3
Pancevo Yugos	54B2
Pandan Phil	79B3
Pandharpur India	87B1
Pandie Pandie Aust	108A1
Panevēžys USSR	58C1
Panfilov USSR	65K5
Pang, R Burma	76B1
Pangani Tanz	99D3
Pangani, R Tanz	99D3
Pangi Zaïre	98C3
Pangkalpinang Indon	78B3
Pangnirtung Can	6D3
Pangtara Burma	76B1
Pangutaran Group, Is Phil	79B4
Panipat India	84D3
Panjao Afghan	84B2
P'anmunjŏm N Korea	74B3
Panna India	86A2
Panorama Brazil	35A2
Pantelleria, I Medit S	53B3
Pantepec Mexico	23B1
Pánuco, R Mexico	23B1
Pan Xian China	73A4
Paola Italy	53C3
Paola USA	18B2
Paoli USA	14A3
Papa Hung	59B3
Papakura NZ	110B1
Papaloapan, R Mexico	23B2
Papantla Mexico	23B1
Papa Stour, I Scot	44D1
Papatoetoe NZ	110B1
Papa Westray, I Scot	44C2
Papua,G of PNG	107D1
Papua New Guinea, Republic S E Asia	107D1
Papudo Chile	34A2
Papun Burma	76B2
Para, State Brazil	33G4
Pará, R Brazil	31B2
Paraburdoo Aust	106A3
Paracas,Pen de Peru	32B6
Paracatu Brazil	35B1
Paracatu, R Brazil	35B1
Parachilna Aust	108A2
Parachinar Pak	84C2
Paracin Yugos	54B2
Pará de Minas Brazil	35C1
Paradise, California USA	21A2
Paragould USA	18B2
Paraguá, R Bol	33E6
Paragua, R Ven	33E2
Paraguai, R Brazil	30E2
Paraguari Par	30E4
Paraguay, Republic S America	30E3
Paraguay, R Par	30E3
Paraiba, State Brazil	31D3
Paraiba, R Brazil	35B2
Paraíba do Sul, R Brazil	35C2
Parakou Benin	97C4
Parakylia Aust	108A2
Paramakkudi India	87B3
Paramaribo Surinam	33F2
Paramushir, I USSR	69H1
Paraná, State Brazil	30F3
Paraná Urug	34C2
Paraná, R Arg	29E2
Paranã, R Brazil	31B4
Paraná, R Brazil	35A2
Paranaguá Brazil	30G4
Paranaiba Brazil	35A1
Paranaiba, R Brazil	35A1
Paranapanema, R Brazil	35A2
Paranavai Brazil	35A2
Parang Phil	79B4
Paraope, R Brazil	35C1
Paraparaumu NZ	110B2
Parbhani India	87B1
Pardes Hanna Israel	94B2
Pardo Arg	34D3
Pardo, R, Bahia Brazil	35D1
Pardo, R, Mato Grosso do Sul Brazil	35A2
Pardo, R, Minas Gerais Brazil	35B1
Pardo, R, Sao Paulo Brazil	35B2
Pardubice Czech	59B2
Parece Vela, Reef Pacific O	69F4
Parent Can	10C2
Parepare Indon	70C4
Parera Arg	34C3
Pariaman Indon	70B4
Paria,Pen de Ven	33E1
Paris France	48C2
Paris, Kentucky USA	14B3
Paris, Texas USA	19A3
Parkersburg USA	14B3
Parkes Aust	109C2
Parkesburg USA	16B3
Park Forest USA	14A2
Parksville Can	20B1
Parli India	87B1
Parma Italy	47D2
Parma USA	14B2
Parnaiba Brazil	31C2
Parnaiba, R Brazil	31C2
Párnon Óros, Mts Greece	55B3
Pärnu USSR	60B2
Paro Bhutan	86B1
Paroo, R Aust	108B1
Paroo Channel, R Aust	108B2
Páros, I Greece	55C3
Parpaillon, Mts France	47B2
Parral Chile	34A3
Parramatta Aust	109D2
Parras Mexico	9C4
Parry B Can	6B3
Parry Is Can	4G2
Parry Sd Can	7C5
Parry Sound Can	14B1
Parsberg W Germ	57C3
Parsnip, R Can	5F4
Parsons, Kansas USA	18A2
Parsons, West Virginia USA	14C3
Parthenay France	48B2
Partinico Italy	53B3
Partizansk USSR	74C2
Paru, R Brazil	33G4
Parys S Africa	101G1
Pasadena, Texas USA	19A4
Pasadena USA	22C3
Pasangkayu Indon	78D3
Pasawing Burma	76B2
Pascagoula USA	19C3
Paşcani Rom	54C1
Pasco USA	20C1
Pas-de-Calais, Department France	46B1
Pasewalk W Germ	39G8
Pashū'īyeh Iran	91C4
Pasley,C Aust	106B4
Paso de los Toros Urug	29E2
Paso Limay Arg	29B4
Paso Robles USA	21A2
Passage West Irish Rep	45B3
Passaic USA	16B2
Passau W Germ	57C3
Passo de los Libres Arg	30E4
Passo di Stelvio, Mt Italy	47D1
Passo Fundo Brazil	30F4
Passos Brazil	35B2
Passy France	47B2
Pastaza, R Peru	32B4
Pasteur Arg	34C3
Pas,The Can	5H4
Pasto Colombia	32B3
Pastol B USA	12B2
Pasubio, Mt Italy	47D2
Pasuruan Indon	78C4
Pasvalys USSR	58C1
Pātan India	85C4
Patan Nepal	86B1
Patchewollock Aust	108B3
Patea NZ	110B1
Patea, R NZ	111B2
Paterno Italy	53B3
Paterson USA	16B2
Paterson Inlet, B NZ	111A3
Pathankot India	84D2
Patiāla India	84D2
Pativilca Peru	32B6
Pátmos, I Greece	55C3
Patna India	86B1
Patnos Turk	93D2
Patos Brazil	31D3
Patos de Minas Brazil	35B1
Patquia Arg	34B2
Pátrai Greece	55B3
Patrocinio Brazil	35B1
Patta, I Kenya	99E3
Pattallasang Indon	78D4
Pattani Thai	77C4
Patterson, California USA	22B2
Patterson, Louisiana USA	19B4
Patterson,Mt Can	12H2
Patterson,Mt USA	22C2
Pattullo,Mt Can	13B1
Patu Brazil	31D3
Patuakhali Bang	86C2
Patuca, R Honduras	25D3
Patzcuaro Mexico	23A2
Pau France	48B3
Paulatuk Can	4F3
Paulista Brazil	31C3
Paulpietersburg S Africa	101H1

Piedade

Piedade Brazil	35B2
Piedra USA	22C2
Piedras Negras Mexico	24B2
Pieksämäki Fin	38K6
Pielinen, L Fin	38K6
Piemonte, Region Italy	47B2
Pierre USA	8C2
Pieštany Czech	59B3
Pietermaritzburg S Africa	101H1
Pietersburg S Africa	100B3
Piet Retief S Africa	101H1
Pietrosu, Mt Rom	60B4
Pietrosul, Mt Rom	54C1
Pieve di Cadore Italy	47E1
Pigeon L Can	13E2
Piggott USA	18B2
Pigüé Arg	34C3
Pikangikum L Can	7A4
Pikes Peak USA	8C3
Piketberg S Africa	100A4
Pikintaleq Greenland	6F3
Pik Kommunizma, Mt USSR	82B2
Pikounda Congo	98B2
Pik Pobedy, Mt China/USSR	82C1
Pila Arg	34D3
Pila Pol	58B2
Pilar Par	30E4
Pilcomayo, R Arg/Par	30D3
Pilibhit India	84D3
Pilica, R Pol	59B2
Pillar,C Aust	109C4
Pílos Greece	55B3
Pilot Point USA	12C3
Pilot Station USA	12B2
Pilottown USA	19C3
Pimenta Brazil	33F4
Pinang, I Malay	77C4
Pinar del Rio Cuba	26A2
Pinas Arg	34B2
Pinche Belg	46C1
Pincher Creek Can	13E2
Pindaré, R Brazil	31B2
Píndhos, Mts Greece	55B3
Pine Bluff USA	19B3
Pine Creek Aust	106C2
Pinecrest USA	22C1
Pinedale, California USA	22C2
Pine Flat Res USA	22C2
Pine Grove USA	16A2
Pine Hills USA	17B2
Pine I USA	17B2
Pineland USA	19B3
Pinellas Park USA	17B2
Pine Point Can	5G3
Pinerolo Italy	47B2
Pines,Lo'the USA	19B3
Pineville USA	19B3
Pingdingshan China	72C3
Pingguo China	73B5
Pingliang China	72B2
Pingluo China	72B2
Pingtan Dao, I China	73D4
P'ing tung Taiwan	73E5
Pingwu China	72A3
Pingxiang, Guangxi China	73B5
Pingxiang, Jiangxi China	73C4
Pinheiro Brazil	31B2
Pini, I Indon	70A3
Piniós, R Greece	55B3
Pinjarra Aust	106A4
Pink Mountain Can	13C1
Pinnaroo Aust	108B3
Pinos,Pt USA	21A2
Pinotepa Nacional Mexico	23B2
Pinrang Indon	70C4
Pinsk USSR	60C3
Pinta, I Ecuador	32J7
Pinyug USSR	61G1
Pioche USA	8B3
Piombino Italy	52B2
Piórsá Iceland	6H3
Piotroków Trybunalski Pol	59B2
Piper, Oilfield N Sea	44E2
Piper Peak, Mt USA	21B2
Pipmuacan Res Can	10C2
Piqua USA	14B2
Piracanjuba Brazil	35B1
Piracicaba Brazil	35B2
Piraçununga Brazil	35B2
Pirai do Sul Brazil	35B2
Piraiévs Greece	55B3
Pirajui Brazil	35B2
Piranhas Brazil	35A1
Pirapora Brazil	35C1
Pirdop Bulg	54B2
Pirenópolis Brazil	35B1
Pires do Rio Brazil	35B1
Pírgos Greece	55B3
Piripiri Brazil	31C2
Pirmasens W Germ	46D2
Pirot Yugos	54B2
Pīr Panjāl Range, Mts Pak	84C2
Piru Indon	71D4
Piru Creek, R USA	22C3
Pisa Italy	49E3
Pisco Peru	32B6
Písek Czech	57C3
Pishin Pak	84B2
Pissis, Mt Arg	30C4
Pistoia Italy	49E3
Pisuerga, R Spain	50B1
Pit, R USA	20B2
Pitalito Colombia	32B3
Pitcairn, I Pacific O	105K5
Pite, R Sweden	38H5
Piteå Sweden	38J5
Pitești Rom	54B2
Pit Gorodok USSR	63B2
Pitkyaranta USSR	38L6
Pitlochry Scot	44C3
Pitrutquén Chile	34A3
Pitt I Can	13B2
Pittsburg, California USA	22B1
Pittsburg, Kansas USA	18B2
Pittsburgh USA	14C2
Pittsfield, Illinois USA	18B2
Pittsfield, Massachusetts USA	16C1
Pittsworth Aust	109D1
Piuthan Nepal	86A1
Pizzo Redorta, Mt Italy	47D1
Pjórsá Iceland	38B2
Pjura Peru	32A5
Placentia B Can	7E5
Placerville USA	22B1
Plaine des Flandres, Plain France/Belg	46B1
Plaine du Tidikelt, Desert, Region	96C2
Plainview, Texas USA	9C3
Planada USA	22B2
Planalto de Mato Grosso, Plat Brazil	30F2
Planalto do Borborema, Plat Brazil	31D3
Planalto do Mato Grosso, Mts Brazil	32A1
Plano USA	19A3
Plantation USA	17B2
Plant City USA	17B2
Plasencia Spain	50A1
Plast USSR	61K3
Plastun USSR	69F2
Plateau du Tademait Alg	96C2
Plateau Lorrain, Plat France	46D2
Plateaux de Limousin, Plat France	48C2
Plateaux du Sersou, Plat Alg	51C2
Plato Colombia	26C5
Plato Ustyurt, Plat USSR	65G5
Platte, R USA	8C2
Plattsburgh USA	15D2
Plattsmouth USA	18A1
Plauen E Germ	57C2
Plavsk USSR	60E3
Playa Azul Mexico	23A2
Playas Ecuador	32A4
Playa Vicente Mexico	23B2
Plaza de Moro Almanzor, Mt Spain	50A1
Pleasanton, California USA	22B2
Pleasantville USA	16B3
Pleasure Ridge Park USA	14A3
Pleiku Viet	76D3
Plenty,B of NZ	110C1
Pleszew Pol	58B2
Pletipi,L Can	7C4
Pleven Bulg	54B2
Pljevlja Yugos	54A2
Ploče Yugos	52C2
Płock Pol	58B2
Ploërmel France	48B2
Ploiești Rom	54C2
Płońsk Pol	60B3
Plovdiv Bulg	54B2
Plummer USA	20C1
Plummer,Mt USA	12C2
Plumtree Zim	100B3
Plymouth, California USA	22B1
Plymouth Eng	43B4
Plymouth, Indiana USA	14A2
Plymouth, Massachusetts USA	16D2
Plymouth, Pennsylvania USA	15C2
Plymouth Sd Eng	43B4
Plynlimon, Mt Wales	43C3
Plzeň Czech	57C3
Pniewy Pol	58B2
Pnyäselkä, L Fin	38K6
Pô U Volta	97B3
Po, R Italy	47E2
Pobé Benin	97C4
Pobedino USSR	69G2
Pocatello USA	8B2
Pocomoke City USA	15C3
Pocos de Caldas Brazil	35B2
Po di Volano, R Italy	47D2
Podkamennaya, R USSR	63B1
Podolsk USSR	60E2
Podol'skaya Vozvyshennost', Upland USSR	59D3
Podporozh'ye USSR	60D1
Podyuga USSR	61F1
Pofadder S Africa	100A3
P'ohang S Korea	74B3
Poinsett,C Ant	112C9
Point Aust	108C2
Pointe-à-Pitre Guadeloupe	27E3
Pointe de Barfleur, Pt France	48B2
Pointe Noire Congo	98B3
Pointe Pongara, Pt Gabon	98A2
Point Fairy Aust	108B3
Point Fortin Trinidad	27L1
Point Hope USA	4B3
Point L Can	4G3
Point Lay USA	12B1
Point Pleasant, New Jersey USA	16B2
Point Pleasant, W Virginia USA	14B3
Point St Bernard, Mt France	47B2
Poitiers France	48C2
Poitou, Region France	48B2
Poix France	46A2
Pokaran India	85C3
Pokataroo Aust	109C1
Pokrovsk USSR	63E1
Poland, Republic Europe	58B2
Polatli Turk	92B2
Polewali Indon	78D3
Poligny France	47A1
Polýiros Greece	55B2
Pollãchi India	87B2
Polollo Is Phil	79B3
Polonnye USSR	59D2
Polotsk USSR	58D1
Poltava USSR	60D4
Pölten Austria	52C1
Poluostrov Kanin, Pen USSR	64F3
Poluostrov Mangyshlak, Pen USSR	61H5
Poluostrov Rybachiy, Pen USSR	38L5
Poluostrov Yamal, Pen USSR	64H2
Polyarnyy, Murmansk USSR	38L5
Polyarnyy, Yakutskaya USSR	1B8
Polynesia, Region Pacific O	105H3
Pomabamba Peru	32B5
Pomba, R Brazil	35C2
Pomona USA	22D3
Pomona Res USA	18A2
Pompano Beach USA	17B2
Pompton Lakes USA	16B2
Ponca City USA	18A2
Ponce Puerto Rico	27D3
Ponce de Leon B USA	17B2
Pondicherry India	87B2
Pond Inlet Can	6C2
Ponferrade Spain	50A1
Pongo, R Sudan	98C2
Pongola, R S Africa	101H1
Ponnãni India	87B2
Ponnyadoung Range, Mts Burma	86C2
Ponoka Can	13E2
Ponoy USSR	64F3
Pons France	48B2
Ponta da Baleia, Pt Brazil	35D1
Ponta Delgada Açores	96A1
Ponta do Padrão, Pt Angola	98B3
Ponta dos Búzios, Pt Brazil	35C2
Ponta Grossa Brazil	30F4
Pontal Brazil	35B2
Pont-à-Mousson France	46D2
Ponta Pora Brazil	30E3
Pontarlier France	49D2
Pontchartrain,L USA	19B3
Pontedera Italy	52B2
Ponte Lecca Corse	52A2
Pontevedra Spain	50A1
Pontiac, Illinois USA	18C1
Pontiac, Michigan USA	14B2
Pontianak Indon	78B3
Pontivy France	48B2
Pontoise France	46B2
Pontotoc USA	19C3
Pontypool Wales	43C4
Pontypridd Wales	43C4
Poole Eng	43D4
Pooncarie Aust	108B2
Poopelloe,L, L Aust	108B2
Poorman USA	12C2
Popayán Colombia	32B3
Poperinge Belg	46B1
Popilta L Aust	108B2
Poplar Bluff USA	18B2
Poplarville USA	19C3
Popndetta PNG	107D1
Popocatepetl, Mt Mexico	23B2
Popokabaka Zaïre	98B3

Popondetta PNG	71F4
Popovo Bulg	54C2
Porbandar India	85B4
Porcher I Can	13A2
Porcupine, R USA/ Can	12F1
Poreč Yugos	52B1
Porecatu Brazil	35A2
Pori Fin	39J6
Porirua NZ	111B2
Porjus Sweden	38H5
Poronaysk USSR	69G2
Porrentruy Switz	47B1
Porsangen, Inlet Nor	38K4
Porsgrunn Nor	39F7
Portadown N Ire	45C1
Portage la Prairie Can	8D2
Port Alberni Can	13C3
Portalegre Port	50A2
Portales USA	9C3
Port Alfred Can	7C5
Port Alfred S Africa	100B4
Port Alice Can	13B2
Port Allen USA	19B3
Port Angeles USA	20B1
Port Antonio Jamaica	26B3
Portarlington Irish Rep	45C2
Port Arthur USA	19B4
Port Augusta Aust	108A2
Port-au-Prince Haiti	26C3
Port Austin USA	14B2
Port Campbell Aust	108B3
Port Canning India	86B2
Port Cartier Can	7D5
Port Chalmers NZ	111B3
Port Charlotte USA	17B2
Port Chester USA	16C2
Port Colborne Can	15C2
Port Credit Can	15C2
Port Davey Aust	109C4
Port-de-Paix Haiti	26C3
Port Dickson Malay	77C5
Port Edward S Africa	100C4
Porteirinha Brazil	35C1
Port Elgin Can	14B2
Port Elizabeth S Africa	100B4
Porter Pt St Vincent	27N2
Porterville USA	21B2
Port Fairy Aust	107D4
Port Gentil Gabon	98A3
Port Gibson USA	19B3
Port Graham USA	12D3
Port Hammond Can	20B1
Port Harcourt Nigeria	89E7
Port Hardy Can	13B2
Port Hawkesbury Can	7D5
Port Hedland Aust	106A3
Porthmadog Wales	43B3
Port Hope Simpson Can	7E4
Port Hueneme USA	22C3
Port Huron USA	14B2
Portimão Port	50A2
Port Jackson, B Aust	109D2
Port Jefferson USA	16C2
Port Jervis USA	16B2
Port Kembla Aust	109D2
Portland, Indiana USA	14B2
Portland, Maine USA	10C2
Portland, New South Wales Aust	109C2
Portland, Oregon USA	20B1
Portland, Victoria Aust	108B3
Portland Bight, B Jamaica	27H2
Portland Bill, Pt Eng	43C4
Portland,C Aust	109C4
Portland Canal USA/ Can	13A1
Portland I NZ	110C1
Portland Pt Jamaica	27H2
Port Laoise Irish Rep	45C2
Port Lincoln Aust	108A2
Port Loko Sierra Leone	97A4
Port Louis Mauritius	101E3
Port MacDonnell Aust	108B3
Port McNeill Can	13B2
Port Macquarie Aust	109D2
Port Moller USA	12B3
Port Moresby PNG	107D1
Port Nolloth S Africa	100A3
Port Norris USA	16B3
Port Novo Benin	89E7
Porto Port	50A1
Pôrto Alegre Brazil	30F5
Pôrto Artur Brazil	33F6
Pôrto 15 de Novembro Brazil	35A2
Pôrto E Cunha Brazil	30F3
Portoferraio Italy	52B2
Portomaggiore Italy	47D2
Porto Novo Benin	97C4
Port Orchard USA	20B1
Port Orford USA	20B2
Porto Santo, I Medeira	96A1
Pôrto Seguro Brazil	31D5
Porto Torres Sardegna	53A2
Porto Vecchio Corse	53A2
Pôrto Velho Brazil	33E5
Port Pegasus, B NZ	111A3
Port Phillip B Aust	108B3
Port Pirie Aust	108A2
Portree Scot	44A3
Port Renfrew Can	20B1
Port Royal Jamaica	27J2
Port Royal Sd USA	17B1
Portrush N Ire	45C1
Port Said Egypt	92B3
Port St Joe USA	17A2
Port St Johns S Africa	100B4
Port Saunders Can	7E4
Port Shepstone S Africa	100C4
Port Simpson Can	13A2
Portsmouth Dominica	27Q2
Portsmouth Eng	43D4
Portsmouth, Ohio USA	14B3
Portsmouth, Virginia USA	11C3
Port Stephens, B Aust	109D2
Port Sudan Sudan	95C3
Port Sulphur USA	19C3
Porttipahdan Tekojärvi Res Fin	38K5
Portugal, Republic Europe	50A2
Port Washington USA	14A2
Port Weld Malay	77C5
Porvenir Bol	32D6
Posadas Arg	30E4
Posadas Spain	50A2
Poschiavo Switz	47D1
Posheim Pen Can	6B2
Posht-e Badam Iran	90C3
Poso Indon	71D4
Postavy USSR	58D1
Post Clinton USA	14B2
Poste-de-la-Baleine Can	7C4
Postmasburg S Africa	100B3
Postojna Yugos	52B1
Pos'yet USSR	74C2
Potchetstroom S Africa	101G1
Poteau USA	19B2
Potenza Italy	53C2
Potgietersrus S Africa	100B3
Potiskum Nig	97D3
Potlatch USA	20C1
Potomac, R USA	15C3
Potosi Bol	30C2
Potrerillos Chile	30C4
Potsdam E Germ	56C2
Pottstown USA	16B2
Pottsville USA	16A2
Poughkeepsie USA	16C2
Pouso Alegre Brazil	35B2
Poverty B NZ	110C1
Povorino USSR	61F3
Povungnituk Can	7C4
Powder, R USA	8C2
Powell Creek Aust	106C2
Powell,L USA	9B3
Powell River Can	13C3
Power, R USA	8C2
Powys, County Wales	43C3
Poyang Hu, L China	73D4
Pozanti Turk	92B2
Poza Rica Mexico	23B1
Poznań Pol	58B2
Pozo Colorado Par	30E3
Pozzuoli Italy	53B2
Pra, R Ghana	97B4
Prachin Buri Thai	76C3
Prachuap Khiri Khan Thai	76B3
Praděd, Mt Czech	59B2
Pradelles France	49C3
Prado Brazil	35D1
Praha Czech	57C2
Praia Cape Verde	97A4
Prainha Brazil	33E5
Prairie Village USA	18B2
Prakhon Chai Thai	76C3
Prata Brazil	35B1
Prata, R Brazil	35B1
Prato Italy	49E3
Prattsville USA	16B1
Prattville USA	17A1
Prawle Pt Eng	48B1
Praya Indon	78D4
Predazzo Italy	47D1
Predivinsk USSR	63B2
Pregolyu, R USSR	58C2
Prek Kak Camb	76D3
Prenzlau E Germ	56C2
Preparis, I Burma	76A3
Preparis North Chan Burma	76A2
Přerov Czech	59B3
Presa del Infiernillo Mexico	23A2
Prescott, Arizona USA	9B3
Prescott, Arkansas USA	19B3
Prescott Can	15C2
Presidencia Roque Sáenz Peña Arg	30D4
Presidente Epitácio Brazil	35A2
Presidente Frei, Base Ant	112C2
Presidente Miguél Aleman, L Mexico	23B2
Presidente Prudente Brazil	35A2
Presidenté Vargas Brazil	30F3
Presidente Venceslau Brazil	35A2
Prešov Czech	59C3
Prespansko Jezero, L Yugos	55B2
Presque Isle USA	10D2
Preston Eng	42C3
Preston, Idaho USA	8B2
Preston, Missouri USA	18B2
Prestwick Scot	42B2
Prêto Brazil	31B6
Prêto, R Brazil	35B1
Pretoria S Africa	101G1
Préveza Greece	55B3
Prey Veng Camb	76D3
Price USA	8B3
Price I Can	13B2
Prichernomorskaya Nizmennost', Lowland USSR	60D4
Prickly Pt Grenada	27M2
Priekule USSR	58C1
Prieska S Africa	100B3
Priest L USA	20C1
Priest River USA	20C1
Prikaspiyskaya Nizmennost', Region USSR	61G4
Prilep Yugos	55B2
Priluki USSR	60D3
Primero, R Arg	34C2
Primorsk USSR	39K6
Primorsko-Akhtarsk USSR	60E4
Primrose L Can	13F2
Prince Albert Can	5H4
Prince Albert,C Can	4F2
Prince Albert Pen Can	4G2
Prince Albert Sd Can	4G2
Prince Charles I Can	6C3
Prince Charles Mts Ant	112B10
Prince Edward I Can	7D5
Prince George Can	13C2
Prince Gustaf Adolp, S Can	4H2
Prince of Wales, I USA	5E4
Prince of Wales I Aust	71F5
Prince of Wales I Can	4H2
Prince of Wales Str Can	4G2
Prince Patrick I Can	4F2
Prince Regent Inlet, Str Can	6A2
Prince Rupert Can	13A2
Princess Charlotte B Aust	107D2
Princess Royal I Can	13B2
Princes Town Trinidad	27L1
Princeton Can	13C3
Princeton, Kentucky USA	18C2
Princeton, Missouri USA	18B1
Princeton, New Jersey USA	16B2
Prince William USA	4D3
Prince William Sd USA	12E2
Principe, I W Africa	97C4
Prineville USA	20B2
Pringle,Mt USA	12E1
Prins Christian Sund, Sd Greenland	6F3
Prinsesse Astrid Kyst, Region Ant	112B12
Prinsesse Ragnhild Kyst, Region Ant	112B12
Prins Karls Forland, I Barents S	64B2
Prinzapolca Nic	25D3
Pripyat', R USSR	58C2
Priština Yugos	54B2
Pritzwalk E Germ	56C2
Privolzhskaya Vozvyshennost', Upland USSR	61F3
Prizren Yugos	54B2
Probolinggo Indon	78C4
Procatello USA	5G5
Proddatür India	87B2
Progreso Mexico	25D2
Project City USA	20B2
Prokhladnyy USSR	61F5
Prokop'yevsk USSR	65K4
Proletarskaya USSR	61F4
Proliv Karskiye Vorota, Str USSR	64G2
Prome Burma	83D4
Propriá Brazil	31D4
Prospect, Oregon USA	20B2
Prosperine Aust	107D3
Prostějov Czech	59B3
Prøven Greenland	6E2
Provence, Region France	49D3
Providence USA	16D2
Provincetown USA	15D2
Provins France	49C2
Provo USA	8B2
Provost Can	13E2
Prudhoe Bay USA	4D2
Prudhoe Land Greenland	6D2
Pruszkow Pol	58C2
Prutul, R USSR	60C4
Pruzhany USSR	58C2
Pryor USA	18A2

Przemys'l

Przemys'l *Pol*	59C3	
Psará, I *Greece*	55C3	
Pskov *USSR*	60C2	
Ptich, R *USSR*	58D2	
Ptolemaïs *Greece*	55B2	
Pucallpa *Peru*	32C5	
Pucheng *China*	73D4	
Pucón *Chile*	34A3	
Pudasjärvi *Fin*	38K5	
Pudukkottai *India*	87B2	
Puebla *Mexico*	23B2	
Puebla, State *Mexico*	23B2	
Puebla de Sanahria *Spain*	50A1	
Puebla de Trives *Spain*	50A1	
Pueblo *USA*	9C2	
Puelches *Arg*	34B3	
Puelén *Arg*	34B3	
Puenta Ixbapa *Mexico*	23A2	
Puente del Inca *Arg*	34B2	
Puerta Aguja *Peru*	32A5	
Puerta Coles *Peru*	30B2	
Puerta de los Llanos *Arg*	34B2	
Puerta do Calcanhar, Pt *Brazil*	31D3	
Puerta Gallinas *Colombia*	32C1	
Puerta Maldonado, Pt *Mexico*	23B2	
Puerta Mariato *Panama*	32A2	
Puerta Médanosa, Pt *Arg*	29C5	
Puerta Mongrove *Mexico*	23A2	
Puerta San Blas, Pt *Panama*	25E4	
Puerta San Telmo *Mexico*	23A2	
Puerto Aisén *Chile*	29B5	
Puerto Armuelles *Panama*	25D4	
Puerto Artur *Brazil*	33F6	
Puerto Asis *Colombia*	32B3	
Puerto Ayacucho *Ven*	32D2	
Puerto Barrios *Guatemala*	25D3	
Puerto Berrio *Colombia*	32C2	
Puerto Cabello *Ven*	32D1	
Puerto Cabezas *Nic*	25D3	
Puerto Carreño *Colombia*	32D2	
Puerto Cortes *Costa Rica*	25D4	
Puerto Cortés *Honduras*	25D3	
Puerto del Rosario *Canary Is*	96A2	
Puerto E Cunha *Brazil*	30F3	
Puerto Fijo *Ven*	32C1	
Puerto Franco *Brazil*	31B3	
Puerto Heath *Bol*	32D6	
Puerto Juarez *Mexico*	25D2	
Puerto la Cruz *Ven*	33E1	
Puertollano *Spain*	50B2	
Puerto Lopez *Colombia*	27C4	
Puerto Madryn *Arg*	29D4	
Puerto Maldonado *Peru*	32D6	
Puerto Marquéz *Mexico*	23B2	
Puerto Montt *Chile*	29B4	
Puerto Murtinho *Brazil*	30E3	
Puerto Natales *Chile*	29B6	
Puerto Peñasco *Mexico*	24A1	
Puerto Pirámides *Arg*	29D4	
Puerto Plata *Dom Rep*	27C3	
Puerto Princesa *Phil*	79A4	
Puerto Rico *Colombia*	32B3	
Puerto Rico, I *Caribbean*	27D3	
Puerto Rico Trench *Caribbean*	27D3	

Puerto San Juan de Lima *Mexico*	23A2	
Puerto Santanga *Brazil*	33G4	
Puerto Suárez *Bol*	30E2	
Puerto Vallarta *Mexico*	24B2	
Puerto Varas *Chile*	29B4	
Puerto Villarroel *Bol*	30D2	
Pugachev *USSR*	61G3	
Pugal *India*	84C3	
Puigcerdá *Spain*	51C1	
Pukaki,L, L *NZ*	111B2	
Pukch'ŏng *N Korea*	74B2	
Pukekobe *NZ*	110B1	
Puketeraki Range, Mts *NZ*	111B2	
Pula *Yugos*	52B2	
Pulaski, New York *USA*	15C2	
Pulau Kolepom, I *Indon*	71E4	
Pulau Pulau Batu, Is *Indon*	70A4	
Pulawy *Pol*	58C2	
Pulicat,L *India*	87C2	
Pul-i-Khumri *Afghan*	84B1	
Puliyangudi *India*	87B3	
Pullman *USA*	20C1	
Pulo Anna Merir, I *Pacific I*	71E3	
Pulog,Mt *Phil*	79B2	
Pulozero *USSR*	38L5	
Pultusk *Pol*	58C2	
Puna de Atacama *Arg*	30C4	
Punakha *Bhutan*	86B1	
Punch *Pak*	84C2	
Pune *India*	87A1	
Punéper *Mexico*	23A2	
Punia *Zaïre*	98C3	
Punitaqui *Chile*	34A2	
Punjab, Province *Pak*	84C2	
Punjab, State *India*	84D2	
Puno *Peru*	30B2	
Punta Abreojos, Pt *Mexico*	24A2	
Punta Alice, Pt *Italy*	53C3	
Punta Alta *Arg*	34C3	
Punta Arenas *Chile*	29B6	
Punta Baja, Pt *Mexico*	24A2	
Punta Curaumilla, Pt *Chile*	34A2	
Punta da Marca, Pt *Angola*	100A2	
Punta de Barra Falsa, Pt *Mozam*	101C3	
Punta del Este *Urug*	29F2	
Punta Eugenia, Pt *Mexico*	24A2	
Punta Gorda *Belize*	25D3	
Punta Gorda *USA*	17B2	
Punta Lavapié, Pt *Chile*	34A3	
Punta Lengua de Vaca Pt *Chile*	34A2	
Punta Licosa, Pt *Italy*	53B2	
Punta Poroto, Pt *Chile*	34A1	
Punta San Antonia, Pt *Mexico*	9B4	
Punta Topocalma *Chile*	34A2	
Puqi *China*	73C4	
Purcell *USA*	19A2	
Purcell Mt *USA*	12C1	
Purcell Mts *Can*	13D2	
Purén *Chile*	34A3	
Puri *India*	86B2	
Pūrna *India*	87B1	
Pūrnia *India*	86B1	
Pursat *Camb*	76C3	
Puruandro *Mexico*	23A1	
Purus, R *Brazil*	33E4	
Purvis *USA*	19C3	
Purwokerto *Indon*	78B4	
Purworejo *Indon*	78C4	
Pusad *India*	85D5	
Pusan *S Korea*	74B3	
Pushkin *USSR*	60D2	
Pustochka *USSR*	58D1	

Puta *Burma*	82D3	
Putaendo *Chile*	34A2	
Putaruru *NZ*	110C1	
Putian *China*	73D4	
Putnam *USA*	16D2	
Puttalam *Sri Lanka*	87B3	
Puttgarden *W Germ*	56C2	
Putumayo, R *Ecuador*	32B4	
Putussibau *Indon*	78C2	
Puulavesl, L *Fin*	38K6	
Puyallup *USA*	20B1	
Puy de Sancy, Mt *France*	49C2	
Puysegur Pt *NZ*	111A3	
Pweto *Zaïre*	99C3	
Pwllheli *Wales*	43B3	
Pyapon *Burma*	76B2	
Pyatigorsk *USSR*	61F5	
P'yŏngyang *N Korea*	74B3	
Pyramid Hill *Aust*	108B3	
Pyramid L *USA*	21B1	
Pyramid,Mt *NZ*	111A2	
Pyrénées, Mts *France*	48B3	
Pytalovo *USSR*	58D1	
Pyu *Burma*	76B2	

Q

Qabatiya *Israel*	94B2	
Qā'el Hafīra, Mud Flats *Jordan*	94C3	
Qa'el Jinz, Mud Flats *Jordan*	94C3	
Qaidam Pendi, Salt Flat *China*	68B3	
Qa Khanna, Salt Marsh *Jordan*	94C2	
Qala'en Nahl *Sudan*	99D1	
Qalat *Afghan*	84B2	
Qal'at al Hisn *Syria*	94C1	
Qal'at Bīshah *S Arabia*	81C3	
Qal'at Sālih *Iraq*	93E3	
Qamdo *China*	68B3	
Qardho *Somalia*	99E2	
Qara *Egypt*	95B2	
Qaςe Shīrin *Iran*	90A3	
Qaryat al Ulyā *S Arabia*	91A4	
Qasr el Kharana *Jordan*	94C3	
Qasr-e-Qand *Iran*	91D4	
Qasr Farafra *Egypt*	95B2	
Qaţana *Syria*	94C2	
Qatar, Emirate *Arabian Pen*	91B4	
Qatrāna *Jordan*	94C3	
Qattāra Depression *Egypt*	95B2	
Qāyen *Iran*	90C3	
Qazvin *Iran*	90A2	
Qena *Egypt*	95C2	
Qeydār *Iran*	90A2	
Qeys, I *Iran*	91B4	
Qian Jiang, R *China*	73B5	
Qian Shan, Upland *China*	72E1	
Qidong *China*	72E3	
Qijiang *China*	73B4	
Qila Saifullah *Pak*	84B2	
Qilian *China*	72A2	
Qilian Shan *China*	68B3	
Qin'an *China*	72B3	
Qingdao *China*	72E2	
Qinghai, Province *China*	72A2	
Qinghai Hu, L *China*	68B3	
Qingjiang, Jiangsu *China*	72D3	
Qingjiang, Jiangxi *China*	73D4	
Qing Jiang, R *China*	72B3	
Qingshuihe *China*	72C2	
Qingshui He, R *China*	72B2	
Qingtonxia *China*	72B2	
Qingyang *China*	72B2	
Qingyuan, Liaoning *China*	74B2	

Qingyuan, Zhejiang *China*	73D4	
Qing Zang, Upland *China*	82C2	
Qinhuangdao *China*	72D2	
Qin Ling, Mts *China*	72B3	
Qinzhou *China*	73B5	
Qionghai *China*	76E2	
Qionglai Shan, Upland *China*	73A3	
Qiongzhou Haixia, Str *China*	76D1	
Qiqihar *China*	69E2	
Qiryat Ata *Israel*	94B2	
Qiryat Gat *Israel*	94B3	
Qiryat Shemona *Israel*	94B2	
Qiryat Yam *Israel*	94B2	
Qishon, R *Israel*	94B2	
Qitai *China*	63A3	
Qiyang *China*	73C4	
Qog Qi *China*	72B1	
Qolleh-ye Damavand, Mt *Iran*	90B2	
Qom *Iran*	90B3	
Qomisheh *Iran*	90B3	
Qornet es Saouda, Mt *Leb*	94C1	
Qôrnoq *Greenland*	6E3	
Qorveh *Iran*	90A2	
Qotābad *Iran*	91C4	
Quabbin Res *USA*	16C1	
Quakertown *USA*	16B2	
Quam Phu Quoc, I *Viet*	77C3	
Quang Ngai *Viet*	76D2	
Quang Tri *Viet*	76D2	
Quan Long *Viet*	77D4	
Quanzhou, Fujian *China*	73D5	
Quanzhou, Guangxi *China*	73C4	
Qu' Appelle, R *Can*	5H4	
Quarayyāt *Oman*	91C5	
Quatsino Sd *Can*	13B2	
Quchan *Iran*	90C2	
Queanbeyan *Aust*	109C3	
Québec *Can*	15D1	
Quebec, Province *Can*	7C4	
Quebra-Anzol, R *Brazil*	35B1	
Quebracho *Brazil*	34D2	
Quedas do Iguaçu *Brazil/Arg*	30F4	
Queen Anne *USA*	16A3	
Queen Bess,Mt *Can*	13B2	
Queen Charlotte, Is *Can*	5E4	
Queen Charlotte Sd *Can*	13B2	
Queen Charlotte Str *Can*	13B2	
Queen Elizabeth Is *Can*	4H1	
Queen Mary Land, Region *Ant*	112B9	
Queen Maud G *Can*	4H3	
Queen Maud Mts *Ant*	80E	
Queens, Borough, New York *USA*	16C2	
Queenscliff *Aust*	108B3	
Queensland, State *Aust*	107D3	
Queenstown *Aust*	109C4	
Queenstown *NZ*	111A3	
Queenstown *S Africa*	100B4	
Queenstown *USA*	16A3	
Quela *Angola*	98B3	
Quelimane *Mozam*	101C2	
Quemuquemú *Arg*	34C3	
Quensel L *Can*	13C2	
Quequén *Arg*	34D3	
Quequén, R *Arg*	34D3	
Querétaro *Mexico*	23A1	
Queretaro, State *Mexico*	23A1	
Quesnel *Can*	13C2	
Quetta *Pak*	84B2	
Quezaltenango *Guatemala*	25C3	

Queziot *Israel*	94B3
Quezon City *Phil*	79B3
Quibala *Angola*	100A2
Quibaxe *Angola*	98B3
Quibdó *Colombia*	32B2
Quiberon *France*	48B2
Quicama Nat Pk *Angola*	98B3
Quijing *China*	73A4
Quilima *Chile*	34A2
Quilino *Arg*	34C2
Quillabamba *Peru*	32C6
Quillacollo *Bol*	30C2
Quillan *France*	48C3
Quill L *Can*	5H4
Quill Lakes *Can*	5H4
Quillota *Chile*	34A2
Quilon *India*	87B3
Quilpie *Aust*	108B1
Quilpué *Chile*	34A2
Quimbele *Angola*	98B3
Quimper *France*	48B2
Quimperlé *France*	48B2
Quincy, California *USA*	21A2
Quincy, Illinois *USA*	10A3
Quincy, Massachusetts *USA*	16D1
Quines *Arg*	34B2
Quinhagak *USA*	12B3
Qui Nhon *Viet*	76D3
Quintanar de la Orden *Spain*	50B2
Quintero *Chile*	34A2
Quinto, R *Arg*	34C2
Quirihue *Chile*	34A3
Quirima *Angola*	100A2
Quirindi *Aust*	109D2
Quissanga *Mozam*	101D2
Quissico *Mozam*	101C3
Quito *Ecuador*	32B4
Quixadá *Brazil*	31D2
Quorn *Aust*	108A2
Quseir *Egypt*	95C2
Qutdligssat *Greenland*	6E3
Qu Xian, Sichuan *China*	73B3
Qu Xian, Zhejiang *China*	73D4
Quynh Luu *Viet*	76D2
Quzhou *China*	72C2
Qüzü *China*	86C1

R

Raahe *Fin*	38J6
Raasay, I *Scot*	44A3
Raasay,Sound of, Chan *Scot*	44A3
Rab, I *Yugos*	52B2
Raba *Indon*	78D4
Rába, R *Hung*	59B3
Rabat *Mor*	96B1
Rabba *Jordan*	94B3
Rabigh *S Arabia*	80B3
Racconigi *Italy*	47B2
Race,C *Can*	7E5
Rachaya *Leb*	94B2
Rachel, Mt *W Germ*	57C3
Rach Gia *Viet*	76D3
Racine *USA*	14A2
Rădăuţi *Rom*	59D3
Radhanpur *India*	85C4
Radix,Pt *Trinidad*	27L1
Radom *Pol*	58C2
Radomsko *Pol*	59B2
Rodviliškis *USSR*	58C1
Rae *Can*	4G3
Räe Bareli *India*	86A1
Rae Isthmus *Can*	6B3
Rae L *Can*	4G3
Raetihi *NZ*	110C1
Rafaela *Arg*	34C2
Rafah *Egypt*	94B3
Rafai *CAR*	98C2
Rafhä Al Jumaymah *S Arabia*	93D3
Rafsanjän *Iran*	91C3

Raga *Sudan*	98C2
Ragged Pt *Barbados*	27R3
Raguba *Libya*	95A2
Ragusa *Italy*	53B3
Rahad, R *Sudan*	99D1
Rahimyar Khan *Pak*	84C3
Rähjerd *Iran*	90B3
Raíces *Arg*	34D2
Räichur *India*	87B1
Raigarh *India*	86A2
Rainbow *Aust*	108B3
Rainbow City *USA*	17A1
Rainier *USA*	20B1
Rainier,Mt *USA*	20B1
Rainy L *Can*	10A2
Rainy P *USA*	12D2
Rainy River *Can*	10A2
Raipur *India*	86A2
Räjahmundry *India*	87C1
Rajang, R *Malay*	78C2
Rajanpur *Pak*	84C3
Räjapälaiyam *India*	87B3
Räjasthan, State *India*	85C3
Räjgarh *India*	84D3
Räjgarh, State *India*	85D4
Räjkot *India*	85C4
Räjmahäl Hills *India*	86B2
Raj Nandgaon *India*	86A2
Räjpipla *India*	85C4
Rajshahi *Bang*	86B2
Rajur *India*	85D4
Rakaia, R *NZ*	111B2
Rakata, I *Indon*	78B4
Raka Zangbo, R *China*	82C3
Rakhov *USSR*	59C3
Rakops *Botswana*	100B3
Rakov *USSR*	58D2
Raleigh *USA*	11C3
Ralny L *Can*	7A5
Rama *Israel*	94B2
Ramallah *Israel*	94B3
Rämanäthapuram *India*	87B3
Ramapo Deep *Pacific Oc*	69G3
Ramat Gan *Israel*	94B2
Rambouillet *France*	46A2
Rämgarh, Bihar *India*	86B2
Rämgarh, Rajosthan *India*	85C3
Rämhormoz *Iran*	90A3
Ramla *Israel*	94B3
Ramlat Al Wahibah, Region *Oman*	91C5
Ramona *USA*	21B3
Rämpur *India*	84D3
Rämpura *India*	85D4
Rämsar *Iran*	90B2
Ramsey *Eng*	42B2
Ramsey *USA*	16B2
Ramsey I *Wales*	43B4
Ramsgate *Eng*	43E4
Ramtha *Jordan*	94C2
Ramu, R *PNG*	71F4
Rancagua *Chile*	34A2
Ränchi *India*	86B2
Ränchi Plat *India*	86A2
Randers *Den*	39G7
Randfontein *S Africa*	101G1
Randolph, Vermont *USA*	15D2
Ranfurly *NZ*	111B3
Rangamati *Bang*	86C2
Rangiora *NZ*	111B2
Rangitaiki, R *NZ*	110C1
Rangitate, R *NZ*	111B2
Rangitikei, R *NZ*	110C1
Rangoon *Burma*	76B2
Rangpur *India*	86B1
Ränibennur *India*	87B2
Ranier,Mt, Mt *USA*	8A2
Räniganj *India*	86B2
Rankins Springs *Aust*	109C2
Ranklin Inlet *Can*	6A3
Rann of Kachchh, Flood Area *India*	85B4
Ranong *Thai*	77B4
Rantauparapat *Indon*	70A3

Rantoul *USA*	18C1
Rapallo *Italy*	49D3
Rapel, R *Chile*	34A2
Raper,C *Can*	6D3
Rapid City *USA*	8C2
Rapid River *USA*	14A1
Rappahannock, R *USA*	15C3
Rapperswil *Switz*	47C1
Raritan B *USA*	16B2
Ras Abu Shagara, C *Sudan*	95C2
Ra's al 'Ayn *Syria*	93D2
Ra's al Hadd, C *Oman*	91C5
Ras al Kaimah *UAE*	91C4
Ras-al-Kuh, C *Iran*	91C4
Ra's al Madrakah, C *Oman*	81D4
Ra's az Zawr, C *S Arabia*	91A4
Räs Bânas, C *Egypt*	95C2
Ras Burûn, C *Egypt*	94A3
Ras Dashan, Mt *Eth*	99D1
Ra's-e-Barkan, Pt *Iran*	90A3
Râs el Kenâyis, Pt *Egypt*	92A3
Ra's Fartak, C *S Yemen*	81D4
Râs Ghârib *Egypt*	95C2
Rashad *Sudan*	99D1
Rashädïya *Jordan*	94B3
Rashîd *Egypt*	92B3
Rasht *Iran*	90A2
Ra's Jibish, C *Oman*	91C5
Ras Khanzira, C *Somalia*	99E1
Ras Koh, Mt *Pak*	84B3
Râs Muhammad, C *Egypt*	95C2
Ras Nouadhibou, C *Maur*	96A2
Rasshua, I *USSR*	69H2
Rasskazovo *USSR*	61F3
Ra's Tanäqib, C *S Arabia*	91A4
Ra's Tannûrah *S Arabia*	91B4
Rastatt *W Germ*	57B3
Ras Xaafuun, C *Somalia*	99F1
Ratangarh *India*	84C3
Rat Buri *Thai*	76B3
Rath *India*	85D3
Rathenow *E Germ*	56C2
Rathkeale *Irish Rep*	45B2
Rathlin, I *N Ire*	45C1
Räth Luirc *Irish Rep*	45B2
Ratläm *India*	85D4
Ratnägiri *India*	87A1
Ratnapura *Sri Lanka*	87C3
Ratno *USSR*	58C2
Rattenberg *Austria*	47D1
Rättvik *Sweden*	39H6
Ratz,Mt *Can*	12H3
Rauch *Arg*	34D3
Raukumara Range Mts *NZ*	110C1
Raul Soares *Brazil*	35C2
Rauma *Fin*	39J6
Raurkela *India*	86A2
Ravänsar *Iran*	90A3
Rävar *Iran*	90C3
Rava Russkaya *USSR*	59C2
Ravena *USA*	16C1
Ravenna *Italy*	52B2
Ravensburg *W Germ*	57B3
Ravenshoe *Aust*	107D2
Ravi, R *Pak*	84C2
Rawalpindi *Pak*	84C2
Rowicz *Pol*	58B2
Rawlinna *Aust*	106B4
Rawlins *USA*	8C2
Rawndiz *Iraq*	93D2
Rawson *Arg*	29C4
Raya, Mt *Indon*	78C3
Räyadurg *India*	87B2
Rayak *Leb*	94C2
Ray,C *Can*	7E5
Räyen *Iran*	91C4

Raymond, California *USA*	22C2
Raymond, Washington *USA*	20B1
Raymond Terrace *Aust*	109D2
Ray Mts *USA*	12D1
Rayon *Mexico*	23B1
Razan *Iran*	90A2
Razgrad *Bulg*	54C2
Razim, L *Rom*	54C2
Reading *Eng*	43D4
Reading *USA*	16B2
Read Island *Can*	4G3
Readsboro *USA*	16C1
Real de Padre *Arg*	34B2
Realicó *Arg*	34C3
Rebiana, Well *Libya*	95B2
Rebiana Sand Sea *Libya*	95B2
Reboly *USSR*	38L6
Recherche,Arch of the Is *Aust*	106B4
Recife *Brazil*	31E3
Récifs D'Entrecasteaux *Nouvelle Calédonie*	107F2
Recklinghausen *W Germ*	46D1
Reconquista *Arg*	30E4
Red, R *USA*	19B3
Redang, I *Malay*	77C4
Red Bank, New Jersey *USA*	16B2
Red Bluff *USA*	21A1
Redcar *Eng*	42D2
Redcliff *Can*	13E2
Redcliffe *Aust*	109D1
Red Cliffs *Aust*	108B2
Red Deer *Can*	13E2
Red Deer, R *Can*	13E2
Redding *USA*	20B2
Red L *USA*	10A2
Red Lake *Can*	7A4
Redlands *USA*	22D3
Red Lion *USA*	16A3
Redmond *USA*	20B2
Red Oak *USA*	18A1
Redon *France*	48B2
Redondo Beach *USA*	22C4
Redoubt V *USA*	12D2
Red River Delta *Vietnam*	73B5
Red Sea *Africa/Arabian Pen*	80B3
Redwater *Can*	13E2
Redwood City *USA*	22A2
Reed City *USA*	14A2
Reedley *USA*	22C2
Reedsport *USA*	20B2
Reefton *NZ*	111B2
Refahiye *Turk*	93C2
Regência *Brazil*	35D1
Regensburg *W Germ*	57C3
Reggane *Alg*	96C2
Reggio di Calabria *Italy*	53C3
Reggio Nell'Emilia *Italy*	47D2
Reghin *Rom*	54B1
Regina *Can*	5H4
Rehoboth *Namibia*	100A3
Rehoboth Beach *USA*	15C3
Rehovot *Israel*	94B3
Reicito *Ven*	32D1
Reigate *Eng*	43D4
Reims *France*	46C2
Reindeer, R *Can*	5H4
Reinosa *Spain*	50B1
Reicterstown *USA*	16A3
Reitz *S Africa*	101G1
Reliance *Can*	4H3
Remarkable,Mt *Aust*	108A2
Rembang *Indon*	78C4
Remeshk *Iran*	91C4
Remscheid *W Germ*	46D1
Rend,L *USA*	18C2
Rendsburg *W Germ*	56B2

Renfrew *Can*	15C1	Ria de Corcubion, B		Rio Grande do Sul,		Rochester, New	
Rengat *Indon*	78A3	Spain	50A1	State *Brazil*	30F4	Hampshire *USA*	15D2
Rengo *Chile*	34A2	Ria de Lage, B *Spain*	50A1	Rio Grande Rise		Rochester, New York	
Reni *USSR*	59D3	Ria de Sta Marta, B		Atlantic O	103G6	USA	10C2
Renk *Sudan*	99D1	Spain	50A1	Riohacha *Colombia*	26C4	Rockford *USA*	10B2
Renland, Pen		Ria de Vigo, B *Spain*	50A1	Riom *France*	49C2	Rock Hill *USA*	11B3
Greenland	6H2	Riäsi *Pak*	84C2	Riombamba *Ecuador*	32B4	Rock Island *USA*	10A2
Renmark *Aust*	108B2	Ribadeo *Spain*	50A1	Rio Mulatos *Bol*	30C2	Rocklands Res *Aust*	108B3
Rennell, I *Solomon Is*	107F2	Ribas do Rio Pardo		Río Negro, State *Arg*	29C3	Rockledge *USA*	17B2
Rennes *France*	48B2	Brazil	35A2	Rio Pardo *Brazil*	30F4	Rock Springs,	
Reno *USA*	21B2	Ribauè *Mozam*	101C2	Rio Tercero *Arg*	34C2	Wyoming *USA*	8C2
Reno, R *Italy*	47D2	Ribble, R *Eng*	42C3	Rio Theodore		Rocks Pt *NZ*	110B2
Renovo *USA*	15C2	Ribeira *Brazil*	35B2	Roosevelt, R *Brazil*	33E6	Rock,The *Aust*	109C3
Rensselaer *USA*	16C1	Ribeirão Prêto *Brazil*	35B2	Rio Turbio *Arg*	29B6	Rockville, Connecticut	
Renton *USA*	20B1	Riberalta *Bol*	32D6	Rio Verde *Brazil*	35A1	USA	16C2
Reo *Indon*	70D4	Rice L *Can*	15C2	Rio Verde *Mexico*	23A1	Rockville, Indiana *USA*	14A3
Reprêsa de Furnas,		Rice Lake *USA*	10A2	Ripley, Ohio *USA*	14B3	Rockville, Maryland	
Dam *Brazil*	35B2	Richard's Bay *S Africa*	101H1	Ripley, West Virginia		USA	16A3
Reprêsa Três Marias,		Richardson *USA*	19A3	USA	14B3	Rocky Island L *Can*	14B1
Dam *Brazil*	35B1	Richardson Mts *Can*	12G1	Ripon *Eng*	42D2	Rocky Mountain	
Republic *USA*	20C1	Richfield *USA*	8B3	Ripon *USA*	22B2	House *Can*	13E2
Republic of Ireland		Richland *USA*	20C1	Rishon le Zion *Israel*	94B3	Rocky Mts *Can/USA*	8B1
NW Europe	41B3	Richmond, California		Rising Sun *USA*	16A3	Rocky Pt *USA*	12B2
Repulse Bay *Can*	6B3	USA	22A2	Risør *Nor*	39F7	Rødbyhavn *Den*	56C2
Réservoir Baskatong,		Richmond, Natal *S*		Ritenberk *Greenland*	6E2	Rodeo *Arg*	34B2
Res *Can*	15C1	Africa	101H1	Ritter,Mt *USA*	22C2	Rodez *France*	49C3
Réservoire Cabonga,		Richmond, New South		Ritzville *USA*	20C1	Ródhos *Greece*	55C3
Res *Can*	7C5	Wales *Aust*	109D2	Rivadavia *Arg*	34B2	Ródhos, I *Greece*	55C3
Réservoire Gouin, Res		Richmond *NZ*	111B2	Rivadavia *Chile*	34A1	Rodi Garganico *Italy*	52C2
Can	7C5	Richmond,		Rivadavia Gonzalez		Rodopi Planina, Mts	
Réservoire		Queensland *Aust*	107D3	Moreno *Arg*	34C3	Bulg	54B2
Manicouagan, Res		Richmond, Virginia		Riva de Garda *Italy*	47D2	Roebourne *Aust*	106A3
Can	10D1	USA	10C3	Rivera *Arg*	34C3	Roer, R *Neth*	46D1
Reshteh-ye Alborz,		Richmond Range, Mts		Rivera *Urug*	29E2	Roermond *Neth*	46C1
Mts *Iran*	90B2	NZ	111B2	Riverbank *USA*	22B2	Roeselare *Belg*	46B1
Reshui *China*	72A2	Rideau,L *Can*	15C2	River Cess *Lib*	97B4	Roes Welcome Sd	
Resistencia *Arg*	30E4	Ridgeland *USA*	17B1	Riverhead *USA*	16C2	Can	6B3
Resita *Rom*	54B1	Ridgway *USA*	15C2	Riverina *Aust*	108B3	Rogers *USA*	18B2
Resolute *Can*	6A2	Riecito *Ven*	27D4	Riversdale *NZ*	111A3	Rogers City *USA*	14B1
Resolution I *NZ*	111A3	Rienza, R *Italy*	47D1	Riverside *USA*	22D4	Rogue, R *USA*	20B2
Resolution Island *Can*	6D3	Riesa *E Germ*	57C2	Rivers Inlet *Can*	13B2	Rohn *Pak*	85B3
Ressano Garcia		Riesco, I *Chile*	29B6	Riverton *NZ*	111A3	Rohtak *India*	84D3
Mozam	101H1	Riet, R *S Africa*	101F1	Riverton *USA*	8C2	Roja *USSR*	58C1
Retamito *Arg*	34B2	Rieti *Italy*	52B2	Riviera Beach *USA*	17B2	Rolândia *Brazil*	35A2
Rethel *France*	46C2	Rif, Mts *Mor*	50B2	Rivière aux Feuilles, R		Rolla *USA*	18B2
Réthimnon *Greece*	55B3	Riga *USSR*	58C1	Can	7C4	Roma *Aust*	109C1
Reunion, I *Indian O*	89K10	Riga,G of *USSR*	60B2	Rivière de la Baleine,		Roma *Italy*	52B2
Reus *Spain*	51C1	Rigän *Iran*	91C4	R *Can*	7D4	Romagnano *Italy*	47C2
Reuss, R *Switz*	47C1	Riggins *USA*	20C1	Rivière du Petit		Romain,C *USA*	17C1
Reutte *Austria*	47D1	Rigolet *Can*	7E4	Mècatina, R *Can*	7D4	Roman *Rom*	54C1
Revda *USSR*	61K3	Riihimaki *Fin*	39J6	Rivigny-sur-Ornain		Romanche Gap	
Revelstoke *Can*	13D2	Rijeka *Yugos*	52B1	France	46C2	Atlantic O	103H5
Revillagigedo, Is		Rimbey *Can*	13E2	Riyadh *S Arabia*	91A5	Romang, I *Indon*	71D4
Mexico	24A3	Rimbo *Sweden*	39H7	Rize *Turk*	93D1	Romania, Republic E	
Revillagigedo I *USA*	12H3	Rimini *Italy*	52B2	Rizhao *China*	72D2	Europe	60B4
Revin *France*	46C2	Rîmnicu Sârat *Rom*	54C1	Rjukan *Nor*	39F7	Romano,C *USA*	17B2
Revivim *Israel*	94B3	Rîmnicu Vîlcea *Rom*	54B1	Roanes Pen *Can*	6B2	Romans sur Isère	
Rewa *India*	86A2	Rimouski *Can*	10D2	Roanne *France*	49C2	France	49D2
Rewari *India*	84D3	Rincón de Romos		Roanoke, Alabama		Romblon *Phil*	79B3
Rexburg *USA*	8B2	Mexico	23A1	USA	17A1	Rome, Georgia *USA*	17A1
Reykjavik *Iceland*	38A2	Ringkøbing *Den*	39F7	Roanoke, Virginia		Rome, New York *USA*	15C2
Reynosa *Mexico*	24C2	Ringkøbing *Den*	39F7	USA	11C3	Romilly-sur-Seine	
Rezé *France*	48B2	Rio Benito *Eq Guinea*	98A2	Roanoke, R *USA*	11C3	France	49C2
Rezekne *USSR*	58D1	Rio Branco *Brazil*	32D5	Roaringwater B *Irish*		Romney *USA*	15C3
Rezh *USSR*	61K2	Rio Bravo del Norte, R		Rep	45B3	Romny *USSR*	60D3
Rhätikon, Mts *Austria/*		USA/Mexico	24B1	Robertsforz *Sweden*	38J6	Rømø, I *Den*	56B1
Switz	47C1	Riochacha *Colombia*	32C1	Robert S Kerr Res		Romont *Switz*	47B1
Rhazir, Republic *Leb*	94B1	Rio Claro *Brazil*	35B2	USA	19B2	Romoratin *France*	48C2
Rhein, R *W Europe*	56B2	Rio Claro *Trinidad*	27L1	Robertsport *Lib*	97A4	Ronda *Spain*	50A2
Rheine *W Germ*	56B2	Rio Colorado *Arg*	34C3	Roberval *Can*	7C5	Rondônia *Brazil*	33E6
Rheinfelden *Switz*	47B1	Rio Cuarto *Arg*	34C2	Robinson Crusoe, I		Rondônia, State *Brazil*	24F6
Rheinland Pfalz,		Rio de Jacuipe *Brazil*	31D4	Chile	30H6	Rondonópolis *Brazil*	30F2
Region *W Germ*	49D2	Rio de Janeiro *Brazil*	35C2	Robinvale *Aust*	108B2	Rong'an *China*	73B4
Rheinwaldhorn, Mt		Rio de Janeiro, State		Robson,Mt *Can*	13D2	Rongchang *China*	73B4
Switz	47C1	Brazil	35C2	Roca Partida, I		Rongcheng *China*	72E2
Rhinebeck *USA*	16C2	Rio de la Plata, Est		Mexico	24A3	Rongjiang *China*	73B4
Rhinelander *USA*	10B2	Arg/Urug	29E3	Rocas, I *Atlantic O*	103G5	Rong Jiang, R *China*	73B4
Rho *Italy*	47C2	Rio Gallegos *Arg*	29C6	Rocas, I *Brazil*	31E2	Rongklang Range, Mts	
Rhode Island, State		Rio Grande *Arg*	29C6	Rocha *Urug*	29F2	Burma	76A1
USA	15D2	Rio Grande *Brazil*	30F5	Rochdale *Eng*	42C3	Rønne *Denmark*	39G7
Rhode Island Sd *USA*	16D2	Rio Grande *Nic*	26A4	Rochefort *France*	48B2	Ronneby *Sweden*	39H7
Rhône, R *France*	49C3	Rio Grande, R		Rocher River *Can*	5G3	Ronne Ice Shelf *Ant*	112B2
Rhyl *Wales*	43C3	Nicaragua	25D3	Rocher River *Can*	5G3	Ronse *Belg*	46B1
Riachão do Jacuipe		Rio Grande, R *USA/*		Rochester *Aust*	108B3	Ronthieu, Region	
Brazil	31D4	Mexico	24B2	Rochester *Can*	7C5	France	46A1
Ria de Arosa, B *Spain*	50A1	Rio Grande de		Rochester *Eng*	43E4	Roof Butte, Mt *USA*	9C3
Ria de Betanzos, B		Santiago *Mexico*	23A1	Rochester, Minnesota		Roorkee *India*	84D3
Spain	50A1	Rio Grande do Norte,		USA	10A2	Roosendaal *Neth*	46C1
		State *Brazil*	31D3				

Roosevelt I *Ant*	80E	Roxas, Palawan *Phil*	79A3	Ruvuma, R *Tanz/*		Şāfītā *Syria*	94C1
Roper, R *Aust*	106C2	Roxas, Panay *Phil*	79B3	Mozam	101D2	Šafwān *Iraq*	93E3
Roraima, State *Brazil*	33E3	Roxburgh *NZ*	111A3	Ruwenzori Range, Mts		Saga *Japan*	75A2
Roraime, Mt *Ven*	33E2	Royal Canal *Irish Rep*	45C2	Uganda/Zaïre	99D2	Sagaing *Burma*	76B1
Røros *Nor*	38G6	Royal Leamington Spa		Ruya, R *Zim*	101C2	Sagami-nada, B *Japan*	75B2
Rorschach *Switz*	47C1	Eng	43D3	Ružomberok *Czech*	59B3	Sāgar *India*	85D4
Rørvik *Nor*	38G6	Royal Oak *USA*	14B2	Rwanda, Republic		Sag Harbor *USA*	16C2
Rosalie *Dominica*	27Q2	Royal Tunbridge Wells		Africa	99C3	Saginaw *USA*	14B2
Rosamond L *USA*	22C3	Eng	43E4	Ryazan' *USSR*	60E3	Saginaw B *USA*	14B2
Rosario *Arg*	34C2	Royan *France*	48B2	Ryazhsk *USSR*	61F3	Saglouc *Can*	6C3
Rosário *Brazil*	31C2	Roye *France*	46B2	Rybinskoye		Sagua de Tánamo	
Rosario del Tala *Arg*	34D2	Royston *Eng*	43D3	Vodokhranilishche,		Cuba	26B2
Roscoff *France*	48B2	Rožňava *Czech*	59C3	Res *USSR*	60E2	Sagua la Grande *Cuba*	26B2
Roscommon, County		Rozoy *France*	46B2	Rycroft *Can*	13D1	Saguenay, R *Can*	7C5
Irish Rep	45B2	Rtishchevo *USSR*	61F3	Ryde *Eng*	43D4	Sagunto *Spain*	51B2
Roscommon *Irish Rep*	41B3	Ruaha Nat Pk *Tanz*	99D3	Rye *Eng*	43E4	Sahāb *Jordan*	94C3
Roscrea *Irish Rep*	45C2	Ruahine Range, Mts		Rye Patch Res *USA*	20C2	Sahagún *Spain*	50A1
Roseau *Dominica*	27E3	NZ	110C1	Ryl'sk *USSR*	60D3	Sahara, Desert *N*	
Rosebery *Aust*	109C4	Ruapehu,Mt *NZ*	110C1	Ryn Peskt, Desert		Africa	96C2
Roseburg *USA*	20B2	Rub al Khālī, Desert *S*		USSR	61G4	Saharanpur *India*	84D3
Rosenberg *USA*	19A4	Arabia	65D3	Ryōtsu *Japan*	74D3	Sahiwal *Pak*	84C2
Rosenheim *W Germ*	57C3	Rubha Hunish *Scot*	44A3	Ryskany *USSR*	59D3	Şahrā al Hijārah,	
Rosetown *Can*	13F2	Rubinéia *Brazil*	35A2	Ryūkyū Retto, Arch		Desert Region *Iraq*	93D3
Rosiorii de Verde *Rom*	54B2	Rubtsoysk *USSR*	65K4	Japan	69E4	Sahuayo *Mexico*	23A1
Roskilde *Den*	39G7	Ruby *USA*	12C2	Rzeszów *Pol*	59C2	Saibai I *Aust*	107D1
Roslavl' *USSR*	60D3	Rudan *Iran*	91C4	Rzhev *USSR*	60D2	Saïda *Alg*	96C1
Roslyatlno *USSR*	61E2	Rūdbār *Iran*	90A2			Säida *Leb*	94B2
Ross *NZ*	111B2	Rudnaya Pristan'				Sa'īdabad *Iran*	91C4
Ross, R *Can*	12H2	USSR	69F2	**S**		Saidia *Mor*	51B2
Rossan, Pt *Irish Rep*	40B3	Rudoka Planina, Mt				Saidpur *India*	86B1
Rossano *Italy*	53C3	Yugos	54B2	Sa'ādatābād *Iran*	91B3	Saidu *Pak*	84C2
Ross Barnet Res *USA*	19C3	Rudong *China*	72E3	Saale, R *E Germ*	56C2	Saigõ *Japan*	75A1
Rosseau L, L *Can*	15C1	Rudyard *USA*	14B1	Saanen *Switz*	47B1	Saigon *Viet*	76D3
Rossel, I *Solomon Is*	107E2	Rue *France*	46A1	Saar, R *W Germ*	46D2	Saiha *India*	86C2
Ross Ice Shelf *Ant*	80E	Ruffec *France*	48C2	Saarbrücken *W Germ*	46D2	Saihan Tal *China*	68D2
Rossiyskaya S.F.S.R.,		Rufiji, R *Tanz*	99D3	Saarburg *W Germ*	46D2	Saijo *Japan*	75A2
Republic *USSR*	60D2	Rufino *Arg*	34C2	Saaremaa, I *USSR*	39J7	Saiki *Japan*	74C4
Ross L *USA*	20B1	Rufisque *Sen*	97A3	Saarland, State *W*		St Abb's Head, Pt	
Rossland *Can*	13D3	Rufunsa *Zambia*	100B2	Germ	46D2	Scot	42C2
Rosslare *Irish Rep*	45C2	Rugby *Eng*	43D3	Saarlouis *W Germ*	46D2	St Albans *Eng*	43D4
Ross,Mt *NZ*	111C2	Rügen, I *E Germ*	39G8	Saavedra *Arg*	34C3	St Albans, Vermont	
Rosso *Maur*	97A3	Ruhr, R *W Germ*	56B2	Šabac *Yugos*	54A2	USA	15D2
Ross-on-Wye *Eng*	43C4	Ruijin *China*	73D4	Sabadell *Spain*	51C1	St Albans, West	
Rossosh *USSR*	60E4	Rujen, Mt *Bulg/Yugos*	54B2	Sabae *Japan*	75B1	Virginia *USA*	14B3
Ross River *Can*	4E3	Rukwa, L *Tanz*	99D3	Sabah, State *Malay*	78D1	St Albans Head, C	
Ross S *Ant*	112B6	Rum, I *Scot*	44A3	Sabanalarga *Colombia*	26C4	Eng	43C4
Rostãq *Iran*	91B4	Ruma *Yugos*	54A1	Sabang *Indon*	70A3	St Albert *Can*	13E2
Rostock *E Germ*	56C2	Rumāh *S Arabia*	91A4	Sabari, R *India*	87C1	St Amand-les-Eaux	
Rostov *USSR*	62E2	Rumbek *Sudan*	98C2	Sabastiya *Israel*	94B2	France	46B1
Rostov-na-Donu *USSR*	61E4	Rum Cay, I *Caribbean*	26C2	Sabaya *Bol*	30C2	St Amand-Mont Rond	
Roswell, Georgia *USA*	17B1	Rumilly *France*	47A2	Sab'Bi'ār *Syria*	93C3	France	48C2
Roswell, New Mexico		Rum Jungle *Aust*	106C2	Sabhā *Jordan*	94C2	St André, C *Madag*	101D2
USA	9C3	Rumphi *Malawi*	101C2	Sabhā *Libya*	95A2	St Andrew B *USA*	17A2
Rota *Pacific O*	71F2	Runanga *NZ*	111B2	Sabi, R *Zim*	101C3	St Andrews *Scot*	44C3
Rotenburg,		Runaway,C *NZ*	110C1	Sabinas *Mexico*	24B2	St Andrew Sd *USA*	17B1
Niedersachsen *W*		Rundu *Namibia*	100A2	Sabinas Hidalgo		St Ann's Bay *Jamaica*	27H1
Germ	56B2	Rungwa *Tanz*	99D3	Mexico	24B2	St Anthony *Can*	7E4
Rothaar-Geb, Region		Rungwa, R *Tanz*	99D3	Sabine, R *USA*	19A3	St Arnaud *Aust*	108B3
W Germ	46E1	Rungwe, Mt *Tanz*	99D3	Sabine L *USA*	19B4	St Augustine *USA*	17B2
Rothera, Base *Ant*	112C3	Ruoqiang *China*	82C2	Sabkhat Matti, Salt		St Austell *Eng*	43B4
Rotherham *Eng*	42D3	Ruo Shui, R *China*	68C2	Marsh *UAE*	91B5	St-Avold *France*	46D2
Rothesay *Scot*	42B2	Rupea *Rom*	54C1	Sabkhet El Bardawîl,		St Bees Head, Pt *Eng*	42C2
Roti, I *Indon*	71D5	Rupert, R *Can*	7C4	Lg *Egypt*	94A3	St-Bonnet *France*	47B2
Roto *Aust*	108C2	Rur, R *W Germ*	46D1	Sablayan *Phil*	79B3	St Brides B *Wales*	43B4
Rotoiti,L *NZ*	111B2	Rurrenabaque *Bol*	32D6	Sable,C *Can*	7D5	St-Brieuc *France*	48B2
Rotorua *NZ*	111B2	Rusape *Zim*	101C2	Sable,C *USA*	17B2	St Catharines *Can*	15C2
Rotorua *NZ*	110C1	Ruse *Bulg*	54C2	Sable I *Can*	7D5	St Catherine,Mt	
Rotorua,L *NZ*	110C1	Rushville, Illinois *USA*	18B1	Sabzevār *Iran*	90C2	Grenada	27M2
Rotterdam *Neth*	56A2	Rushworth *Aust*	108B3	Sacajawea Peak *USA*	20C1	St Catherines I *USA*	17B1
Roubaix *France*	46B1	Rusk *USA*	19A3	Sachigo, R *Can*	10A1	St Catherines Pt *Eng*	43D4
Rouen *France*	48C2	Ruskin *USA*	17B2	Sachs Harbour *Can*	4F2	St Chamond *France*	49C2
Rough, Oilfield *N Sea*	42E3	Russell *NZ*	110B1	Säckingen *W Germ*	47B1	St Charles, Missouri	
Round I *Mauritius*	101E3	Russellville, Arkansas		Sacramento *USA*	22B1	USA	18B2
Round Mt *Aust*	109D2	USA	18B2	Sacramento, R *USA*	22B1	St Clair *USA*	14B2
Roundup *USA*	8C2	Russellville, Kentucky		Sacramento, V *USA*	21A1	St Clair,L *USA/Can*	14B2
Rousay, I *Scot*	44C2	USA	18C2	Sacramento Mts *USA*	9C3	St Clair Shores *USA*	14B2
Roussillon, Region		Russian, R *USA*	21A2	Sa'dah *Yemen*	81C4	St Claud *France*	49D2
France	48C3	Russian Socialist		Sadiya *India*	82D3	St Cloud *USA*	10A2
Rouyn *Can*	10C2	Federated Soviet		Sado, R *Port*	50A2	Ste Croix *Switz*	47B1
Rovaniemi *Fin*	38K5	Rep *USSR*	60B3	Sado-shima, I *Japan*	74D3	St Croix, I *Caribbean*	27E3
Rovereto *Italy*	47D2	Rustavi *USSR*	93E1	Sādri *India*	85C3	St Davids Head, Pt	
Rovigo *Italy*	47D2	Rustenburg *S Africa*	101G1	Safed Koh, Mts		Wales	43B4
Rovinj *Yugos*	52B1	Ruston *USA*	19B3	Afghan	84A2	St Denis *France*	46B2
Rovno *USSR*	59D2	Rutana *Burundi*	99C3	Saffle *Sweden*	39G7	St Denis *Réunion*	101E3
Row'ān *Iran*	90A2	Rüthen *W Germ*	46E1	Safi *Jordan*	92C3	St Dizier *France*	46C2
Rowena *Aust*	109C1	Rutla *Mexico*	23B2	Safi *Mor*	96B1	St Elias,Mt *USA*	12F2
Rowley I *Can*	6C3	Rutland *USA*	15D2	Safidabeh *Iran*	90D3	St Elias Mts *Can*	12G2
Rowley Shoals *Aust*	106A2	Rutog *China*	84D2			Saintes *France*	48B2

St Étienne

St Étienne France	49C2	St Mary Peak, Mt		Salar de Uyuni, Salt		Salto del Angel,	
St Francis, R USA	18B2	Aust	108A2	Pan Bol	30C3	Waterfall Ven	33E2
St Francis,C S Africa	100B4	St Marys Aust	109C4	Salasomaggiore Italy	47C2	Salto del Guaira,	
St Gallen Switz	47C1	St Marys USA	15C2	Salavat USSR	61J3	Waterfall Brazil	30E3
St-Gaudens France	48C3	St Marys, R USA	17B1	Salayar Indon	70D4	Salto Grande,	
St George Aust	109C1	Ste-Menehould France	46C2	Sala y Gomez, I		Waterfall Colombia	32C4
St George, South		St Michael USA	12B2	Pacific O	105L5	Salt Range, Mts Pak	84C2
Carolina USA	17B1	St Michaels USA	16A3	Salazar Arg	34C3	Salt River Jamaica	27H2
St George, Utah USA	9B3	St-Michel France	47B2	Salbris France	48C2	Saluda USA	17B1
St George I, Florida		St-Mihiel France	46C2	Salcha, R USA	12E2	Saluzzo Italy	47B2
USA	17B2	St Moritz Switz	47C1	Saldanha S Africa	100A4	Salvador Brazil	31D4
St George,Pt USA	20B2	St-Nazaire France	48B2	Saldhad Syria	94C2	Salvador,L USA	19B4
St-Georges Can	15D1	St-Niklaas Belg	46C1	Saldungaray Arg	34C3	Salvatierra Mexico	23A1
St George's Grenada	27E4	St-Omer France	46B1	Saldus USSR	58C1	Salwah Qatar	91B5
St Georges Chan Irish		St Paul Can	13E2	Sale Aust	109C3	Salween, R Burma	76B1
Rep/Wales	45C3	St Paul, Minnesota		Salem, Illinois USA	18C2	Sal'yany USSR	93E2
St Germain-en-Laye		USA	10A2	Salem India	87B2	Salzburg Austria	57C3
France	46A2	St Paul, R Lib	97A4	Salem, Massachusetts		Salzgitter W Germ	56C2
St-Gervais France	47B2	St Petersburg USA	17B2	USA	16D1	Salzwedel E Germ	56C2
St Gotthard, P Switz	47C1	St Pierre Can	7E5	Salem, New Jersey		Samagaltay USSR	68B1
St Govans Head, Pt		St Pierre,L Can	15D1	USA	16B3	Samales Group, Is Phil	79B4
Wales	43B4	St-Pol-Sur-Ternoise		Salem, Oregon USA	20B2	Samaná Dom Rep	27D3
St Helena USA	22A1	France	46B1	Salembu Besar, I		Samandaği Turk	92C2
St Helena, I Atlantic O	103H5	St Pölten Austria	59B3	Indon	78C4	Samangan Afghan	84B1
St Helena B S Africa	100A4	St Quentin France	46B2	Salen Sweden	39G6	Samar, I Phil	79C3
St Helena Sd USA	17B1	St Raphaël France	49D3	Salerno Italy	53B2	Samarai PNG	107E2
St Helens Aust	109C4	St Sébastien, C		Salford Eng	42C3	Samarinda Indon	78D3
St Helens Eng	42C3	Madag	101D2	Salgót Hung	54A1	Samarkand USSR	80E2
St Helens USA	20B1	St Simons I USA	17B1	Salgótarjan Hung	59B3	Sämarrā' Iraq	93D3
St Helens,Mt USA	20B1	St Stephen USA	17B1	Salgueiro Brazil	31D3	Samar S Phil	79B3
St Helier Jersey	48B2	St Thomas Can	14B2	Salihli Turk	55C3	Sambalpur India	86A2
St Hippolyte France	47B1	St-Tropez France	49D3	Salima Malawi	101C2	Sambas Indon	78B2
St-Hubert Belg	46C1	St Truiden Belg	46C1	Salimaa, L Fin	39K6	Sambava Madag	101E2
St-Hyacinthe Can	7C5	St-Valéry-sur-Somme		Salina, Kansas USA	18A2	Sambhal India	84D3
St Ignace USA	14B1	France	46A1	Salina, I Italy	53B3	Samboja Indon	78D3
St Ives Eng	43B4	St Vincent, C Madag	101D3	Salina Cruz Mexico	23B2	Sambor USSR	59C3
St James, Missouri		St Vincent, I		Salina de Arizato Arg	30C3	Sambre, R France	46B1
USA	18B2	Caribbean	27E4	Salina Grande, Salt		Samch'ŏk S Korea	74B3
St James,C Can	5E4	St Vincent,G Aust	108A2	pan Arg	34B3	Same Tanz	99D3
St Jean Can	15D1	St-Vith W Germ	46D1	Salina La Antigua, Salt		Samedan Switz	47C1
St Jean-d'Angely		St Wendel W Germ	46D2	pan Arg	34B2	Samer France	46A1
France	48B2	Saipan, I Pacific O	71F2	Salinas Brazil	35C1	Samfya Zambia	100B2
St-Jean-de-Maurienne		Saiydabad Afghan	84B2	Salinas USA	22B2	Samka Burma	76B1
France	47B2	Sajama, Mt Bol	30C2	Salinas, R USA	22B2	Sam Neua Laos	76C1
St Jean,L Can	10C2	Sakai Japan	74D4	Salinas de Llancaneb,		Sámos, I Greece	55C3
St-Jérôme Can	15D1	Sakaidi Japan	75A2	Salt Pan Arg	34B3	Samothráki, I Greece	55C2
St Joe, R USA	20C1	Sakaiminato Japan	75A1	Salinas Grandes, Salt		Sampacho Arg	34C2
Saint John Can	7D5	Sakākah S Arabia	93D4	Pan Arg	34B2	Sampaga Indon	78D3
St John's Can	7E5	Sakami,L Can	10C1	Saline, R, Arkansas		Sampit Indon	78C3
St Johns, Michigan		Sakania Zaïre	100B2	USA	19B3	Sampit, R Indon	78C3
USA	14B2	Sakaraha Madag	101D3	Salines,Pt Grenada	27M2	Sam Rayburn Res	
St Johns, R USA	17B2	Sakarya, R Turk	60D5	Salinópolis Brazil	31B2	USA	19B3
St Johnsbury USA	15D2	Sakasleja USSR	58C1	Salins France	47A1	Samrong Camb	76C3
St-Joseph Can	15D1	Sakata Japan	74D3	Salisbury Eng	43D4	Samsø, I Den	56C1
St Joseph, Louisiana		Saketél Benin	97C4	Salisbury, Maryland		Samsun Turk	92C1
USA	19B3	Sakhalin, I USSR	69G1	USA	15C3	San Mali	97B3
St Joseph, Michigan		Sakishima gunto, Is		Salisbury I Can	6C3	San, R Camb	76D3
USA	14A2	Japan	69E4	Salisbury Plain Eng	43D4	San, R Pol	59C2
St Joseph, Missouri		Sal, I Cape Verde	97A4	Salla Fin	38K5	San'ã' Yemen	81C4
USA	18B2	Sal, R USSR	61F4	Sallanches France	47B2	Sanaga, R Cam	98B2
St Joseph Trinidad	27L1	Sala Sweden	39H7	Sallisaw USA	18B2	San Agustín Arg	29C2
St Joseph, R USA	14B2	Saladillo Arg	34D3	Sallyana Nepal	86A1	San Agustin,C Phil	79C4
St Joseph I Can	14B1	Saladillo, R Arg	34C2	Salmas Iran	93D2	Sanandaj Iran	90A2
St Joseph,L Can	7A4	Salado, R, Buenos		Salmi USSR	38L6	San Andreas USA	22B1
St Julien France	47B1	Aires Arg	34D3	Salmo Can	20C1	San Andrés Tuxtla	
St-Junien France	48C2	Salado, R, Mendoza/		Salmon USA	8B2	Mexico	25C3
St-Just-en-Chaussée		San Luis Arg	34B3	Salmon Arm Can	13D2	San Angelo USA	9C3
France	46B2	Salado, R, Sante Fe		Salmon River Mts		San Antioco Sardegna	53A3
St Kilda, I Scot	4B2	Arg	30D4	USA	8B2	San Antioco, I Medit	
St Kitts, I Caribbean	27E3	Salaga Ghana	97B4	Salo Fin	39J6	S	53A3
St-Laurent France	47A1	Sala Hintoun Camb	76C3	Salò Italy	47D2	San Antonio Chile	34A2
St Lawrence, R Can	7D5	Salal Chad	98B1	Salon-de-Provence		San Antonio, New	
Saint Lawrence,G of		Salālah Oman	81D4	France	49D3	Mexico USA	9C3
Can	7D5	Salamanca Chile	34A2	Salonta Rom	54B1	San Antonio Phil	79B2
St Lawrence I USA	4A3	Salamanca Mexico	23A1	Salpausselka, Region		San Antonio, R, Texas	
St Lawrence Seaway		Salamanca Spain	50A1	Fin	38K6	USA	9D4
Can/USA	15C2	Salamanca USA	15C2	Salsacate Arg	34B2	San Antonio Abad	
St Lô France	48B2	Salamat, R Chad	98B2	Sal'sk USSR	61F4	Spain	51C2
St Louis Sen	97A3	Salamaua PNG	71F4	Salt Jordan	94B2	San Antonio,C Cuba	25D2
St Louis USA	11A3	Salamonica USA	15C2	Salta Arg	30C3	San Antonio de los	
St Lucia, I Caribbean	27E4	Salang Indon	78D1	Salta, State Arg	30C3	Banos Cuba	26A2
St Lucia,L S Africa	101H1	Salangen Nor	38H5	Saltillo Mexico	24B2	San Antonio,Mt USA	22D3
St Magnus, I Scot	44D1	Salar de Arizaro Arg	30C3	Salt Lake City USA	8B2	San Antonio Oeste	
St Malo France	48B2	Salar de Atacama,		Salto Arg	34C2	Arg	29C4
Ste Marie, C Madag	101D3	Salt Pan Chile	30C3	Salto Urug	34D2	San Augustin Arg	34D3
St Maries USA	20C1	Salar de Coipasa, Salt		Salto Angostura,		San Augustin de Valle	
St Martin, I Caribbean	27E3	Pan Bol	30C2	Waterfall Colombia	32C3	Féril Arg	34B2
		Salto da Divisa Brazil	35D1			Sanawad India	85D4

Santiago de Compostela

San Bartolo *Mexico*	23A1
San Benedicto, I *Mexico*	24A3
San Benito, R *USA*	22B2
San Benito Mt *USA*	22B2
San Bernardino *USA*	22D3
San Bernardo *Chile*	34A2
San Blas,C *USA*	17A2
San Carlos *Chile*	34A3
San Carlos *Nic*	32A1
San Carlos *Phil*	79B2
San Carlos de Bariloche *Arg*	29B4
San-chung *Taiwan*	69E4
Sanchursk *USSR*	61G2
San Clemente *Chile*	34A3
San Clemente *USA*	22D4
San Clemente I *USA*	21B3
San Cristóbal *Arg*	34C2
San Cristóbal *Mexico*	25C3
San Cristóbal *Ven*	32C2
San Cristóbal, I *Ecuador*	32J7
San Cristobal, I *Solomon Is*	107F2
Sancti Spíritus *Cuba*	25E2
Sandai *Indon*	78C3
Sandakan *Malay*	70C3
Sanday, I *Scot*	44C2
Sanderson *USA*	9C3
Sandfly L *Can*	13F1
San Diego *USA*	21B3
Sandikli *Turk*	92B2
Sandila *India*	86A1
Sandnes *Nor*	39F7
Sandnessjøen *Nor*	38G5
Sandø *Faroes*	38D3
Sandoa *Zaïre*	98C3
Sandomierz *Pol*	59C2
Sandpoint *USA*	20C1
Sandrio *Italy*	49D2
Sand Springs *USA*	18A2
Sandstone *Aust*	106A3
Sandu *China*	73C4
Sandusky *USA*	14B2
Sandviken *Sweden*	39H6
Sandy L *Can*	7A4
San Elcano *Arg*	34C2
San Felipe, Baja Cal *Mexico*	9B3
San Felipe *Chile*	34A2
San Felipe, Guanajuato *Mexico*	23A1
San Felipe *Ven*	27D4
San Feliu de Guixols *Spain*	51C1
San Felix, I *Pacific O*	28A5
San Fernando *Chile*	34A2
San Fernando *Phil*	79B2
San Fernando *Phil*	79B2
San Fernando *Spain*	50A2
San Fernando *Trinidad*	27E4
San Fernando *USA*	22C3
San Fernando *Ven*	32D2
Sanford, Florida *USA*	17B2
Sanford,Mt *USA*	12F2
San Francisco *Arg*	34C2
San Francisco *Dom Rep*	27C3
San Francisco *USA*	22A2
San Francisco B *USA*	22A2
San Francisco del Oro *Mexico*	24B2
San Francisco del Rincon *Mexico*	23A1
San Gabriel Mts *USA*	22D3
Sangamner *India*	85C5
Sangamon, R *USA*	18C2
Sangan, I *Pacific O*	71F2
Sangāreddi *India*	87B1
Sangeang, I *Indon*	78D4
Sanger *USA*	22C2
Sanggan He, R *China*	72C2
Sanggau *Indon*	78C2
Sangha, R *Congo*	98B2
Sangkhar *Pak*	85B3
Sangkhla Buri *Thai*	76B3
Sangkulirang *Indon*	78D2
Sāngli *India*	87A1
Sangmélima *Cam*	98B2
San Gorgonio Mt *USA*	9B3
Sangre de Cristo, Mts *USA*	9C3
San Gregorio *Arg*	34C2
San Gregorio *USA*	22A2
Sangrür *India*	84D2
San Ignacio *Arg*	30E4
San Isidro *Phil*	79B3
San Jacinto *Colombia*	32B2
San Jacinto Peak, Mt *USA*	21B3
San Javier *Chile*	34A3
San Javier, Sante Fe *Arg*	34D2
Sanjō, I *Japan*	74D3
San João del Rei *Brazil*	31C6
San Joaquin, R *USA*	22B2
San Joaquin Valley *USA*	22B2
San José *Costa Rica*	32A1
San José *Guatemala*	25C3
San Jose, Luzon *Phil*	79B2
San Jose, Mindoro *Phil*	79B3
San Jose *USA*	22B2
San José, I *Mexico*	9B4
San José de Chiquitos *Bol*	30D2
San José de Feliciano *Arg*	34D2
San José de Jachal *Arg*	34B2
San José de la Dormida *Arg*	34C2
San José do Rio Prêto *Brazil*	31B6
San José del Cabo *Mexico*	24B2
San Juan *Arg*	34B2
San Juan *Puerto Rico*	27D3
San Juan, State *Arg*	34B2
San Juan *Trinidad*	27L1
San Juan *Ven*	32D2
San Juan, Mt *Cuba*	26B2
San Juan, Mts *USA*	8C3
San Juan, R *Arg*	34B2
San Juan, R *Mexico*	23B2
San Juan, R *Nicaragua/Costa Rica*	25D3
San Juan Bautista *Mexico*	23B2
San Juan Bautista *Par*	30E4
San Juan Bautista *USA*	22B2
San Juan del Norte *Nic*	25D3
San Juan de los Cayos *Ven*	27D4
San Juan de loz Lagoz *Mexico*	23A1
San Juan del Rio *Mexico*	23A1
San Juan del Sur *Nicaragua*	25D3
San Juan Is *USA*	20B1
San Juan Tepozcolula *Mexico*	23B2
San Julián *Arg*	29C5
San Justo *Arg*	34C2
Sankuru, R *Zaïre*	98C3
San Leandro *USA*	22A2
San Lorenzo *Ecuador*	32B3
San Lorenzo *Arg*	34C2
San Lucas *USA*	22B2
San Luis *Arg*	34B2
San Luis, State *Arg*	34B2
San Luis de la Paz *Mexico*	23A1
San Luis Obispo *USA*	21A2
San Luis Potosi *Mexico*	23A1
San Luis Res *USA*	22B2
Sanluri *Sardegna*	53A3
San Maigualida, Mts *Ven*	33D2
San Manuel *Arg*	34D3
San Marcos *Chile*	34A2
San Marcos *Mexico*	23B2
San Marino, Republic Europe	52B2
San Martin, Mendoza *Arg*	34B2
San Martin, Base *Ant*	112C3
San Martino di Castroza *Italy*	47D1
San Martin Tuxmelucan *Mexico*	23B2
San Mateo *USA*	22A2
San Matias *Bol*	30E2
Sanmenxia *China*	72C3
San Miguel *El Salvador*	25D3
San Miguel, I *USA*	22B3
San Miguel del Allende *Mexico*	23A1
San Miguel del Monte *Arg*	34D3
San Miguel de Tucumán *Arg*	30C4
Sanming *China*	73D4
San Nicolas, I *USA*	9B3
San Nicolás de los Arroyos *Arg*	34C2
Sannieshof *S Africa*	101G1
Sanniquellie *Lib*	97B4
Sanok *Pol*	59C3
San Onofore *Colombia*	26B5
San Onofre *USA*	22D4
San Pablo *Phil*	79B3
San Pablo B *USA*	22A1
San Pedro, Buenos Aires *Arg*	34D2
San Pédro *Ivory Coast*	97B4
San Pedro, Jujuy *Arg*	30D3
San Pedro *Par*	30E3
San Pedro Chan *USA*	22C4
San Pedro de los Colonias *Mexico*	9C4
San Pedro Sula *Honduras*	25D3
San Pietro, I *Medit S*	53A3
San Quintin *Mexico*	24A1
San Rafael *Arg*	34B2
San Rafael *USA*	22A2
San Rafael Mts *USA*	22C3
San Remo *Italy*	49D3
San Salvador *Arg*	34D2
San Salvador, I *Caribbean*	26C2
San Salvador, I *Ecuador*	32J7
San Salvador de Jujuy *Arg*	30C3
San Sebastian *Spain*	51B1
San Severo *Italy*	53C2
Santa Ana *Bol*	30C2
Santa Ana *Guatemala*	25C3
Santa Ana *USA*	22D4
Santa Ana Mts *USA*	22D4
Santa Bárbara *Chile*	34A3
Santa Barbara *Mexico*	24B2
Santa Barbara *USA*	22C3
Santa Barbara, I *USA*	22C4
Santa Barbara Chan *USA*	22B3
Santa Barbara Res *USA*	22C3
Santa Catalina, I *USA*	22C4
Santa Catalina,G of *USA*	22C4
Santa Catarina, State *Brazil*	30F4
Santa Clara *Cuba*	26B2
Santa Clara, R *USA*	22C3
Santa Cruz *Arg*	29C6
Santa Cruz *Bol*	30D2
Santa Cruz *Chile*	34A2
Santa Cruz *Phil*	79B3
Santa Cruz, State *Arg*	29B5
Santa Cruz *USA*	22A2
Santa Cruz, I *USA*	22C4
Santa Cruz Cabrália *Brazil*	35D1
Santa Cruz Chan *USA*	22C3
Santa Cruz de la Palma *Canary Is*	96A2
Santa Cruz del Sur *Cuba*	26B2
Santa Cruz de Tenerife *Canary Is*	96A2
Santa Cruz do Cuando *Angola*	100B2
Santa Cruz do Rio Pardo *Brazil*	35B2
Santa Cruz Mts *USA*	22A2
Santa Elena *Arg*	34D2
Santa Elena *Ven*	33E3
Santa Fe *Arg*	34C2
Santa Fe, State *Arg*	34C2
Santa Fe *USA*	9C3
Santa Helena de Goiás *Brazil*	35A1
Santai *China*	73B3
Santa Inés, I *Chile*	29B6
Santa Isabel, La Pampa *Arg*	34B3
Santa Isabel, Sante Fe *Arg*	34C2
Santa Isabel, I *Solomon Is*	107E1
Santa Lucia, Ra *USA*	21A2
Santa Lucia Range, Mts *USA*	21A2
Santa Luzia, I *Cape Verde*	97A4
Santa Margarita, I *Mexico*	9B4
Santa Margarita, R *USA*	22D4
Santa Maria *Brazil*	30F4
Santa Maria *Colombia*	26C4
Santa Maria *USA*	21A3
Santa Maria, I *Açores*	96A1
Santa Maria, R, Queretaro *Mexico*	23B1
Santa Maria del Rio *Mexico*	23A1
Santa Marta *Colombia*	32C1
Santa Monica *USA*	22C3
Santa Monica B *USA*	22C4
Santana do Livramento *Brazil*	29E2
Santander *Colombia*	32B3
Santander *Spain*	50B1
Santañy *Spain*	51C2
Santa Paula *USA*	22C3
Santa Quitéria *Brazil*	31C2
Santarem *Brazil*	33G4
Santarém *Port*	50A2
Santa Rosa, California *USA*	22A1
Santa Rosa *Honduras*	25D3
Santa Rosa, La Pampa *Arg*	34C3
Santa Rosa, Mendoza *Arg*	34B2
Santa Rosa, San Luis *Arg*	34B2
Santa Rosa, I *USA*	22B3
Santa Rosalía *Mexico*	24A2
Santa Rosa Range, Mts *USA*	20C2
Santa Talhada *Brazil*	31D3
Santa Teresa *Brazil*	35C1
Santa Teresa de Gallura *Sardegna*	53A2
Santa Ynez, R *USA*	22B3
Santa Ynez Mts *USA*	22B3
Santee, R *USA*	17C1
Santhia *Italy*	47C2
Santiago *Chile*	34A2
Santiago *Dom Rep*	27C3
Santiago *Panama*	32A2
Santiago *Phil*	79B2
Santiago, R *Peru*	32B4
Santiago de Compostela *Spain*	50A1

63

Santiago de Cuba

Santiago de Cuba Cuba	26B2	Sapulpa USA	18A2	Satilla, R USA	17B1	Schleswig Holstein,
Santiago del Estero Arg	30D4	Saqqez Iran	90A2	Satka USSR	61J2	State W Germ	56B2
Santiago del Estero, State Arg	30D4	Saquenay, R Can	10C2	Satluj, R India	84D2	Schoharie USA	16B1
		Saráb Iran	90A2	Satna India	86A2	Schouten, Is PNG	71F4
Santiago Peak, Mt USA	22D4	Sarafa USSR	54C1	Sätpura Range, Mts India	85C4	Schreiber Can	7B5
		Sarajevo Yugos	54A2			Schurz USA	21B2
Santo, State Brazil	31C5	Sarakhs Iran	90D2	Satu Mare Rom	54B1	Schuykill Haven USA	16A2
Santo Anastatácio Brazil	35A2	Saraktash USSR	61J3	Sauce Arg	34D2	Schuylkill, R USA	16B2
Santo Angelo Brazil	30F4	Sarala USSR	63A2	Sauda Nor	39F7	Schwabische Alb,
Santo Antão, I Cape Verde	97A4	Saranac L USA	15D2	Saudi Arabia, Kingdom Arabian Pen	80C3	Upland W Germ	57B3
		Saranac Lake USA	15D2			Schwarzwald, Mts W Germ	49D2
Santo Antonio da Platina Brazil	35A2	Sarandë Alb	55B3			
		Sarangani Is Phil	79C4	Sauer, R W Germ/Lux	46D2	Schwarzwald, Upland W Germ	57B3
Santo Domingo Dom Rep	27D3	Saransk USSR	61G3	Sauerland, Region W Germ	46D1	
		Sarapul USSR	61H2			Schwatka Mts USA	12C1
Santos Brazil	35B2	Sarasota USA	17B2	Sauðárkrókur Iceland	38B1	Schwaz Austria	47D1
Santos Dumont Brazil	35C2	Saratoga Springs USA	15D2	Saugatuck USA	14A2	Schweinfurt W Germ	57C2
Santo Tomé Arg	30E4	Saratok Malay	78C2	Saugerties USA	16C1	Schweizer Reneke S Africa	101G1
San Valentin, Mt Chile	29B5	Saratov USSR	61G3	Saugstad,Mt Can	13B2	
San Vicente Chile	34A2	Saratovskoye Vodokhranilishche, Res USSR	61G3	Sault Sainte Marie Can	7B5	Schwerin E Germ	56C2
Sanza Pomba Angola	98B3					Schwyz Switz	47C1
São Borja Brazil	30E4	Sarawak, State Malay	67F4	Sault Ste Marie Can	14B1	Sciacca Italy	53B3
São Carlos Brazil	35B2	Saraykoy Turk	92A2	Sault Ste Marie USA	14B1	Scioto, R USA	14B3
São Félix, Mato Grosso Brazil	33G5	Sarbisheh Iran	90C3	Saumlaki Indon	71E4	Scone Aust	109D2
		Sarca, R Italy	47D1	Saumur France	48B2	Scoresby Sd Greenland	6H2
São Fidélis Brazil	35C2	Sardalais Libya	95A2	Saurimo Angola	98C3	
São Francisco Brazil	35C1	Sar Dasht Iran	90A2	Sauteurs Grenada	27M2	Scotia Ridge Atlantic O	103F7
São Francisco, R Brazil	31D3	Sardegna, I Medit S	52A2	Sava, R Yugos	54A2	
		Sarektjåkkå, Mt Sweden	38H5	Savalou Benin	97C4	Scotia S Atlantic O	103F7
São Francisco do Sul Brazil	30G4			Savannah, Georgia USA	17B1	Scotland, Country U K	44B3
		Sargodha Pak	84C2			Scott, Base Ant	112B7
São Gotardo Brazil	35B1	Sarh Chad	98B2	Savannah, R USA	17B1	Scott,C Can	13B2
Sao Hill Tanz	99D3	Sārī Iran	90B2	Savannakhet Laos	76C2	Scott City USA	9C2
São João da Barra Brazil	35C2	Sarida, R Isreal	94B2	Savanna la Mar Jamaica	26B3	Scott I Ant	112C6
		Sarikamiş Turk	93D1			Scott Inlet, B Can	6C2
São João da Boa Vista Brazil	35B2	Sarina Aust	107D3	Savant Lake Can	7A4	Scott,Mt USA	20B2
		Sarine, R Switz	47B1	Savarane Laos	76D2	Scott Reef Timor S	106B2
São João da Ponte Brazil	35C1	Sar-i-Pul Afghan	84B1	Savé Benin	97C4	Scottsbluff USA	8C2
		Sarir Libya	95B2	Save, R Mozam	101C3	Scottsboro USA	17A1
São João del Rei Brazil	35C2	Sarir Tibesti, Desert Libya	95A2	Sāveh Iran	90B3	Scottsdale Aust	109C4
				Saverne France	46D2	Scranton USA	10C2
São Joaquim da Barra Brazil	35B2	Sariwŏn N Korea	74B3	Savigliano Italy	47B2	Scuol Switz	47D1
		Sark, I UK	48B2	Savigny France	46B2	Seal, R Can	5J4
São Jorge, I Açores	96A1	Šarkišla Turk	92C2	Savoie, Region France	49D2	Sea Lake Aust	108B3
São José do Rio Prêto Brazil	35B2	Sarmi Indon	71E4	Savona Italy	49D3	Searcy USA	18B2
		Sarmiento Arg	29C5	Savonlinna Fin	38K6	Seaside, California USA	22B2
São José dos Campos Brazil	35B2	Särna Sweden	39G6	Savoonga USA	4A3	
		Sarnen Switz	47C1	Savukoski Fin	38K5	Seaside, Oregon USA	20B1
São Luis Brazil	31C2	Sarnia Can	14B2	Savu S Indon	71D4	Seaside Park USA	16B3
São Marcos, R Brazil	35B1	Sarny USSR	58D2	Saw Burma	76A1	Seattle USA	20B1
São Maria do Suaçui Brazil	35C1	Saroaq Greenland	6E2	Sawai Mädhopur India	85D3	Sebastopol USA	22A1
		Sarobi Afghan	84B2	Sawang Indon	78A2	Sebez USSR	58D1
São Mateus Brazil	35D1	Sarolangun Indon	78A3	Sawankhalok Thai	76B2	Sebring USA	17B2
São Mateus, R Brazil	35C1	Saronikós Kólpos, G Greece	55B3	Sawara Japan	75C1	Secretary I NZ	111A3
São Miguel, I Açores	96A1			Sawknah Libya	95A2	Sedalia USA	18B2
Saône, R France	49C2	Saronno Italy	47C2	Sawtooth Mt USA	12E1	Sedan France	46C2
São Nicolau, I Cape Verde	97A4	Saros Körfezi, B Turk	55C2	Sawu, I Indon	106B2	Seddonville NZ	111B2
		Sarpsborg Nor	39G7	Say Niger	97C3	Sede Boqer Israel	94B3
São Paulo Brazil	35B2	Sarralbe France	46D2	Sayghan Afghan	84B1	Sederot Israel	94B3
São Paulo, State Brazil	35A2	Sarrebourg France	46D2	Sayhandulaan Mongolia	72B1	Sédhiou Sen	97A3
São Raimundo Nonato Brazil	31C3	Sarreguemines France	46D2	Sayhūt S Yemen	91B5	Sedom Israel	94B3
		Sarre-Union France	46D2	Saykhin USSR	61G4	Seeheim Namibia	100A3
São Romão Brazil	35B1	Sarrion Spain	51B1	Saynshand Mongolia	68D2	Sefton,Mt NZ	111B2
São Sebastia do Paraiso Brazil	35B2	Sartanahu Pak	85B3	Say-Utes USSR	61H5	Segamat Malay	77C5
		Sartène Corse	53A2	Sayville USA	16C2	Segorbe Spain	51B2
São Simão, Goias Brazil	35A1	Sarthe, R France	48B2	Sayward Can	13B2	Ségou Mali	97B3
		Sarykamys USSR	61H4	Sázava, R Czech	57C3	Segovia Spain	50B1
São Simão, Sao Paulo Brazil	35B2	Sarysu, R USSR	65H5	Sbisseb, R Alg	51C2	Segre, R Spain	51C1
		Sasarām India	86A2	Scafell Pike, Mt Eng	42C2	Séguéla Ivory Coast	97B4
São Tiago, I Cape Verde	97A4	Sasebo Japan	74B4	Scalloway Scot	44D1	Seguia el Hamra, Watercourse Mor	96A2
		Saskatchewan, Province Can	5H4	Scapa Flow, Sd Scot	44C2	
Sápai Greece	55C2			Scarborough Can	15C2	Segundo, R Arg	34C2
Sape Indon	78D4	Saskatchewan, R Can	5H4	Scarborough Eng	42D2	Seguntur Indon	78D2
Sapele Nig	97C4	Saskatoon Can	13F2	Scarborough Tobago	27E4	Segura, R Spain	50B2
Sapporo Japan	74E2	Sasolburg S Africa	101G1	Scarp, I Scot	44A2	Sehwan Pak	85B3
Sapri Italy	53C2	Sasovo USSR	61F3	Scarriff Irish Rep	45B2	Seille, R France	46D2
		Sassandra Ivory Coast	97B4	Schaffhausen Switz	52A1	Seinäjoki Fin	38J6
		Sassandra, R Ivory Coast	97B4	Scharding Austria	57C3	Seine, R France	48C2
		Sassari Sardegna	53A2	Scharteberg, Mt W Germ	46D1	Seine-et-Marne, Department France	46B2
		Sassnitz E Germ	56C2			
		Sassuolo Italy	47D2	Schefferville Can	7D4	Sekenke Tanz	99D3
		Sastre Arg	34C2	Schelde, R Belg	46B1	Selah USA	20B1
		Sātāra India	87A1	Schenectady USA	10C2	Selaru, I Indon	71E4
		Satellite B Can	4G2	Schio Italy	47D2	Selat Alas, Str Indon	78D4
		Satengar, Is Indon	78D4	Schleiden W Germ	46D1	Selat Bangka, Str Indon	78B3
		Säter Sweden	39H6	Schleswig W Germ	56B2	Selat Berhala, B Indon	78A3

Shikoku-sanchi

Selat Dampier, Str Indon	71E4
Selat Gaspar, Str Indon	78B3
Selat Lombok, Str Indon	78D4
Selat Sape, Str Indon	78D4
Selat Sunda, Str Indon	78B4
Selat Wetar, Chan Indon	71D4
Selawik USA	12B1
Selawik, R USA	12C1
Selawik L USA	12B1
Selby Eng	42D3
Selçuk Turk	55C3
Seldovia USA	12D3
Selebi Pikwe Botswana	100B3
Selfoss Iceland	6H3
Selima Oasis Sudan	95B2
Selkirk Can	5J4
Selkirk Scot	42C2
Selkirk Mts Can	13D2
Selma, California USA	22C2
Selouane Mor	50B2
Selous,Mt Can	12H2
Selta Karimata, Str Indon	78B3
Selvas, Region Brazil	32C5
Selwyn Aust	107D3
Selwyn Mts Can	4E3
Semarang Indon	78C4
Semenov USSR	61E2
Semidi Is USA	12C3
Semiluki USSR	60E3
Seminole, Oklahoma USA	19A2
Seminole,L USA	17B1
Semipalatinsk USSR	65K4
Semirara Is Phil	79B3
Semirom Iran	90B3
Semitau Indon	78C2
Semnān Iran	90B2
Semois, R Belg	46C2
Sempoala, Hist Site Mexico	23B2
Sena Madureira Brazil	32D5
Senanga Zambia	100B2
Senatobia USA	19C3
Sendai, Honshū Japan	74E3
Sendai, Kyūshū Japan	74C4
Sendwha India	85D4
Seneca Falls USA	15C2
Senegal, Republic Africa	97A3
Sénégal, R Maur Sen	97A3
Senekal S Africa	101G1
Senhor do Bonfim Brazil	31D4
Senigallia Italy	52B2
Senj Yugos	52C2
Senkaku Gunto, Is Japan	69E4
Senlis France	46B2
Sennar Sudan	99D1
Senneterre Can	7C5
Sens France	49C2
Senta Yugos	54A1
Sentery Zaïre	98C3
Sentinel Peak, Mt Can	13C2
Seoni India	85D4
Separation Pt NZ	110B2
Sepone Laos	76D2
Sept-Iles Can	7D4
Séquédine Niger	95A2
Sequoia, Nat Pk USA	21B2
Seram, I Indon	71D4
Serang Indon	78B4
Serasan, I Indon	78B2
Sorbia, Region Yugos	54A2
Serdobsk USSR	61F3
Seremban Malay	77C5
Serengeti Nat Pk Tanz	99D3
Serenje Zambia	100C2
Seret, R USSR	59D3
Sergach USSR	61G2
Sergino USSR	65H3
Sergipe, State Brazil	31D4
Seria Brunei	78C2
Serian Malay	78C2
Sérifos, I Greece	55B3
Serio, R Italy	47C2
Serir Calanscio, Desert Libya	95B2
Sermaize-les-Bains France	46C2
Sermata, I Indon	71D4
Sernovodsk USSR	61H3
Serov USSR	65H4
Serowe Botswana	100B3
Serpa Port	50A2
Serpukhov USSR	60E3
Serra da Canastra, Mts Brazil	35B2
Serra da Estrela, Mts Port	50A1
Serra da Mantiqueira, Mts Brazil	35B2
Serra da Mombuca Brazil	35A1
Serra do Cabral, Mt Brazil	35C1
Serra do Cachimbo, Mts Brazil	33F5
Serra do Caiapó, Mts Brazil	35A1
Serra do Cantu, Mts Brazil	35A2
Serra do Caparaó, Mts Brazil	35C2
Serra do Chifre Brazil	31C5
Serra do Espinhaço, Mts Brazil	35C1
Serra do Mar, Mts Brazil	35B2
Serra do Mirante, Mts Brazil	35A2
Serra do Navio Brazil	33G3
Serra do Paranapiacaba, Mts Brazil	35B2
Serra dos Caiabis, Mts Brazil	33F6
Serra dos Dourados, Mts Brazil	35A2
Serra dos Parecis, Mts Brazil	33E6
Serra dos Pilões, Mts Brazil	35B1
Serra Dourada, Mts Brazil	35A1
Serra Formosa, Mts Brazil	33F6
Sérrai Greece	55B2
Serrana Bank, Is Caribbean	25D3
Serrana de Cuenca, Mts Spain	51B1
Serranópolis Brazil	35A1
Serra Pacaraima, Mts Brazil/Ven	33E3
Serra Parima, Mts Brazil	33E3
Serra Tumucumaque Brazil	33G3
Serre, R France	46B2
Serrezuela Arg	34B2
Serrinha Brazil	31D4
Serrmilik Greenland	6G3
Serro Brazil	35C1
Sertanópolis Brazil	35A2
Sêrtar China	72A3
Seruyan, R Indon	78C3
Sesfontein Namibia	100A2
Sesheke Zambia	100B2
Sestriere Italy	47B2
Setana Japan	74D2
Sète France	49C3
Sete Lagoas Brazil	35C1
Sétif Alg	96C1
Seto Japan	75B1
Seto Naikai, S Japan	75A2
Settat Mor	96B1
Settle Eng	42C2
Settler Can	5G4
Sêtubal Port	50A2
Sevan,Oz, L USSR	93E1
Sevastopol' USSR	60D5
Severn, R Can	7B4
Severn, R Eng	43C3
Severnaya Zemlya, I USSR	1B9
Severo-Baykalskoye Nagorye, Mts USSR	63C2
Severo Donets USSR	60E4
Severodvinsk USSR	64E3
Severo Sos'va, R USSR	64H3
Sevier, R USA	8B3
Sevier L USA	8B3
Sevilla Spain	50A2
Sevlievo Bulg	54C2
Sewa, R Sierra Leone	97A4
Seward, Alaska USA	12E2
Seward, Nebraska USA	18A1
Seward Pen USA	12A1
Sexsmith Can	13D1
Seychelles, Is Indian O	89K8
Seyðisfjörður Iceland	38C1
Seyhan Turk	92C2
Seym, R USSR	60E3
Seymour Aust	108C3
Seymour, Connecticut USA	16C2
Seymour, Indiana USA	14A3
Sézanne France	46B2
Sfax Tunisia	96D1
Sfîntu Gheorghe Rom	54C1
's-Gravenhage Neth	56A2
Shaanxi, Province China	72B3
Shabunda Zaïre	98C3
Shache China	82B2
Shackleton Ice Shelf Ant	112C9
Shadadkot Pak	85B3
Shādhām, R Iran	91B3
Shaftesbury Eng	43C4
Shag Rocks, Is South Georgia	29G8
Shāhābād Iran	90A3
Shāhbā Syria	94C2
Shahdap Iran	91C3
Shahdol India	86A2
Shāhīn Dezh Iran	90A2
Shāh Kūh Iran	90C3
Shahr-e Bābak Iran	91C3
Shahr Kord Iran	90B3
Shājābād India	87B1
Shājahānpur India	84D3
Shājāpur India	85D4
Shakhty USSR	61F4
Shakhun'ya USSR	61G2
Shaki Nig	97C4
Shaktoolik USA	12B2
Shamary USSR	61J2
Shambe Sudan	99D2
Shamokin USA	16A2
Shandaken USA	16B1
Shandong, Province China	72D2
Shangchuan Dao, I China	73C5
Shangdu China	72C1
Shanghai China	73E3
Shangnan China	72C3
Shangombo Zambia	100B2
Shangra China	73D4
Shangsi China	73B5
Shang Xian China	72C3
Shannon, R Irish Rep	41B3
Shanqiu China	72D3
Shansonggang China	74B2
Shantarskiye Ostrova, I USSR	63F2
Shantou China	73D5
Shanxi, Province China	72C2
Shan Xian China	72D3
Shaoguan China	73C5
Shaoxing China	73E4
Shaoyang China	73C4
Shapinsay, I Scot	44C2
Shaqqā Syria	94C2
Sharīfābād Iran	90C2
Sharjah UAE	91C4
Shark B Aust	106A3
Sharlauk USSR	90C2
Sharon,Plain of Israel	94B2
Sharya USSR	61G2
Shashamanna Eth	99D2
Shashi China	73C3
Shasta L USA	20B2
Shasta,Mt USA	20B2
Shaṭṭ al Gharrat, R Iraq	93E3
Shaubak Jordan	94B3
Shaunavon Can	13F3
Shaver L USA	22C2
Shawangunk Mt USA	16B2
Shawinigan Can	15D1
Shawnee, Oklahoma USA	19A2
Sha Xian China	73D4
Shay Gap Aust	106B3
Shaykh Miskīn Syria	94C2
Shaykh 'Uthmān S Yemen	99E1
Shchigry USSR	60E3
Shchors USSR	60D3
Shchuchinsk USSR	65J4
Sheboygan USA	14A2
Shebshi, Mts Nig	98B2
Sheenjek, R USA	12F1
Sheep Haven, Estuary Irish Rep	45C1
Sheerness Eng	43E4
Shefar'am Israel	94B2
Sheffield Eng	42D3
Shekhupura Pak	84C2
Shelagyote Peak, Mt Can	13B1
Shelburne Falls USA	16C1
Shelby, Michigan USA	14A2
Shelby, Montana USA	8B2
Shelbyville, Indiana USA	14A3
Sheldon,Mt Can	12H2
Shelikof Str USA	12D3
Shellharbour Aust	109D2
Shelter Pt NZ	111A3
Shelton USA	20B1
Shemakha USSR	93E1
Shenandoah USA	18A1
Shenandoah, R USA	15C3
Shenandoah Nat Pk USA	15C3
Shendam Nig	97C4
Shendi Sudan	95C2
Shenmu China	72C2
Shenyang China	72E1
Shenzhen China	73C5
Sheopur India	85D3
Shepetovka USSR	59D2
Shepparton Aust	108C3
Sherard,C Can	6B2
Sherborne Eng	43C4
Sherbro I Sierra Leone	97A4
Sherbrooke Can	15D1
Shergarh India	85C3
Sheridan, Arkansas USA	19B3
Sheridan, Wyoming USA	8C2
Sherman USA	19A3
s-Hertogenbosh Neth	56B2
Sheslay Can	12H3
Shetland, Is Scot	40C1
Shevchenko USSR	61H5
Sheyk Sho'eyb, I Iran	91B4
Shiashkotan, I USSR	69H2
Shibarghan Afghan	84B1
Shibata Japan	74D3
Shibeli, R Eth	99E2
Shibin el Kom Egypt	95C1
Shibukawa Japan	75B1
Shijiazhuang China	72C2
Shikarpur Pak	84B3
Shikoku, I Japan	67G3
Shikoku-sanchi, Mts Japan	75A2

65

Shiliguri

Sitkalidak I USA	12D3
Sitkinak, I USA	12D3
Sittang, R Burma	76B2
Sittard Neth	46C1
Sittwe Burma	86C2
Situbondo Indon	78C4
Sivas Turk	92C2
Siverek Turk	93C2
Sivrihisar Turk	92B2
Siwa Egypt	95B2
Siwalik Range, Mts India	84D2
Siwalik Range, Mts Nepal	86A1
Siyang China	72D3
Sjaelland, I Den	56C1
Skagen Den	39G7
Skagerrak, Str Nor/Den	39F7
Skagit, R USA	20B1
Skagit Mt Can	20B1
Skagway USA	4E4
Skara Sweden	39G7
Skarzysko-Kamienna Pol	59C2
Skeena, R Can	5F4
Skeena Mts Can	13B1
Skeenjek, R USA	4D3
Skegness Eng	42E3
Skellefte, R Sweden	38H5
Skellefteå Sweden	38J6
Skíathos, I Greece	55B3
Skibbereen Irish Rep	45B3
Skidegate Can	5E4
Skiemiewice Pol	58C2
Skien Nor	39F7
Skikda Alg	96C1
Skikoku, I Japan	74C4
Skipton Eng	42D3
Skíros, I Greece	55B3
Skive Den	39F7
Skjern Den	56B1
Skjoldungen Greenland	6F3
Skokie USA	14A2
Skópelos, I Greece	55B3
Skopje Yugos	54B2
Skövde Sweden	39G7
Skovorodino USSR	63E2
Skwentna USA	4C3
Skwierzyna Pol	58B2
Skye, I Scot	40B2
Slagelse Den	39G7
Slaney, R Irish Rep	45C2
Slatina Rom	54B2
Slaung Indon	78C4
Slav Brod Yugos	54A1
Slave, R Can	5G3
Slave Lake Can	13E1
Slavgorod, Rossiyskaya USSR	65J4
Slavuta USSR	59D2
Slavyansk USSR	60E4
Sleat,Sound of, Chan Scot	44B3
Sleetmute USA	12C2
Sleeve Bloom, Mts Irish Rep	45C2
Slidell USA	19C3
Slide Mt USA	16B2
Sligo, County Irish Rep	45B1
Sligo Irish Rep	41B3
Sligo, B Irish Rep	41B3
Sliven Bulg	54C2
Slobozia Rom	54C2
Slocan Can	13D3
Slonim USSR	58D2
Slough Eng	43D4
Slough, R USA	22B2
Slovensko, Region Czech	59B3
Słubice Pol	56C2
Sluch', R USSR	59D2
Sludyanka USSR	68C1
Słupsk Pol	58B2
Slutsk USSR	58D2
Slutsk, R USSR	58D2
Slyne Head, Pt Irish Rep	41A3
Slyudyanka USSR	63C2
Smallwood Res Can	7D4
Smara Mor	96A2
Smederevo Yugos	54B2
Smederevska Palanka Yugos	54B2
Smela USSR	60D4
Smethport USA	15C2
Smith Can	13E1
Smith Arm, B Can	4F3
Smithers Can	13B2
Smith I Can	7C3
Smith Sd Can	13B2
Smiths Falls Can	15C2
Smithton Aust	109C4
Smoky, R Can	13D1
Smoky C Aust	109D2
Smoky Lake Can	13E2
Smøla, I Nor	38F6
Smolensk USSR	60D3
Smólikas, Mt Greece	55B2
Smolyan Bulg	54B2
Smorgon' USSR	58D2
Smyrna, Delaware USA	16B3
Smyrna, Georgia USA	17B1
Snaefell, Mt Eng	42B2
Snafell, Mt Iceland	38B2
Snake, R USA	8B2
Snake River Canyon USA	8B2
Sneek Neth	56B2
Sneem Irish Rep	45B3
Snelling USA	22B2
Snežka, Mt Pol/Czech	59B2
Snøhetta, Mt Nor	38F6
Snohomish USA	20B1
Snoqualmie P USA	20B1
Snoul Camb	76D3
Snowdon, Mt Wales	43B3
Snowdonia Nat Pk Wales	43B3
Snowdrift Can	4G3
Snow Lake Can	5H4
Snowtown Aust	108A2
Snowy Mts Aust	109C3
Snyder USA	9C3
Soan-kundo, I S Korea	74B4
Sobat, R Sudan	99D2
Sobral Brazil	31C2
Sochaczew Pol	58C2
Sochi USSR	61E5
Socorro USA	9C3
Socorro, I Mexico	24A3
Socos Chile	34A2
Socotra, I S Yemen	81D4
Sodankylä Fin	38K5
Soddo Eth	99D2
Soderhamn Sweden	39H6
Södertälje Sweden	39H7
Sodiri Sudan	99C1
Soest W Germ	46E1
Sofala Mozam	101C2
Sofiya Bulg	54B2
Sofu Gan, I Japan	69G4
Sogamoso Colombia	32C2
Sognefjorden, Inlet Nor	39F6
Sog Xian Indon	82D2
Sohâg Egypt	95C2
Sohipat India	84D3
Soignies Belg	46B1
Soissons France	46B2
Sojat India	85C3
Sójosŏn-man, B N Korea	74A3
Söke Turk	92A2
Sokodó Togo	97C4
Sokol USSR	61E2
Sokołka Pol	58C2
Sokolo Mali	97B3
Søkongens Øy, I Greenland	6H3
Sokota Eth	99D1
Sokoto Nig	97C3
Sokoto, R Nig	97C3
Solander I NZ	111A3
Solano Phil	79B2
Solapur India	87B1
Solbad Hall Austria	47D1
Sölden Austria	47D1
Soldotna USA	12D2
Soledad Colombia	26C4
Solent, Sd Eng	43D4
Solesmes France	46B1
Soligorsk USSR	58D2
Solikamsk USSR	61J2
Solimões Peru	32C4
Solingen W Germ	46D1
Sol'Itesk USSR	65G4
Sollefteå Sweden	38H6
Sol'Iltsk USSR	61H3
Solok Indon	70B4
Solomon, Is Pacific O	105G4
Solothurn Switz	47B1
Soltau W Germ	39F8
Solvang USA	22B3
Solway Firth, Estuary Scot/Eng	42C2
Solwezi Zambia	100B2
Sōma Japan	75C1
Soma Turk	55C3
Somalia, Republic E Africa	81C5
Sombor Yugos	54A1
Somerset Aust	107D2
Somerset, County Eng	43C4
Somerset, Massachusetts USA	16D2
Somerset, Pennsylvania USA	15C2
Somerset East S Africa	100B4
Somerset I Can	6A2
Somers Point USA	16B3
Somerville USA	16B2
Somerville Res USA	19A3
Somes, R Rom	54B1
Somme, Department France	46B2
Somme, R France	46B2
Sommesous France	46C2
Son, R India	86A2
Sŏnch'ŏn N Korea	74A3
Sønderborg Den	39F8
Søndre Strømfjord Greenland	6E3
Sondrio Italy	47C1
Song Ba, R Viet	76D3
Song Cau Viet	76D3
Songea Tanz	101C2
Songjiang China	73E3
Songkhla Thai	77C4
Songnim N Korea	74B3
Sông Pahang, R Malay	77C5
Songpan China	72A3
Sŏngd Youqi China	72C1
Son La Viet	76C1
Sonmiani Pak	85B3
Sonmiani Bay Pak	85B3
Sonoma USA	22A1
Sonora, California USA	22B2
Sonora, R Mexico	24A2
Sonoran Desert USA	9B3
Sonora P USA	22C1
Sonsonate El Salvador	25D3
Sonsorol, I Pacific O	71E3
Soo Canals USA/Can	10B2
Sooke Can	13C3
Sopot Pol	58B2
Sopron Hung	59B3
Soquel USA	22B2
Sora Italy	53B2
Sored, R Israel	94B3
Sorel Can	15D1
Sorell Aust	109C4
Sorgun Turk	92C2
Soria Spain	50B1
Sørkjosen Nor	38J5
Sørksop, I Barents S	64C2
Sor Mertvyy Kultuk, Plain USSR	61H4
Sorocaba Brazil	35B2
Sorochinsk USSR	61H3
Soroi, I Pacific O	71F3
Sorok USSR	60C4
Sorong Indon	71E4
Sorong, Province Indon	71E4
Soroti Uganda	99D2
Sørøya, I Nor	38J4
Sorrento Italy	53B2
Sorsatunturi, Mt Fin	38K5
Sorsele Sweden	38H5
Sorsogon Phil	79B3
Sortavala USSR	38L6
Sôsan S Korea	74B3
Sosnowiec Pol	59B2
Sos'va USSR	65H4
Souanké Congo	98B2
Soubré Ivory Coast	97B4
Souderton USA	16B2
Soufrière St Lucia	27P2
Soufrière, V St Vincent	27N2
Souillac France	48C3
Souk Ahras Alg	96C1
Soul S Korea	74B3
Soummam, R Alg	51C2
Sources,Mt aux Lesotho	101G1
Sousa Brazil	31D3
Sousse Tunisia	96D1
South Africa, Republic Africa	100B4
South Amboy USA	16B2
Southampton Can	14B2
Southampton Eng	43D4
Southampton USA	16C2
Southampton I Can	6B3
South Atlantic O	28F6
South Aulatsivik I Can	7D4
South Australia, State Aust	106C3
South Australian Basin Indian O	104E5
Southaven USA	19C3
South Bay USA	17B2
South Baymouth Can	14B1
South Bend, Indiana USA	14A2
South Bend, Washington USA	20B1
Southbridge USA	16D1
South Carolina, State USA	11B3
South China S S E Asia	70C2
South Dakota, State USA	8C2
South Deerfield USA	16C1
South Downs Eng	43D4
South East C Aust	109C4
Southen Alps, Mts NZ	111A2
Southend Can	5H4
Southend-on-Sea Eng	43E4
Southern Alps, Mts NZ	111A2
Southern Cross Aust	106A4
Southern Indian L Can	5J4
Southfield Jamaica	27H2
South Fiji Basin Pacific O	105G5
South Fork, R, Alaska USA	12D2
South Fork, R, California USA	22B1
South Georgia, I S Atlantic O	28F8
South Glamorgan, County Wales	43C4
South Haven USA	14A2
South Henik L Can	5J3
South I Ionshu Ridgo Pacific O	104F3
South I NZ	111A2
Southington USA	16C2
South Korea, Republic S E Asia	74B3
South Lake Tahoe USA	21A2

South Magnetic Pole

South Magnetic Pole
Ant 112C8
South Miami *USA* 17B2
South Mt *USA* 16A3
South Nahanni, R *Can* 4F3
South Negril Pt
Jamaica 26G1
South Orkney, Is
Atlantic O 103F8
South Platte, R *USA* 8C2
South Pole *Ant* 80E
Southport *Eng* 42C3
South Pt *Barbados* 27R3
South River *USA* 16B2
South Ronaldsay, I
Scot 44C2
South Sandwich
Trench *Atlantic O* 103G7
South San Francisco
USA 22A2
South Saskatchewan,
R *Can* 5H4
South Shields *Eng* 42D2
South Taranaki Bight,
B *NZ* 110B1
South Uist, I *Scot* 44A3
South West C *Aust* 107D5
South West Pacific
Basin *Pacific O* 105J5
South West Peru
Ridge *Pacific O* 103D5
South Yemen,
Republic *Arabian
Pen* 81C4
South Yorkshire,
County *Eng* 43D3
Sovetsk, RSFSR *USSR* 58C1
Sovetsk, RSFSR *USSR* 61G2
Soyo Congo *Angola* 98B3
Sozh, R *USSR* 60D3
Spa *Belg* 46C1
Spain, Kingdom 37
Spalding *Eng* 43D3
Spanish, R *Can* 14B1
Spanish Town
Jamaica 26B3
Sparks *USA* 21B2
Spartanburg *USA* 11B3
Spartí *Greece* 55B3
Spassk Dal'niy *USSR* 69F2
Speightstown
Barbados 27R3
Spenard *USA* 12E2
Spencer, Indiana *USA* 14A3
Spencer, Iowa *USA* 8D2
Spencer Bay *Can* 6A3
Spencer,C *Aust* 108A3
Spencer G *Aust* 108A2
Spencer I *Can* 6C3
Spenser Mts *NZ* 111B2
Sperrin, Mts *N Ire* 45C1
Spey, R *Scot* 44C3
Speyer *W Germ* 57B3
Speyside *Tobago* 27K1
Spiez *Switz* 47B1
Spike Mt *USA* 12F1
Spirit Lake *USA* 20C1
Spirit River *Can* 5G4
Spitsbergen, I *Barents
S* 64C2
Spittal *Austria* 57C3
Spjelkavik *Nor* 38F6
Split *Yugos* 52C2
Splügen *Switz* 47C1
Spokane *USA* 20C1
Sporádhes, Is *Greece* 55C3
Spray *USA* 20C2
Spree, R *E Germ* 56C2
Springbok *S Africa* 100A3
Springdale *USA* 18B2
Springfield, Illinois
USA 10B3
Springfield,
Massachusetts *USA* 10C2
Springfield, Missouri
USA 18B2

Springfield, Oregon
USA 20B2
Springfield, Vermont
USA 15D2
Springfontein *S Africa* 100B4
Springs *S Africa* 101G1
Spurn Head, Pt *Eng* 41D3
Squamish *Can* 13C3
Sredne-Russkaya
Vozvyshennost,
Upland *USSR* 60E3
Sredne Sibirskoye
Ploskogorye,
Tableland *USSR* 63B1
Sredniy Ural, Mts
USSR 61J2
Srepok, R *Camb* 76D3
Sretensk *USSR* 68D1
Sre Umbell *Camb* 76C3
Sri Lanka, Republic *S
Asia* 83C5
Srinagar *Pak* 84C2
Srivardhan *India* 87A1
Sroda *Pol* 58B2
Sta Clara, I *Chile* 30H6
Sta Cruz, I *Ecuador* 32J7
Stade *W Germ* 56B2
Staffa, I *Scot* 44A3
Stafford, County *Eng* 43C3
Stafford *Eng* 43C3
Stafford Springs *USA* 16C2
Stallworthy,C *Can* 6A1
Stalowa Wola *Pol* 59C2
Sta Maria, I *Ecuador* 32J7
Stamford, Connecticut
USA 16C2
Stamford, New York
USA 16B1
Stampriet *Namibia* 100A3
Standerton *S Africa* 101G1
Standish *USA* 14B2
Stanger *S Africa* 101H1
Stanislaus, R *USA* 22B2
Stanke Dimitrov *Bulg* 54B2
Stanley *Aust* 109C4
Stanley *Falkland Is* 29E6
Stanley Res *India* 87B2
Stann Creek *Belize* 25D3
Stanovoy Khrebet,
Mts *USSR* 63E2
Stans *Switz* 47C1
Stanthorpe *Aust* 109D1
Starachowice *Pol* 59C2
Stara Planiná, Mts
Bulg 54B2
Staraya Russa *USSR* 60D2
Stara Zagora *Bulg* 54C2
Stargard *Pol* 58B2
Starkville *USA* 19C3
Starnberg *W Germ* 57C3
Starogard Gdanski *Pol* 58B2
Starokonstantinov
USSR 59D3
Start Pt *Eng* 43C4
Staryy Oskol *USSR* 60E3
State College *USA* 15C2
Staten I *USA* 16B2
Statesboro *USA* 17B1
Staunton *USA* 15C3
Stavanger *Nor* 39F7
Stavelot *Belg* 46C1
Stavropol' *USSR* 61F4
Stawell *Aust* 108B3
Stawno *Pol* 58B2
Stayton *USA* 20B2
Stebbins *USA* 12B2
Steele,Mt *Can* 12F2
Steelton *USA* 16A2
Steens Mt *USA* 20C2
Steenstrups Gletscher,
Gl *Greenland* 6E2
Stefansson I *Can* 4H2
Stegi *Swaziland* 101H1
Steinach *Austria* 47D1
Steinback *Can* 8D2
Steinkier *Nor* 38G6
Stein Mt *Can* 13C2
Stemaco *Mexico* 23B2

Stenay *France* 46C2
Stendal *E Germ* 56C2
Stephens,C *NZ* 110B2
Stephens Creek *Aust* 108B2
Stephenson *USA* 14A1
Stephens Pass *USA* 12H3
Stephenville *Can* 7E5
Sterkstroom *S Africa* 100B4
Sterling, Colorado
USA 8C2
Sterling Heights *USA* 14B2
Sterlitamak *USSR* 61J3
Stettler *Can* 13E2
Steubenville *USA* 14B2
Stevens Village *USA* 4D3
Stewart *Can* 13B1
Stewart *USA* 21B2
Stewart, R *Can* 12G2
Stewart Crossing *Can* 12G2
Stewart I *NZ* 111A3
Stewart Is *Solomon Is* 107F1
Stewart River *Can* 4E3
Stewartstown *USA* 16A3
Steyn *S Africa* 101G1
Steyr *Austria* 57C3
Stika *USA* 12G3
Stikine, R *Can* 12H3
Stikine Ranges, Mts
Can 12H3
Stillwater, Oklahoma
USA 18A2
Stillwater Range, Mts
USA 21B2
Stirling *Aust* 108A2
Stirling *Scot* 44C3
Stockbridge *USA* 16C1
Stockerau *Austria* 59B3
Stockholm *Sweden* 39H7
Stockport *Eng* 42C3
Stockton, California
USA 22B2
Stockton *Eng* 42D2
Stockton L *USA* 18B2
Stoke-on-Trent *Eng* 43C3
Stokkseyri *Iceland* 38A2
Stokmarknes *Nor* 38G5
Stolbtsy *USSR* 39K8
Stolin *USSR* 58D2
Stone Harbor *USA* 16B3
Stonehaven *Scot* 44C3
Stonewall *USA* 19A3
Stony, R *USA* 12D2
Storavan, L *Sweden* 38H5
Støren *Nor* 38G6
Storm B *Aust* 109C4
Stornoway *Scot* 44A2
Storozhinets *USSR* 59D3
Storrs *USA* 16C2
Storsjön, L *Sweden* 38G6
Storuman *Sweden* 38H5
Stoughton *USA* 16D1
Stowmarket *Eng* 43E3
Strablane *N Ire* 45C1
Strahan *Aust* 109C4
Stralsund *E Germ* 56C2
Stranda *Nor* 38F6
Strängnäs *Sweden* 39H7
Stranraer *Scot* 42B2
Strasbourg *France* 49D2
Strasburg *USA* 15C3
Stratford *Can* 14B2
Stratford, Connecticut
USA 16C2
Stratford *NZ* 110B1
Stratford-on-Avon *Eng* 43D3
Strathalbyn *Aust* 108A3
Strathclyde, Region
Scot 42B2
Strathmore *Can* 13E2
Streator *USA* 18C1
Stresa *Italy* 47C2
Stretto de Messina,
Str *Italy/Sicily* 53C3
Stroboli, I *Italy* 53C3
Strømfjord *Greenland* 6E3
Stromness *Scot* 44C2
Strømø *Faroes* 38D3
Stromsburg *USA* 18A1

Stromsund *Sweden* 38H6
Ströms Vattudal, L
Sweden 38G6
Stronsay, I *Scot* 44C2
Stroud *Eng* 43C4
Stroudsburg *USA* 16B2
Struma, R *Bulg* 54B2
Strumble Head, Pt
Wales 43B3
Strumica *Yugos* 55B2
Stryy *USSR* 59C3
Stryy, R *USSR* 59C3
Strzelecki Creek, R
Aust 108B1
Stuart, Florida *USA* 17B2
Stuart, R *Can* 13C2
Stuart I *USA* 12B2
Stuart L *Can* 13C2
Stubaier Alpen, Mts
Austria 47D1
Stuch, R *USSR* 60C3
Stung Sen *Camb* 76D3
Stung Treng *Camb* 76D3
Stura, R *Italy* 52A2
Sturge I *Ant* 112C7
Sturgeon Bay *USA* 14A2
Sturgeon Falls *Can* 14C1
Sturgis, Kentucky *USA* 18C2
Sturgis, Michigan *USA* 14A2
Sturt Creek, R *Aust* 106B2
Sturt Desert *Aust* 108B1
Stuttemeim *S Africa* 100B4
Stuttgart *USA* 19B3
Stuttgart *W Germ* 57B3
Stykkishólmur *Iceland* 38A1
Styr, R *USSR* 59D2
Suaçuí Grande, R
Brazil 35C1
Suakin *Sudan* 81B4
Su-ao *Taiwan* 73E5
Suardi *Arg* 34C2
Subi, I *Indon* 78B2
Subotica *Yugos* 54A1
Suceava *Rom* 60C4
Suck, R *Irish Rep* 45B2
Sucre *Bol* 30C2
Sucuriú, R *Brazil* 35A1
Sudan, Republic
Africa 98C1
Sudbury *Can* 14B1
Sudbury *Eng* 43E3
Sudd, Swamp *Sudan* 99C2
Suddie *Guyana* 33F2
Sue, R *Sudan* 98C2
Suerdrup Is *Can* 4H2
Suez *USA* 92B4
Suez Canal *Egypt* 92B3
Suez,G of *Egypt* 92B4
Suffern *USA* 16B2
Suffolk, County *Eng* 43E3
Sugarloaf Pt *Aust* 109D2
Suhâr *Oman* 91C5
Sühbaatar *Mongolia* 68C1
Sui *Pak* 84B3
Suide *China* 72C2
Suihua *China* 69E2
Suining *China* 73B3
Suippes *France* 46C2
Suir, R *Irish Rep* 41B3
Sui Xian *China* 73C3
Suizhong *China* 72E1
Sujângarth *India* 85C3
Sukabumi *Indon* 78B4
Sukadana, Borneo
Indon 78C3
Sukadana, Sumatra
Indon 78B4
Sukagawa *Japan* 74E3
Sukaraya *Indon* 78C3
Sukhinichi Shchekino
USSR 60E3
Sukhona, R *USSR* 61F2
Sukhumi *USSR* 61F3
Sukkertoppen
Greenland 6E3
Sukkertoppen, L
Greenland 6E3
Sukkozero *USSR* 38L6

Sukkur *Pak*	85B3		Surinam, Republic	33F3		Sylarna, Mt *Sweden*	38G6		Taiping *Malay*	77C5
Sukma *India*	87C1		Surrey, County *Eng*	43D4		Sylhet *Bang*	86C2		Taira *Japan*	75C1
Sukses *Namibia*	100A3		Sursee *Switz*	47C1		Sylt, I *W Germ*	56B1		Tais *Indon*	78A3
Sukumo *Japan*	75A2		Surtsey, I *Iceland*	38A2		Sylvania *USA*	14B2		Taisha *Japan*	75A1
Sukunka, R *Can*	13C1		Susa *Italy*	47B2		Syowa, Base *Ant*	112C11		Taitao,Pen de *Chile*	29B5
Sula, R *USSR*	60E3		Susa *Japan*	75A2		Syracuse, New York			T'ai-tung *Taiwan*	73E5
Sulaiman Range, Mts			Susaki *Japan*	75A2		USA	10C3		Taivelkoski *Fin*	38K5
Pak	84B3		Susanville *USA*	21A1		Syracuse *USA*	15C2		Taiwan, Republic	
Sulawesi, I *Indon*	70C4		Süsch *Switz*	47D1		Syrdal'ya, R *USSR*	65H5		China	69E4
Sulaymānīyah *Iraq*	93E3		Susitna, R *USA*	12E2		Syria, Republic *S W*			Taiyuan *China*	72C2
Sulina *Rom*	54C1		Susquehanna, R *USA*	16A3		*Asia*	93C2		Taizhou *China*	72D3
Sulitjelma *Nor*	38H5		Sussex *USA*	16B2		Sysert' *USSR*	61J2		Ta 'izz *Yemen*	81C4
Sullana *Peru*	32A4		Sussex West *Eng*	43D4		Syzran' *USSR*	61G3		Tajo, R *Spain*	50B1
Sullivan *USA*	18B2		Sustut Peak, Mt *Can*	13B1		Szczecin *Pol*	56C2		Tak *Thai*	76B2
Sullivan Bay *Can*	13B2		Sutherland *S Africa*	100B4		Szczecinek *Pol*	58B2		Takada *Japan*	74D3
Sullivan L *Can*	13E2		Sutlej, R *Pak*	84C2		Szczytno *Pol*	58C2		Takahashi *Japan*	75A2
Sulmona *Italy*	52B2		Sutter Creek *USA*	21A2		Szeged *Hung*	59C3		Takaka *NZ*	110B2
Sulphur, Louisiana			Sutton *USA*	14B3		Székesfehérvar *Hung*	59B3		Takamatsu *Japan*	74C4
USA	19B3		Sutwik I *USA*	12C3		Szekszard *Hung*	59B3		Takaoka *Japan*	74D3
Sulphur, Oklahoma			Suwa *Japan*	74D3		Szolnok *Hung*	59B3		Takapuna *NZ*	110B1
USA	19A3		Suwałki *Pol*	58C2		Szombathely *Hung*	59B3		Takasaki *Japan*	74D3
Sulphur Springs *USA*	19A3		Suwannee, R *USA*	17B2		Szprotawa *Pol*	58B2		Takayama *Japan*	75B1
Sultānpur *India*	86A1		Suweilih *Jordan*	94B2					Takefu *Japan*	74D3
Sulu Arch *Phil*	79B4		Suwŏn *S Korea*	74B3		**T**			Takeo *Camb*	76C3
Sulu S *Philip*	70C3		Su Xian *China*	72D3					Takeo *Japan*	75A2
Sumampa *Arg*	30D4		Suzaka *Japan*	75B1		Tabas *Iran*	90C3		Takestān *Iran*	90A2
Sumba, I *Indon*	70C4		Suzhou *China*	73E3		Tabasco *Mexico*	23A1		Taketa *Japan*	75A2
Sumbawa, I *Indon*	78D4		Suzu *Japan*	74D3		Tabatinga *Brazil*	32D4		Takingeun *Indon*	70A3
Sumbawa Besar *Indon*	78D4		Suzuka *Japan*	75B2		Tabelbala *Alg*	96B2		Takjvak L *Can*	4G3
Sumbawanga *Tanz*	99D3		Suzu-misaki, C *Japan*	75B1		Tabeng *Camb*	76C3		Takkaze, R *Eth*	99D1
Sumbe *Angola*	100A2		Svalbard, Is *Barents S*	64C2		Taber *Can*	13E2		Takla L *Can*	13B1
Sumburgh Head, Pt			Svalyava *USSR*	59C3		Tablas, I *Phil*	79B3		Takla Landing *Can*	13B1
Scot	44D2		Svartisen, Mt *Nor*	38G5		Table Mt *S Africa*	100A4		Takslesluk L *USA*	12B2
Sumenep *Indon*	78C4		Svay Rieng *Camb*	76D3		Table Mt *USA*	12F1		Taku Arm, R *Can*	12H2
Sumisu, I *Japan*	69G3		Sveg *Sweden*	38G6		Table Rock Res *USA*	18B2		Tala *Mexico*	23A1
Summerland *Can*	13D3		Svendborg *Den*	39G7		Taboali *Indon*	78B3		Talabanya *Hung*	59B3
Summit Lake *Can*	5F4		Sverdlovsk *USSR*	65H4		Tabor *Czech*	57C3		Talagang *Pak*	84C2
Summit Mt *USA*	21B2		Sverdrup Chan *Can*	6A1		Tabora *Tanz*	99D3		Talagante *Chile*	34A2
Sumner,L *NZ*	111B2		Svetlaya *USSR*	69F2		Tabou *Ivory Coast*	97B4		Talaimannar *Sri Lanka*	87B3
Sumoto *Japan*	75A2		Svetlogorsk *USSR*	58C2		Tabrīz *Iran*	90A2		Talak, Desert, Region	
Sumter *USA*	17B1		Svetogorsk *USSR*	39K6		Tabūk *S Arabia*	92C4		*Niger*	97C3
Sumy *USSR*	60D3		Svetozarevo *Yugos*	54B2		Tacámbaro *Mexico*	23A2		Talangbetutu *Indon*	78A3
Sunbury *USA*	16A2		Svilengrad *Bulg*	54C2		Tacheng *China*	82C1		Talara *Peru*	32A4
Sunchales *Arg*	34C2		Svir' *USSR*	58D2		Tacloban *Phil*	79C3		Talavera de la Reina	
Sunch'ŏn *N Korea*	74B3		Svitavy *Czech*	59B3		Tacna *Peru*	30B2		*Spain*	50B2
Sunch'ŏn *S Korea*	74B4		Svobodnyy *USSR*	69E1		Tacoma *USA*	8A2		Talca *Chile*	34A3
Sundargarh *India*	86A2		Svolvaer *Nor*	38G5		Tadjoura *Djibouti*	99E1		Talcahuano *Chile*	34A3
Sunderbans, Swamp			Swain Reefs *Aust*	107E3		Tādpatri *India*	87B2		Tälcher *India*	86B2
India	86B2		Swainsboro *USA*	17B1		Tadzhen *USSR*	65H6		Taldy Kurgan *USSR*	82B1
Sunderland *Eng*	42D2		Swakopmund *Namibia*	100A3		Tadzhikskaya SSR,			Taliabu *Indon*	71D4
Sundre *Can*	13E2		Swale, R *Eng*	42D2		Republic *USSR*	82A2		Taligan *Afghan*	84B1
Sundridge *Can*	15C1		Swallow Reef, I *S E*			Taebaek Sanmaek,			Tali Post *Sudan*	99D2
Sundsvall *Sweden*	38H6		*Asia*	70C3		Mts *S Korea*	74B3		Taliwang *Indon*	78D4
Sungaianyar *Indon*	78D3		Swāmihalli *India*	87B2		Taegu *S Korea*	74B3		Talkeetna *USA*	12D2
Sungaisalak *Indon*	78A3		Swan, I *Honduras*	25D3		Taehüksan, I *S Korea*	74B4		Talkeetna Mts *USA*	12E2
Sunnyside *USA*	20C1		Swanage *Eng*	43D4		Taejŏn *S Korea*	74B3		Talladega *USA*	17A1
Sunnyvale *USA*	21A2		Swan Hill *Aust*	108B3		Tafalla *Spain*	51B1		Tall 'Afar *Iraq*	93D2
Suntar *USSR*	63D1		Swan Hills *Can*	13D2		Tafassaset,			Tallahassee *USA*	17B1
Sunyani *Ghana*	97B4		Swan Hills, Mts *Can*	13D2		Watercourse *Alg*	96C2		Tall Bīsah *Syria*	94C1
Suō-nada, B *Japan*	75A2		Swan I *Caribbean*	26A3		Taff, R *Wales*	43C4		Tallinn *USSR*	60B2
Suonejoki *Fin*	38K6		Swan River *Can*	5H4		Tafila *Jordan*	94B3		Tall Kalakh *Syria*	92C3
Supaul *India*	86B1		Swansea *Wales*	43C4		Tagant, Region *Maur*	97A3		Tallulah *USA*	19B3
Superior, Nebraska			Swansea B *Wales*	43C4		Tagbilaran *Phil*	79B4		Tal'noye *USSR*	60D4
USA	18A1		Swartruggens *S Africa*	101G1		Taguenout			Talpaki *USSR*	58C2
Superior, Wisconsin			Swaziland, Kingdom *S*			Hagguerete, Well			Taltal *Chile*	30B4
USA	10A2		*Africa*	101H1		*Maur*	96B2		Talwood *Aust*	109C1
Superior,L *USA/Can*	10B2		Sweden, Kingdom *N*			Tagula, I *Solomon Is*	107E2		Tamabo Range, Mts	
Suphan Buri *Thai*	76C3		*Europe*	39G7		Tagum *Phil*	79C4		*Malay*	78D1
Süphan Daği *Turk*	93D2		Sweet Home *USA*	20B2		Tahat, Mt *Alg*	96C2		Tamale *Ghana*	97B4
Supiori, I *Indon*	71E4		Sweetwater *USA*	9C3		Tahiti, I *Pacific O*	105J4		Tamanrasset *Alg*	96C2
Suq ash Suyukh *Iraq*	93E3		Swellendam *S Africa*	100B4		Tahlequah *USA*	18A2		Tamanrasset,	
Suqian *China*	72D3		Świdnica *Pol*	59B2		Tahoe City *USA*	21A2		Watercourse *Alg*	96C2
Sūr *Oman*	91C5		Świdwin *Pol*	58B2		Tahoe,L *USA*	21A2		Tamaqua *USA*	16B2
Surabaya *Indon*	78C4		Świebodzin *Pol*	58B2		Tahoua *Niger*	97C3		Tamazula, Jalisco	
Suraga-wan, B *Japan*	75B2		Świecie *Pol*	58B2		Tahuna *Indon*	71D3		*Mexico*	23A2
Surakarta *Indon*	78C4		Swift Current *Can*	5H4		Tai'an *China*	72D2		Tamazulapán *Mexico*	23B2
Surar, R *USSR*	61G3		Swindon *Eng*	43D4		Taibai Shan, Mt *China*	72B3		Tamazunchale *Mexico*	23B1
Surat *Aust*	109C1		Swinford *Irish Rep*	45B2		Taibus Qi *China*	72D1		Tambacounda *Sen*	97A3
Sūrat *India*	85C4		Swift Current *Can*	56C2		T'ai-chung *Taiwan*	73E5		Tambov *USSR*	61F3
Sūratgarh *India*	84C3		Świnoujście *Pol*	56C2		Taieri, R *NZ*	111B3		Tambre, R *Spain*	50A1
Surat Thani *Thai*	77B4		Switzerland, Federal			Talhang Shan *China*	72C2		Tambura *Sudan*	98C2
Surendranagar *India*	85C4		Republic *Europe*	49D2		Taihape *NZ*	110C1		Tamchaket *Maur*	97A3
Surf City *USA*	16B3		Swords *Irish Rep*	45C2		Tai Hu, L *China*	72E3		Tamega, R *Port*	50A1
Surgut *USSR*	64J3		Syderø *Faeroes*	38D3		Tailem Bend *Aust*	108A3		Tamiahua *Mexico*	23B1
Suriāpet *India*	87B1		Sydney *Aust*	109D2		Tain *Scot*	44B3		Tamil Nādu, State	
Sürich *Switz*	49D2		Sydney *Can*	7D5		T'ai-nan *Taiwan*	73E5		*India*	87B2
Surigao *Phil*	79C4		Syktyvkar *USSR*	64G3		Taiobeiras *Brazil*	35C1		Tamis, R *Rom*	54B1
Surin *Thai*	76C3		Sylacauga *USA*	17A1		T'ai pei *Taiwan*	73E5		Tam Ky *Viet*	76D2

Tampa

Tampa *USA*	17B2
Tampa B *USA*	17B2
Tampere *Fin*	39J6
Tampico *Mexico*	23B1
Tamsagbulag *Mongolia*	68D2
Tamu *Burma*	86C2
Tamuis *Mexico*	23B1
Tamworth *Aust*	109D2
Tamworth *Eng*	43D3
Tana *Nor*	38K4
Tana, L *Eth*	99D1
Tana, R *Kenya*	99E3
Tana, R *Nor/Fin*	38K5
Tanabe *Japan*	75B2
Tanafjord, Inlet *Nor*	38K4
Tanahgrogot *Indon*	78D3
Tanahmerah *Indon*	71E4
Tanana *USA*	12D1
Tanana, R *USA*	12E2
Tanaro, R *Italy*	47C2
Tanch'ŏn *N Korea*	74B2
Tandaho *Eth*	99E1
Tandil *Arg*	34D3
Tandjong Datu, Pt *Indon*	78B2
Tandjung d'Urville, C *Indon*	71E4
Tandjung Layar, C *Indon*	78D3
Tandjung Lumut, C *Indon*	78B3
Tandjung Mangkalihet C *Indon*	78D2
Tandjung Sambar, C *Indon*	78C3
Tandjung Sirik, C *Malay*	78C2
Tandjung Vals, C *Indon*	71E4
Tando Adam *Pak*	85B3
Tando Muhammad Khan *Pak*	85B3
Tandou L *Aust*	108B2
Tändür *India*	87B1
Taneatua *NZ*	110C1
Tanen Range, Mts *Burma/Thai*	76B2
Tanezrouft, Desert Region *Alg*	96B2
Tang *Iran*	91C4
Tanga *Tanz*	99D3
Tanganrog *USSR*	60E4
Tanganyika,L *Tanz/Zaïre*	99C3
Tanger *Mor*	96B1
Tanggula Shan, Mts *China*	82C2
Tangjungpinang *Indon*	78A2
Tangra Yumco, L *China*	82C2
Tangshan *China*	72D2
Tangub *Phil*	79B4
Tanguy *USSR*	63C2
Tanjay *Phil*	79B4
Tanjong Bugel, C *Indon*	78C4
Tanjong Cangkuang, C *Indon*	78B4
Tanjong Puting, C *Indon*	78C3
Tanjong Selatan, C *Indon*	78C3
Tanjung *Indon*	78D3
Tanjungbalai *Indon*	70A3
Tanjung Jabung, Pt *Indon*	78A3
Tanjungpandan *Indon*	78B3
Tanjung Priok *Indon*	78B4
Tanjungredeb *Indon*	78D2
Tanjungselor *Indon*	78D2
Tank *Pak*	84C2
Tannu Ola, Mts *USSR*	68B1
Tano, R *Ghana*	97B4
Tanout *Niger*	97C3
Tanquián *Mexico*	23B1
Tan-shui *Taiwan*	73E4
Tansing *Nepal*	86A1
Tanta *Egypt*	95C1
Tan-Tan *Mor*	96A2
Tanunak *USA*	4B3
Tanzania, Republic *Africa*	99D3
Tao He, R *China*	72A3
Taolañaro *Madag*	101D3
Taole *China*	72B2
Taourirt *Mor*	96B1
Tapa *USSR*	60C2
Tapachula *Mexico*	25C3
Tapajós, R *Brazil*	33F4
Tapalquén *Arg*	34C3
Tapan *Indon*	70B4
Tapanui *NZ*	111A3
Tapauá, R *Brazil*	32D5
Tapi, R *India*	85D4
Taplejung *Nepal*	86B1
Tapuaeniku, Mt *NZ*	111B2
Tapuaritinga *Brazil*	35B2
Tapul Group, Is *Phil*	79B4
Tapurucuara *Brazil*	33E4
Tara *Aust*	109D1
Tara *USSR*	65J4
Tara, R *USSR*	65J4
Tara, R *Yugos*	54A2
Taraba, R *Nig*	97D4
Tarabuco *Bol*	30D2
Taracón *Spain*	50B1
Taradale *NZ*	110C1
Tarakan *Indon*	78D2
Taransay, I *Scot*	44A3
Taranto *Italy*	53C2
Tarapoto *Peru*	32B5
Tarare *France*	49C2
Tararua Range, Mts *NZ*	110C2
Tarat *Alg*	96C2
Tarawera *NZ*	110C1
Tarazona *Spain*	51B1
Tarbat Ness, Pen *Scot*	44C3
Tarbela Res *Pak*	84C2
Tarbert, Strathclyde *Scot*	42B2
Tarbert, Western Isles *Scot*	44A3
Tarbes *France*	48C3
Tarcoola *Aust*	106C4
Tarcoon *Aust*	109C2
Taree *Aust*	109D2
Tarfaya *Mor*	96A2
Tarhünah *Libya*	95A1
Tarïf *UAE*	91B5
Tarija *Bol*	30D3
Tarikere *India*	87B2
Tarim *S Yemen*	81C4
Tarime *Tanz*	99D3
Tarim He, R *China*	82C1
Tarim Pendi, Basin *China*	82C2
Tarin Kut *Afghan*	84B2
Tarkio *USA*	18A1
Tarlac *Phil*	79B2
Tarma *Peru*	32B6
Tarn, R *France*	49C3
Tarnobrzeg *Pol*	59C2
Tarnów *Pol*	59C3
Taroom *Aust*	107D3
Tarragona *Spain*	51C1
Tarraleah *Aust*	109C4
Tarrasa *Spain*	51C1
Tarrytown *USA*	16C2
Tarsus *Turk*	92B2
Tartan, Oilfield *N Sea*	44D2
Tartaro, R *Italy*	47D2
Tartu *USSR*	60C2
Tartūs *Syria*	92C3
Tarumirim *Brazil*	35C1
Tarutung *Indon*	70A3
Tarvisio *Italy*	52B1
Tashauz *USSR*	80D1
Tashigang *Bhutan*	86C1
Tashkent *USSR*	82A1
Tashtagol *USSR*	65K4
Tashtyp *USSR*	63A2
Tasikmalaya *Indon*	78B4
Tasil *Syria*	94B2
Tasiussaq *Greenland*	6E2
Tasker, Well *Niger*	95A3
Tasman B *NZ*	110B2
Tasmania, I *Aust*	107D5
Tasman Mts *NZ*	111B2
Tasman Pen *Aust*	109C4
Tasman S *NZ Aust*	107E4
Taşova *Turk*	92C1
Tassili du Hoggar, Desert, Region *Alg*	96C2
Tassili N'jjer, Desert, Region *Alg*	96C2
Tata *Mor*	96B2
Tataouine *Tunisia*	96D1
Tatarsk *USSR*	65J4
Tatarskaya ASSR, Republic *USSR*	61G2
Tatarskiy Proliv, Str *USSR*	69G2
Tateyama *Japan*	75B1
Tathlina L *Can*	5G3
Tatitlek *USA*	12E2
Tatla Lake *Can*	13C2
Tatry, Mts *Pol/Czech*	59B3
Tatsuno *Japan*	75A2
Tatta *Pak*	85B4
Tatuí *Brazil*	35B2
Tatvan *Turk*	93D2
Tauá *Brazil*	31C3
Taubaté *Brazil*	35B2
Taumarunui *NZ*	110C1
Taung *S Africa*	101F1
Taungdwingyi *Burma*	76B2
Taung-gyi *Burma*	76B1
Taungup *Burma*	76A2
Taunsa *Pak*	84C2
Taunton *Eng*	43C4
Taunton *USA*	16D2
Taunus, Region *W Germ*	46E1
Taupo *NZ*	110C1
Taupo,L *NZ*	110C1
Taurage *USSR*	58C1
Tauranga *NZ*	110C1
Tauranga Harbour, B *NZ*	110C1
Tauroa Pt *NZ*	110B1
Tavani *Can*	7A3
Tavira *Port*	50A2
Tavistock *Eng*	43B4
Tavoy *Burma*	76B3
Tavoy Pt *Burma*	76B3
Tavsanli *Turk*	92A2
Tawa *NZ*	111B2
Tawakoni,L *USA*	19A3
Tawas City *USA*	14B2
Tawau *Malay*	70C3
Taweisha *Sudan*	98C1
Tawitawi, I *Phil*	79B4
Tawitawi Group, Is *Phil*	79B4
Taxco *Mexico*	23B2
Taxcoco *Mexico*	23B2
Tay, R *Scot*	44C3
Tayan *Indon*	78C3
Taylor, Alaska *USA*	12B1
Taylor *Can*	13C1
Taylor, Michigan *USA*	14B2
Taylor, Texas *USA*	19A3
Taylorville *USA*	18C2
Taymä' *S Arabia*	80B3
Taymura, R *USSR*	63B1
Tay Ninh *Viet*	76D3
Tayshet *USSR*	63B2
Tayshir *Mongolia*	68B2
Tayside, Region *Scot*	44C3
Taytay *Phil*	79A3
Tayyebät *Iran*	90D3
Taza *Mor*	96B1
Tazerbo, Region *Libya*	95B2
Tazlina L *USA*	12E2
Tazovskiy *USSR*	64J3
Tbilisi *USSR*	65F5
Tchibanga *Gabon*	98B3
Tchigai,Plat du *Niger*	95A2
Tchin Tabaradene *Niger*	97C3
Tcholliré *Cam*	98B2
Tczew *Pol*	58B2
Te Anau *NZ*	111A3
Te Anau,L *NZ*	111A3
Te Aroha *NZ*	110C1
Te Awamutu *NZ*	110C1
Tébessa *Alg*	96C1
Teboman *Mexico*	23A2
Tecailtlán *Mexico*	23A2
Tecate *Mexico*	21B3
Techa, R *USSR*	61K2
Tecolotlán *Mexico*	23A1
Tećpan *Mexico*	23A2
Tecuci *Rom*	54C1
Tecumseh *USA*	18A1
Tedzhen *USSR*	80E2
Tedzhen, R *USSR*	65H6
Tees, R *Eng*	42D2
Tefé *Brazil*	33E4
Tegal *Indon*	78B4
Tegineneng *Indon*	78B4
Tegucigalpa *Honduras*	25D3
Tehachapi Mts *USA*	21B3
Tehachapi P *USA*	21B2
Tehek L *Can*	4J3
Tehrän *Iran*	90B2
Tehuacán *Mexico*	23B2
Tehuantepec *Mexico*	23B2
Tehuitzingo *Mexico*	23B2
Teifi, R *Wales*	43B3
Tejo, R *Port*	50A2
Tejupilco *Mexico*	23A2
Tekapo,L *NZ*	111B2
Tekeli *USSR*	82B1
Tekirdağ *Turk*	92A1
Tekir Dağlari, Mts *Turk*	55C2
Teknaf *Bang*	86C2
Te Kuiti *NZ*	110C1
Tela *Honduras*	25D3
Tel Aviv Yafo *Israel*	94B2
Telén *Arg*	34B3
Telescope Peak, Mt *USA*	21B2
Teles Pires, R *Brazil*	33F5
Telfs *Austria*	47D1
Teli *USSR*	63A2
Tell el Meise, Mt *Jordan*	94B3
Teller *USA*	12A1
Tellicherry *India*	87B2
Telok Anson *Malay*	77C5
Tělok Darvel *Malay*	78D2
Tělok Flamingo, B *Indon*	71E4
Tělok Kumai, B *Indon*	78C3
T14elok Pelabuanratu, B *Indon*	78B4
Tělok Saleh, B *Indon*	78D4
Tělok Sampit, B *Indon*	78C3
Tělok Sukadona, B *Indon*	78B3
Teloloapán *Mexico*	23B2
Telšiai *USSR*	58C1
Telukbatang *Indon*	78C3
Teluk Berau, B *Indon*	71E4
Telukbetung *Indon*	78B4
Teluk Bone, B *Indon*	70D4
Teluk Cendrawasih, B *Indon*	71E4
Teluk Mandar, B *Indon*	78D3
Teluk Tolo, B *Indon*	71D4
Teluk Tomini, B *Indon*	70D3
Tëluk Weda, B *Indon*	71D3
Temagami,L *Can*	14B1
Temascal *Mexico*	23B2
Tembesi, R *Indon*	78A3
Tembilahan *Indon*	78A3
Temblador *Ven*	27E5
Temerloh *Malay*	77C5
Temir *USSR*	65G5
Temirtau *USSR*	65J4
Temiscaming *Can*	15C1
Temora *Aust*	109C2
Tempe *Aust*	9B3
Temple *USA*	19A3
Templemore *Irish Rep*	45C2
Tempoal *Mexico*	23B1
Temuco *Chile*	34A3

Tlaquepaque *Mexico*	23A1	
Tlaxcala *Mexico*	23B2	
Tlaxcala, State *Mexico*	23B2	
Tlaxiaco *Mexico*	23B2	
Tlemcem *Alg*	96B1	
Toamasina *Madag*	101D2	
Toay *Arg*	34C3	
Toba *Japan*	75B2	
Toba and Kakar Ranges, Mts *Pak*	84B2	
Tobago, I *Caribbean*	27E4	
Toba Inlet, Sd *Can*	13C2	
Tobelo *Indon*	71D3	
Tobermory *Can*	14B1	
Iobermory *Scot*	44A3	
Tobi, I *Pacific O*	71E3	
Tobin,Mt *USA*	21B1	
Tobol, R *USSR*	65H4	
Toboli *Indon*	70D4	
Tobol'sk *USSR*	65H4	
Tocantins, R *Brazil*	31B2	
Toccoa *USA*	17B1	
Toce, R *Italy*	47C1	
Tocopilla *Chile*	30B3	
Tocorpuri, Mt *Chile*	30C3	
Tocuyo, R *Ven*	32D1	
Toda *India*	85D3	
Tôdi, Mt *Switz*	47C1	
Todong *S Korea*	75A1	
Todos Santos *Mexico*	9B4	
Tofield *Can*	13E2	
Tofino *Can*	13B3	
Togiak *USA*	12B3	
Togiak B *USA*	12B3	
Togo, Republic *Africa*	97C4	
Togtoh *China*	72C1	
Tok *USA*	12F2	
Tokachi, R *Japan*	74E2	
Tokamachi *Japan*	75B1	
Tokar *Sudan*	95C3	
Tokara Retto, Arch *Japan*	69E4	
Tokat *Turk*	92C1	
Tŏkchŏk-kundo, Arch *S Korea*	74B3	
Tok-do, I *S Korea*	75A1	
Tokmak *USSR*	82B1	
Tokomaru Bay *NZ*	110C1	
Toku, R *Can/USA*	12H3	
Tokung *Indon*	78C3	
Tokuno, I *Japan*	69E4	
Tokushima *Japan*	74C4	
Tokuyama *Japan*	75A2	
Tŏkyŏ *Japan*	74D3	
Tolaga Bay *NZ*	110C1	
Toledo *Brazil*	30F3	
Toledo *Spain*	50B2	
Toledo *USA*	14B2	
Toledo Bend Res *USA*	19B3	
Toliara *Madag*	101D3	
Toliman *Mexico*	23B1	
Tolina, Mt *Colombia*	32B3	
Tolosa *Spain*	51B1	
Toltén *Chile*	29B3	
Toluca *Mexico*	23B2	
Tol'yati *USSR*	61G3	
Tomakomai *Japan*	74E2	
Tomani *Malay*	78D1	
Tomaszów Mazowiecka *Pol*	58C2	
Tombigbee, R *USA*	11B3	
Tomboco *Angola*	98B3	
Tombos *Brazil*	35C2	
Tombouctou *Mali*	97B3	
Tombua *Angola*	100A2	
Tomé *Chile*	34A3	
Tomelloso *Spain*	50B2	
Tomer *Port*	50A2	
Tomkinson Range, Mts *Aust*	106B3	
Tommot *USSR*	63E2	
Tomorrit, Mt *Alb*	55B2	
Tomsk *USSR*	65K4	
Toms River *USA*	16B3	
Tonalá *Mexico*	25C3	
Tonasket *USA*	20C1	
Tonawanda *USA*	15C2	
Tonga, Is *Pacific O*	105H4	
Tongaat *S Africa*	101H1	
Tongcheng *China*	73D3	
Tongchuan *China*	72B2	
Tongde *China*	72A2	
Tongeren *Belg*	46C1	
Tonggu Jiao, I *China*	76E2	
Tonghai *China*	73A5	
Tonghua *China*	74B2	
Tongjosŏn-man *N Korea*	74B3	
Tongkin,G of *Viet/ China*	76D1	
Tonglia *China*	72E1	
Tongling *China*	73D3	
Tongo *Aust*	108B2	
Tongoy *Chile*	34A2	
Tongren, Guizhou *China*	73B4	
Tongren, Qinghai *China*	72A2	
Tongsa *Bhutan*	86C1	
Tongta *Burma*	76B1	
Tongtian He, R *China*	68B3	
Tongue *Scot*	44B2	
Tong Xian *China*	72D2	
Tongxin *China*	72B2	
Tongzi *China*	73B4	
Tonhil *Mongolia*	63B3	
Tonich *Mexico*	9C4	
Tonj *Sudan*	99C2	
Tonk *India*	85D3	
Tonkawa *USA*	18A2	
Tonle Sap, L *Camb*	76C3	
Tonopah *USA*	21B2	
Tonsina *USA*	12E2	
Tooele *USA*	8B2	
Toogoolawah *Aust*	109H1	
Toompine *Aust*	108B1	
Toowoomba *Aust*	109D1	
Topaz L *USA*	22C1	
Topeka *USA*	18A2	
Topolobampo *Mexico*	9C4	
Toppenish *USA*	20B1	
Torbali *Turk*	55C3	
Torbat-e-Heydarīyeh *Iran*	90C2	
Torbat-e Jäm *Iran*	90D2	
Torbay *Eng*	43C4	
Torbert,Mt *USA*	12D2	
Tordesillas *Spain*	50A1	
Torgau *E Germ*	56C2	
Torhout *Belg*	46B1	
Tori *Eth*	99D2	
Tori, I *Japan*	69G3	
Torino *Italy*	47B2	
Torit *Sudan*	99D2	
Torixoreu *Brazil*	35A1	
Tormes, R *Spain*	50A1	
Tornado Mt *Can*	13E2	
Torne, L *Sweden*	38J5	
Torneträsk *Sweden*	38H5	
Torngat, Mts *Can*	7D4	
Tornio *Fin*	38J5	
Tornquist *Arg*	34C3	
Toronto *Can*	15C2	
Toropets *USSR*	60D2	
Tororo *Uganda*	99D2	
Toros Dağlari, Mts *Turk*	92B2	
Torrance *USA*	22C4	
Torrão *Port*	50A2	
Torreblanca *Spain*	51C1	
Torre del Greco *Italy*	53B2	
Torrelavega *Spain*	50B1	
Torremolinos *Spain*	50B2	
Torrens,L *Aust*	108A2	
Torreón *Mexico*	24B2	
Torre Pellice *Italy*	47B2	
Torres Str *Aust*	107D2	
Torres Vedras *Port*	50A2	
Torrington, Connecticut *USA*	16C2	
Torrington, Wyoming *USA*	8C2	
Torrón *Mexico*	9C4	
Torshavn *Faeroes*	38D3	
Tortona *Italy*	47C2	
Tortosa *Spain*	51C1	
Torūd *Iran*	90C2	
Toruń *Pol*	58B2	
Tory, I *Irish Rep*	40B2	
Torzhok *USSR*	60D2	
Tosa *Japan*	75A2	
Tosa-shimizu *Japan*	74C4	
Tosa-wan, B *Japan*	74C4	
To-shima, I *Japan*	75B2	
Tosno *USSR*	39L7	
Tosno *USSR*	60D2	
Tosu *Japan*	75A2	
Tosya *Turk*	92B1	
Tot'ma *USSR*	61F1	
Totnes *Eng*	43C4	
Totness *Surinam*	33F2	
Totolapan *Mexico*	23B2	
Totona *Spain*	51B2	
Tottenham *Aust*	109C2	
Tottori *Japan*	74C3	
Touba *Ivory Coast*	97B4	
Touba *Sen*	97A3	
Toubkal, Mt *Mor*	96B1	
Tougan *U Volta*	97B3	
Touggourt *Alg*	96C1	
Tougué *Guinea*	97A3	
Toul *France*	46C2	
Toulon *France*	49D3	
Toulouse *France*	48C3	
Toumodi *Ivory Coast*	97B4	
Toungoo *Burma*	76B2	
Tourcoing *France*	46B1	
Tourine *Maur*	96A2	
Tournai *Belg*	46B1	
Tours *France*	48C2	
Towada *Japan*	74E2	
Towada-ko, L *Japan*	74E2	
Towanda *USA*	15C2	
Townsville *Aust*	107D2	
Towson *USA*	16A3	
Towy, R *Wales*	43C4	
Toyama *Japan*	74D3	
Toyama-wan, B *Japan*	75B1	
Toyohashi *Japan*	75B2	
Toyonaka *Japan*	75B2	
Toyooka *Japan*	75A1	
Toyota *Japan*	74D3	
Tozeur *Tunisia*	96C1	
Traben-Trarbach *W Germ*	46D2	
Trabzon *Turk*	93C1	
Tracy, California *USA*	22B2	
Traiguén *Chile*	34A3	
Trail *Can*	13D3	
Tralee *Irish Rep*	41B3	
Tralee B *Irish Rep*	45B2	
Tramore *Irish Rep*	45C2	
Tranås *Sweden*	39G7	
Trang *Thai*	77B4	
Trangan, I *Indon*	71E4	
Trangie *Aust*	109C2	
Transalaskan Pipeline *USA*	12E2	
Transvaal, Province *S Africa*	100B3	
Trapani *Italy*	53B2	
Traralgon *Aust*	109C3	
Trarza, Region *Maur*	97A3	
Trat *Thai*	76C3	
Traveller's, L *Aust*	108B2	
Travemünde *W Germ*	56C2	
Traverse City *USA*	14A2	
Traverse Peak, Mt *USA*	12C1	
Travers,Mt *NZ*	111B2	
Trebbia, R *Italy*	47C2	
Třebíč *Czech*	59B3	
Trebinje *Yugos*	54A2	
Trebon *Czech*	57C3	
Treinta y Tres *Urug*	29F2	
Trelew *Arg*	29C4	
Trelleborg *Sweden*	39G7	
Tremadog B *Wales*	43B3	
Tremblant,Mt *Can*	15D1	
Trembleur L *Can*	13C2	
Tremont *USA*	16A2	
Trenčín *Czech*	59B3	
Trenque Lauquén *Arg*	34C3	
Trent, R *Eng*	43D3	
Trentino, Region *Italy*	47D1	
Trento *Italy*	47D1	
Trenton *Can*	15C2	
Trenton, Missouri *USA*	18B1	
Trenton, New Jersey *USA*	16B2	
Trepassey *Can*	7E5	
Tres Arroyos *Arg*	34C3	
Tres Corações *Brazil*	35B2	
Três Lagoas *Brazil*	30F3	
Tres Lomas *Arg*	34C3	
Tres Pinos *USA*	22B2	
Três Rios *Brazil*	35C2	
Treviglio *Italy*	47C2	
Treviso *Italy*	47E2	
Trezzo *Italy*	47C2	
Trichūr *India*	87B2	
Trida *Aust*	108C2	
Trier *W Germ*	46D2	
Trieste *Italy*	52B1	
Trim *Irish Rep*	45C2	
Trincomalee *Sri Lanka*	87C3	
Trinidad *Bol*	33E6	
Trinidad *Urug*	29E2	
Trinidad *USA*	9C3	
Trinidad, I *Arg*	34C3	
Trinidad, I *Caribbean*	27E4	
Trindade, I *Atlantic O*	103G6	
Trinidad & Tobago, Republic *Caribbean*	27E4	
Trinity *USA*	19A3	
Trinity, R *USA*	9D3	
Trinity B *Can*	7E5	
Trinity Is *USA*	12D3	
Trion *USA*	17A1	
Tripoli *Leb*	94B1	
Tripoli *Libya*	95A1	
Trípolis *Greece*	55B3	
Tripura, State *India*	86C2	
Tristan da Cunha, Is *Atlantic O*	103H6	
Trivandrum *India*	87B3	
Trnava *Czech*	59B3	
Trobriand Is *PNG*	107E1	
Trois-Riviéres *Can*	15D1	
Troitsk *USSR*	65H4	
Trollhättan *Sweden*	39G7	
Trollheimen, Mt *Nor*	38F6	
Tromelin, I *Indian O*	89K9	
Tromsø *Nor*	38H5	
Trondheim *Nor*	38G6	
Trondheimfjord, Inlet *Nor*	38G6	
Troon *Scot*	42B2	
Tropic of Cancer	102J3	
Tropic of Capricorn	103J6	
Troudenni *Mali*	96B2	
Trout L, Ontario *Can*	7A4	
Troy, Alabama *USA*	17A1	
Troy, New York *USA*	16C1	
Troy, Ohio *USA*	14B2	
Troyan *Bulg*	54B2	
Troyes *France*	49C2	
Trucial Coast, Region *UAE*	91B5	
Truckee, R *USA*	21A2	
Trujillo *Honduras*	25D3	
Trujillo *Peru*	32B5	
Trujillo *Spain*	50A2	
Trujillo *Ven*	32C2	
Trundle *Aust*	109C2	
Truro *Can*	7D5	
Truro *Eng*	43B4	
Trust Territories of the Pacific Is *Pacific O*	71E3	
Tsagaan Nuur, L *Mongolia*	68B2	
Tsagan-Tologoy *USSR*	68B1	
Tsaratanana *Madag*	101D2	
Tsau *Botswana*	100B3	
Tsavo *Kenya*	99D3	
Tsavo Nat Pk *Kenya*	99D3	
Tselinograd *USSR*	65J4	
Tses *Namibia*	100A3	
Tsetserleg *Mongolia*	68B2	
Tsetserleg *Mongolia*	68C2	
Tsévié *Togo*	97C4	

Tshabong *Botswana*	100B3	Tungabhadra, R *India*	87B1	Tuxpan, Jalisco
Tshane *Botswana*	100B3	Tung-Chiang *Taiwan*	68D4	Mexico	23A2
Tshela *Zaïre*	98B3	Tungnafellsjökull, Mts		Tuxpan, Nayarit
Tshibala *Zaïre*	98C3	Iceland	38B2	Mexico	24B2
Tshikapa *Zaïre*	98C3	Tungsten *Can*	12J2	Tuxpan, Veracruz
Tshuapa, R *Zaïre*	98C3	Tunguska, R *USSR*	63B1	Mexico	23B1
Tsihombe *Madag*	101D3	Tuni *India*	87C1	Tuxtepec *Mexico*	23B2
Tsimlyanskoye		Tunis *Tunisia*	96D1	Tuxtla Gutiérrez
Vodokhranilishche,		Tunisia, Republic *N*		Mexico	25C3
Res *USSR*	61F4	Africa	88E4	Túy *Spain*	50A1
Tsiroanomandidy		Tunja *Colombia*	32C2	Tuy Hoa *Viet*	76D3
Madag	101D2	Tuntutuliak *USA*	12B2	Tuz Gölü, Salt L *Turk*	92B2
Tsitsutl Peak, Mt *Can*	13B2	Tununak *USA*	12B2	Tuz Khurmātū *Iraq*	93D3
Tsna, R *USSR*	58D2	Tunuyán *Arg*	34B2	Tuzla *Yugos*	54A2
Tsogt Ovoo *Mongolia*	72B1	Tunuyán, R *Arg*	34B2	Tweed, R *Scot/Eng*	42C2
Tsu *Japan*	75B2	Tunxi *China*	73D4	Tweed Heads *Aust*	109D1
Tsubata *Japan*	75B1	Tuolumne Meadows		Tweedsmuir Hills *Scot*	42C2
Tsuchira *Japan*	74E3	USA	22C2	Twillingate *Can*	7E5
Tsugaru-kaikyō, Str		Tupã *Brazil*	35A2	Twin Falls *USA*	8B2
Japan	74E2	Tupaciguara *Brazil*	35B1	Twins,The, Mt *NZ*	111B2
Tsumeb *Namibia*	100A2	Tupelo *USA*	19C3	Two Rivers *USA*	14A2
Tsumis *Namibia*	100A3	Tupiza *Bol*	30C3	Tygda *USSR*	63E2
Tsunugi *Japan*	75B1	Tupper Lake *USA*	15D2	Tyler *USA*	19A3
Tsuruga *Japan*	74D3	Tupungato *Arg*	34B2	Tymovskoye *USSR*	69G1
Tsuruoka *Japan*	74D3	Tupungato, Mt *Arg*	29C2	Tyne, R *Eng*	42D2
Tsushima *Japan*	75B1	Tura *India*	86C1	Tyne and Wear,
Tsushima, I *Japan*	74B4	Tura *USSR*	63C1	Metropolitan County
Tsuyama *Japan*	74C3	Tura, R *USSR*	61K2	Eng	42D2
Tua, R *Port*	50A1	Turān *Iran*	90C2	Tynemouth *Eng*	42D2
Tuam *Irish Rep*	45B2	Turan *USSR*	63B2	Tynset *Nor*	38G6
Tuapse *USSR*	60E5	Turayf *S Arabia*	93C3	Tyonek *USA*	12D3
Tuatapere *NZ*	111A3	Turbat *Pak*	80E3	Tyr *Leb*	94B2
Tubarão *Brazil*	30G4	Turbo *Colombia*	32B2	Tyrone, County *N Ire*	45C1
Tubas *Israel*	94B2	Turda *Rom*	54B1	Tyrrell,L *Aust*	108B3
Tubbataha Reefs, Is		Turfan Depression		Tyrrhenian S *Italy*	53B2
Phil	79A4	China	63A3	Tyumen' *USSR*	65H4
Tübingen *W Germ*	57B3	Turgay *USSR*	65H4	Tywyn *Wales*	43B3
Tubruq *Libya*	95B1	Turgen Uul, Mt		Tzoumérka, Mt
Tuckerton *USA*	16B3	Mongolia	63B3	Greece	55B3
Tucson *USA*	9B3	Turgutlu *Turk*	92A2		
Tucumán, State *Arg*	30C4	Turhal *Turk*	92C1	**U**	
Tucunuco *Arg*	34B2	Türi *USSR*	39K7		
Tucupita *Ven*	33E2	Turia, R *Spain*	51B2	Uarsciek *Somalia*	99E2
Tudela *Spain*	51B1	Turinsk *USSR*	61K2	Ubá *Brazil*	35C2
Tudmur *Syria*	93C3	Turiy Rog *USSR*	69F2	Ubaí *Brazil*	35C1
Tugela, R *S Africa*	101H1	Turkana,L *Kenya/Eth*	99D2	Ubangi, R *CAR*	98B2
Tuggerah, L *Aust*	109D2	Turkestan, Region *C*		Ubaye, R *France*	47B2
Tugidak, I *USA*	12D3	Asia	80E1	Ube *Japan*	75A2
Tuguegarao *Phil*	79B2	Turkestan *USSR*	82A1	Ubeda *Spain*	50B2
Tugur *USSR*	63F2	Turkey, Republic *W*		Ubekendt Ejland, I
Tuhai He, R *China*	72D2	Asia	92C2	Greenland	6E2
Tuktoyaktuk *USA*	4E3	Turkmenskaya, SSR,		Uberaba *Brazil*	35B1
Tukums *USSR*	58C1	Republic *USSR*	80D1	Uberlândia *Brazil*	35B1
Tukuyu *Tanz*	99D3	Turkmenskiy Zaliv, B		Ubon Ratchathani
Tukzar *Afghan*	84B1	USSR	90B2	Thai	76C2
Tula *USSR*	60E3	Turks Is *Caribbean*	27C2	Ubort, R *USSR*	58D2
Tulancingo *Mexico*	23B1	Turku *Fin*	39J6	Ubundu *Zaïre*	98C3
Tulangbawang, R		Turkwel, R *Kenya*	99D2	Ucayali, R *Peru*	32C5
Indon	78A3	Turlock *USA*	22B2	Uch *Pak*	84C3
Tulcán *Colombia*	32B3	Turlock L *USA*	22B2	Uchiura-wan, B *Japan*	74E2
Tulcea *Rom*	60C5	Turnagain,C *NZ*	110C2	Uchur, R *USSR*	63F2
Tuli *Zim*	100B3	Turneffe I *Belize*	25D3	Udaipur *India*	85C4
Tulkarm *Israel*	94B2	Turners Falls *USA*	16C1	Udaipur Garhi *Nepal*	86B1
Tulle *France*	48C2	Turnhout *Belg*	46C1	Udaquoila *Arg*	34D3
Tullos *USA*	19B3	Turnor L *Can*	13F1	Uddevalla *Sweden*	39G7
Tullow *Irish Rep*	45C2	Turnu Măgurele *Rom*	54B2	Uddjaur, L *Sweden*	38H5
Tulsa *USA*	18A2	Turnu-Severin *Rom*	54B2	Udgir *India*	87B1
Tulūl ash Shāmīyah,		Turpan *China*	63A3	Udhampur *India*	84D2
Desert Region		Turquino, Mt *Cuba*	26B2	Udmurtskaya, ASSR,
Syria/S Arabia	93C3	Turtkul' *USSR*	80E1	Republic *USSR*	61H2
Tulun *USSR*	63C2	Turtle Creek Res *USA*	18A2	Udon Thani *Thai*	76C2
Tulungagung *Indon*	78C4	Turtle L *Can*	13F2	Udskaya Guba, B
Tumaco *Colombia*	32B3	Turukhansk *USSR*	63A1	USSR	63F2
Tumbarumba *Aust*	109C3	Turuntayevo *USSR*	68C1	Udupi *India*	87A2
Tumbes *Ecuador*	32A4	Turvo, R, Goias *Brazil*	35A1	Ueda *Japan*	75B1
Tumby Bay *Aust*	108A2	Turvo, R, São Paulo		Uele, R *Zaïre*	99C2
Tumen *China*	74B2	Brazil	35B2	Uelzen *W Germ*	56C2
Tumkür *India*	87B2	Tur'ya, R *USSR*	58C2	Uere, R *Zaïre*	98C2
Tumpat *Malay*	77C4	Tuscaloosa *USA*	19C3	Ufa *USSR*	61J3
Tumsar *India*	86D4	Tuscola *USA*	18C2	Ufa, R *USSR*	61J2
Tumu *Ghana*	97B3	Tusharīk *Iran*	90C3	Ugab, R *Namibia*	100A3
Tumut *Aust*	109C3	Tuticorin *India*	87B3	Ugaila, R *Tanz*	99D3
Tumut, R *Aust*	109C3	Tutrakan *Bulg*	54C2	Ugak B *USA*	12D3
Tunapuna *Trinidad*	27L1	Tuttlingen *W Germ*	57B3	Uganda, Republic
Tunceli *Turk*	93C2	Tuul Gol, R *Mongolia*	68C2	Africa	99D2
Tunduma *Zambia*	99D3	Tuvalu, Is *Pacific O*	105G4	Ugashik B *USA*	12C3
Tunduru *Tanz*	101C2	Tuvinskaya, Republic		Ugashik L *USA*	12C3
Tundzha, R *Bulg*	54C2	USSR	63B2	Ugine *France*	47B2

Uglegorsk *USSR*	69G2
Uglich *USSR*	60E2
Ugra, R *USSR*	60E3
Uig *Scot*	44A3
Uige *Angola*	98B3
Uil *USSR*	61H4
Uinta Mts *USA*	8B2
Uitenhage *S Africa*	100B4
Ujfehértó *Hung*	59C3
Uji *Japan*	75B2
Ujiji *Tanz*	99C3
Ujina *Chile*	30C3
Ujjain *India*	85D4
Ujung Pandang *Indon*	70C4
Ukerewe, I *Tanz*	99D3
Ukhrul *India*	86C1
Ukiah, California *USA*	21A2
Ukiah, Oregon *USA*	20C1
Ukmerge *USSR*	58C1
Ukrainskaya, Republic
USSR	60C4
Ulaanbaatar *Mongolia*	68C2
Ulaangom *Mongolia*	68B2
Ulaan Uul *Mongolia*	72C1
Ulangar Hu, L *China*	82C1
Ulan Ude *USSR*	68C1
Ulan Ul Hu, L *China*	68B3
Ulapes *Arg*	34B2
Ulchin *S Korea*	74B3
Ulcinj *Yugos*	54A2
Uldz *Mongolia*	68D2
Uliastay *Mongolia*	68B2
Ulla *USSR*	58D1
Ulladulla *Aust*	109D3
Ullapool *Scot*	44B3
Ullsfjorden, Inlet *Nor*	38H5
Ullswater, L *Eng*	42C2
Ullung-do, I *S Korea*	74C3
Ulm *W Germ*	57C3
Uloowaranie,L *Aust*	108A1
Ulsan *S Korea*	74B3
Ulster, Region *N Ire*	45C1
Ulungur He, R *China*	65K5
Ulungur Hu, L *China*	65K5
Ulva, I *Scot*	44A3
Ulverston *Eng*	42C2
Ulverstone *Aust*	109C4
Ulya, R *USSR*	63G2
Ul'yanovsk *USSR*	61G3
Uman *USSR*	60D4
Umanak *Greenland*	6E2
Umaria *India*	86A2
Umarkot *Pak*	85B3
Umaroona,L *Aust*	108A1
Umatilla *USA*	20C1
Umba *USSR*	38L5
Umba, R *Tanz*	99D3
Ume, R *Sweden*	38H6
Umea *Sweden*	38J6
Umfolozi, R *S Africa*	101H1
Umiat *USA*	4C3
Umm al Qaiwain *UAE*	91C4
Umm as Samīm, Salt
Marsh *Oman*	91C5
Umm Bell *Sudan*	99C1
Umm Hagar *Eth*	99D1
Umm Keddada *Sudan*	98C1
Umm Ruwaba *Sudan*	99D1
Umm Sa'id *Qatar*	91B5
Umnaiti, R *Zim*	100B2
Umpqua, R *USA*	20B2
Umred *India*	85D4
Umtata *S Africa*	100B4
Umuarama *Brazil*	35A2
Una, R *Yugos*	52C1
Unai *Brazil*	35B1
Unalakleet *USA*	12B2
Unayzah *S Arabia*	80C3
Uncasville *USA*	16C2
Underberg *S Africa*	101G1
Unecha *USSR*	60D3
Uneisa *Jordan*	94B3
Ungava B *Can*	7D4
União de Vitória *Brazil*	30F4
Unión *Arg*	34B3
Union, Missouri *USA*	18B2
Union, S Carolina
USA	17B1

Union City

Union City, Pennsylvania *USA*	14C2	Ústi nad Labem *Czech*	57C2	Valença, Bahia *Brazil*	31D4	Varde *Den*	39F7
Union of Soviet		Ust'Ishim *USSR*	65J4	Valença, Rio de		Vardø *Nor*	38L4
Socialist Reps *Asia*	62C3	Ustka *Pol*	58B2	Janeiro *Brazil*	35C2	Varéna *USSR*	58C2
Union Springs *USA*	17A1	Ust'-Kamenogorsk		Valence *France*	49C3	Varenna *Italy*	47C2
Uniontown *USA*	15C3	*USSR*	65K5	Valencia, Region		Varese *Italy*	47C2
United Arab Emirates		Ust Karabula *USSR*	63B2	Spain	51B2	Varginha *Brazil*	35B2
Arabian Pen	91B5	Ust'Katav *USSR*	61J2	Valencia *Spain*	51B2	Varkaus *Fin*	38K6
United Kingdom,		Ust'-Kut *USSR*	63C2	Valencia *Ven*	32D1	Varna *Bulg*	54C2
Kingdom *W Europe*	36C3	Ust Labinsk *USSR*	61E4	Valencia, I *Irish Rep*	45A3	Värnamo *Sweden*	39G7
United States of		Ust'Maya *USSR*	63F1	Valencia de Alcantara		Varnville *USA*	17B1
America	2H4	Ust'Nera *USSR*	1C8	Spain	50A2	Várzea da Palma *Brazil*	35C1
United States Range,		Ust'Nyukzha *USSR*	63E2	Valenciennes *France*	46B1	Varzi *Italy*	47C2
Mts *Can*	6B1	Ust'Ordynskiy *USSR*	63C2	Valenza *Italy*	47C2	Vascongadas, Region	
Unity *Can*	13F2	Ust'Tsil'ma *USSR*	64G3	Valera *Ven*	32C2	Spain	50B1
Unity *USA*	20C2	Ust'Umal'ta *USSR*	63F2	Valga *USSR*	39K7	Vasil'kov *USSR*	60D3
Unna *W Germ*	46D1	Usuki *Japan*	75A2	Valikiyo *USSR*	64E4	Vassar *USA*	14B2
Unnão *India*	86A1	Usumacinta, R		Valjevo *Yugos*	54A2	Västerås *Sweden*	39H7
Unst, I *Scot*	44D1	Guatemala/Mexico	25C3	Valkeakoski *Fin*	39J6	Västervik *Sweden*	39H7
Unuk, R *USA*	13A1	Usutu, R *Swaziland*	101H1	Valladolid *Mexico*	25D2	Vasto *Italy*	52B2
Ünye *Turk*	92C1	Utah, State *USA*	8B3	Valladolid *Spain*	50B1	Vatnajökull, Mts	
Unzha, R *USSR*	61F2	Utah L *USA*	8B2	Valle d'Aosta, Region		Iceland	38B2
Upata *Ven*	33E2	Utena *USSR*	58D1	Italy	47B2	Vatneyri *Iceland*	38A1
Upemba Nat Pk *Zaïre*	98C3	Uthal *Pak*	85B3	Valle de la Pascua		Vatra Dornei *Rom*	54C1
Upernavik *Greenland*	6E2	Utica *USA*	10C2	Ven	27D5	Vättern, L *Sweden*	39G7
Upland *USA*	22D3	Utiel *Spain*	51B2	Valle de Santiago		Vaughn *USA*	9C3
Uplington *S Africa*	100B3	Utikuma L *Can*	13D1	Mexico	23A1	Vaupés, R *Colombia*	32C3
Upper Arlington *USA*	14B2	Utrecht *Neth*	56B2	Valle d'Isére *France*	47B2	Vauxhall *Can*	13E2
Upper Arrow L *Can*	13D2	Utrecht *S Africa*	101H1	Valledupar *Colombia*	32C1	Vavunija *Sri Lanka*	87C3
Upper Hutt *NZ*	111C2	Utrera *Spain*	50A2	Vallée de l'Azaouak, V		Växjö *Sweden*	39G7
Upper Klamath L *USA*	20B2	Utsjoki *Fin*	38K5	Niger	97C3	Vedia *Arg*	34C2
Upper L *USA*	20B2	Utsunomiya *Japan*	74D3	Vallée Tilemis, V *Mali*	97C3	Vega, I *Nor*	38G5
Upper Lough Erne, L		Uttaradit *Thai*	76C2	Valle Grande *Bol*	30D2	Vegreville *Can*	13E2
N Ire	45C1	Uttar Pradesh, State		Vallejo *USA*	22A1	Vejer de la Frontera	
Upper Manzanilla		India	86A1	Vallenar *Chile*	30B4	Spain	50A2
Trinidad	27L1	Uval *USSR*	65H4	Valley City *USA*	8D2	Vejle *Den*	39F7
Upper Seal,L *Can*	7C4	Uvéa, I *Nouvelle*		Valley Falls *USA*	20B2	Velebit, Mts *Yugos*	52C2
Upper Volta, Republic		Calédonie	107F3	Valleyfield *Can*	15D1	Velenje *Yugos*	52C1
Africa (see Burkina)	97B3	Uvinza *Tanz*	99D3	Valleyview *Can*	13D1	Velhas, R *Brazil*	35C1
Uppsala *Sweden*	39H7	Uvira *Zaïre*	99C3	Valli di Comacchio, Lg		Velikaya, R *USSR*	39K7
Urad Qianqi *China*	72B1	Uvkusigssat *Greenland*	6E2	Italy	47E2	Velikiye Luki *USSR*	60D2
Urairah *S Arabia*	91A4	Uvsikaupunki *Fin*	39J6	Valls *Spain*	51C1	Velikiy Ustyug *USSR*	61G1
Ural, R *USSR*	61H3	Uvs Nuur, L *China*	68B1	Valmiera *USSR*	58D1	Veliko Tŭrnovo *Bulg*	54C2
Uralla *Aust*	109D2	Uwajima *Japan*	74C4	Valparaiso *Brazil*	35A2	Vélingara *Sen*	97A3
Ural'sk *USSR*	61H3	Uxin Qi *China*	72B2	Valparaiso *Chile*	34A2	Vellore *India*	87B2
Uralskiy Khrebet, Mts		Uyar *USSR*	63B2	Valparaiso *Mexico*	23A1	Vel'sk *USSR*	61F1
USSR	65G4	Uyuni *Bol*	30C3	Valparaiso *USA*	17A1	Vembanad L *India*	87B3
Uranium City *Can*	5H4	Uzbekskaya, S.S.R.,		Vals, R *S Africa*	101G1	Venado Tuerto *Arg*	34C2
Urawa *Japan*	75B1	Republic *USSR*	80E1	Valsäd *India*	85C4	Vençeslau Braz *Brazil*	35B2
Urbana, Illinois *USA*	18C1	Uzerche *France*	48C2	Valuyki *USSR*	60E3	Vendôme *France*	49C2
Urbana, Ohio *USA*	14B2	Uzhgorod *USSR*	59C3	Valverde del Camino		Venetie *USA*	12E1
Urbino *Italy*	52B2	Uzlovaya *USSR*	60E3	Spain	50A2	Veneto, Region *Italy*	47D2
Ure, R *Eng*	42C2	Uzunköprü *Turk*	92A1	Vammala *Fin*	38J6	Venezia *Italy*	47E2
Uren' *USSR*	61G2			Van *Turk*	93D2	Venezuela, Republic *S*	
Urfa *Turk*	93C2			Vanavara *USSR*	63C1	America	32D2
Urgench *USSR*	80E1	# V		Van Buren, Arkansas		Vengurla *India*	87A1
Urgun *Afghan*	84B2			USA	18B2	Veniaminof V *USA*	12C3
Urla *Turk*	55C3	Vaal, R *S Africa*	101F1	Vancouver *Can*	13C3	Venkatagiri *India*	87B2
Uroševac *Yugos*	54B2	Vaal Dam, Res *S*		Vancouver *USA*	20B1	Venlo *Neth*	56B2
Uruaçu *Brazil*	31B4	Africa	101G1	Vancouver I *Can*	5F5	Venta, R *USSR*	58C1
Uruapan *Mexico*	23A2	Vaalwater *S Africa*	100B3	Vancouver,Mt *Can*	12G2	Ventersburg *S Africa*	101G1
Urucuia *Brazil*	35B1	Vaasa *Fin*	38J6	Vandalia, Illinois *USA*	18C2	Ventspils *USSR*	58C1
Uruguaiana *Brazil*	30E4	Vác *Hung*	59B3	Vandalia, Ohio *USA*	14B3	Ventuari, R *Ven*	32D3
Uruguay, Republic *S*		Vacaria *Brazil*	30F4	Vanderhoof *Can*	13C2	Ventura *USA*	22C3
America	29E2	Vacaria, R, Minas		Van Diemen G *Aust*	106C2	Vepsovskaya	
Uruguay, R *Urug*	29E2	Gerais *Brazil*	35C1	Vänern, L *Sweden*	39G7	Vozvyshennost',	
Ürümqi *China*	82C1	Vacaville *USA*	21A2	Vänersborg *Sweden*	39G7	Upland *USSR*	60D1
Urup, I *USSR*	69H2	Vadsø *Nor*	38K4	Vangaindrano *Madag*	101D3	Vera *Arg*	30D4
Uruzgan *Afghan*	84B2	Vaduz *Leichtenstein*	47C1	Van Gölü, Salt L *Turk*	93D2	Vera *Spain*	51B2
Uryupinsk *USSR*	61F3	Va Gesell *Arg*	29E3	Vang Vieng *Laos*	76C2	Veracruz *Mexico*	23B2
Urzhum *USSR*	61H2	Vågø *Faroes*	38D3	Van Horn *USA*	9C3	Veracruz, State	
Urziceni *Rom*	54C2	Váh, R *Czech*	59B3	Vanier *Can*	15C1	Mexico	23B1
Usa *China*	82C1	Vaigai, R *India*	87B2	Vankarem *USSR*	1C6	Veräval *India*	85C4
Usa *Japan*	75A2	Vâlcea *Rom*	60B4	Vännäs *Sweden*	38H6	Verbania *Italy*	47C2
Uşak *Turk*	92A2	Valcheta *Arg*	29C4	Vannes *France*	48B2	Vercelli *Italy*	47C2
Usakos *Namibia*	100A3	Valdagno *Italy*	47D2	Vanoise, Mts *France*	47B2	Verde, R, Goias *Brazil*	35A1
Ushashi *Tanz*	99D3	Valday *USSR*	60D2	Vanrhynsdorp *S Africa*	100A4	Verde, R, Jalisco	
Ush Tobe *USSR*	65J5	Valdayskaya		Vansittart I *Can*	6B3	Mexico	23A1
Ushuaia *Arg*	29C6	Vozvyshennost'		Vanuatu, Is *Pacific O*	105G4	Verde, R, Mato	
Ushumun *USSR*	63E2	Upland *USSR*	60D2	Van Wert *USA*	14B2	Grosso do Sul *Brazil*	35A1
Usk, R *Wales*	43C4	Val de la Pascua *Ven*	32D2	Varallo *Italy*	47C2	Verde, R, Oaxaca	
Üsküdar *Turk*	92A1	Valdepeñas *Spain*	50B2	Varāmīn *Iran*	90B2	Mexico	23B2
Usol'ye Sibirskoye		Valdez *USA*	12E2	Vārānasi *India*	86A1	Verde Grande, R *Brazil*	35C1
USSR	63C2	Valdivia *Chile*	29B3	Varangerfjord, Inlet		Verde,Pen *Arg*	34C3
Uspallata *Arg*	34B2	Val d'Oise,		Nor	38K4	Verdon, R *France*	49D3
Ussuriysk *USSR*	69F2	Department *France*	46B2	Varangerhalvøya, Pen		Verdun *France*	46C2
Uster *Switz*	47C1	Valdosta *USA*	17B1	Nor	38K4	Vereeniging *S Africa*	101G1
Ustica, I *Italy*	53B3	Vale *USA*	20C2	Varazdin *Yugos*	52C1	Vereshchagino *USSR*	61H2
		Valemount *Can*	13D2	Varberg *Sweden*	39G7	Verga,C *Guinea*	97A3

Vukovar

Vukovar *Yugos*	54A1
Vulcan *Can*	13E2
Vulcano, I *Italy*	53B3
Vung Tau *Viet*	77D3
Vuollerim *Sweden*	38J5
Vyartsilya *USSR*	38L6
Vyatka, R *USSR*	61H2
Vyazemskiy *USSR*	69F2
Vyaz'ma *USSR*	60D2
Vyazniki *USSR*	61F2
Vyborg *USSR*	60C1
Vyrnwy, R *Wales*	43C3
Vyshiy Volochek *USSR*	60D2
Vyškuv *Czech*	59B3
Vytegra *USSR*	60E1

W

Wa *Ghana*	97B3
Wabasca *Can*	13E1
Wabasca, R *Can*	5G4
Wabasca L *Can*	13E1
Wabash *USA*	14A2
Wabash, R *USA*	14A3
Wabowden *Can*	5J4
Wabush *Can*	7D4
Waccasassa B *USA*	17B2
Wachusett Res *USA*	16D1
Waco *USA*	19A3
Wad *Pak*	85B3
Waddān *Libya*	95A2
Waddington,Mt *Can*	5F4
Wadi al Bātin, Watercourse *Iraq*	93E4
Wadi al Ghudāf, Watercourse *Iraq*	93D3
Wadi al Harīr, V *Syria*	94C2
Wadi al Mirah, Watercourse S *Arabia/Iraq*	93D3
Wadi al Ubayyid, Watercourse *Iraq*	93D3
Wadi Ar'ar, Watercourse S *Arabia*	93D3
Wadi as Hsabā', Watercourse S *Arabia*	91A5
Wadi as Sirhān, V *Jordan/S Arabia*	92C3
Wadi az Zaydi, V *Syria*	94C2
Wadi edh Dhab'i, V *Jordan*	94C3
Wadi el 'Arish, V *Egypt*	94A3
Wadi el Ghadaf, V *Jordan*	94C3
Wadi el Hasa, V *Jordan*	94B3
Wadi el Janab, V *Jordan*	94C3
Wadi el Jeib, V *Israel/ Jordan*	94B3
Wadi el Milk, Watercourse *Sudan*	95B3
Wadi el Natrun, Watercourse *Egypt*	92A3
Wadi es Sir *Jordan*	94B3
Wadi Fidan, V *Jordan*	94B3
Wadi Hareidin, V *Egypt*	94B3
Wadi Hawrān, R *Iraq*	93D3
Wadi Howa, Watercourse *Sudan*	95B3
Wadi Ibra, Watercourse *Sudan*	98C1
Wadi Luhfi, Watercourse *Jordan*	94C2
Wadi Mujib, V *Jordan*	94B3
Wadi Qîtaiya, V *Egypt*	94B3
Wadi Sha'it, Watercourse *Egypt*	80B3
Wad Medani *Sudan*	99D1
Wafra *Kuwait*	93E4
Wager B *Can*	6B3
Wager Bay *Can*	6A3
Wagga Wagga *Aust*	109C3

Wagin *Aust*	106A4
Waha *Libya*	95A2
Wahaiwa *Hawaiian Is*	21C4
Wahoo *USA*	18A1
Wahpeton *USA*	8D2
Wai *India*	87A1
Waiau *NZ*	111B2
Waiau, R *NZ*	111A3
Waiau, R *NZ*	111B2
Waigeo, I *Indon*	71E3
Waihi *NZ*	110C1
Waikaremoana,L *NZ*	110C1
Waikato, R *NZ*	110C1
Waikerio *Aust*	108A2
Waikouaiti *NZ*	111B3
Wailuku *Hawaiian Is*	21C4
Waimakariri, R *NZ*	111B2
Waimate *NZ*	111B2
Waimea *Hawaiian Is*	21C4
Waingapu *Indon*	106B1
Wainwright *Can*	13E2
Wainwright *USA*	4B2
Waipara *NZ*	111B2
Waipukurau *NZ*	110C2
Wairarapa,L *NZ*	111C2
Wairau, R *NZ*	111B2
Wairoa *NZ*	110C1
Wairoa, R *NZ*	110C1
Waitaki, R *NZ*	111B2
Waitara *NZ*	110B1
Waitomo *NZ*	110C1
Waiuku *NZ*	110B1
Wajima *Japan*	75B1
Wajir *Kenya*	99E2
Wakasa-wan, B *Japan*	75B1
Wakatipu,L *NZ*	111A3
Wakayama *Japan*	74D4
Wakefield *Eng*	42D3
Wakefield *Jamaica*	27H1
Wakefield, Rhode Island *USA*	16D2
Wakema *Burma*	76B2
Wakkanai *Japan*	69G2
Wakool, R *Aust*	108B3
Walbrzych *Pol*	59B2
Walcha *Aust*	109D2
Walcz *Pol*	58B2
Waldbröl *W Germ*	46D1
Walden *USA*	16B2
Waldia *Eth*	99D1
Wales, Country *U K*	43C3
Wales *USA*	12A1
Wales I *Can*	6B3
Walgett *Aust*	109C2
Walgreen Coast, Region *Ant*	112B4
Walikale *Zaïre*	99C3
Walker, L *USA*	21B2
Walkerton *Can*	14B2
Wallace *USA*	8B2
Wallaroo *Aust*	108A2
Walla Walla *Aust*	109C3
Walla Walla *USA*	20C1
Wallingford *USA*	16C2
Wallis and Futuna, Is *Pacific O*	105H4
Wallowa *USA*	20C1
Wallowa Mts, Mts *USA*	20C1
Wallumbilla *Aust*	109C1
Walnut Ridge *USA*	18B2
Walouru *NZ*	110C1
Walsall *Eng*	43D3
Walsenburg *USA*	9C3
Walsenburgh *USA*	9C3
Walterboro *USA*	17B1
Walter F George Res *USA*	17A1
Waltham *USA*	16D1
Walvis Bay *S Africa*	100A3
Walvis Ridge *Atlantic O*	103J6
Wamba *Nig*	97C4
Wamba, R *Zaïre*	98B3
Wamego *USA*	18A2
Wana *Pak*	84B2
Wanaaring *Aust*	108B1
Wanaka *NZ*	111A2

Wanaka,L *NZ*	111A2
Wanapitei L *Can*	14B1
Wandoan *Aust*	109C1
Wanganella *Aust*	108B3
Wanganui *NZ*	110B1
Wanganui *NZ*	110C1
Wanganui, R *NZ*	110C1
Wangaratta *Aust*	109C3
Wanle Weyne *Somalia*	99E2
Wanning *China*	76E2
Wanparti *India*	87B1
Wanxian *China*	73B3
Wanyuan *China*	73B3
Wapiti, R *Can*	13D2
Wappapello,L *USA*	18B2
Wappingers Falls *USA*	16C2
Warangal *India*	87B1
Waratah *Aust*	109C4
Waratah B *Aust*	108C3
Warburton *Aust*	108C3
Warburton, R *Aust*	108A1
Ward, R *Aust*	109C1
Warden *S Africa*	101G1
Warder *Eth*	99E2
Wardha *India*	85D4
Ward,Mt *NZ*	111A3
Ware *Can*	5F4
Ware *USA*	16C1
Wareham *USA*	16D2
Warialda *Aust*	109D1
Warin Chamrap *Thai*	76C2
Warmbad *S Africa*	100B3
Warminster *USA*	16B2
Warm Springs *USA*	21B2
Warnemünde *E Germ*	56C2
Warner Mts *USA*	20B2
Warner Robins *USA*	17B1
Warracknabeal *Aust*	108B3
Warrandirinna,L *Aust*	108A1
Warrego, R *Aust*	107D3
Warren, Arkansas *USA*	19B3
Warren *Aust*	109C2
Warren, Massachusetts *USA*	16D2
Warren, Ohio *USA*	14B2
Warren, Pennsylvania *USA*	15C2
Warrenpoint *N Ire*	45C1
Warrensburg *USA*	18B2
Warrenton *S Africa*	101F1
Warrenton *USA*	15C3
Warri *Nig*	97C4
Warrina *Aust*	108A1
Warrington *Eng*	42C3
Warrnambool *Aust*	108B3
Warszawa *Pol*	58C2
Warta, R *Pol*	59B2
Warwick *Aust*	109D1
Warwick, County *Eng*	43D3
Warwick *Eng*	43D3
Warwick, New York *USA*	16B2
Warwick, Rhode Island *USA*	16D2
Wasatch Range, Mts *USA*	8B3
Wasbank *S Africa*	101H1
Wasco *USA*	21B2
Washburn L *Can*	4H2
Wāshīm *India*	85D4
Washington, District of Columbia *USA*	10C3
Washington, Georgia *USA*	17B1
Washington, Indiana *USA*	14A3
Washington, Missouri *USA*	18B2
Washington, New Jersey *USA*	16B2
Washington, Pennsylvania *USA*	14B2
Washington, State *USA*	8A2
Washington Court House *USA*	14B3
Washington Land *Can*	6D1

Washington,Mt *USA*	15D2
Wash,The *Eng*	43E3
Washuk *Pak*	85A3
Wasilla *USA*	12E2
Waspán *Nic*	26A4
Watampone *Indon*	70D4
Waterbury *USA*	16C2
Waterford, County Irish Rep	45C2
Waterford *Irish Rep*	41B3
Waterford Harbour *Irish Rep*	45C2
Waterloo *Belg*	46C1
Waterloo *USA*	10A2
Watertown, New York *USA*	15C2
Waterval-Boven S *Africa*	101H1
Waterville, Maine *USA*	10D2
Watervliet *USA*	16C1
Waterways *Can*	5G4
Watford *Eng*	43D4
Watkins Bjerge, Mt *Greenland*	6H3
Watkins Glen *USA*	15C2
Watrous *Can*	8C1
Watsa *Zaïre*	99C2
Watson Lake *Can*	12J2
Watsonville *USA*	22B2
Wau *PNG*	71F4
Wau *Sudan*	99C2
Waua *Can*	7B5
Wauchope *Aust*	109D2
Wauchula *USA*	17B2
Waukegan *USA*	14A2
Wausau *USA*	10B2
Wauwatosa *USA*	14A2
Wave Hill *Aust*	106C2
Waveney, R *Eng*	43E3
Waverly, Ohio *USA*	14B3
Wavre *Belg*	46C1
Wawa *Can*	10B2
Wāw Al Kabīr *Libya*	95A2
Wāw an Nāmūs, Well Libya	95A2
Wawona *USA*	22C2
Waxahachie *USA*	19A3
Waycross *USA*	17B1
Waynesboro, Georgia *USA*	17B1
Waynesboro, Mississippi *USA*	19C3
Waynesboro, Pennsylvania *USA*	16A3
Waynesboro, Virginia *USA*	15C3
Waynesville, Missouri *USA*	18B2
Wazi Khwa *Afghan*	84B2
Weald,The, Upland *Eng*	43E4
Wear, R *Eng*	42C2
Weatherford, Texas *USA*	19A3
Weaverville *USA*	20B2
Webbwood *Can*	14B1
Webster *USA*	16D1
Webster Groves *USA*	18B2
Weddell I *Falkland Is*	29D6
Weddell S *Ant*	112C2
Wedge Mt *Can*	13C2
Weed *USA*	20B2
Weenen *S Africa*	101H1
Wee Waa *Aust*	109C2
Weichang *China*	72D1
Weiden *W Germ*	57C3
Weifang *China*	72D2
Weihai *China*	72E2
Wei He, R, Henan *China*	72C3
Wei He, R, Shaanxi *China*	72C2
Weilmoringle *Aust*	109C1
Weining *China*	73A4
Weipa *Aust*	107D2
Weirton *USA*	14B2
Weiser *USA*	20C2

Witney

Ziller

Ziller, R *Austria*	**47D1**	Ziya He, R *China*	**72D2**	Zrenjanin *Yugos*	**54B1**	Zuyevka *USSR*	**61H2**
Zillertaler Alpen, Mts		Ziyang *China*	**72A3**	Zug *Switz*	**47C1**	Zvishavane *Zim*	**100B4**
Austria	**47D1**	Zlatoust *USSR*	**61J2**	Zugspitze, Mt *W*		Zvolen *Czech*	**59B3**
Zilupe *USSR*	**58D1**	Zmeinogorsk *USSR*	**65K4**	*Germ*	**47D1**	Zvornik *Yugos*	**54A2**
Zima *USSR*	**63C2**	Znin *Pol*	**58B2**	Zújar, R *Spain*	**50A2**	Zweibrücken *W Germ*	**46D2**
Zimapan *Mexico*	**23B1**	Znoimo *Czech*	**59B3**	Zumbo *Mozam*	**100C2**	Zweisimmen *Switz*	**47B1**
Zimatlan *Mexico*	**23B2**	Zofinger *Switz*	**47B1**	Zumpango *Mexico*	**23B2**	Zwickau *E Germ*	**57C2**
Zin, R *Israel*	**94B3**	Zoigê *China*	**72A3**	Zungeru *Nig*	**97C4**	Zwolle *Neth*	**56B2**
Zinacatepec *Mexico*	**23B2**	Zolochev *USSR*	**59D3**	Zunyi *China*	**73B4**	Zyrardów *Pol*	**58C2**
Zinapécuaro *Mexico*	**23A2**	Zomba *Malawi*	**101C2**	Zuo, R *China*	**76D1**	Zyryanovsk *USSR*	**65K5**
Zinder *Niger*	**97C3**	Zongo *Zaïre*	**98B2**	Zuo Jiang, R *China*	**73B5**	Żywiec *Pol*	**59B3**
Zi Shui *China*	**73C4**	Zonguldak *Turk*	**92B1**	Zürich *Switz*	**47C1**	Zyyi *Cyprus*	**94A1**
Zitácuaro *Mexico*	**23A2**	Zorzor *Lib*	**97B4**	Zürichsee, L *Switz*	**47C1**		
Zittau *E Germ*	**57C2**	Zouerate *Maur*	**96A2**	Zuwārah *Libya*	**95A1**		